THIRD EDITION

Introduction to
RESEARCH AND
MEDICAL LITERATURE
for Health Professionals

Introduction to
RESEARCH AND MEDICAL LITERATURE
for Health Professionals

THIRD EDITION

EDITED BY

J. Dennis Blessing, PhD, PA
Associate Dean
School of Health Professions
UT Health Science Center San Antonio
San Antonio, TX

J. Glenn Forister, MS, PA-C
Associate Professor and Program Director
Department of Physician Assistant Studies
School of Health Professions
UT Health Science Center San Antonio
San Antonio, TX

JONES & BARTLETT
LEARNING

World Headquarters
Jones & Bartlett Learning
5 Wall Street
Burlington, MA 01803
978-443-5000
info@jblearning.com
www.jblearning.com

Jones & Bartlett Learning books and products are available through most bookstores and online booksellers. To contact Jones & Bartlett Learning directly, call 800-832-0034, fax 978-443-8000, or visit our website, www.jblearning.com.

Substantial discounts on bulk quantities of Jones & Bartlett Learning publications are available to corporations, professional associations, and other qualified organizations. For details and specific discount information, contact the special sales department at Jones & Bartlett Learning via the above contact information or send an email to specialsales@jblearning.com.

Production Credits
Publisher: David D. Cella
Acquisitions Editor: Katey Birtcher
Managing Editor: Maro Gartside
Editorial Assistant: Teresa Reilly
Associate Production Editor: Cindie Bryan
Production Assistant: Sean Coombs
Marketing Manager: Grace Richards
Manufacturing and Inventory Control Supervisor: Amy Bacus
Composition: Circle Graphics, Inc.
Cover Design: Kristin E. Parker
Cover Image: © Ka Ho Leung/Dreamstime.com
Printing and Binding: Malloy, Inc.
Cover Printing: Malloy, Inc.

Some images in this book feature models. These models do not necessarily endorse, represent, or participate in the activities represented in the images.

To order this product use ISBN: 978-1-4496-5035-3

Library of Congress Cataloging-in-Publication Data
Introduction to research and medical literature for health professionals / edited by J. Dennis Blessing, J. Glenn Forister.—3rd ed.
    p.; cm.
  Rev. ed. of: Physician assistant's guide to research and medical literature / [edited by] J. Dennis Blessing. 2nd ed. Philadelphia : F. A. Davis, c2006.
  Includes bibliographical references and index.
  ISBN 978-1-4496-0481-3 (pbk.)
  I. Blessing, J. Dennis. II. Forister, J. Glenn. III. Physician assistant's guide to research and medical literature.
  [DNLM: 1. Allied Health Personnel. 2. Research. 3. Allied Health Personnel—education. 4. Research Design. W 20.5]
  610.73'7069—dc23

                                         2011035624

6048
Printed in the United States of America
16 15 14 13 12   10 9 8 7 6 5 4 3 2 1

Contents

Dedication

This book is dedicated to all the people who made it happen. The contributors to this book have put forth their effort to improve the research capabilities of all healthcare professionals, present and future. It is rare for authors from so many professions to collaborate on such an effort.

We further dedicate this book to our friends and colleagues at Jones & Bartlett Learning. They work behind the scenes to make us look good.

Ultimately, contributors and publishers want this to be a successful book that helps every reader in their understanding of research and what it means to the people who benefit from our healthcare efforts.

JDB

JGF

Preface

The editors and contributors of this book are dedicated teachers, researchers, administrators, and practitioners in healthcare professions. They have worked tirelessly to make this book readable, understandable, and useful for students and practitioners in healthcare professions. Our intent is to provide a tool that can be the first step in understanding research and, perhaps, the first step in a research career.

For most of our readers, this book will help you understand research in health care and your field so that you can make best use of research for your patients. Research articles, news flashes, and advertisements bombard us daily. To make sense of it all, we must be able to interpret and apply the information in the best interest of our patients. This skill is a critical requirement of clinical practice in today's world.

We have tried to present our material in a step-by-step fashion, from idea development to publication and presentation. Our contributors represent a wide range of healthcare professionals who ultimately want you to succeed.

This is book is not the last research book you will need. Consider it the starting point.

JDB

JGF

Foreword

Douglas L. Murphy, PhD
Dean, College of Health Related Professions
University of Arkansas for Medical Sciences

Over the past two decades, I have devoted thousands of hours, as a teacher, advisor, and thesis or dissertation committee member, to working with scores of students dealing with a research project of some type. These students in the allied health professions, nursing, dentistry, and biomedical sciences requested assistance with refining research questions, tying theories together, laying out research designs, planning for data collection and analyses, and relating their research findings to their research goals and specific aims. Other students required assistance in interpreting published research and applying the results to their anticipated practice. In the process, I often scoured my personal library of references on research methods and statistics to find just the right chapter or article that would enable the student to gain the insight they required to become more independent as a "consumer" of research literature or fledgling researcher. I often came up short because the book wasn't exactly what the student needed. The examples were from a different discipline, making the information difficult to apply; the content was too basic and theoretical, making the information difficult to understand; or the information was outdated, not taking into account technological advances that make the conduct of research easier.

I wish now that I had had a book such as *Introduction to Research and Medical Literature for Health Professionals, Third Edition,* to lend. It would have made my task simpler and would have enlightened the student far better than what I was able to provide at the time. This book, edited by my colleagues J. Dennis Blessing and J. Glenn Forister, is the first research methods textbook written specifically for students in the allied health professions. Both Dr. Blessing and Mr. Forister are respected physician assistant educators, researchers, and scholars. Dr. Blessing has received numerous national awards for his contributions to education and research, and Mr. Forister is recognized as an outstanding teacher and researcher.

Why a book on allied health research methods? On one hand, one may argue that research methods are research methods and data analysis techniques are data analysis techniques, regardless of the discipline, and that is true to some extent. On the other hand, there are many good reasons for a book specifically for allied health professions students.

First, the allied health professions are maturing at a rapid rate and are evolving into distinctive professions in their own right, with their own professional concerns, clinical techniques, roles within healthcare systems, and practice traditions. These factors often lead to research questions that can and should be answered and, in turn, research findings must be understood and applied by students and practitioners.

Second, as the allied health professions evolve, greater demands are placed on practitioners for responsibility and accountability in health care. Increasingly, practitioners are expected to participate as full members of healthcare teams who contribute expertise on par with physicians, nurses, dentists, and other team members. Therefore, allied health professionals must stay current on the research in their disciplines and must understand how research finding A or technique X applies to the care of their patients or clients, because it is unlikely that other members of the team will be able to contribute that same expertise.

Third, allied health professionals must demonstrate the efficacy of their contributions to health and wellness. Evidence-based care, economic imperatives, and professional ethics require us to show concretely that research finding A or technique X actually does result in better outcomes or reduce costs. The days of justifying a procedure or clinical practice by invoking tradition are quickly fading away.

Finally, allied health research tends to be grounded in the real-life experiences of allied health clinicians, many of whom have extended therapeutic care relationships with patients, clients, and their families. Other allied health personnel such as laboratory scientists and health information professionals may have no or limited direct contact with patients or clients. Their vital contributions lead to other research opportunities that range from basic scientific mechanisms to investigations into human factors (person-program or person-machine interfaces) that result in more accurate laboratory tests or more efficient, productive, and useful information systems. The nature of these relationships and their role in treatment, healing, and wellness can and should shape the kinds of research questions that are posed, methods used for answering the questions, and even the theory that shapes practice.

Fulfilling as a research career may be, it is unlikely that a large proportion of students reading

Introduction to Research and Medical Literature for Health Professionals, Third Edition, will pursue a career in allied health research. Some will practice in clinical settings as clinician-researchers, research partners, or research participants. The majority, however, will be informed "consumers" of research as they apply new knowledge, new procedures, and new techniques to day-to-day clinical care. All will require competencies in reading and comprehending research reports, interpreting and applying results, judging the adequacy of research practices, and drawing justifiable conclusions.

The editors and authors of this book are expert educators, researchers, and academics, who have "been there and done that." They speak from experience in guiding students and conducting research. This book is a valuable introduction to the major considerations in planning and carrying out research projects, guidelines for judging the quality of investigations, cautions for interpreting and applying findings, and essential resources. The topics range from the process for identifying a "researchable" problem and focusing research questions to finding the appropriate journal for your manuscript. Research techniques are explained from positivist and post-positivist paradigms to qualitative methods. Ethical considerations of human research are described, and guidelines for writing a research report are provided. Community-based participatory research, an emerging expectation in biomedical research, is explained and guidelines are provided for planning and conducting such research. Chapters and sections that describe the full array of study types that fall under the term "research" are particularly valuable because they can stimulate creative thinking about options for answering research questions and, even, what kinds of questions are "legitimate."

Regardless of the ultimate career aspirations of the allied health professions student reading this book, it is the one that you will keep on your shelf and refer to often. I know that I will keep a copy (or two or three) handy for that student who knocks on my door asking for some advice about a perplexing research project.

Contributors

Salah Ayachi, PhD, PA-C
Associate Professor
Department of Physician Assistant Studies
School of Health Professions
University of Texas Medical Branch
Galveston, TX

Rhonda L. Barnard, MS, CIP
Expedited Reviewer
Institutional Review Board
UT Health Science Center San Antonio
San Antonio, TX

J. Dennis Blessing, PhD, PA
Associate Dean
School of Health Professions
UT Health Science Center San Antonio
San Antonio, TX

Christopher E. Bork, PhD, FASAHP
Professor
Department of Public Health and Preventive Medicine
College of Medicine
The University of Toledo
Toledo, OH

James F. Cawley, MPH, PA-C
Professor and Interim Chair, Department of Prevention
   and Community Health
School of Public Health and Health Services
Professor of Health Care Sciences
School of Medicine and Health Sciences
The George Washington University
Washington, DC

Meredith Davison, PhD, MPH
Associate Dean for Academic Services
School of Community Medicine
Associate Director
Physician Assistant Program
University of Oklahoma, College of Medicine
Tulsa, OK

Richard Dehn, MPA, PA-C
Professor, College of Health and Human Services
Chair, Department of Physician Assistant Studies
Northern Arizona University
Flagstaff, AZ

Roy R. Estrada, PhD, PA-C, CIP
Associate Professor/Research, School of Health
   Professions
Associate Director, Institutional Review Board
UT Health Science Center San Antonio
San Antonio, TX

J. Glenn Forister, MS, PA-C
Associate Professor, Program Director
Department of Physician Assistant Studies
School of Health Professions
UT Health Science Center San Antonio
San Antonio, TX

Donna (De De) Gardner, MSHP, RRT, FAARC
Associate Professor, Interim Chair
Department of Respiratory Care
School of Health Professions
UT Health Science Center San Antonio
San Antonio, TX

Christine S. Gaspard, MSLS
Head of Access Services and Interlibrary Loan
Librarian, Briscoe Library
UT Health Science Center San Antonio
San Antonio, TX

Anita Duhl Glicken, MSW
Associate Dean for Physician Assistant Studies
University of Colorado School of Medicine
Director, CHA/PA Program
Professor and Section Head, Pediatrics
University of Colorado Anshutz Medical Campus
Aurora, CO

William D. Hendricson, MS, MA
Assistant Dean, Education and Faculty Development
Dental School
UT Health Science Center San Antonio
San Antonio, TX

Robert Jarski, PhD, PA
Professor, School of Health Sciences and
The OU William Beaumont School of Medicine
Director, Complementary Medicine and
   Wellness Program
Oakland University
Rochester, MI

Vasco Deon Kidd, DHSc, MPH, MS, PA-C
Assistant Professor
Department of Physician Assistant Studies
School of Health Professions
UT Health Science Center San Antonio
San Antonio, TX

George B. Kudolo, PhD, CPC, FACB
Distinguished Teaching Professor
Department of Clinical Laboratory Sciences
School of Health Professions
UT Health Science Center San Antonio
San Antonio, TX

Linda Levy, MSW, MLS, AHIP
Assistant Library Director for Branch Libraries and
   Database Services, Librarian IV
Briscoe Library
UT Health Science Center San Antonio
San Antonio, TX

Anthony A. Miller, MEd, PA-C
Professor and Director
Division of Physician Assistant Studies
School of Health Professions
Shenandoah University
Winchester, VA

Bruce R. Niebuhr, PhD
Susan Brown Logan Distinguished Professor in
   Teaching Excellence
Distinguished Teaching Professor
Department of Physician Assistant Studies
School of Health Professions
University of Texas Medical Branch
Galveston, TX

Catherine Ortega, EdD, PT, ATC, OCS
Associate Professor, Interim Chairperson
Distinguished Teaching Professor
Department of Physical Therapy
School of Health Professions
UT Health Science Center
San Antonio, TX

Suzanne M. Peloquin, PhD, OTR, FAOTA
Professor
Department of Occupational Therapy
School of Health Professions
University of Texas Medical Branch
Occupational Therapist, Alcohol and Drug Abuse Center
Galveston, TX

Bridgett Piernik-Yoder, PhD, OTR
Assistant Professor
Department of Occupational Therapy
School of Health Professions
UT Health Science Center San Antonio
San Antonio, TX

Katherine A. Prentice, MSIS
Head of Education and Information Services
Librarian, Briscoe Library
UT Health Science Center San Antonio
San Antonio, TX

Richard R. Rahr, EdD, PA-C
Professor and Chair
Department of Physician Assistant Studies
School of Health Professions
University of Texas Medical Branch
Galveston, TX

Scott D. Rhodes, PhD, MPH
Professor
Division of Public Health Sciences
Wake Forest School of Medicine
Winston-Salem, NC

Joseph O. Schmelz, PhD, RN, CIP, FAAN
Director, Research Regulatory Programs
Professor of Research, School of Nursing
UT Health Science Center San Antonio
San Antonio, TX

Albert Simon, DHS, PA
Vice Dean and Associate Professor
School of Osteopathic Medicine in Arizona
A.T. Still University
Mesa, AZ

Eric Willman, MSIS
Systems Librarian
Briscoe Library
UT Health Science Center San Antonio
San Antonio, TX

Reviewers

Amy L. Frith PhD, MPH, MS
Assistant Professor
School of Health Sciences and Human Performance
Ithaca College
Ithaca, NY

Dawn LaBarbera, PhD, PA-C
Associate Professor and Chair
Department of Physician Assistant Studies
University of Saint Francis
Fort Wayne, IN

Kenneth Ebersole, Med
Academic Dean
Dragon Rises College of Oriental Medicine
Gainesville, FL

Andrew J. Starsky MPT, PhD
Clinical Assistant Professor
Department of Physical Therapy
Marquette University
Milwaukee, WI

Antonio F. Cardoso, PhD
St. Joseph's University
Philadelphia, PA

Antoinette Marks, DHEd
Dean, Associate Studies
Former Asst. Dean College of Health Sciences
Grand Canyon University
Phoenix, AZ

Ashley Dulle, MBA, RRT, AE-C
Respiratory Therapy Program Director
Bossier Parish Community College
Bossier City, LA

Karen A. Wright, PhD, PA-C
Director of Research, Physician Assistant Program
School of Medicine and Health Sciences
The George Washington University
Washington, DC

WHY RESEARCH

CHAPTER OVERVIEW

This book is meant to be useful for students in the healthcare professions and for healthcare professionals beginning a research agenda. The goal of this book is to provide an introduction to research. At best, it is a beginner's guide. The contributors are experienced educators, practitioners, and researchers from many professions. Certainly, there are many ways to approach research beyond those in this book. Two things this book is not: (1) a complete research guide, and (2) a statistics book. Other references and resources will be needed. This book is designed to help the reader begin his or her research efforts and to advance his or her research skills and abilities. Each small piece of research that can add to the whole body of medical knowledge results in improvement in the healthcare professions and in the physical, mental, and social health of those for whom care is provided.

Introduction

J. Dennis Blessing, PhD, PA

J. Glenn Forister, MS, PA-C

"If we knew what it was we were doing, it would not be called research, would it?"

—Albert Einstein

INTRODUCTION

From my own retrospective viewpoint of a student in a healthcare profession and eventually as a healthcare practitioner, research has determined almost everything that is practiced now and in the future. The word "research" often evokes a panic reaction. Students often see research as a mysterious process that is difficult to understand and even more difficult to conduct. Often students cannot see the connection between a required research project and their healthcare careers. Similarly, many clinicians may not connect their job to research. However, the exact opposite is more likely to be true. Research is an opportunity to explore, understand, and explain. Mastery of research methods can expand opportunities for healthcare professionals and can lead to improved health care.

Many clinical practices are becoming involved with clinical trials and studies. This makes understanding the scientific process and research even more important. Beyond the possibility of being directly involved in research, every healthcare professional must understand research processes in order to interpret healthcare literature. The decision to incorporate a new treatment modality depends on the ability to evaluate and understand the research that led to that modality. Additionally, healthcare professionals must be able to evaluate the literature in terms of how it relates to patients and to evaluate the best treatment options.

RESEARCH AND STUDENTS IN HEALTHCARE PROFESSIONS

The word "research" conjures up images:

1. Egghead nerds hidden away in a lab doing something that seems to have little relationship to the everyday world.
2. Dr. Frankenstein.
3. Boring work forced on students.
4. Pursuit of information that has little application in the real world.
5. Not something a health professional does in clinical practice.

For many people, the research process is difficult to understand. Research requires manipulations of impossible-to-learn formulations that end up in language that only other researchers comprehend. Research sometimes produces contradictory results that often leave healthcare professionals wondering what to do. Research frightens clinicians and keeps educators from taking tenure-track positions. Research conjures up an image of boring, regimented work that may have little to do with the "real world."

However frightening the concept of research is for students, faculty, and practitioners, it provides the basis for practice of the healthcare profession. Research is the key to the present and future, regardless of profession or position and function in health care. The practice of medicine, nursing, and other forms of health care is based in scientific research that is applied to every patient. The only way health care can advance is by research, that is, developing evidence of what works and applying the results. Practitioners who are not actively involved in research must possess a basic understanding of the process and what research results mean. This understanding allows practitioners to interpret results, to differentiate between conflicting results, and to discern what is useful AND best for patients. As evidence-based medicine becomes the basis for health care, understanding and conducting research also become more important. More and more practicing healthcare professionals are finding that research or some aspect of research has become part of their day-to-day job.

RESEARCH EQUALS CURIOSITY

Whether they realized it or not, everyone has done research in some manner. Seeking an answer to a question is a form of research. Even looking up a word in a dictionary can be considered a form of research. Curiosity and the need for information create the drive to find answers in health care and in everyday life. Finding those answers is research. Certainly, much "research" is informal and without the systematic constraints required in formal research, but it occurs every day. A parent's admonition to "Look it up!" sends children off on a research effort whether they realize it or not. Practitioners do research every day as they investigate the literature for solutions to patients' problems. Students do research as part of their education and preparation to enter their profession. The very act of study is investigation in some ways, regardless of what it is called. Preparation for an examination is a form of research.

Research occurs in the laboratory, classroom, office, practice, and society at large. It is directly applicable to a problem or only a small piece of larger solutions. Research can help prepare for what will happen and understand what has happened. Individual and personal needs and desires direct how research is used and the part it plays in careers and lives. Research is a tool to be used. Learning to use this tool helps relieve anxieties and increases the ability to appreciate and to even enjoy the process.

Research that involves interests or needs for discovery is most important. In some ways research may be more important to the practitioner than to the student, but research skills are introduced during education. Similarly, what interests a healthcare practitioner or student may be mundane but necessary to the profession or livelihood. For example, an occupational therapist may have little interest in the differences in practice census flows by disability type, but that information may have a great impact on patient scheduling and clinical assignments. Research may provide answers that allow for the most efficient use of time and expertise in a practice. Many questions about one's practice can be answered by research. It may or may not require great statistical analysis, but it requires the systematic gathering, analysis, and interpretation of information.

Another example of research application in practice is patient outcomes. What is the difference in outcomes in a practice if a disease is treated with regime A versus regime B? There may be a wealth of information in texts and the literature, but what about a specific practice? Personal research is needed to determine the answer, whether a formal or informal process is used. The values of informal versus formal research may be equal, but a formal investigation might lead to benefits beyond a single setting if the investigation yields significant information.

RESEARCH AND THE STUDENTS OF HEALTHCARE PROFESSIONS

For a student, research is part of the task of discovery and learning. Research provides the information needed to build a fund of knowledge that will determine what a student will do as a healthcare provider. Every student must learn to interpret the literature and be an informed consumer of medical research and healthcare literature. At a minimum, learning what research means and how to interpret research findings is useful in a professional career. These skills allow healthcare practitioners to deliver an acceptable level of care. In many ways, the research process is comparable to clinical reasoning and critical thinking skills. Much of the discipline needed to develop and conduct research is

Table 1–1 Types of Research*

Type	Description
Pure	Abstract and general, concerned with generating new theory and gaining new knowledge for the knowledge's sake. Example: theory development.
Experimental	Manipulation of one variable to see its effect on another variable, while controlling for as many other variables as possible and randomly assigning subjects to groups. Example: double-blind random assignment control groups, response to an intervention.
Clinical	Performed in the clinical setting where control over variables is quite difficult. Examples: drug trials, therapeutic outcomes.
Applied	Designed to answer a practical question, to help people do their jobs better. Examples: time use studies, evaluation of different types of interventions with the same purpose.
Descriptive	Describing a group, a situation, or an individual to gain knowledge that may be applied to further groups or situations, as in case studies or trend analyses. Examples: surveys, qualitative research, measurement of characteristics, response to phenomena.
Laboratory	Performed in laboratory surroundings that are tightly controlled. Example: basic science research.

*Adapted from Bailey,[1] p. xxii.

the same as the discipline needed to systematically assess and manage disease processes.

Education in the healthcare professions should be consistent with adult learning theory. All healthcare practitioners should be lifelong learners; the healthcare professional who stops building his or her knowledge base and abilities will soon be hopelessly behind. Experience is part of that knowledge base, but continuing to understand and interpret the literature is the foundation for maintaining, redefining, and increasing that base. Research can help meet future healthcare challenges. Research is one tool that helps practitioners to "learn how to learn."

FEAR OF THE UNKNOWN

Research can be a monster. The unknowns and seemingly complex methods of systematic research and its processes frighten many people. Analysis, statistics, and interpretation can be daunting as well. Research as a discipline even has its own language. Research may be held in high regard by many and in low regard (almost thought of as a dirty word?) by others. Many healthcare professionals want to leave research to others. But as healthcare professionals become more involved in and invested with their careers and practices, they may find that their roles involve research and additional responsibilities in a research arena. Society expects healthcare professionals to understand healthcare research and to apply this to the needs of the individual patient.

RESEARCH TAKES MANY FORMS

Research takes many different forms (**Table 1–1**). Research can be categorized in several ways, including pure research, experimental research, clinical research, applied research, descriptive research, laboratory research,[2] and outcomes research. These forms depend on many factors.

The design of a research study is an important factor that confuses many beginning investigators.[1] Some research can be done without any special knowledge or skills, such as counting how many patients have a particular diagnosis. Some research requires specialized skills and must follow an exact methodology, such as clinical drug trials. Research has a language of its own that must be learned and understood. The recording of experimental results and writing of research have special requirements that must be learned, practiced, and perfected. For most, research is about phenomena (something that can be perceived) that affects what is done and what is needed to know. It is about observation and interpretation of what is learned in order to answer the questions posed.

Research can be challenging and difficult. It also can be enjoyable and rewarding. At every level and in every format and design, it should add to knowledge. It is unlikely that any single piece of research will make headlines. However, answering questions and making small contributions to the larger body of medical knowledge is very satisfying. Health care at every level continually creates questions that need answering. Society has questions that need answering. When healthcare professionals accept the challenge of answering those questions, a basic understanding of research and how to apply it is necessary. Learning the research process offers the greatest likelihood of finding those answers. One does not have to be a genius to do research. One does not have to be mathematically gifted. One must only have the interest. Research and its results can be used in the classroom, laboratory, or clinic. It is a process to be learned and used to help healthcare practitioners, patients, students, and others.

OUR GOAL

This book is just one tool in developing research expertise. The student should use this book as an introductory tool, a starting point, and add to it from other resources. Learning the process of research is as important as understanding the research results. Students should use many books and resources. The goal of this text is to help students in healthcare professions and healthcare pro-

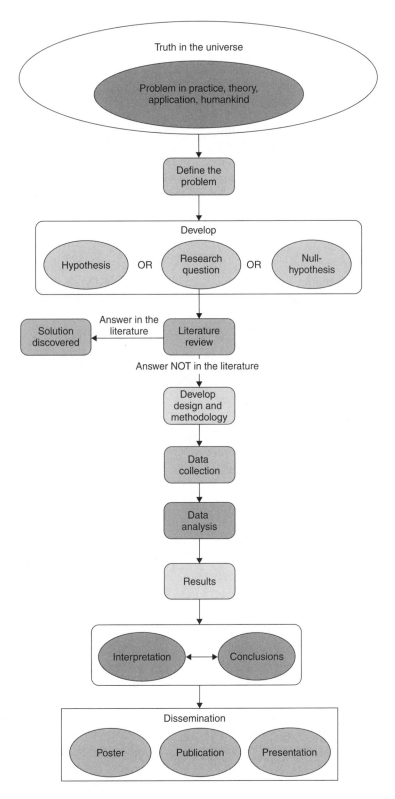

Figure 1–1 Outline of the scientific process.

fessionals develop research skills to acquire and contribute knowledge that benefits their patients.

DEVELOPING A RESEARCH PROJECT

If a research project is part of education and training, it may take many forms. Choosing a project and developing its design depends on a number of factors. The first is to understand exactly what is expected. Schools or institutions may have specific guidelines. These parameters must be known before beginning any project. Many programs and institutions prescribe a scientific writing format. Student investigators must know which style and style manual is required and should, of course, buy a copy or acquire an electronic copy.

Schools or institutions may assign research topics and/or a specific design to follow. Development of a research project depends on many factors. Some introspection and consideration are required with regard to time, effort, cost, resources, and ability needed for any project. This introspection must include an assessment of personal attributes, interests, resources, and expectations of self.[3] Part of this assessment must consider strengths as a researcher and abilities to accomplish a project. One cannot do quantum physics without the education and skills necessary, no matter how interested one may be in quantum physics. Students and inexperienced investigators must be able to concentrate their research efforts to develop or use their expertise to the maximum benefit. It is better to be an expert in one small, specific area, than somewhat of an expert in several. Every beginning researcher needs mentors and collaborators. Students and beginning investigators should seek out people who have skills in their area of interest and ask for their help. They should explore the possibilities of collaborating with someone on their research as a learning activity. Another key element to a successful research effort is the allotment of adequate time for investigations. For students, time may be very limited by schedules, class obligations, planned graduation date, etc. A timeline for a research project and should be created and followed.

The first step of developing a research project is brainstorming. This activity should be as expansive as possible by making a list (by hand or on the computer) of everything of interest in any way. Once these ideas are recorded, a short break of a few minutes or a few days should be taken (the key is NOT to think about the project for a short while). Then the list can be refined; new items can be added, and those that do not seem important can be eliminated. This process can or may be repeated more than once before a project is defined. A student, for example, may have an assigned topic, which makes things a little easier, but with an assigned topic there may be many ways to approach the assigned project. Once a list of possibilities has been developed, then the defining process can be done in this way:

1. Make a list of everything of interest or questions that need to be answered.
2. Prioritize the list in the order of interests.
3. Make a second ordered list (from the first) of the things that are within the capabilities of the investigator.
4. Make a third ordered list (from the first) of the things that are important to the effort.
5. Make a fourth ordered list (from the first) of the things that are important to society or health, or your particular profession.
6. Compare the lists. Items that appear at the top of all four lists should then be prioritized and merged into a single list.
7. Make the decisions about what can and cannot be done. Mark off the things that cannot be done. This includes financing the study. Financial support is just as important as time and expertise to the success of a project.
8. The topic that survives, becomes, or is central to the lists is the basis of the research project. This topic represents a process of summation that includes challenges that need to be researched; challenges to the capability of the researcher; challenges that are important to the individual, the program, and the topic of interest. What could be better?

9. Develop a timeline for the study; set aside research time and plan the step-by-step process and then . . .

10. GET STARTED. A respected educator said, "Time goes by regardless of what you do. When it does, make sure you are not still waiting for the best time to begin."[4] A student may have a defined end date (e.g., project due date, end of semester, graduation, etc.). Do not hesitate to get started.

SUMMARY

Whether one loves it, dislikes it, or would rather not think about it, research is a part of professional life in health care. Research will certainly be part of a healthcare career. Research provides the basis for all that healthcare providers do. Individual research is unlikely to change the world or win a Nobel Prize; however, each small addition to our knowledge of the world and health care improves them both. Remember, research is not a dirty word, it is a powerful tool that every healthcare provider must learn to use. Research is a tool to be mastered in order to care for others.

REFERENCES

1. Bailey DM. *Research for the Health Professional: A Practical Guide,* 2nd ed. Philadelphia, PA: FA Davis; 1997, xxii.
2. Campbell DT, Stanley JC. *Experimental and Quasi-Experimental Designs for Research.* Boston, MA: Houghton Mifflin; 1963:1.
3. Jones PE. Personal communication; 2004.
4. Rahr RR. Personal communication; 2004.

CHAPTER OVERVIEW

This chapter contains several essays on research from several healthcare professionals. In no way does this list represent all the healthcare professions; the selected professions provide but a sample.

Essays on Research in the Health Professions

George B. Kudolo, PhD, FACB, *Clinical Laboratory Sciences*
Bridgett Piernik-Yoder, PhD, OTR, *Occupational Therapy*
Vasco Deon Kidd, Dr.HS, PA-C, *Physician Assistant*
Donna D. Gardner, MSHP, RRT, FAARC, *Respiratory Care*
Catherine Ortega, EdD, PT, ATC, OCS, *Physical Therapy*

RESEARCH IN THE CLINICAL CHEMISTRY LABORATORY

The Importance of Research in the Clinical Chemistry Laboratory

George B. Kudolo, PhD, FACB

Clinical laboratory sciences (CLS) is one of the least recognized of the healthcare professions, primarily because it involves very little direct contact with patients. Yet, clinical laboratory scientists play a very crucial role in patient care. There are several disciplines within CLS, including clinical chemistry, microbiology, and hematology. CLS professionals work with blood, urine, and other body fluids as well as microorganisms. CLS is estimated to provide more than seventy percent of the objective data used by healthcare providers in the diagnosis and treatment of patients.[1] In cases of national emergencies, such as a bioterrorist attack (e.g., anthrax or ricin) or epidemic disease outbreak (e.g., the swine flu, H1N1), CLS professionals play leading roles in the identification of the causative organisms or insulting chemicals. Clinical chemistry scientists may also specialize in the area of forensic toxicology, providing data from postmortem toxicology. Research is very important in all these areas. Research reveals the best test procedures with the highest diagnostic specificity (i.e., to test negative when the patient has no disease) and diagnostic sensitivity (i.e., to test positive when a disease is present in the patient).

Scientific research involves systematic investigation. Research often involves grouping facts (data) so that conclusions can be drawn regarding disease processes, for example, how they are acquired and how they can be detected and treated. The primary objective of most of the research in CLS is to discover new data that may improve the diagnosis of disease. For example, diabetes mellitus is a debilitating disease affecting approximately 25 million people in the United States. Because of its morbidity and mortality, we must understand how best to diagnose and manage this disease. Laboratory evaluation is key to management of the disease and its sequellae. Clinical laboratory scientists play a major role in this arena. More investigation of blood and body fluid markers for diabetes are needed. We need to understand what changes occur in this disease process, and this is the type of research undertaken by the CLS. For the test results to be meaningful to the patient, healthcare providers must interpret the results correctly. In many instances, interferences complicate the interpretation of results.[2] The role of the clinical laboratory scientist is to research those interfering factors and provide clear results. For example, the CLS professional may help the healthcare provider prescribe drugs that are adjusted to the patient's biochemistry. From CLS research, additional tests may be developed that help to monitor drug toxicity and efficacy.[3]

One important area in which CLS research continues to make significant strides is forensic investigation, which includes workplace drug testing and the justice system. CLS research provides the basis for much of the forensic evidence that is so important in today's crime scene and other investigations.[4]

In conclusion, CLS research produces data and information on which clinical decisions are made. Research ensures that the results are reliable and reproducible. CLS research can influence life-and-death decisions. CLS research can show who is innocent and who is guilty. Every CLS professional must understand what research means and how to use it effectively.

REFERENCES

1. Forsman RW. Why is the laboratory an afterthought for managed care organizations? *Clinical Chemistry.* 1996;42(5):813–816.
2. Dasgupta A. The effects of adulterants and selected ingested compounds on drugs-of-abuse testing in urine. *Am J Clin Pathol.* 2007;128(3):491–503.
3. Kaldy J. Personalized medicine: Genetic component to providing quality care. *Consult Pharm.* 2011;26(9): 618–627.
4. Flanagan RJ, Connally G. Interpretation of analytical toxicology results in life and at postmortem. *Toxicol Rev.* 2005; 24(1):51–62.

RESEARCH IN OCCUPATIONAL THERAPY

The Importance of Research to Occupational Therapy

Bridgett Piernik-Yoder, PhD, OTR

Like other healthcare professions, occupational therapy (OT) has the obligation to provide evidence that the services provided for clients have a benefit. While the notion of this responsibility is readily accepted, it is often stated that the OT profession has not always been as aggressive as it should be in demonstrating the efficacy and efficiency of OT treatments through empirical evidence.[1] Occupational therapy is a healthcare profession that uses a holistic approach to understand and address how people with and without disabilities live their daily lives in the context of their environments.[2] In examining research activity in OT, it is important to understand the current status of research in the field, barriers to the production and utilization of research, and opportunities for growth in OT research.

The Status of Occupational Therapy Research

In March 1917, when OT was formalized as a profession, the founders recognized the need to disseminate knowledge about the therapeutic effect of OT. The profession's first scientific journal, *Archives of Occupational Therapy,* was published in 1922.[3] More than 80 years later, in preparation for the profession's 100th anniversary in 2017, the American Occupational Therapy Association developed the Centennial Vision. The Centennial Vision, intended to be vision statement for the profession as well as a call to action, states that by 2017, "occupational therapy is a *powerful, widely recognized, science-driven,* and *evidence-based* profession . . ."[4] This expression is a clear mandate to the profession to not only continue but to increase its research efforts.

Gutman, editor of the *American Journal of Occupational Therapy (AJOT)*, outlined the publication priorities of the journal. Occupational therapy—like other health professions—has not fully answered questions regarding treatment efficacy and efficiency.[5] Consequently, third-party payers have been placed in the decision-making role regarding many aspects of treatments, including who receives services, for how long, and even what treatments are denied.[5] In an effort to build the evidence needed to respond to these external challenges, the publication goals of *AJOT* were aligned to match the research needs of the profession. The stated publication priorities of *AJOT* include the following: high-quality effectiveness studies; efficiency studies including cost and time efficiency, patient satisfaction, safety, and patient compliance; studies addressing the psychometric properties of occupational therapy assessment measures; studies demonstrating the relationship between participation in occupation and health indicators; and analyses of current professional issues.

With regard to research methodology, it has been stated that *AJOT*'s publication preference is not based on a specific study design but rather on the appropriateness of the study design selection to answer the research question. For instance, quantitative study designs are the most appropriate to answer research questions about intervention efficacy, cost, and time efficiency. Qualitative study designs best answer research questions related to needs of patients and their caregivers from novel populations or in areas where OT services are emerging. Additionally, mixed-method study designs provide answers about patient satisfaction, compliance, and safety.[5]

Barriers to Occupational Therapy Research

While the research priorities for the profession have been clearly articulated, it is important to consider the barriers that exist in both the production and the utilization of evidence in OT. With regard to the production of resources, challenges that face the OT profession are similar to those encountered in many other healthcare professions. First, the paucity of advanced, research-intensive degrees available in the field lead to occupational therapists pursuing advanced degrees in non-OT fields.[6] While cross-disciplinary study does provide many benefits, the result is that most research conducted by occupational therapists at the doctoral level is outside the OT field.

Most occupational therapy academicians come to the educational setting after a number of years in clinical practice. While a strong clinical background is extremely important to teaching future practitioners, this background does not typically include an established line of research.[6]

It has been suggested that occupational therapists must be prepared to critically evaluate the evidence-based literature and apply it to their practice. Some recommendations include incorporating evidence-based practice into the OT educational curriculum. Thus, occupational therapists entering the profession have a strong foundation in an evidence-based approach.[7]

Growth Opportunities

As resources in healthcare and education settings become increasingly competitive, it is critical that the benefit of OT services to individual, families, and societies be unequivocally demonstrated. Given the importance of this task, opportunities must be explored to not only expand the research capacity within the field but also to produce clinically relevant research.

Although it will always be necessary to address the support needed to build career scientists in the profession, it is also important to consider building partnerships between researchers and clinicians.[2] This important endeavor will provide an opportunity for researchers and clinicians to collaborate on clinical questions that will have true utility for the OT and other clinicians, while providing the researcher access to an applied setting in which to collect data.

As Keilhofner aptly stated, "the existence of occupational therapy depends on societal support."[8] While much as been accomplished over the past decade with regard to increasing the amount of evidence available in occupational therapy, we must embrace the obligation to demonstrate the benefit of our services in order to maintain a strong place in the health and education settings.

REFERENCES

1. Gutman S. State of the journal, 2010. *Am J Occup Ther.* 2010; 64(6):832–840.
2. Clark F. High-definition occupational therapy: HD OT. *Am J Occup Ther.* 2010;64(6):848–854.
3. Punwar A, Peloquin S. *Occupational Therapy: Principles and Practice.* Baltimore, MD: Lippincott, Williams & Wilkins; 2000.
4. American Occupational Therapy Association. *The Road to the Centennial Vision.* Published in 2006. http://www.aota.org/News/Centennial/Background/36516.aspx?FT=.pdf. Accessed on August 26, 2011.
5. Gutman S. AJOT publication priorities. *Am J Occup Ther.* 2010;64(5):679–681.
6. Gutman S. Why haven't we generated sufficient evidence? Part I: Barriers to applied research. *Am J Occup Ther.* 2009; 63(3):235–237.
7. Lin SH, Murphy SL, Robinson JC. The issue is—facilitating evidence-based practice: Process, strategies, and resources. *Am J Occup Ther.* 2010;64(1):164–171.
8. Keilhofner G. *Research in Occupational Therapy: Methods of Inquiry for Enhancing Practice.* Philadelphia, PA: FA Davis; 2006.

RESEARCH IN THE PHYSICIAN ASSISTANT PROFESSION

Why Is Research Important to the Physician Assistant Profession?

Vasco Deon Kidd, Dr.HS, PA-C

Research is as important to the physician assistant (PA) profession as it is to all healthcare disciplines. Research is vital to our efforts in improving patient care, clinical guidelines, healthcare policies, and expanding the PA scope of practice. However, a crucial challenge facing the PA profession is the lack of PA clinical, educational, and bench researchers whose research interests revolve around PA issues.

Historically, most educational institutions are focused on fulfilling the mandate of producing quality, competent, primary care clinicians. Therefore, PA training programs did not teach research in the didactic curriculum. However, the trend is changing; many PA programs have placed a greater emphasis on educating students about research methodology, data collection, and critically appraising research findings. In addition, more PA faculty are becoming involved in clinical, educational, and workforce research. This increase in faculty expertise will translate to improved PA student understanding.

As new PA programs open and existing programs are expanded, formulating best practices in teaching and learning derived from educational research will become increasingly important. Therefore, it is imperative that PA educators advance PA education to address the needs of the twenty-first century adult learner.

For students and practicing PAs, having the requisite skills for appraising and conducting primary research is extremely important, especially in the era of evidence-based medicine and healthcare reform. Not only is it important for PAs to know how to formulate and answer research questions, but it is also important to understand the research priorities and the needs of the health service sector. For example, more research is needed on how the PA profession can reduce healthcare costs while providing quality care.

Unless PAs plug the data gaps surrounding the PA profession and the care PAs deliver, it will be difficult if not impossible for policy makers to understand the value that PAs bring to the table. Evidence-based medicine will be used to guide educational policies and practices that influence all healthcare disciplines. Those healthcare professions that have data to support their practice decisions will be able to shape policy and garner resources most effectively.

Another benefit of research is that it opens up opportunities that were not readily available to PAs a decade ago. These opportunities include being a primary investigator for clinical trials, director of research, working for a think tank, acting as a policy and content expert, etc. For those PAs that are effective clinicians and researchers, the opportunity to carve out a niche in the PA profession is tremendous.

As important as it is for PAs to acquire research knowledge and to publish, at times conducting research can seem tedious, time-consuming, and monotonous. Many clinicians may not have the time to develop their research interests and may have no desire to publish for fear of being scrutinized. However, the sense of accomplishment an investigator feels after finishing and submitting a research manuscript for publication is an exhilarating experience.

More PA researchers are needed to answer the looming professional questions in order to garner the respect this unique profession deserves. PAs can no longer sit on the sidelines and allow non-PAs to determine their professional worth. PAs must take hold of the profession's destiny by answering critical questions through research.

RESEARCH IN RESPIRATORY CARE

Types of Research in Respiratory Care

Donna D. Gardner, MSHP, RRT, FAARC

First, very few respiratory therapists (RTs) are employed as researchers.[1] Many RT researchers are also clinicians, teachers, and managers.[1] Respiratory therapists and other healthcare providers must be able to read and understand scientific research even though they may not be directly involved in research.[2] Respiratory therapists are primary investigators in research in a variety of settings and opportunities. Some RTs began their careers in bench, laboratory, clinical, educational, or management research. These types of research lead to changes in the practice of respiratory therapy. The one area of research in which RTs can participate is patient care. Research may occur anywhere RTs work. The research type and topic can be broad, from equipment to technological advances to disease management or education.

Because many RT tasks are equipment and technology based, evaluating new equipment is an area for research almost all RTs can do. This includes evaluating new medical equipment that is used to diagnose or support the patient. The question is this: "Is it better than what we have?" New products, modes of ventilation, medications, educational methods, and electronic medical records lend themselves to investigation. The RT must take the lead to make sure new equipment is necessary.[2]

Many RTs participate in industry research. In addition to understanding the scientific methods, RT investigators must be knowledgeable about regulatory and ethical standards. This means following the Institutional Review Board (IRB) protocols and legal and ethical policies to ensure safety and the protection of their subjects' rights.

Another avenue for research is respiratory therapy academic research, that is, keeping educators up to date with technology, treatment, and educational practices.[1] Respiratory therapy educators must ensure that new technology, medications, and equipment being introduced to the student are applicable for the profession and have met the scientific rigor required for patient care.[2] The RT academician must be knowledgeable about new and developing products and technologies. Respiratory therapy faculty must be able to evaluate and compare new and existing treatment modalities. Educators must be able to critically evaluate and interpret the research literature concerning respiratory therapy and educational practices. Many academicians are expected to conduct their own investigational research.[2]

The purpose of research is to advance the scientific knowledge of respiratory therapy. Some RTs participate in device and equipment evaluation; some participate in prospective and retrospective clinical trials. Respiratory therapy managers are involved in quality improvement activities, which can be valuable research projects.[1] Many RTs use survey research to investigate attitudes, knowledge, and interests in the various dynamics of respiratory therapy.[1] Many RTs use case reports to provide teaching lessons important to respiratory care practice.[1]

Research is the basis for making changes in respiratory care practices. Decision making regarding therapeutics, new technology, and approaches to patient problems must be based in research and, preferably, evidence-based practice.[3] Prospective clinical studies are the best tools for evidence-based clinical practice.[4] These types of investigations change the practice of respiratory therapy. Case reports are a great method for students to examine unusual or educational cases in terms of patient signs, symptoms, treatment, or a combination of these items.[5]

Respiratory therapy often requires processes that change existing modes of care or implement new processes to achieve the best patient care. Research helps determine the best method for delivering the care.[6] Quality assurance or quality improvement programs help RT managers and practitioners to improve practice. For example, misallocation of respiratory therapy services is a problem among many hospitals. This type of research can determine quality assurance and guide selection of indicated services.[6]

Although not all RTs are involved in research, there is no doubt that research is becoming a greater part of respiratory therapy practice. Each year, more research reports and abstracts are presented at the profession's international congress. This research that has been completed by RTs worldwide. Much of what RTs are doing becomes part of the evidence that supports RT practice. It is the duty of all RTs to move the respiratory therapy research agenda forward.

REFERENCES

1. Pearson DJ. Research and publication in respiratory care. *Respir Care.* 2004:49(10):1145–1146.
2. Chatburn RL. Overview of respiratory care research. *Respir Care.* 2004;49(10):1149–1157.
3. Fink J. Device and equipment evaluations. *Respir Care.* 2004;49(10):1158–1164.
4. Schwenzer KJ, Durbin CG. The spectrum of respiratory care research: Prospective clinical research. *Respir Care.* 2004;49(10):1165–1170.
5. Hess DR. Retrospective studies and chart reviews. *Respir Care.* 2004;49(10):1171–1174.
6. Stoller JK. Quality assurance research: Studying process of care. *Respir Care.* 2004:49(10)1175–1180. http://www.aarc.org/daz/rcjournal/rcjournal/x.RCJOURNAL.COM%2002.21.07/contents/10.04/10.04.1175.pdf. Accessed on August 29, 2011.
7. Rubenfeld GD. Surveys: An introduction. *Respir Care.* 2004;49(10):1181–1185. https://research.chm.msu.edu/Resources/Surveys_an_introduction.pdf. Accessed on August 29, 2011.
8. Restrepo, RD. AARC clinical practice guidelines: From referenced-based to evidence-based. *Respir Care.* 2010;55(6):787–789. http://www.rcjournal.com/contents/06.10/06.10.0787.pdf. Accessed on August 29, 2011.

RESEARCH IN PHYSICAL THERAPY

The Relevance of Research to the Profession of Physical Therapy

Catherine Ortega, EdD, PT, ATC, OCS

The physical therapy profession was founded in response to a national need during World War I.[1] Early practitioners provided care with interventions derived from deduction, empirical evidence, and clinical experience. The height of the polio epidemic and increased numbers of injured veterans from World War II combined to increase the demand for physical therapy and thus provide impetus for the establishment of curricula and formal education in the profession.[1,2] Even with this increased demand for patient care, much of the intervention was passive and based on clinical expertise.

Though exercise as an intervention was added to the profession during the 1960s and in subsequent years, much of physical therapy clinical practice continued to be supported by experiential evidence and minimal research. With the advent and development of evidence-based medicine, it became clear that physical therapy had to demonstrate therapy outcomes. Evidence-based practice has three primary components: (1) patient preference, (2) research evidence, and (3) clinical expertise.[3] The profession of physical therapy, similar to other branches of medicine, is challenged to provide systematic reasoning and scientific investigations to support interventions.

The initial trend in evidence-based practice was to search for research evidence and, where it was not available, to regard interventions with skepticism. Research was initially given more merit than patient preference and clinical expertise. This dearth of research evidence in the field of physical therapy provided rationale for the elevation of the entry-level degree from a bachelor's to a master's degree. Physical therapy programs across the country transitioned to the master's degree level and added research components to physical therapy curricula.[2] All students were encouraged to perform research as they progressed through the master's level programs. It was proposed that all clinicians would then be able to contribute to the body of evidence to support interventions and promote patient care.

With the creation of the Vision 2020 statement from the American Physical Therapy Association (www.apta.org),[4] which included the component of physical therapy as a "doctoring profession," came an understanding that not all physical therapists should perform research. There was improved clarity with regard to the place of research as a component of evidence-based practice. Therefore, though research continues to be valued to support the high standards for patient care, the role of the physical therapist with regard to research and the place of research within the practice of physical therapy is more clear.

Specifically, physical therapists must understand research and be able to critically appraise the evidence. All physical therapy curricula now must contain activities that promote critical thinking with regard to the assessment of research. Activities and didactic content are included to promote an understanding of the application of statistical procedures, assessment of the validity of evidence, and the appropriate application of evidence to clinical practice.

Current physical therapy graduates enter the clinical setting with an understanding of research and are able to apply the steps of evidence-based practice. Their first step is to assemble a clinical question using the P-I-C-O (Patient, Intervention, Comparison, Outcome) format. This format defines a patient problem and allows for the search of the evidence for answers. Physical therapists then use the information gained to attain competence and assess the validity of each investigation found. By doing so, physical therapists can better apply research evidence to make the best choice with patient care. Though the performance of research is critical to provide evidence for interventions, the critical thinking and systematic steps of evidence-based practice give relevance to research in physical therapy.

The current state of health care in our country provides further support for the relevance of research to physical therapy. Insurance providers and governmental oversight mechanisms merit justifications for physical therapy. Often justification is required to approve physical therapy services, and even after approval, specific interventions require validation. The ability to apply the steps of evidence-based practice efficiently allow clinicians to provide patient care with less disruption of services due to lack of approval. Research in and of itself is relevant to physical therapy. Without data, without sound, rigorous investigations and systematic conclusions, professionals will continue to perform trial-and-error interventions.

In summary, physical therapy professionals have progressed from using passive trial-and-error interventions to using critical thinking to assess evidence and apply the steps of evidence-based practice. Doctor of physical therapy programs include education to perform and assess research, always with the intent to apply the highest standard of care to patients. The current understanding of the relevance of research has placed this third leg of the evidenced-based practice stool in perspective for academicians, students, and clinicians alike.

REFERENCES

1. Moffat M. History of physical therapy practice in the United States. *The Journal of Physical Therapy Education,* Winter 2003.
2. Murphy W. Healing the Generations: A History of Physical Therapy and the American Physical Therapy Association. 1995. Lyme, CT: Greenwich Publishing Group.
3. Sackett D. Evidence-based medicine: What it is and what it isn't. *BMJ.* 1996; 312:71–72. http://www.bmj.com/cgi/content/full/312/7023/71. Accessed on September 12, 2011.
4. American Physical Therapy Association. www.apta.org. Accessed on September 12, 2011.
5. American Physical Therapy Association. *Guide to Physical Therapy Practice,* 2nd ed. Alexandria, VA: APTA, 1997.

CHAPTER OVERVIEW

This chapter discusses a sampling of the ethical considerations involved in research that may not immediately come to mind. Most individuals understand that ethical behaviors are important in the treatment of human subjects who participate in research studies and that such ethical treatment is essential. Recently, U.S. officials formally apologized after a medical historian unearthed what they called a reprehensible experiment within which U.S. researchers deliberately infected prisoners and patients with syphilis in a mental hospital in Guatemala from 1946 to 1948. The research process taps many ethical considerations beyond this clear violation of human rights, however. Research in healthcare practice is a multifaceted process with interpersonal and ethical challenges that transcend the ethical demands associated with the science that occurs in a laboratory. Scientific inquiry demands that healthcare practitioners make critical decisions, act morally, and interact responsibly with others. They must consider personal value systems, make critical decisions, and interact responsibly with others. This chapter is designed to provoke the reader to think more deeply about what it means to be ethical in the practice of research, to touch the reader's mind according to Allen's description above, to provoke the reader to "think about action and see the uses in experience of acting one way rather than another."[1(p53)]

Ethics in Research

Suzanne M. Peloquin, PhD, OTR, FAOTA

"Even if we cannot, strictly speaking, teach people to act properly, we can prepare minds to think about action and to see the uses in experience of acting one way rather than another."

—J. Allen[1(p53)]

THINKING ABOUT ETHICS IN RESEARCH

We begin by examining a provocative fable entitled, "The Glass in the Field."[2] A fable is a story about animals that aims to teach moral lessons about persons. This fable features a goldfinch, several large birds (a seagull, a hawk, and an eagle) and one small swallow, and provides analogues for many aspects of research. As its title suggests, the story turns around a large piece of plate glass left standing in a field by a construction crew. The first bird to encounter the glass was a goldfinch who was knocked out after flying into it. When asked by the seagull what had happened, the recovered goldfinch considered the question carefully and concluded that the air had crystallized. The seagull, the eagle, and the hawk all laughed at the unlikely assumption. They offered other hypotheses: the goldfinch was struck by a hailstone; the goldfinch had had a stroke. They asked for the swallow's opinion, and the swallow said that perhaps the air *had* crystallized.

The large birds then took wagers from the goldfinch, who, annoyed at their laughter, predicted that they would also hit the hardened air if they flew the same course. They took the goldfinch's bet of a dozen worms each and invited the swallow to join them in testing their hypotheses. The swallow, having empirically observed the health outcome experienced by the goldfinch, declined. Together the large and more powerful birds flew the exact course described by the goldfinch and, as predicted, were knocked unconscious. The swallow, who had chosen to observe, remained unscathed.

The moral that James Thurber attached to his fable was this: "He who hesitates is sometimes saved."[2] Certainly, the swallow that stayed behind was the one bird saved. The fable does not reveal whether the swallow's choice emerged from a moral stand on gambling over health outcomes, a healthy sense of skepticism, or a sound belief in what he had witnessed empirically. The moral of this fable is a whimsical twist on the old adage, "He who hesitates is lost."[2]

The fable can relate much about research functions such as experiencing reality, asking questions, formulating hypotheses, and testing hypotheses in the field. It conveys that precision and observation are needed to test assumptions. It demonstrates the kinds of speculations that lead to experimentation in the first place. It illustrates the manner in which researchers can sometimes be at odds with one another about whether and how hypotheses should be tested. It highlights the risks that some investigators take in formulating and testing their assumptions and the prudence that others exercise when the risk of harm is present. It shows how incentives to investigate a reality can grow when funding is thrown into the mix.

This fable was chosen to introduce a discussion of ethics in research because its strong moral theme about hesitation targets the work of this chapter. Other chapters in this book point to the cognitive and technical demands of research, and these are vital discussions. But many affective challenges, both intrapersonal (within an individual) and interpersonal (between or among individuals), also characterize the quest for knowledge, and these must not be taken lightly or dismissed as peripheral. "The Glass in the Field" supports the

necessity for reflection, an action that is vital to ethical practice. Often, in moments of critical decision making, little time is available to ponder the best choice. Time spent beforehand pondering issues set forth in this chapter is a proactive way to prepare for such moments.

THE NATURE OF ETHICS AND RESEARCH

When a person habitually, or even regularly, thinks about the ends and means of actions and accordingly acts to achieve the best ends, that person can be said to have learned virtue, or grace.[1(p53)] Allen's words show his broad understanding of ethics as a deliberation that keeps the following thoughts in mind simultaneously: the best outcomes of any action, the goodness of the means or methods used, and the call to honor virtue. Allen's understanding characterizes the good researcher who would agree that any responsible discussion of the *ethics of research* must occur within discussion of the broader disciplines of ethics and science. This discussion of the ethics of research considers the affective dimension of science alongside its intellectual rigor.

Ethics as a discipline seeks to understand the moral duties and obligations associated with any action. Ethics relies heavily on personal thought, value systems, and the interpersonal responsibilities of those who live their lives and practice their professions in communities. Science has a different focus. Science as a discipline is a search for knowledge. Although the practice of science is best known for its intellectual or cognitive rigor, science also taps the affective or emotional side of human nature. If one agrees that the affective dimension of human nature includes creativity, imagination, motivation, will, and courage, then the link between science and the affective performance of scientists becomes clear. Research, remember, is but one of many of the methods of science, alongside other forms of scientific inquiry, such as theoretical, philosophical, and historical work. Scholars in history, philosophy, or the humanities would be the first to agree that their work taps both intellectual and affective competence. But even the practice of highly focused medical research is commonly understood to have affective demands such as those for personal integrity, interpersonal accountability, and collaborative teamwork.

There is much to consider, then, when the two terms *ethics* and *research* are juxtaposed; the call becomes one of considering moral action while seeking knowledge. The challenge to be ethical in research is far greater than can be met through memorization of any guidelines for research found in ethical codes published by professional groups. The scope of the phrase *the ethics of research* includes any issues that may emerge when the practice of honoring moral duties and obligation (ethics) intersects with the practice of discovering new knowledge (research). Such issues may include the affective energy that it takes to prompt and sustain scientific inquiry, the principles and values that drive a personal or professional quest for knowledge, and the intrapersonal and interpersonal challenges that structure the investigatory process. The values that surface as important to researchers include honesty, beneficence, integrity, altruism, respect, prudence, justice, equality, and fidelity. Because each of these values is known in psychology as either an intrapersonal or interpersonal aspect of personal functioning, this examination of the ethics of research is very much about the affective dimension of science.

THE AFFECTIVE DIMENSION OF SCIENCE

In an essay some years ago about the art of science, I noted that science, as a human practice, taps personal characteristics such as passion, imagination, and intuition, each considered affective.[3] Science demands the exercise of these personal characteristics, alongside intellectual rigor. In 1986 Bruner noted that science builds on wild and artful metaphors that also rise from the affective domain:

> Let me say now what Niels Bohr told me. The idea of complementarity in quantum theory, he said to me, came to him as he thought of the impossibility of considering his son simultaneously in the light of love and in the light of justice, the son having just voluntarily confessed that he had stolen a pipe from a local shop. His brooding set him to thinking about the vases and the faces in the trick figure-ground pictures: you can see only one at a time. And then the impossibility of thinking simultaneously about the position and the velocity of a particle occurred to him.[4(p49)]

How little known is the fact that *quantum theory* sprang from a father's emotional musings about how to love his son!

Perhaps because such stories are not widespread, there is a sad tendency to dichotomize affect and cognition in ways that resemble the longstanding and more popular *art-from-science* split. This ideology makes distinctions that name science as the worthier source of knowledge and that value thought more than emotion. In this same scheme, adjectives like *soft, fuzzy,* or *subjective* attach to affective and interpersonal realms. But science is a human endeavor and as such both requires and reflects the thinking–feeling nature of humans. Being engaged in a *scientific* endeavor does not mean that one is free from having to make affective or ethical considerations.

In the early and mid-nineteenth century, scientist-physician Bernard argued against such dichotomies.[5] He said, "Discovery inheres in a feeling about things."[5(p34)] He supported engaging in intuitive feelings *for the sake of science.* Affect, in his view, makes science happen. Most will agree that the forces behind science, such as curiosity, motivation, and a desire to know, seem as much affective as intellectual. In 1976 philosopher Goodman reiterated this point as he spoke of the tools and talk in science:

> To suppose that science is flatfootedly linguistic, literal, and denotational, would be to overlook the analog instruments often used. . . . and the talk in current physics and astronomy of charm and strangeness and black holes. Even if the ultimate artifact of science, unlike that of art, is literal, verbal, or mathematical denotational theory, science and art proceed in much the same way with their searching and building.[6(p107)]

Simply said, the point is this: As a human enterprise, science demands affect *and* cognition from its practitioners, often in equal measures.

AFFECTIVE CONCERNS IN RESEARCH SCENARIOS

A few specific examples can demonstrate the practice of science as affective in the sense that it challenges researchers to use their intrapersonal strengths. More specifically, these scenarios may help to illuminate the manner in which the work of conducting research involves values-based conflicts. A brief overview of what is meant by *values* may be a helpful point at which to start.

The fable that introduced this chapter gave a few examples of strongly held values: The workers who left the plate glass standing upright in the field must have valued trust in that they left something so costly out in the open. In addition to being trusting, they perhaps also valued risk-taking: much could have happened to damage that glass. We might also assume from the fact that they were construction workers that they valued physical work. We deduce that the swallow, having declined to risk flying over the course that had knocked the goldfinch cold, valued prudence. He also valued independent thought, choosing to stay behind even when the large birds ridiculed him. The seagull, having challenged both the goldfinch and the swallow, seemed to value boldness of idea and action. He clearly valued risk and adventure and perhaps also the leadership role of rallying the larger birds to join him in wager and flight.

Knowing one's personal values requires reflection. The process is a matter of first determining one's preferences and dislikes, then thinking more deeply about what draws one to make those judgments. Most often, a particular value or set of values is at the foundation of our choices and decisions, preferences, or dislikes.

Examples of situations that may involve value-based conflicts are presented here in the form of highly plausible research scenarios. Some of the scenarios may feel quite familiar. Others may require an imaginative leap into a future within which more advanced roles related to research are assumed. For each of the scenarios, consider these questions:

1. What feelings might surface within the individuals in the case?
2. What personal values might lead the individuals to experience conflict?
3. Which values might make peace or compromise possible?
4. What actions might be taken that could be perceived as good or virtuous?

Scenario 1. You are a student. As part of a larger class project, you have been invited to participate in a research project conducted by one of your faculty members. You have been told that your participation is voluntary and anonymous, but you know that if you leave the room it will be apparent that you have chosen to abstain. You prefer not to complete the required personal questionnaires. You worry that your nonparticipation in this project will suggest to your faculty that you lack a commitment to the research agenda of the department and may cause some ill will and recrimination.

Scenario 2. You are in your first year of practice and have developed a documentation form to gather numerical data on the progress of patients with chronic diseases. You have monitored its use for the past four months and are pleased that your supervising physician seems so responsive to its use. You have heard from a reliable friend that this same physician supervisor recently gave a presentation to staff at a hospital out of state. She presented "her" documentation form without mentioning your role in either developing or piloting it.

Scenario 3. You are a first-year practitioner in a rehabilitation setting for individuals with head injuries, a population unfamiliar to you. Your supervisor asked you a week ago to invite each client to give consent to participate in an ongoing research project. Not quite sure that you know how to do this with individuals who have significant cognitive impairments, you have been asking them, "Do you want to help us with our research?" You hope that this request will suffice. You feel rather awkward asking your supervisor if this approach is sufficient, because the question would suggest the extent to which you feel yourself a novice with this population and with research.

Scenario 4. In your study of child abuse, you understand that your responsibility in obtaining informed consent includes initiating a dialogue with each participant regarding the possible consequences of participating in your research. Your project requires that participants review their early childhood histories of abuse and neglect. Your task is to discuss fully with each individual the fact that possibly difficult thoughts and emotions may surface as they remember their pasts. You hope to recruit numerous participants for your project and do not want to scare them off. How will you proceed?

Scenario 5. You walk into the main office of an outpatient clinic in psychiatry on a Monday morning. A new member of the clerical staff, seated among several other workers, looks up and says to you, "Well, Mr. F. certainly has little emotional sensitivity, according to his answers on the scale you're using! He dropped the research form onto my desk, and I have rated it for you. I thought I would just keep up with them as they come in." This staff member was *supposed* to have followed your instructions to have each participant place an anonymous code number on his or her completed scale, drop it into a large box with a slot, and rate all accumulated forms at the same time in two weeks.

Scenario 6. You are one among several individuals who have worked on a committee that decides to publish the results of a recently completed project on immunizing children in the community. You come from different disciplines. In your group are two administrators who endorsed the project, each very invested in their status and their leadership roles. You are meeting as a group to decide who shall be first author and in which order the rest of the names shall appear in the journal. You have been the strongest and primary writer for the group thus far, and you anticipate that you will also do most of the writing on this article. You predict that the two administrators will want to be first or primary authors.

Scenario 7. You are a departmental chair working on an interdisciplinary healthcare team. You conceived of a joint research project with your brother's firm. The team thinks that the project is worth pursuing. Your administrator tells you in the meeting that it seems best that you disengage yourself from the project because of your close relationship with your brother. You see no conflict of interest because the nature of the research is such that your being a relative of a coresearcher will not matter. You want to be part of the team; this was your original idea.

Scenario 8. You are a junior faculty member with a master's degree. You teach an innovative course that you think is a good fit for submission to a well-known state agency as a project for grant funding. The chair of your department has a doctoral degree and says that the grant would stand a much better chance of funding if her name was listed as the primary investigator and yours was listed in the lesser role of project coordinator. You know that you would earn less credit and hold less status within your setting as a project coordinator, but you believe that your chair has a valid suggestion.

Scenario 9. You have practiced in your town for 20 years, and you are known as a master clinician. You receive a phone call from a faculty member who teaches in a local university and who has a strong research background. He tells you that he has a research idea on which he hopes that you might collaborate. He asks if he may send you his proposal. You later read the proposal and realize that the research agenda would mean you doing much more work than you think possible or reasonable. You also see that it reflects a lack of understanding of your patients and the constraints within your practice. You realize that this faculty member is naïve about your clinical practice. You are scheduled to meet with him to discuss the proposal.

Scenario 10. You are a senior faculty member with a reputation for theoretical inquiry in your profession. You have thought of yourself as a historical scholar for years, and your profession values your scholarship. Your university president has announced that funded grants will be prized as the most prestigious form of scholarship, and all of the schools within your university are revising their salary merit systems to reward such work. You know that merit raises will be hard to come by if you do historical work, and you resent this apparent dismissal of valuable research.

Within each scenario are both a research issue and an intrapersonal or interpersonal challenge that invites attention, reflection, and virtuous action. What are the intrapersonal issues in each scenario? What possible differences in personal values among those involved might be at play in each scenario, considering the questions posed at the start of this section. Some of the challenges that surface within each scenario may seem trivial at first, but the manner in which they are handled can have a significant impact on the researcher, the research process, or its outcome. These scenarios may become more meaningful when they are thoughtfully discussed with others. Some of these scenarios will be further examined as the chapter moves forward.

VALUES THAT SHAPE GOOD PRACTICE

Beyond the individual values held by any one practitioner, several *professional* values relate to good practice in research. Some professions have articulated the core values that should guide their practice. Both the nursing and occupational therapy professions uphold the following values,[7] and some of the links between these values and the practice of research have been interpreted:

Altruism in scientific inquiry is the unselfish concern of a researcher for the well-being of others.

Equality in scientific inquiry requires that the researcher perceive individuals as having the same fundamental human rights and opportunities.

Freedom in scientific inquiry presses the researcher to allow individuals to exercise choice and to demonstrate self-direction.

Justice in scientific inquiry mandates that the researcher act with fairness, equity, truthfulness, and objectivity.

Dignity in scientific inquiry requires that the researcher emphasize the importance of valuing the inherent worth of each person.

Truth in scientific inquiry requires that the researcher be faithful to facts and reality.

Prudence in scientific inquiry is the researcher's ability to discipline the self through the use of reason.

The previously presented scenarios can be examined to determine which of the above values might prompt better interpersonal outcomes as well as virtuous actions in each. For example, how would a strong value of altruism (the unselfish concern of a researcher for the well-being of others) shape communications with the individuals in Scenario 4, who have a history of child abuse? In all likelihood, with altruism *foremost* in mind, practitioners would convey real concern for each candidate. You would openly acknowledge that although the research project is important to you, at least equally important is the fact that participation could be emotionally painful. You would make every effort to ensure that study participants could easily secure help from counselors made accessible to them. You would communicate your empathy and the availability of this resource to your participants. Considering the list of several other of the core values of two healthcare professions, how might they help direct a virtuous course of action in the other scenarios?

Although a list of professional values with accompanying definitions seems a helpful enough tool, research dilemmas (like those that arise in clinics) often present more complex considerations, pressing researchers and/or healthcare professionals to choose one highly important value over another. Many matters are not as straightforward the example of the application of altruism to Scenario 4.

For example, Scenario 8 involves a junior faculty member's dilemma over whether to accept the chair's suggestion to yield the leadership role to her on a research grant. Perhaps the junior faculty member ultimately chose to exercise *prudence* by yielding to the chair's suggestion. Given her personal lack of a higher educational status that promises a better review by experts, she abandoned the thought of being a principal investigator. In deliberations over what to do in this dilemma, she reflected on several points. She believed that she would end up doing the most work and that *justice* would be compromised if the grant proposal indicated otherwise. And although having *equality* of status with the chair in this project, the faculty member reasoned that prudent promotion of the chair's educational status and experience in research would result in funding that would get this project off the ground. She considered several values (e.g., prudence, justice, and equality) as well as their meanings and consequences to her and her project. She chose prudence. And so it is, in practice, that no list of professional values can remove from a practitioner the responsibility to reflect upon the broader context within which moral action occurs and to make difficult decisions about which values should take priority. In this case, the novice researcher, feeling admittedly torn when it came to upholding her sense of equality and justice, chose to value prudence most.

COMMUNICATIONS WITHIN ETHICAL RESEARCH

The research scenarios considered in this chapter also call up this question: What interpersonal challenges are present in research and how might they be met? It is an excellent question. Qualities of assertiveness, setting limits, active listening, and negative inquiry contribute to the formulation of these answers. Many challenges in the practice of research call for competence in communicating. The hope is for the best possible outcome—that a healthcare practitioner will interact professionally and effectively. To reinforce that hope, a brief review of foundational communication competencies is presented.

One important communication capacity in the practice of research is that of conveying desires and needs assertively. To assert a personal opinion or position is not to dominate or to be aggressive, but to calmly state one's view in a deferential manner. "I statements" often characterize assertive communications. Here are some examples of

self-assertions that might work in some of the research scenarios presented in this chapter:

> "Although I appreciate the opportunity to be involved in this project, I don't feel comfortable filling out this questionnaire." *(Scenario 1)*
> "If you have time, I'd like to discuss something that's bothering me. I have heard from a reliable source that you are making presentations and using the form that I developed while referring to it as your own." *(Scenario 2)*
> "I really do appreciate the work that you have done. As soon as you get a chance, I'd like to speak with you privately about the aims of this project." *(Scenario 5)*
> "I don't agree with you on that point. I believe that, as originator of the idea for this project, I should be on the team." *(Scenario 7)*
> "I think that you have a very exciting idea, but I can't assume the level of responsibility that you have assigned to me in this proposal." *(Scenario 9)*
> "I understand that grant work is considered to be of utmost importance on this campus, but I believe that merit raises should follow the execution of quality historical work as well." *(Scenario 10)*

Another communication capacity helpful in the ethical practice of research is that of setting limits or assertively declaring personal boundaries. An individual can set limits effectively with members of a research team in a number of ways that include offering alternatives, compromising, refusing empathically, and responsive repetition. Scenario 9 lends itself to illustrating each of these methods. In this scenario, remember, the master clinician has been asked by a local university faculty member to participate in an enormous way in a research project that has little personal appeal for many reasons. The clinician might set limits in these ways:

> *Offer alternatives:* "I can't do all that you have assigned to me in your proposal, but I *would* be willing to take the lead in gathering some data for you."

Compromise: "If you would be willing to take over a few of my clinical responsibilities, I might be able to help you more."

Empathic refusal: "I understand that you need my involvement, but I can't help you in all of the ways that you've specified."

Responsive repetition: In response to several overtures initiated in rapid sequence by the academic researcher, the practitioner might respond to each, in turn, in this way: "I'm not comfortable with the level of responsibility that you've assigned me". . . . . . . "No, I can't do that". . . . . "I'm sorry, I'm not able to do that". . . . "There are too many responsibilities for me to handle."

By setting limits respectfully, a practitioner shares important values and personal intentions that manifest virtue.

The capacity to actively listen is a critical aspect of ethical research. Both research colleagues and participants need to be heard, particularly when they are sharing strongly held ideas or opinions. To meet such needs, active listening must be mastered. The process of active listening consists of a series of exchanges that convey a desire to really hear and understand.[8] An active listener does the following:

Focuses complete attention on the individual who is speaking and communicates interest through eye contact, posture, facial expression, movement, or gestures

Reflects back what was said through a paraphrase, including the feeling and content of the communication, by using variations of the formula for the understanding response: "You feel _____ because _____."

Seeks confirmation and clarification (Sometimes this step can be incorporated with reflecting.)

Offers empathy and support

Explores events and feelings further

Facilitates problem solving

As an example, consider Scenario 3. A first-year practitioner working among individuals with traumatic brain injury, hearing that the supervisor had the reputation for being understanding, approached him to share his lack of knowledge in discussing research protocols with patients who are cognitively challenged.

Using active listening, the supervisor might say, "You're feeling a bit awkward about how to approach some patients, and that is totally understandable. I felt the same way when I started to explain protocols. Tell me how you have been approaching the task so far, and maybe we can figure out ways that will work for you." The first sentence is a variation on the how you feel/because formula; next the supervisor offer support. Finally, the supervisor explores the situation and moves toward solving the problem.

Another communication competency that is closely related to active listening is that of negative inquiry. Negative inquiry consists of listening fully, without interruptions or defensive responses, to a complaint that someone wants to make. Instead of either responding defensively or prematurely to justify the offensive behavior, the person first *hears* the complaint, and evidence of listening occurs through paraphrasing. Negative inquiry invites the expression of divergent thoughts and feelings so that the air can be cleared, the problem addressed, and better relations resumed.

In Scenario 2, for example, the practitioner has a significant complaint about the use of a documentation form that she developed. Note here how the supervisor, using negative inquiry, might respond to the complaint:

Practitioner: "I'm really upset that you have been using the documentation form that I developed when you do presentations at conferences."

Supervisor: "I've really angered you by using your form."

Practitioner: "Yes. I have heard that you are not acknowledging me for having developed it."

Supervisor: "You think that I have not clarified your role in developing it?"

Practitioner: "Yes, and it looks to others as if you developed it yourself."

Supervisor: "Is there anything else about this situation that troubles you?"

Practitioner: "No, it just seems unfair to me that you have been doing this."

Supervisor: "So if I were to use the form but acknowledge your efforts, that would be acceptable?"

Practitioner: "Yes."

Supervisor: "May I tell you what I have been doing? On the bottom of the form, I have listed you as its primary developer. I'm sorry that I failed to share this with you beforehand. Maybe I should point that out more directly to my audiences in the future."

THE HAZARDS OF PLAGIARISM

This last dialogue between a practitioner and supervisor highlighted ethical concerns about ownership in research. In this case, it was ownership of a documentation form that was useful in gathering research data. In some of the other scenarios, ownership questions emerged relative to ideas and projects (Scenarios 6 and 7). Ownership clashes can occur around use of the titles of *primary* or first author of an article or *primary investigator* on a grant. Often the discussion turns on who should get credit for the work and how fair that determination seems in light of who did either the most work or the most important parts of the work.

One aspect of ownership in research that is familiar to those who are still in a student role is that of plagiarism. Commonly understood as taking the idea or work of another and passing it off as one's own, plagiarism is a growing concern today because so many resources are so readily available. The guidelines established in the American Medical Association's *Manual of Style*[9] in a section entitled "Scientific Misconduct" are helpful in clarifying various forms of plagiarism.

The first definition of scientific misconduct was released by the U.S. Public Health Service in 1989 as "fabrication, falsification, plagiarism, or other practices that seriously deviate from those that are commonly accepted within the scientific community for proposing, conducting, or reporting research."[10]

This definition, known as FFP (fabrication, falsification, and plagiarism), remains the official one. Although in 1993 the Commission on Research Integrity defined scientific misconduct further at the request of the U.S. Public Health Service,[11] the new definition, known as MMI (misappropriation, misrepresentation, and interference), has not replaced the old because it does not apply to all governmental departments as well as the old one does.[9]

Iverson et al. described four common kinds of plagiarism[9]:

1. *Direct plagiarism:* Lifting passages word for word without placing the material in quotation marks or crediting the author.
2. *Mosaic:* Borrowing ideas from an original source by using a few word-for-word phrases woven into one's own work without crediting the original author.
3. *Paraphrase:* Restating a phrase or paragraph so that, although the words differ, the meaning is the same and the author is not credited.
4. *Insufficient acknowledgement:* Noting only a small part of what is borrowed so that a reader cannot know exactly what is original and what is not.[9]

Within the discussion that follows their descriptions, Iverson et al. said that plagiarism often occurs because of careless note taking.[9] For example, consider a student sitting in the library or at a computer and recording good ideas to include in a paper. The student does not, near each idea, either note the precise source or insert quotation marks. Prompted by these good ideas of other authors, the student then jots down personal thoughts alongside ideas from his other sources. Days later, when the student begins writing a paper from his notes, he forgets or confuses which ideas were original and which came from the resources being used, mixing them in a way that constitutes plagiarism.

Even if it can be argued as having been inadvertent, plagiarism can be a violation of copyright law and a breach of honesty. Should the holders of the original copyright discover the breach of ethics and law and file suit, penalties could be imposed by the courts. In most academic centers, violations of academic integrity policies can result in serious consequences for students, such as expulsion or suspension.

PRINCIPLES AND GUIDELINES FOR ETHICAL RESEARCH

In addition to intrapersonal and interpersonal approaches that guide research, ethical principles (the guidelines that direct moral action) merit consideration. Typically, most individuals understand the phrase *ethics of research* to mean adherence to sets of principles that are part of institutional policy, ethics committee protocols, professional codes of ethics, or grant-funding guidelines. Although this understanding is sound, it is restrictive in light of the broad affective competence required for successful research, as seen in the discussion of research scenarios. Although some professional codes of ethics do not specify conduct related to research, certainly general guidelines within any code shape research directives. Examples of general phrases that apply to research practices as much as they apply to clinical practice are the following:

> ". . . providing competent . . . care . . ."
> ". . . to the full measure of their ability . . ."
> ". . . adhere to . . . laws governing informed consent . . ."
> ". . . uphold the doctrine of confidentiality . . ."
> ". . . place service before material gain . . ."[12]

Codes of ethics from many professions mandate more specific behaviors for the professional who engages in research. A sampling of such behaviors may be helpful:

- Obtain informed consent from subjects.
- Respect the individual's right to refuse involvement in research.
- Protect the confidential nature of research gained from investigational activities.
- Be honest in receiving and disseminating information.
- Give credit and recognition when using the work of others.
- Do not fabricate data, falsify information, or plagiarize.

The codes of ethics for most health professionals invoke ethical responsibilities for research. Ultimately, all professionals are guided by the principle of nonmaleficence, the principle that prohibits physical, mental, and social harm and includes honoring patient confidentiality. In a broad sense, the conduct of healthcare practitioners must be beyond reproach and must *transcend* guidelines for nonmaleficence articulated in ethical codes. The call to follow the major tenets of honesty, sound communication, ensuring the common good, competence, and confidentiality extends to practice in research. The admonition against conflicts of interest, sexual relationships, and impaired practice generalizes to research as well.

The manner in which research issues require the kind of thinking that this chapter encourages can be illustrated by considering the research scenarios and the ethical guidelines mentioned here. Eight of the scenarios in this chapter relate in some way to the six principles listed above that come from various professional codes. In Scenario 5, for example, the outcome must include consideration of the principle of confidentiality with the newly hired clerical staff. The ethical behaviors mentioned here can be easily matched to the scenarios considered. Taking time to think more deeply about these issues is an important part of developing a functional research ethic.

SUMMARY

Research holds many affective challenges. In fact, the research enterprise is enhanced when affective standards are integrated into the research process alongside intellectual and technical rigors. Ethical choices in the realm of research have intrapersonal, interpersonal, and ethical implications. Healthcare researchers who lack awareness damage not only their own careers, but the research and healthcare professions as well.

At its best, ethical science is a virtuous quest for knowledge. Ethical research enhances the knowledge base of practitioners and medical science as a whole, with a good end in mind. As a means toward that good end, researchers must support the dignity and the values of persons who perform and participate in research projects. Researchers must possess a desire to do the right thing and persistence in a course of moral action in spite of obstacles. Consideration of what it means to be ethical in research should be part of any research plan and will certainly enhance the quality of health care. The results are the manifestation of learning virtue, or grace (Allen, 1987).[1]

ACKNOWLEDGMENT

This chapter derives from a larger work prepared by the author for the American Occupational Therapy Foundation.

Opportunities for Reflection

In the spirit of provoking deeper thought about ethics in research, I propose the viewing of movies that can prompt lively discussion of the principles explored in this and other chapter of this text.

1. **Awakenings (1990):** A new doctor finds himself with a ward full of comatose patients. When he finds a possible chemical cure, he gets permission to try it on one of them. The film delights in the new awareness of the patients and then on the reactions of their relatives to the changes.
2. **Away from Her (2006):** A man coping with the institutionalization of his wife because of Alzheimer's disease faces an epiphany when she transfers her affections to another patient, a mute man in a wheelchair.
3. **Brainstorm (2001):** This odyssey is lived by Neto, a middle-class teenager, who lives a normal life until his father sends him to a mental institution after finding drugs in his pocket. In the mental institution, Neto is forced to mature.
4. **Crash (2004):** Several stories interweave during two days in Los Angeles involving a collection of interrelated characters in a film that examines cultural differences in a powerful way.
5. **Extreme Measures (1996):** Thriller about a British doctor working at a hospital in New York who starts making unwanted inquiries when the body of a man who died in his emergency room disappears. The doctor soon finds himself in danger from people who want the hospital's secret to remain undiscovered.
6. **Good Will Hunting (1997):** A janitor at MIT, Will Hunting has a gift for math that can take him light-years beyond his blue-collar roots, but to achieve his dream he must turn his back on his neighborhood and his best friend. Two strangers enter the equation: a washed-up shrink and a medical student.
7. **I Am Legend (2007):** Years after a plague kills most of humanity and transforms the rest into monsters, the sole survivor in New York City struggles valiantly to find a cure.
8. **The Insiders (1999):** A research chemist comes under personal and professional attack when he decides to appear in a "60 Minutes" exposé on Big Tobacco.
9. **John Q (2002):** A down-on-his-luck father, whose insurance will not cover his son's heart transplant, takes the hospital's emergency room hostage until the doctors agree to perform the operation.
10. **The Laramie Project (2002):** This is a film version of the play based on more than 200 interviews they conducted in Laramie, Wyoming. It follows and in some cases re-enacts the chronology of Shepherd's visit to a local bar, his kidnapping and beating, the discovery of his body tied to a fence, the vigil at the hospital, his death and funeral, and the trial of his killers.
11. **Lorenzo's Oil (1992):** A boy develops a disease so rare that nobody is working on a cure, so his father decides to learn all about it and tackle the problem himself.
12. **Miss Evers' Boys (1997):** The true story of the U.S. Government's 1932 Tuskegee Syphilis Experiments, in which a group of black test subjects were allowed to die, despite a cure having been developed.

13. **My Sister's Keeper (2009):** Anna Fitzgerald seeks medical emancipation from her parents who until now have relied on their youngest child to help their leukemia-stricken daughter Kate remain alive.

14. **Nell (1994):** Nell is a girl who has been brought up in an isolated world. The only people she knew were her mother and twin sister. After her mother's death, she is discovered by the local doctor Jerome. He's fascinated by her because she speaks a mangled "twin speak" language, developed by her sister and herself growing up. But Paula, a psychology student, wants her observed in a laboratory.

15. **One Flew over the Cuckoo's Nest (1975):** Upon arrival at a mental institution, a brash rebel rallies the patients together to take on the oppressive Nurse Ratchet, a woman more dictator than nurse.

16. **Philadelphia (1993):** When a man with AIDS is fired by a conservative law firm because of his condition, he hires a homophobic small-time lawyer as the only willing advocate for a wrongful dismissal suit.

17. **The Rainmaker (1997):** Rudy Baylor is a jobless young attorney. However, he is also the only hope of an elderly couple whose insurance company will not pay for an operation that could save their son's life. In this judicial drama, Rudy learns to hate corporate America as he falls in love with a battered young married woman.

18. **Something the Lord Made (2004 TV):** Cardiologist Alfred Blalock leaves Vanderbilt for Johns Hopkins, taking with him his lab technician, Vivien Thomas. Thomas, an African American without a college degree, is a gifted mechanic and tool-maker with hands splendidly adept at surgery. In 1941, Blalock and Thomas take on the challenge of blue babies and invent bypass surgery. Blalock brings Thomas into the surgery to advise him, but when *Life* magazine and kudos come, Thomas is excluded.

19. **Whose Life Is it Anyway (1981):** Ken Harrison is an artist who makes sculptures. One day he is involved in a car accident and is paralyzed from his neck down. All he can do is talk, and he wants to die. In the hospital he makes friends with some of the staff, and they support him when he goes to trial to be allowed to die.

REFERENCES

1. Allen J. The use and abuse of humanistic education. In: Christensen RC, ed. *Teaching and the Case Method.* Boston, MA: Harvard Business School; 1987:50–53.
2. Thurber J. *Fables for Our Times.* New York: Harper and Brothers; 1940:59.
3. Peloquin SM. Occupational therapy as an art and science: Should the older definition be reclaimed? *Am J Occup Ther.* 1994;48:1093–1096.
4. Bruner J. *Actual Minds, Possible Worlds.* Cambridge, MA: Harvard University Press; 1986:49.
5. Bernard C. *An Introduction to the Study of Experimental Medicine.* (Greene HC, trans.). New York; Dover; 1957:34. (Original work published in 1927.)
6. Goodman N. *Languages of Art: An Approach to a Theory of Symbols.* Indianapolis: Hackett; 1976:107.
7. American Occupational Therapy Association. Core values and attitudes in occupational therapy practice. *Am J Occup Ther.* 1993;47:1085–1087.
8. Davidson DA, Peloquin SM. *Making Connection with Others.* Bethesda, MD: The American Occupational Therapy Association; 1998.
9. Iverson C, Flanagin A, Fontanarosa PB, Glass RM, Glitman P, Lantz JC, Meyer HS, Smith JM., Winker MA, Young RK. *American Medical Association Manual of Style. A Guide for Authors and Editors.* Philadelphia, PA: Williams & Wilkins; 1998.
10. U.S. Public Health Service. Editor's report: Scientific misconduct and the responsibility of journal editors. 1989;80(4):399–400.
11. Commission on Research Integrity. *Integrity and Misconduct in Research.* Washington, DC: Office of Research Integrity; 1993.
12. American Academy of Physician Assistants. *Code of Ethics.* Alexandria, VA: American Academy of Physician Assistants; 1999.

CHAPTER OVERVIEW

The protection of human subjects in research is paramount to any research effort. Research that uses human subjects is highly regulated by federal, state, and institutional policies and requirements. Protection is extended to almost every type of research that involves people, even if only survey research. The purpose of this chapter is to explain the federal regulations that govern research involving humans, to clarify the authority of the Institutional Review Board (IRB), and to address the responsibilities of investigators conducting research using human subjects.

Regulatory Protection of Human Subjects in Research

Joseph O. Schmelz, PhD, RN, CIP, FAAN
Rhonda Barnard, MS, CIP
Roy R. Estrada, PhD, CIP

INTRODUCTION AND OBJECTIVE

During the course of academic study, it is common for students in healthcare professions to perform projects or other activities that involve data collection, analysis, and interpretation. The use of data for the purpose of drawing conclusions and solving problems is not unique to research. Many other activities, such as quality improvement and program evaluation, share many of the data collection and analysis methods used by researchers. However quality improvement[1] and program evaluation are generally not considered research because they serve different purposes. Students and faculty may find it difficult to determine whether a particular activity is research and whether it requires the approval of an institutional review board (IRB). After reading this chapter the reader should have a basic understanding of what constitutes human research, how it is regulated, and what responsibilities a person who performs research has.

HOW IS RESEARCH APPROVED?

Before involving living individuals in research, the project and the protections provided by the investigator must be reviewed by the institution's committee designated to oversee such research. This committee is commonly referred to as the institutional review board (IRB). An IRB is comprised of scientists, nonscientists, and individuals who are not affiliated with the institution (sometimes referred to as community members). Members of the IRB are selected based on their expertise in the types of research typically reviewed by the board or on the diversity of their background or experience. The goal of the IRB review is to ensure that the individuals participating in the research are adequately protected. To achieve this goal, the IRB reviews the written plan for conducting the research and the safeguards that will be provided to protect participants. The IRB must conclude that the research fulfills the basic principles for conducting ethical research established by the National Commission for the Protection of Human Subjects in Biomedical and Behavioral Research.[2]

In 1979 the National Commission released the "Belmont Report" that established three basic ethical principles for conducting research involving humans.[2] See Table 4-1. The Belmont principles are autonomy, beneficence, and justice. The National Commission was established by Congress in the National Research Act of 1974. As part of the act, the requirement for IRB approval and obtaining informed consent for research funded by the Department of Health, Education and Welfare (now the Department of

Health and Human Services, HHS) was included in the regulations that were codified as 45 CFR Part 46, Subpart A.[3] This regulation became known as the "Common Rule" when it was adopted by 16 federal agencies in 1991.[4] In addition to the Common Rule, the Food and Drug Administration's (FDA) regulations[5,6] for the protection of human subjects (21 CFR Parts 50 & 56) require IRB approval and informed consent for research involving drugs, devices, or biologics, regardless of the funding source. Finally, the Privacy Rule (45 CFR Part 164)[7] requires additional approval by a Privacy Board when research involves identifiable health information held by health-related entities, regardless of the funding source or whether the research uses a drug, device, or biologic. See Figure 4-1.

WHEN IS IRB APPROVAL REQUIRED?

IRB approval is needed whenever a project meets the regulatory definitions of human-subject research provided in either the Common Rule[3] or the FDA regulations.[5,6] The Common Rule is generally applicable to most research conducted by students in healthcare professions. Although the Common Rule is technically only applicable to federally funded or supported research, most institutions apply it to all research, regardless of the funding source. The Common Rule requires IRB approval of all "human subjects research." To understand when an activity is considered human-subject research, it is helpful to ask two questions: "Is this research?" and "Are human subjects involved?"

Is This Research?

The Belmont Report noted that the distinction between research and practice (nonresearch) is blurred. The Common Rule defines research as "a systematic investigation, including research development, testing and evaluation, designed to develop or contribute to generalizable knowledge."[3]

Unfortunately, the two key concepts in the definition "systematic investigation" and "generalizable

---

Table 4–1 Belmont Principles

⬥ **Respect for Persons**
  • Treat individuals as autonomous agents capable of making informed choices and acting on them.
  • Individuals with diminished autonomy are entitled to protection.

⬥ **Beneficence**
  • Maximize possible benefits and minimize possible harms

⬥ **Justice**
  • Fairness in distribution of the benefits and burdens

Source: Joseph O. Schmelz

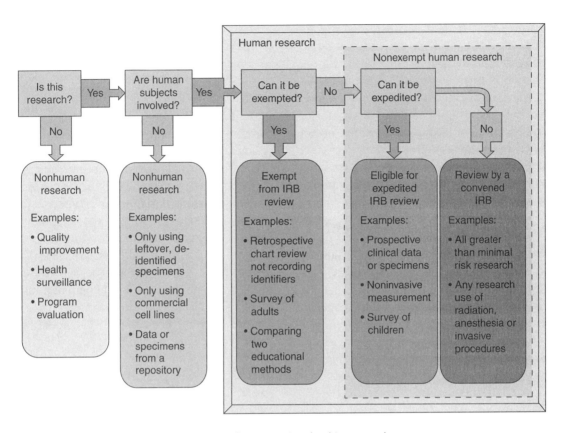

Figure 4–1 Determining whether human subjects are involved in research.

knowledge" are not defined by the regulation. Because many activities other than research would be considered systematic investigations, for example, evaluation of patient satisfaction in a clinic or the incidence of infections on a nursing unit, this part of the definition is not particularly helpful in defining research. Jeff Cooper (personal communication, May 2010) notes that a major problem with the definition of "research" is the question, "What constitutes generalizable knowledge?" He suggests that "generalizable" should be interpreted as a matter of policy to mean "widely applicable." This interpretation has the advantage that it meets the common intuitive interpretation of "research" and maximally carves out scholarly activities.[8]

In general, the purpose of research is to fill a gap in the current knowledge. The Belmont Report describes research as ". . . an activity designed to test a hypothesis, permit conclusions to be drawn"[8 (p4)]. If the conclusions that are drawn from the activity

are widely applicable, one could say the results are generalizable.

Are Human Subjects Involved?

When it has been determined that an activity meets the regulatory definition of research, the next step is to decide whether the research involves human subjects. Research involves human subjects if the researcher either obtains data through interacting or intervening with a living individual or obtains private identifiable information about a living individual. Interacting means that the researcher communicates or has interpersonal contact with the individual (e.g., makes phone contact for recruitment or obtains consent to participate). Intervening includes physical procedures (e.g., obtaining blood) or manipulating the individual (e.g., providing a treatment), or manipulating the individual's environment (e.g., changing room temperature). Information is considered private when it is provided for a specific purpose by an individual and the individual can expect will not be made public. Private information is considered individually identifiable if the identity of the individual may be ascertained by the investigator or associated with the information. Whether or not an activity meets these criteria it is still necessary when considering whether or not it is research under the FDA human protections regulations.[5]

Is this FDA-Regulated Research?

Although it is uncommon for students in healthcare professions to conduct research that is FDA regulated, it is important to consider FDA regulations when determining whether IRB approval and informed consent are required. The FDA often uses the term "clinical investigation" to indicate research. FDA-regulated research includes the following[9]:

- Use of an unapproved drug or biologic
- Use of an FDA approved drug other than the use of a marketed drug in the course of medical practice
- Use of a device to evaluate safety or effectiveness of that device, or
- Data from the use of a drug or device will be submitted to the FDA for advertising or a change in labeling

If a study involves any of these, the IRB must be contacted for guidance. Not only will IRB approval and informed consent be required, but additional FDA permissions may be necessary before the research can begin. If the activity meets either the Common Rule or FDA definition of human subject research discussed earlier, it will generally be reviewed by the IRB unless it qualifies for an exemption to the Common Rule.

Can It Be Exempted?

If a research project is not subject to the FDA human protection regulations (as described previously) and does not involve incarcerated individuals (i.e., prisoners), it may qualify for exemption.

Certain human research studies that involve very little or no risk and fall completely within one or more specific exemption categories may qualify for exempt status. This means that the institution is not required to follow the Common Rule with respect to the research (e.g., obtain IRB approval).[10] However, other rules are applicable to an exempt study. In general, the institution or a higher authority establishes policy for exempt human research. For example, because IRB approval is not required, most institutions designate an office or official to make a determination that the research is exempt. Currently, the Office for Human Research Protections (OHRP, a subdivision of HHS) does not recommend that investigators be given the authority to make an independent judgment. Most local policies applicable to exempt research are based on the Belmont Principles (IRBs should be consulted for specific guidance).

Examples of the most common types of research that can be exempted include (1) educational research involving normal educational practices such as comparing different curricula or instructional techniques, (2) surveys (not involving children) that collect information that would not likely pose a risk to those completing the survey if their answers were released (either because the information is not sensitive in nature or because it cannot be traced back to the individual), or (3) chart reviews of health information that is both preexisting and is not traceable back to the individual. An institution's IRB generally provides the complete list of exemptions from the Common Rule.

If a research project does not meet the criteria for exemption (nonexempt human-subject research) it must be reviewed by the IRB. In reviewing nonexempt research, the IRB can use one of two review processes: (1) expedited review or (2) review by a meeting of the IRB.

Can It Be Expedited?

Some nonexempt studies that involve no more than minimal risk to participants and fall completely within one or more specific expedited categories may be eligible for an expedited review procedure.

Expedited review may be carried out by the IRB chairperson or one or more experienced members of the IRB instead of the convened board. To understand whether a study is eligible for expedited review, the concept of risk as it is used in the federal regulations must be understood.[3] Risk is a measure of harm. It refers to both the likelihood (i.e., probability) that harm may occur and the magnitude of possible harm. Although investigators often focus on physical harms when developing their IRB application, the IRB views harm more broadly. Harm can be categorized as physical (e.g., injury or pain), psychological (e.g., anxiety or shame), social (e.g., adverse effect on relationships), economic (e.g., financial costs), legal (e.g., arrest or lawsuits), or dignitary (e.g., violates personal values).[4]

Like the regulatory definition of human-subject research discussed earlier, the meaning of minimal risk is a source for debate and may be defined differently by different IRBs. In general, minimal risk means that the risks from the research activities is not greater than those ordinarily encountered in daily life. Recognizing the debate over whether daily life should be taken to refer to an absolute (i.e., daily life of healthy individuals) or relative (i.e., daily life of subjects of the research), many IRBs consider activities outside those used during a routine physical or psychological examination as carrying more than minimal risk.[3,5] Examples of minimal-risk procedures that meet this definition include simple venipuncture, surveys or interviews, etc. If the risk is no more than minimal, the next step in determining whether the study is eligible for expedited review can be undertaken. The list of research activities is then compared with the expedited review categories.

The categories of research eligible for expedited review include the following[3,6]: the use of approved drugs or devices in an approved manner; collection of blood in limited quantities over specific time periods, noninvasive collection of biological specimens (e.g., urine, leftover specimens collected for other purposes); noninvasive data collected routinely in clinical practice that does not involve x-rays, general anesthesia, or sedation (e.g., MRI, weight, blood pressure); use of information or specimens that have been or will be collected solely for nonresearch purposes (e.g., chart reviews); recordings (e.g., voice recordings, digital images); and surveys or interviews.

It is important to remember that the study cannot include any procedures that involve more than minimal risk and that all research procedures must fall into one or more of the expedited categories. An example of a research study that may involve minimal risk but does not fall completely within the expedited review categories is a study involving use of health information normally collected as part of routine dental care and a dental x-ray being completed for research purposes. The risk of all the research procedures can be categorized as no more than minimal risk. However, the dental x-ray procedure does not fit into any of the expedited review categories (i.e., noninvasive data collection routinely used in clinical practice cannot be used because this procedure involves x-rays). Therefore, although the risk to the participants may be no more than minimal, the research study is not eligible for expedited review (at least initially) and would be reviewed by the convened IRB. If the convened IRB determines the study involves no more than minimal risk, future IRB reviews of the study may be completed using the expedited review procedure.

What If a Research Project Is Not Eligible for Expedited Review?

Research that does not meet criteria as either exempt or nonexempt expedited must be reviewed by the convened IRB (i.e., the full committee). A convened IRB is a committee of at least five members, each with varying expertise (scientific and nonscientific) and affiliations (both affiliated and not affiliated with the institution).[3,6] Notably, the IRB uses the same criteria for evaluating a study regardless of whether it is reviewed by expedited review or by the full board. The Common Rule and the FDA human-protection regulations impose specific criteria for approval of nonexempt research. As an investigator it is important to develop the study plan with the specific criteria in mind. Many investigators assume that their scientific plan is all the IRB needs to approve their research. Although there are significant overlaps, they are not the same. In general, the IRB application calls for additional information not commonly found in a grant application or academic degree proposal. The criteria used by the IRB to approve nonexempt research are presented in Figure 4-2.

How Will the IRB Review My Research?

For the IRB to approve research, it must determine the following:

The risks to the participants have been minimized. In other words, the probability and magnitude of the reasonably expected research harms have been minimized. However, the nature of the study may limit the extent to which risks can be minimized. An example of minimizing risk is choosing a procedure that would pose less risk to the subjects over another or designing the study to use procedures that would be performed regardless of whether the individual was enrolled in the research.

The risks are reasonable in relation to anticipated benefits. Once the risks have been minimized, the possible benefits associated with the research are considered. In general, research can potentially benefit individual subjects (direct benefit) and/or society (important knowledge gained). The assessment of risks to potential benefits is often referred to as the risk–benefit ratio. The IRB will only approve research where the probability of a benefit outweighs the risks of participating in the research.

The selection of subjects is equitable. With a clear understanding of the risks and potential benefits in the study, consider whether the selected population fairly distributes the burdens and benefits of research. In mak-

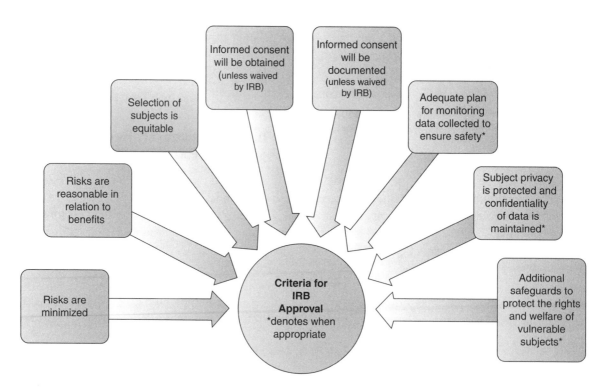

Figure 4–2 Criteria for IRB approval of nonexempt research.

ing this determination, the IRB considers whether the study targets individuals who will likely benefit from the outcome of the research. For example, the board may ask whether there are subjects who may benefit more from the study.

The informed consent will be sought from each prospective subject or the subject's legally authorized representative. Because in-

formed consent is one of the three basic protections provided by the Common Rule, the IRB will require it in most cases. The human-protection regulations define the basic information that must be provided while obtaining informed consent (see **Table 4–2**). In some cases, a request may be made that some or all of the elements of consent be waived by the IRB. For example,

---

Table 4–2 Elements of Informed Consent

Basic Elements of Informed Consent Provide Subjects with the Following Information

◇ **A statement that the study involves research**
  - An explanation of the purposes of the research
  - The expected duration of the subject's participation
  - A description of the procedures to be followed
  - Identification of any procedures that are experimental

◇ **Description of any reasonably foreseeable risks or discomforts**

◇ **Benefits that may reasonably be expected**
  - To the subject (if applicable)
  - To others

◇ **Alternative procedures or treatment, if any, that might be advantageous to the subject**

◇ **Confidentiality of records**
  - The extent, if any, to which confidentiality will be maintained

◇ **Injury related care or compensation** (for research involving more than minimal risk)
  - Whether any compensation and medical treatments are available if injury occurs
  - If so, what they consist of, or where further information may be obtained

◇ **Contact information—whom to contact**
  - For answers to pertinent questions about the research and subjects' rights
  - In the event of a research related injury to the subject

◇ **Participation remains voluntary**—no penalty or loss of entitled benefits
  - By refusing to participate
  - By discontinuing participation at any

Additional information when determined to be appropriate by the IRB
  ✓ A statement that the particular treatment or procedure may involve unforeseeable risks
  ✓ Anticipated circumstances under which the subject's participation may be terminated by the investigator without regard to the subject's consent
  ✓ Any additional costs to the subject that may result from participation in the research
  ✓ The consequences of a subject's decision to withdraw from the research and procedures for orderly termination of participation by the subject
  ✓ A statement that significant new findings developed during the course of the research that may relate to the subject willingness to continue participation will be provided to the subject
  ✓ The approximate number of subjects involved in the study

a waiver of consent may be appropriate for a study using existing health information that was collected for clinical purposes where it is not feasible to obtain consent from the individual patients. An example of an alteration of informed consent would include a study where some of the required information is not appropriate for the research. In this case the investigator can request an alteration in consent if the study meets the criteria for alteration or waiver. In addition to the information provided during the consent process, the IRB also evaluates each plan for obtaining informed consent. A recruitment plan should provide ample opportunity for prospective subjects (or their surrogate) to make an informed choice. Considerations include the study setting, how and by whom the consent interview will be conducted, and timing for obtaining consent (to minimize the possibility that prospective subjects may perceive undue pressure to enroll or feel coerced).

The informed consent will be appropriately documented. The investigator must have clear plans for obtaining appropriate signatures of subjects (or their legally authorized representative) to document the informed consent process. Most IRBs provide a consent document template that provides the basic elements of consent. If this documentation is not possible (e.g., telephone surveys), the investigator may request a waiver of documentation of informed consent which must be approved by the IRB.

The research plan makes adequate provision for monitoring the data collected to ensure the safety of subjects (when appropriate). When required, a plan for monitoring the safety of the study using the data collected should be developed. This plan should include (1) how often safety data is compiled and reviewed, (2) by whom (an individual or committee), and (3) whether limits are needed for stopping the research procedures to ensure safety of the subjects.

There are adequate provisions to protect the privacy of subjects and to maintain the confidentiality of data (when appropriate).[11] For example, assigning study codes to subjects rather than using names and storing the key to decipher the code in a separate, secure location accessible only to the investigators is way of demonstrating this type of protection.

In addition to the seven determinations listed previously, if a study involves populations vulnerable to coercion or undue influence, such as children, prisoners, pregnant women, or mentally disabled people, the IRB will evaluate whether the study provides safeguards capable of protecting the rights and welfare of those individuals.

In preparing a research project for review by the IRB, the study plan should be designed with the required determinations in mind. While it is the IRB's responsibility to determine whether these requirements for approval are met, it is the investigator's responsibility to design and carrying out the study plan in such a way that the criteria for approval are met. This is one of several responsibilities assumed by the investigator responsible for the research.

WHAT ARE THE INVESTIGATOR'S RESPONSIBILITIES?

Obtaining IRB approval for a new project is only the first of many responsibilities for the principal investigator (PI).[12] The PI must ensure that the study continues to meet the criteria used by the IRB for the initial approval (e.g., the risks continue to be minimized, informed consent continues to be obtained and documented, safety data is collected and monitored, etc.).[13] The PI is also responsible for communicating regularly with the IRB under certain circumstances such as those described in the following sections.

Continuing Review

Many investigators do not realize that the approval they get when a study is first reviewed by the IRB has a time limit that cannot exceed one year. To request reapproval so that the research can continue uninterrupted, the PI must submit a status report to the IRB before the approval period expires. The report must include information about the number of subjects accrued (if any); a description of any adverse events, unanticipated problems, subject withdrawals or complaints; a summary of relevant new information (either published or learned in the research); and a copy of the current consent document(s) being used. The IRB reviews the status report, including any other new information and reconsiders the required determinations for approval of research (e.g., risks continue to be minimized, risks continue to be reasonable in relation to the benefits, informed consent continues to be obtained and appropriately documented, etc.). If the study continues to meet the criteria for approval, the IRB will reapprove the study for up to one additional year.

Sometimes the IRB may decide to issue an approval for less than a year (e.g., for particularly high risk studies the IRB may only approve the study for three months). It is the responsibility of the investigator to contact the IRB to request reapproval prior to the expiration of the original IRB approval.[12] If the IRB has not reapproved the study before the current approval period expires, research procedures may not be performed.

Modifications

When changes to a research study are needed, IRB approval must first be obtained before the modification is implemented.[12] The only time changes may be made to a study is when the modification is necessary to eliminate an immediate hazard to the subjects. Examples of changes that must be approved by the IRB are changes in the number of subjects needed to enroll; changes to the study design, methods or procedures; study staff changes; study sites or locations changes; changes in consent procedures and/or consent document; changes in recruitment materials; changes in compensation amounts. Each IRB establishes a mechanism for requesting approval of modifications. Like new studies, the IRB may use expedited or full-committee review procedures. Minor changes to already approved studies are generally eligible for expedited review.

Tracking Adverse Events and Reporting UPIRSOs

Adverse events can be expected in research. A good data safety monitoring plan allows investigators to track adverse events that occur during a research study and to continuously monitor them to determine whether changes should be made to the research plan to minimize risks to participants.[14] While adverse events should be tracked, not all occurrences must be reported to the IRB immediately.

Only adverse events which meet the criteria of an UPIRSO (Unanticipated Problem Involving Risks to Subjects or Others) must be reported immediately to the IRB. A UPIRSO is any incident, experience, or outcome that meets *all* of the following criteria[14]:

1. Unexpected (in terms of nature, severity or frequency), *and*
2. Related or possibly related to participation in the research, *and*
3. Suggests that the research places subjects (or others) at a greater risk of harm (including physical, psychological, economic, or social harm) than was previously known or recognized

While some UPIRSOs are also adverse events, keep in mind that not all UPIRSOs are adverse events. UPIRSOs may result from other problems such as unintentional loss of identifiable private information that represents increased likelihood of harm, rather than actual harm. The IRB will review the UPIRSO and determine whether the research should continue and whether modifications should be made to the research to offer additional protection to the participants or others.

Reporting Noncompliance

Instances of noncompliance should be reported by the PI to the IRB. Noncompliance is an action by the investigator or member of the research team that disregards or violates federal regulations, IRB requirements and determinations, or institutional policies and procedures.[12] When noncompliance is discovered, the IRB reviews the events surrounding the incident, the seriousness of the event and whether it has occurred before, and the event's effect on the subject's rights, welfare, and safety. The IRB often requires a written report from the investigator that includes a corrective action plan. The IRB may decide that additional actions are necessary to address the noncompliance; such actions may range from retraining to suspension or termination of the research depending upon the severity of the event. If the IRB determines the noncompliance is either serious or continuing, the event is reported to the OHRP (for research funded by HHS) and/or the FDA (for certain FDA-regulated research).[3]

Inactivation

The investigator should notify the IRB when the study has concluded or when the IRB approval is no longer necessary. An IRB approval may be inactivated if *all* of the following are true:

1. Enrollment is permanently closed to new subjects.
2. Data, private information, and/or specimens are no longer being collected for research purposes (including long term follow up).
3. Participants are no longer being treated under the research protocol and there are no plans for future research treatment.
4. Research assessments or procedures are no longer being performed and there are no plans for future research procedures.
5. Data or specimen analysis has been completed, or if analysis continues, the materials will be deidentified.
6. Federal research funding for the study is closed (if applicable).
7. The study is closed at all participating sites that are under the investigator's supervision.

The investigator notifies the IRB of the intent to inactivate the IRB approval by providing a final status report to the IRB. The IRB reviews the status of the study and determines whether inactivating the approval is appropriate.

Additional Responsibilities

In addition to the responsibilities of the investigator to the IRB as outlined above, additional responsibilities are expected of PIs[15,16]:

1. Complete and maintain training on human subjects protection. Confirm the institution's training requirements. [Several courses are available on the Internet. As a public service, the NIH Office of Extramural Research offers a free tutorial on "Protecting Human Research Participants" that institutions may elect to use to meet the human-subjects protections education requirement.]
2. Follow the IRB approved protocol and the regulations and policies related to research and privacy.
3. Supervise everyone working on the project to ensure they follow the protocol and rules that govern research.
4. Place the protection of research participants first.
5. Verify IRB approval before allowing research to begin or before implementing changes.
6. Keep participants informed and ensure they are willing to continue participating. Informed consent occurs at the beginning of research participation and should continue throughout a participant's involvement in the research.
7. Regularly collect and assess information about safety or unexpected problems. This includes conducting regular literature reviews for new information that may affect the study or the study participants.
8. Ensure those working on the project are qualified and are authorized to perform delegated tasks. This includes education, training, experience, and certifications.
9. Provide ongoing communication with study staff. This communication allows the PI to assess problems as they arise and to make swift changes as necessary.
10. Confirm that the data is accurate.
11. Maintain organized records.

By following these guidelines, the PI protects research participants and improves the quality of the research conducted.

SUMMARY

In conclusion, a number of complex federal regulations govern research involving human subjects. This chapter provided a brief introduction to the major concepts involved in complying with the regulations. Understanding these concepts is essential for students in healthcare professions who must understand the basic ethical principles that guide research and their responsibilities to comply with the rules and regulations applicable to the type of research they may conduct. Investigators and their IRBs must work together to ensure that research is conducted safely and in an ethical manner. When any human-subject research project is planned, the local IRB should be contacted for assistance.

REFERENCES

1. Tolleson-Rinehart S. A collision of noble goals: protecting human subjects, improving health care, and a research agenda for political science. *PS.* 2008;41:507–511.
2. National Commission for the Protection of Human Subjects of Biomedical and Behavioral Research. The Belmont report: ethical principles and guidelines for the protection of human subjects of research. Published 1979. http://ohsr.od.nih.gov/guidelines/belmont.html. Accessed on February 25, 2011.
3. U.S. Department of Health and Human Services, National Institutes of Health, and Office for Human Research Protections The Common Rule, Title 45 (Public Welfare), Code of Federal Regulations, Part 46 (Protection of Human Subjects). Published 1991, revised 2009. http://www.hhs.gov/ohrp/humansubjects/guidance/45cfr46.html. Accessed on February 25, 2011.
4. National Bioethics Advisory Commission. Ethical and policy issues in research involving human participants. Bethesda, MD; published August 2001. http://bioethics.georgetown.edu/pcbe/reports/past_commissions/nbac_human_part.pdf. Accessed on March 4, 2011.
5. U.S. Department of Health and Human Services, Food and Drug Administration. Title 21 (Food and Drugs), Code of Federal Regulations, Part 50 (Protection of Human Subjects). Published 1981. http://www.accessdata.fda.gov/scripts/cdrh/cfdocs/cfCFR/CFRSearch.cfm?CFRPart=50. Accessed on February 25, 2011.
6. U.S. Department of Health and Human Services, Food and Drug Administration. Title 21 (Food and Drugs), Code of Federal Regulations, Part 56 (Institutional Review Boards). Published 1981. http://www.accessdata.fda.gov/scripts/cdrh/cfdocs/cfCFR/CFRSearch.cfm?CFRPart=56. Accessed on March 2, 2011.
7. U.S. Department of Health and Human Services. Title 45 (Public Welfare), Code of Federal Regulations, Part 164 (Security and Privacy). Published 2003. http://ecfr.gpoaccess.gov/cgi/t/text/text-idx?c=ecfr&tpl=/ecfrbrowse/Title45/45cfr164_main_02.tpl. Accessed on March 3, 2011.
8. Cooper JA. Responsible conduct of radiology research. IV. The boundary of research and practice. *Radiology.* 2005;237:383–384.
9. Food and Drug Administration. Protection of Human Subjects: Standards for Institutional Review Boards for Clinical Investigations 21 CFR Parts 16 and 56 [Docket No. 77N-0350] 46 FR 8958. Published 1981. http://www.fda.gov/ScienceResearch/SpecialTopics/RunningClinicalTrials/ucm118296.htm. Accessed on February 26, 2011.
10. Bankurt EA, Amdur RJ. *Institutional Review Board: Management and Function,* 2nd ed. Sudbury, MA: Jones and Bartlett; 2006.
11. Shaughnessy M, Beidler SM, Gibbs K, Michael K. Confidentiality challenges and good clinical practices in human subjects research: Striking a balance. *Top Stroke Rehabil.* 2007;14(2): 1–4.
12. U.S. Department of Health and Human Services, Office for Human Research Protections. Investigator responsibilities, FAQs: What are investigators' responsibilities during the conduct of an approved research study? Published January 20, 2011. http://answers.hhs.gov/ohrp/questions/7216. Accessed on February 26, 2011.
13. Emanuel EJ, Wendler D, Grady C. What makes clinical research ethical? *JAMA.* 2000;283:2701–2711.
14. U.S. Department of Health and Human Services, Office for Human Research Protections. Guidance on reviewing and reporting unanticipated problems involving risks to subjects or others and adverse events. Published 2007. http://www.hhs.gov/ohrp/policy/advevntguid.html. Accessed on February 26, 2011.
15. U.S. Department of Health and Human Services, Office for Human Research Protections. Investigator FAQs: investigator responsibilities, FAQs. Published January 20, 2011. http://answers.hhs.gov/ohrp/categories/1567. Accessed on February 26, 2011.
16. Merritt MW, Labrique AB, Katz J, Rashid M, West KP Jr, Pettit J. A field training guide for human subjects research ethics. *PLoS Med.* 2010;7(10):1–4.

CHAPTER OVERVIEW

Research is not free or inexpensive. In fact, it can be very expensive. For many researchers or potential researchers, finding funding is as much a part of the job as the research itself. Grant support is one funding method that is available from many sources, from the federal government to foundations. This chapter discusses writing grant proposals, and the techniques and suggestions presented can be applied to many grant opportunities.

Funding the Research: Grants

William D. Hendricson, MA, MS
J. Dennis Blessing, PhD, PA

INTRODUCTION

There is nothing worse than having a great idea for a research problem and not enough money to do the investigation. This is a big problem for cash-strapped students or for anyone undertaking an expensive project. One answer to money and cost problems is a grant. Writing a grant proposal is an intellectual undertaking that requires time and effort, and it can be emotionally intense if funding is the only way a project can be completed. Submitting a grant proposal can be a high-risk endeavor. There are no guarantees of success; in fact, failure is common, although the percentage of grants that ultimately receive funding is higher than related mythology might lead one to believe, especially for investigators who are persistent. However, writing a grant proposal can also accrue a high reward. In 2003, an estimated $35 billion of funding was provided to grant seekers from various sources. It is estimated that more than a million grant proposals are submitted to various types of funding agencies every year in the United States that range from small family-based foundations (e.g., the Joe and Sally Smith Charitable Trust) to the National Institutes of Health (NIH) and other federal organizations. Numerous sources of funding lie in between small, private foundations and the NIH, including church-based foundations, professional associations, the military, the business sector, nonprofit organizations, and government agencies at city, county, and state levels. In addition, many colleges, universities, and statewide higher education coordinating boards operate grant programs to stimulate research or educational innovation.

The information presented in this chapter is drawn from four sources: (1) the authors' experiences writing grant proposals, (2) personal favorites among the mass of literature on grant writing (i.e., a Google search in January 2010 yielded 7.3 million citations for "books, grant writing"), (3) workshops conducted by the authors, and (4) experiences as writers and as reviewers of grant proposals. Information and help are abundantly available in a number of formats. While the major concentration of this chapter focuses on the NIH format, the information can be used for any type of grant application.

There are many categories of grants in the biomedical sciences and health professions. These categories include

1. education *training grants* designed to support educational programs for healthcare providers,
2. *program development grants* designed to help institutions establish centers of excellence that promote research, education, and community service in focused areas, often centered on a public health problem (e.g., diabetes, alcoholism, health problems of the elderly, rural access to care),
3. *infrastructure grants* designed to help schools create core support services and facilities that will enhance research or education for the entire campus,
4. *career development grants* of many types that are designed to enhance the professional growth of faculty and help establish research careers,
5. and a multitude of *research grants* designed to support investigations of scientific unknowns in the basic, clinical, and behavioral sciences as well as to explore research questions pertinent to health services delivery, public health issues, organizational dynamics within healthcare service institutions,

and best practices for educating healthcare providers and patients. Many professional organizations have grants specifically for students.

This chapter focuses on the development of research grants because many of the writing strategies that are critical for creation of a competitive research applications are also essential for other types of grant proposals. Grantsmanship issues are addressed herein, but the primary focus of the chapter is on writing strategies that can make a grant application, such as the three C's (Clear, Compelling, and Convincing) shown in **Table 5–1**. The three C's are universal principles that apply to telling "the story" in any type of grant application. The grant writer's primary job is to communicate the scientific plan in an easy-to-understand and persuasive manner so that the grant application stands out from the many other proposals that a reviewer is likely to be critiquing at the same time.

Figure 5–1 presents the three components of any successful grant application. First and foremost, a *clear need* must exist for the project proposed in the application. In the biomedical world, needs often involve deficits in our understanding of "how things work," ranging from gaps in knowledge of how breakdowns in cellular mechanisms

Table 5–1 The Grant Writer's Goal: Communicate the Scientific Plan with the Three C's

Clear	Grant application is reviewer friendly. It is succinct, easy to comprehend, well organized, and easy to follow.
Compelling	Grant application presents a persuasive case for the importance and value of the project.
Convincing	The description of the project makes it seem exciting and unique. The proposal grabs the attention of reviewers and makes them want to be an advocate for the research question, "Why hasn't this been studied before?"

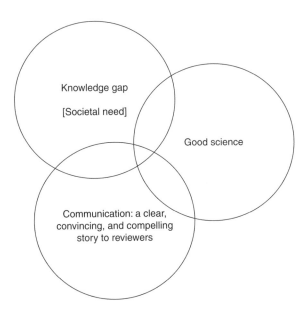

Figure 5–1 Components of a successful grant application.

or genetic structure can trigger disease to lack of understanding about how to effectively implement healthcare services for the public. A grant writer's success hinges on the ability to clearly articulate a knowledge gap and convince reviewers that this gap needs to be addressed now AND by the specific applicant. A second ingredient in the formula for a successful grant application is *good science,* that is, using up-to-date and appropriate scientific principles and methodology to investigate the knowledge gap. The third ingredient is *persuasive communication,* or the use of language to communicate the need for the project (e.g., the knowledge gap) and the scientific plan in a clear, convincing, and compelling manner that distinguishes the proposal from all the other applications being considered.

The first section of this chapter reviews three important considerations related to "getting into the grant writing game" often known as grantsmanship, including an examination of grant writing from the reviewer's perspective. The second section presents writing strategies for the six major sections of a research grant application: the abstract, specific aims (e.g., project objectives), background and significance, preliminary studies, research methods, and the budget justification. The format and level of detail for the budget section of grant applications

varies considerably depending on the nature of the funding agency. Therefore, the material on budget in this chapter will focus primarily on how to write compelling justifications for project personnel using a effective and proven template. Format requirements (e.g., page length, word count, or sequencing) for the other components of a research grant proposal also vary depending on the funding agency, but the core information that needs to be provided in each section is basically the same whether the application is for a small amount of money to support a student project or a million-dollar proposal to the NIH or the National Science Foundation. This chapter outlines and explores goals and writing strategies (e.g., presentation and sequencing of ideas) of successful grant writers as well as critical red flags to avoid for each of the "narrative" components of a research grant application. The term narrative is used because the grant writer's primary task is to employ the written word to explain the concept and rationale for the proposed project. Successful grant writers tell a story with words to build a compelling case for the project.

GETTING INTO THE GRANT-WRITING GAME

In this section, three questions are addressed: What is a grant? What do grant writers need to know about funding agencies? And what do grant writers need to know about reviewers? Let us start with the basics. *What is a grant?* A grant is basically a financial award given by an organization to help implement a project that is consistent with the mission and priorities of the grantor (i.e., the organization that is awarding money to sponsor projects). Essentially, the agency that provides grant monies is making an investment in the investigator or grant requestor. In return for the monies provided to support the research, the funding agency is anticipating a pay-off on its investment in terms of answers to "gap(s) in knowledge" in a particular area or field. Grantors may also expect to garner notoriety and enhanced public image from their support of a project. A grantor in the business sector, such as a company that makes medical instruments, may expect to gain a marketplace advantage over competitors as a result of products that evolve from research that they support. Thus, grants provide recipients with the financial support to conduct a project under conditions that meet the expectations and desired outcomes of the grantor. Many award mechanisms are globally called "grants." The three most common award mechanisms are (1) grants, which can be either unsolicited or submitted in response to a solicitation (request) for applications, (2) contracts, and (3) cooperative agreements. The key characteristics of each mechanism are described in **Table 5–2**.

Table 5–2 Characteristics of Funding Mechanisms

Grants: Unsolicited	• The grantor (funding agency) agrees to support a project that has been proposed by the applicant. • The research question, project conceptualization, and methodology are originated by the applicant. • Recipients of unsolicited grants typically have considerable freedom to configure and conduct the project as they see fit. • The funding organization typically plays no active role in project implementation other than to receive progress reports.
Grants: Solicited	• Solicited grants are often called RFAs, Request For Applications. • The funding agency has already identified a problem or issue that needs to be studied. • The agency sends out a request for applications to solicit projects to study the problem or issue. • Generally RFAs come with certain stipulations to guide grant writers in creation of their proposals (e.g., types of research protocols that are acceptable, specific aspects of the overall problem that have high priority, study populations that need to be addressed, and healthcare providers that need to be involved in the project). • Awards made in response to RFAs are typically monitored more closely that unsolicited grants, but investigators often have a fair degree of latitude in structuring the project.
Contracts	• The agency solicits proposals to perform specified tasks that are often tightly prescribed. Contract-based solicitations are often called Requests For Proposals, or RFPs. • Contracts are frequently issued for applied research (e.g., implementation of projects that attempt to incorporate a biomedical science breakthrough into clinical practice or to evaluate the "real world" effectiveness of a technique that has had promising results in an experimental and well-controlled environment). • The funding agency is often more involved in the day-to-day details of a contract-supported project than in a project supported by a grant. • The funding agency expects stricter financial accountability and project reporting than with grants.
Cooperative Agreements	• Cooperative agreements are similar to RFAs (Requests For Applications, or solicited grants) except that the funding agency works closely with investigators on project implementation details, basically functioning as co-investigators. • This funding mechanism is used by the NIH and by many state agencies to pursue research in specific areas where pooling of resources is needed. • Conceptually, a project supported by a cooperative agreement is a shared research protocol between the grantor and grantee. • Most faculty are not likely to be involved in a cooperative agreement project unless they are well-established investigators in their discipline.

For RFAs and RFPs, it is important to carefully analyze what the funding agency wants initially. Understanding the funding agency's "want" is absolutely critical to constructing a grant application so that it "gives them what they want." Many applications submitted in response to an RFA are rejected because the grant writers did not pay enough attention to the information in the solicitation announcement. RFAs can be quite detailed, often 10–15 pages in length. Many are prescriptive in describing what types of projects they want and the conditions under which the research should be conducted. Failing to respond to the "wish list" communicated in the announcement of the RFA is usually fatal to the application. Some RFA announcements can be found on the NIH website for the Office of Extramural Research (http://grants.nih.gov/grants/guide/index.html). This link accesses the Funding Opportunities and Notices page, where Requests for Applications (RFAs) under "Browse Funding Opportunities" can be further explored. Dozens of currently active RFAs are listed at this site and can be reviewed online. **Exhibit 5–1**

Exhibit 5–1 Summary of Information Available to Grant Writers in a RFA

Title: Interventions for Control of Asthma Among African American and Hispanic Children

Goal: Develop reproducible model programs that reduce asthma morbidity, decrease inappropriate use of health resources, and increase quality of life of asthmatic patients and families among target populations.

Support: $1.6 million annually for four grants. Awards for up to five years.

Key project design considerations:
- Projects should seek multidisciplinary approaches involving medicine, public health, and behavioral sciences.
- Applicants must demonstrate access to target populations.
- Projects should focus on children up to 18 years old and parents and/or care providers.
- Interventions can include changing knowledge and behavior of healthcare providers.

Research design should include the following:
- Well-defined population with asthma
- Reliable asthma assessment and long-term monitoring methods
- Appropriate theoretical basis for intervention
- Sufficient population for a control group
- Social and cultural characteristics of intervention population
- Health status and behavioral change measurements
- Follow-up data for two years postintervention

Examples of questions that could be answered by programs developed through this solicitation include the following:
- How can patients at high risk be targeted for early intervention in order to avoid emergency room visits and hospitalizations for asthma?
- How can patient education be integrated into healthcare systems used by these populations?
- How can education of healthcare providers contribute to improved management of asthma among minority children?
- What strategies are needed to ensure that patients receive an appropriate treatment regimen?
- What are the relationships between interventions and medical outcomes?
- What is the effect of intervention on quality of life and family functioning?
- What interventions are most effective among Hispanic and African American populations?

Source: NIH-95-HL-11-L (RFA Number)
National Heart, Lung, and Blood Institute
Original application date: December 1, 1995

illustrates the type of information typically available in an RFA, including the goal of the solicitation (which should be read carefully and addressed directly in the proposal), level and duration of support, key project design considerations, guidelines for creating the research plan (which are imperative to a successful application), and examples of research questions that the funding agency would like to see answered by funding projects. The research questions presented in the proposal should closely paraphrase (although not verbatim) one or more of the questions that appear in the RFA. Similar sites exist for a number of funding agencies. Many healthcare professional organizations also offer grant opportunities.

What Information About the Funding Agency Is Needed?

In a word—*everything*. One of the most common reasons for rejection of grant applications at all levels below NIH is that the topic (i.e., area of emphasis) and goals of the proposal do not match the mission and priorities of the funding agency. Unfortunately, these mismatches are quite common, even at the federal level. One peer-review coordinator for one of NIH's institutes who works closely with the institutes' study sections (i.e., peer review panels) indicates that proposal–mission mismatches account for twenty percent of the applications that are rejected prior to peer review in the prescreening (triage) system employed by NIH. A common misconception is that the scientific mission of the NIH is to support biomedical research, when in fact the actual mission of the NIH is to "improve the health of the people of the United States."[1] NIH study-section reviewers are not likely to endorse a project if they cannot see a connection between the research question and how the answer to that question or results of the proposed study can be applied to enhance public health. This is usually true of all grant agencies. An investigator may have a great idea, but if it does not fit with the mission and priorities of the grantor, it will not be funded.

In this electronic era, grant writers can obtain a wealth of information about almost any potential funding source in local, state, and federal government, among the thousands of private foundations that have grant award programs and among the numerous corporations in the business and industry sectors that support biomedical research. Various military agencies also operate award programs (e.g., RFP contract mechanisms) to support biomedical research. An entire book could be written on the topic of search strategies to find sources of funding to support research. These are three of the most common elements of a successful strategy:

1. *Make voice contact.* In-person or by phone, contact the grant program managers at the funding sources that have identified as potential recipients of the grant application.
2. *Do the homework.* Learn everything about the funding sources being considered.
3. *Be proactive.* Take advantage of online resources and searchable databases to stay informed about funding opportunities and what the competitors for grant dollars are doing.

The first rule of grantsmanship is to never submit a grant application to any organization without talking to a grant program coordinator about the proposed project. It is essential to make sure that the funding agency has an interest in a research idea before investing in proposal development. It is also important to determine whether the funding agency has particular interests within the general topic of research that may help focus the proposal on a specific aspect. With private foundations and with county and state governments, it is critical to determine whether they have recently funded projects similar to the proposal being developed. A research idea may have great merit and address a clear need, but if the agency has funded several similar projects in the past couple of years, they may hesitate to provide financial support for yet another project in the same area. One strategy for approaching foundations is to telephone the grant program manager (who is usually listed on the website) to discuss project ideas. If the grant manager is encouraging, a one-page synopsis should be sent as an email attachment within 24 hours as a follow-up. This email should be followed by a second phone call within 48 hours to determine whether the project still seems to fit with the objectives of the foundation's award program after the grant manager has examined the project details. Most grant program managers will be candid about informing investigators if the idea does not fit, but their responses may require some interpretation. In general, any degree of hesitancy about a project synopsis indicates that at least some aspect of the project should be reconsidered.

The second rule of grantsmanship is to do the homework. This means identifying and researching potential funding sources, which can be a time-consuming process. Here are suggestions for identifying potential sponsors among philanthropic foundations, the private sector (business and industry), and the federal government, including the military, and recommendations for communicating with foundations and private businesses.

Philanthropic foundations. A wide variety of print and electronic resources are available to help locate "best fit" target foundations for grant applications. Exhibit 5–2 describes several print resources that may be helpful; most of these have companion electronic versions that can be

---

Exhibit 5–2 Funding Resource Directories in Print

The Foundation Directory. New York: Sage Publications.
This annual publication provides information on the finances, governance, and giving interests of the nations' 10,000 largest grant-making foundations. Information is arranged by the state where the foundation is located. Entries explain each foundation's purpose and activities, fields of interest, type of support, and limitations. Many entries list examples of grants funded in the last reported year.

Annual Register of Grant Support. Medford, NJ: Information Today, Inc.
The *Annual Register* describes nearly 4000 grant support programs, including government agencies, public and private foundations, corporations, community trusts, unions, educational and professional associations, and special-interest organizations. Eleven broad categories, including "Life Sciences," are subdivided into more specific fields, including medicine (multiple disciplines), dentistry, nursing, pharmacology, as well as allergy, immunology, infectious diseases, and several other specialties.

Directory of Texas Foundations. San Antonio: Nonprofit Resource Center of Texas.
Information about nearly 2500 foundations located in Texas is listed alphabetically in the *Directory of Texas Foundations*. Indices include areas of interest and type of support, headquarter city, trustees, and officers. This directory also includes information about foundation support in geographic areas of the state and a breakdown of types of grants given in each city (e.g., medical research received 7.7 percent of grants given in San Antonio in 2003). It also includes analyses of the top 100 Texas grant-making foundations and breaks down the types of grants given by each foundation.

Guide to U.S. Foundations, Their Trustees, Officers, and Donors. New York: The Foundation Center.
This publication includes entries for nearly 60,000 large and small foundations. Foundation listings are arranged alphabetically by state. Within each state, foundations are listed in descending order by total grants awarded. Indexes include lists of trustees, officers, and donors, a foundation name index and a locator for independent, company-sponsored, and operating foundations and a community foundation name index and locator for community foundations.

Directory of Biomedical and Health Care Grants. Phoenix: Oryx Press.
More focused in scope than other directories, the Directory of Biomedical and Health Care Grants includes brief information on 2500 funding programs. Arranged alphabetically, each entry explains the foundation's purpose, requirements, restrictions, grant amounts, and contact and sponsor information. Indexes include subject listings, program type, and sponsoring organization, in addition to a geographic index by state.

accessed online. The bible of information about private foundations is *The Foundation Directory*, which is updated annually and now includes information on more than 20,000 foundations with award programs. This is a searchable database that can be used to pinpoint potential targets for the proposals. Access to this database requires a subscription. The Foundation Center (http://fdncenter.org/), which publishes *The Foundation Directory*, has an elaborate website with links to other directories, literature on grant writing, support services, and training opportunities available through the center. The Foundation Center's link to "Medical Research" at its RFP Bulletin (http://fdncenter.org/pnd/rfp/cat_medical_research.jhtml) is a valuable inventory of information about recently announced solicitations from a wide variety of foundations and other nonprofit organizations, and it can be accessed without a subscription fee.

There are organizations within virtually all states that print directories of state-based foundations, and many of these are available online as well as in print. Directories of state and national foundations are usually available in university libraries. For example, the *2010 Directory of Texas Foundations* (Exhibit 5–2). This directory is produced by the Center for Nonprofit Support (http://www.nprc.org/) located in San Antonio, Texas. This organization also offers personal consultation on search strategies to help grant writers find funding sources. Most major metropolitan areas have similar organizations that function as grant information clearinghouses and sources of consultation or training. Foundations typically provide detailed information about their grant programs at their websites. Usually, the banner running vertically along the left margin of the website or horizontally across the top of the page includes a link labeled in one of the following ways: Grant Program, Grants, Award Program, or Funding Opportunities. Such links lead to information about the foundation's grant mechanisms. Whether an investigator uses one of the foundation directories, either print or online, or goes directly to a foundation's website, answers to most of the following questions are usually readily available. If not, the foundation should be contacted directly prior to writing the proposal.

- What is the overall purpose or mission of the grant program? Does the foundation have a priority list of problems, issues, and topics?
- Does the foundation have geographic limits on funding? For example, awards may be limited to specific counties within the state. Will the foundation fund out-of-state projects?
- Does the foundation provide grants to support higher education and specifically, healthcare professions education?
- Does the foundation target certain population groups?
- Does the foundation have specific areas of interest? For foundations that support education in the healthcare professions or research in the biomedical sciences, certain public health issues such as alcoholism, or diseases such as diabetes, are often identified as high priorities.
- What types of projects does the foundation support? Foundations may support many of the following categories of grants or may focus on just one or two types: education and training, research, community service, scholarship programs, capital improvement projects, physical plant renovations, endowment funds, start-up funding (seed money), land acquisition, equipment purchase, endowed chairs in academic institutions, continuing education for professionals, and public education campaigns.
- Are there any specific restrictions on who can receive grants? Many foundations will not award grants to individuals who are not affiliated with an institution, and they might not make awards to religious organizations.
- How many grants are awarded annually, and what is the range in funding provided to applicants?
- What were the titles of grants awarded in the past 2–3 years and what organizations received these funds?

- What is the application process, including deadlines?
- Most importantly, who is the person identified as the grant program director for the foundation?

Answering these questions will help determine whether a particular foundation is a good fit for a proposal. An investigator should not submit a grant application to an organization unless the answers to these questions are clear.

Business and industry. Strategies for securing funding support from the private sector are generally similar to those employed with foundations. However, finding information on corporate award programs is more difficult. Fewer directories of corporate grant programs are available, and priorities and availability of funds shift in concert with marketplace factors more rapidly in the private sector. Generally, the website of the corporation provides information about award mechanisms. One starting point is the corporate funding website of the Foundation Center (http://foundation center.org/). As with foundations, personal contact with the grant program manager is extremely important. Before approaching a private company, potential applicants must be clear about how the project can benefit this company. In other words, they must be able to present solid reasons that the foundation would want to invest in the investigator and the project. In general, corporate entities are not likely to sponsor biomedical research unless it opens the door to a new and potentially profitable product line, provides them with resources (e.g., the research and the expertise of the investigative team) that give them a competitive edge over marketplace challengers, or enhances their image within the business community or among the public.[2] Therefore, some preliminary market analysis needs to be done before approaching potential sponsors. Companies are not likely to fund a project that "starts from scratch." They will expect to see that the project is already underway and has produced tangibles products or outcomes. The decision-making process about a proposal in the private sector can range from a single empowered corporate officer making the "call" to a deliberate and well-researched process that parallels NIH peer review. In contrast to public foundations, the first approach should be a brief personalized letter sent to an individual responsible for the company's grant program. The letter should accomplish four objectives: (1) define the product or concept, (2) identify commercial potential for the company, (3) discuss progress already made by the investigator, and (4) outline the next steps in development, and thus the need for collaboration and support. An example of a hypothetical introductory letter to a private company appears in **Exhibit 5–3.** A list of helpful suggestions for composing this approach letter appears below.

- Address the letter to a specific individual in a "decision-making position" within the company.
- Mention any previous contact in first paragraph (indicate where and when met).
- Ensure that the style is consistent and brief (two pages maximum). The letter should be clearly written and informative without making grandiose claims or boasting. Overly technical language should be avoided.
- Discuss why the company should be involved in product development (e.g., market expansion, "edge" over competition, ownership of a potential "breakthrough" product).
- Describe the status of work in progress (show that project is ready for expansion).
- Outline future plans (illustrate why support is needed).
- Request an opportunity to meet in person without sounding over-ambitious.

Within seven days, a follow-up phone call to the company's grant program manager should be made to make sure the letter was received, to elaborate on the letter, to answer questions that hopefully will arise (i.e., questions are a good sign), and to offer to send additional information. If the grant manager is receptive to receiving additional information, these materials should be sent within twenty-four hours. Follow-up materials can include reports detailing work accomplished to date,

Exhibit 5–3 Example of an Approach Letter to a Private Company

October 22, 1998

Douglas Morgan, PhD
Vice-President for Research & Development
Silver Star Biotechnologies
2344 S. 31st Street
Carson City, Nevada 77011

Dear Dr. Morgan:

This letter is a follow-up to our meeting at the Western States Conference in Portland. We appreciated your willingness to meet with us. As you may recall, we are attempting to produce a safe, effective, and commercially viable vaccine against respiratory syntial virus (RSV), the primary cause of lower respiratory tract infection among children under 6 years of age. RSV disease is now the leading cause of morbidity and mortality world-wide among children in this age group. In the past decade, there also has been a marked increase in deaths from RSV in the United States, Germany, Spain, and Great Britain. There have been many attempts to produce a vaccine against RSV, but all efforts to manufacture such a vaccine have been unsuccessful, including attempts to use a formalin-inactivated virus vaccine in the 1970s and efforts in the 1980s to use attenuated temperature sensitive mutants. Advances in biotechnology now provide legitimate opportunities for the production of a RSV vaccine that will embrace an international market due to the incidence of RSV disease throughout the world.

Because of Silver Star's commitment to vaccine development and the collaboration with the World Health Organization's vaccine research team, we thought you would appreciate an update on our progress since we met in Portland. The goals of our project are to produce an RSV vaccine that (1) can be administered to infants as young as six months, (2) has minimal immune-response side effects, and (3) is economically viable as a mass vaccination in both developing and industrialized nations.

Viral proteins with well-defined sequences can be produced using recombinant DNA technology. During phase I of this project, we produced noninfectious RSV-like particles (virus-like particles; VLPs) without the RSV genome. As you are aware, creation of such particles is a goal of the WHO's vaccine development team. This task was accomplished by coexpressing the envelope glycoproteins (F and G) and the envelope matrix proteins (M1 and M2) in cells using vaccinia virus (VV) recombinants. We then used Western blot analysis and immuno-electron microscopy to characterize the VLPs for the presence of four RSV proteins and the presence of vaccinia virus and cell proteins. We are now determining the immunogenicity of the VLPs by immunizing rabbits.

Phase I has been supported by institutional seed money, departmental resources, and two foundations that underwrite biomedical research but at modest funding levels. To continue with this project, we are seeking a collaborator in the private sector with similar research priorities. Phase II of this project will involve three tasks:

- Evaluate the humoral (mucosal and systemic) and cell-mediated immune responses induced by RSV-like particles with novel adjuvant/delivery systems such as dehydroepiandrosterone (DHEA) and vitamin D3.
- Evaluate the degree to which this immune response protects the respiratory tract after virus challenge.
- Determine whether this immune response will exacerbate the disease or induce significant side effects.

A prospectus is attached that reviews our phase I accomplishments and describes the objectives, methodology, needed resources, and timetable for phase II. Two abstracts describing our progress to date are also enclosed. They will be presented at next month's North American Virology Conference. We look forward to continued discussion of our mutual interests in production of a RSV vaccine.

Sincerely,

James Bosworth, PhD   Janet Gunderson, MD
Associate Professor   Associate Professor
Division of Virology   Division of Pulmonary Medicine

reprints of publications, newspaper articles, pictures of the product, and links to websites. Reports should be professionally packaged because corporate managers are accustomed to receiving polished and attractive documents. After another seven days, a second follow-up telephone call should be made to make sure the materials were received and answer any questions. Hopefully, a follow-up meeting will be invited at this point. If not, turn the attention to another potential source of funding. If a meeting is scheduled, two items should be discussed:

1. A development budget that specifically identifies the financial support needed for clearly defined future tasks
2. Any new products, outcomes, or reports that have evolved since the start of communication with the company.

During the meeting, a request for a decision-making timeframe about the funding should be made.

Federal government. Exhibit 5–4 describes online resources that can be used to stay abreast of funding opportunities at the federal level. Two helpful government websites are http://www.grants. gov/ and http://science careers.sciencemag.org/ funding. Investigators can arrange to have the *NIH Guide for Grants and Contracts* (http://grants. nih.gov/grants/guide/description.htm) sent weekly by email. Directions for subscribing to the *Guide* are available at this website. The *Guide* announces the availability of NIH RFAs for biomedical and behavioral research and for research training, and it also disseminates policy and administrative information. A number of online sources provide information about research sponsored by the military, which is more substantial than most people realize. For example, the link to Department of Defense Medical Research Programs is http:// cdmrp.army.mil/. The U.S. Army Medical Research and Material Command can be accessed at http:// www.usamraa.army.mil/pages/index.cfm.

The third rule of grantsmanship is to be proactive. This can be accomplished by collecting recent information about funding opportunities automatically online via email. An excellent way to stay current is to subscribe to an information organization, such as InfEd International (http://www. infoed.org/new_spin/spinmain.asp). InfoEd International has a searchable database that provides information on more than 1000 sponsoring agencies and more than 10,000 separate funding opportunities. All of the information is obtained directly from the funding agency and is updated frequently. Investigators can enter a detailed profile of their research interests and priorities with key words. The system automatically conducts daily searches of its database using the research interest information supplied and sends daily emails to registrants that contain announcements of RFAs, RFPs, and other research support opportunities. The service typically available by subscription or free of charge through the grants management office of universities or sometimes the library. A vast array of other funding alert systems are available online. Most are proprietary and vary greatly in quality and accuracy, so care should be taken to examine and investigate each opportunity thoroughly.

Proactive grantsmanship includes taking advantage of a powerful database known as CRISP (Computer Retrieval of Information on Scientific Projects, http://www.ninds.nih.gov). CRISP is a searchable database of federally funded biomedical research projects conducted at universities, hospitals, and other research institutions. At the present time, the database reaches back to 1972 and can be searched using key words to define research topics, to locate the titles, federal grant numbers, and names of the principle investigators for current or previously funded research projects. The database, maintained by the Office of Extramural Research at the NIH, includes projects funded by the NIH, Substance Abuse and Mental Health Services (SAMHSA), the Health Resources and Services Administration (HRSA), FDA, the Centers for Disease Control and Prevention (CDCP), the Agency for Health Care Research and Quality (AHRQ), and the Office of Assistant Secretary of Health (OASH). CRISP can be used to search for scientific concepts and emerging trends, or to identify specific projects and/or investigators. For example,

---

Exhibit 5–4 Online Sources of Information About Federal Grants

---

The Catalog of Federal Domestic Assistance (CFDA) (http://12.46.245.173/cfda/cfda.html)
The Catalog of Federal Domestic Assistance (CFDA) is a government-wide compendium of Federal programs, projects, services, and activities that provide assistance or benefits to the American public. It contains financial and nonfinancial assistance programs administered by departments and establishments of the Federal government.

Federal Register, National Archives and Records Administration
(http://www.archives.gov/federal_register/index.html)
The Federal Register is the official publication for presidential documents and executive orders as well as notices, rules, and proposed rules from federal agencies and organizations. Many federal programs and deadlines are announced in the Federal Register.

Grants.gov (http://www.grants.gov/)
Grants.gov is the electronic storefront for federal grants. The Department of Health and Human Services is the managing partner for the federal E-Grants initiative, designed to improve access to government services by the Internet. Grants.gov is a single access point for over 900 grant programs offered by the 26 federal grant-making agencies. Grants.gov allows organizations to electronically find and apply for competitive grant opportunities from all federal grant-making agencies.

GrantsNet (http://www.grantsnet.org/)
GrantsNet is a searchable database of Funding Opportunities for Training in the Biological and Medical Sciences. The American Association for the Advancement of Science (AAAS) and the Howard Hughes Medical Institute (HHMI) created this searchable database of biomedical funding options aimed at scientists in training, that is, graduate students, postdoctoral fellows, and junior faculty members.

Guide to U.S. Department of Education Programs and Resources
(http://web99.ed.gov/GTEP/Program2.nsf)
The Guide to U.S. Department of Education Programs and Resources website provides information about programs and resources administered by the U.S. Department of Education. Information is also available on financial assistance offered to state and local education agencies, institutions of higher education, post-secondary vocational institutions, public and private nonprofit organizations, and individuals to help serve a variety of education needs, including those of students, teachers, administrators, and researchers. It also includes information about laboratories, centers, and other research-oriented entities that produce resources important to education.

NIH Guide to Grants and Contracts (http://grants.nih.gov/grants/guide/index.html)
The official publication of NIH policies, procedures, and availability of funds. At this website, the NIH Guide issues can be searched, beginning with 1992.

NSF Guide to Programs; Funding Opportunities (http://www.nsf.gov/home/programs/recent.cfm)
The Guide to Programs website lists funding opportunities offered by the National Science Foundation (NSF) for research and education in science, mathematics, engineering, and technology. The NSF Guide includes broad, general descriptions of programs and activities for each NSF Directorate, as well as sources for more information. It also offers links to various NSF websites, program announcements, and solicitations that contain additional proposal or eligibility information, including the NSF E-Bulletin for proposal deadlines.

---

a CRISP search run in July 2004 with the key words "screening" and "diabetes" identified 247 current or previously funded grants. Specific titles can be selected from the CRISP return search items; in this case one of the projects that the CRISP system rated as a close match to the key words was selected, and the abstract that appears in **Exhibit 5–5** was retrieved. Although not displayed in this figure, CRISP searches indicate the names of the investigators for each project that appears on the hit list. The thesaurus terms listed with the project abstract can serve as a guide to help grant seekers further refine and focus their searches.

APPEALING TO THE GRANT REVIEWER

Most grant agencies use volunteers or reviewers who receive relatively low compensation. A grant writer must make the reviewer's task of critiquing the grant as easy as possible. (Recall the three C's of grant writing.) One of the grant writer's top priorities is to write a "reviewer friendly" proposal. The writer's job is to communicate the scientific plan and underlying rationale for the project in a clear, compelling, and convincing manner, with a major emphasis on clarity. The reviewer's job is to provide an objective, scientifically sound, and thoughtful critique of the proposal. If the proposal is written in a way that makes it difficult for reviewers to do their job, the chances for a favorable review decrease. So another critical goal of effective grantsmanship is to make it easy and painless for reviewers to critique the grant, that is, to facilitate the reviewers. To accomplish this critical goal, it is important to understand what reviewers value and conversely what they dislike. An annoyed reviewer is much more likely to look for excuses to reject a grant application. The initial impression of the application package can be critical. Good grammar, correct spelling, readable font, as well as professional layout and overall appearance are important. Many reviewers may do a general, quick review of a proposal and then decide if it warrants further or in-depth review. If a proposal looks like it will be a hard read (e.g., single-spaced text, smaller 10-point font, no

paragraph breaks or attractive headings, tables, and figures), the reviewer may set it aside. Moreover, if a proposal is difficult to read or understand on first review, regardless of its agreeable appearance, it is unlikely to get a second review. No reviewer wants to slog through a poorly written proposal.

What annoys reviewers? Here are six prominent annoyances in poorly written grant proposals:

1. *Detail drift.* Reviewers are highly sensitive to a red flag known as *detail drift,* which is sometimes called "sliding precision" or "moving targets." For example, in the abstract, the grant writer states that a study will be conducted at six community-based clinics in three cities, involving a total of 200 patients. However, in two subsequent sections of the proposal, the number of clinics and patients is reported differently each time. Detail drift is disconcerting for reviewers and can lead them to question whether the investigators are organized enough to perform a successful study. Additionally, sloppiness with key details in the proposal often leads reviewers to conclude that the project may be managed in a similar manner.

2. *Lack of precision in explaining project implementation.* When the "who, what, where, when, and how" details are unclear, reviewers become annoyed and are prevented from doing their job.

3. *Convoluted and obtuse writing style.* Lack of concise language, especially in the explanation of concepts or project rationale, is potentially fatal. If grant writer makes the reviewer S-A-T (<u>S</u>top <u>A</u>nd <u>T</u>hink) too many times, the proposal may be in trouble. Grant proposals laden with S-A-Ts that force reviewers to guess about the writers' intended meaning rarely result in a positive review. Liane Reif-Lehrer's famous statement about grant writing is well worth remembering: "The best writing cannot turn a bad idea into a good grant proposal. However, bad writing can turn a good idea into a poor grant proposal."[3]

Exhibit 5–5 Example of Abstract Obtained by CRISP Search of Funded Projects

---

Title: Screening for IGT: Glucose Challenge vs. Predictive Model

Source of Funding: National Institute of Diabetes and Digestive and Kidney Diseases (NIDDK) NIDDK and the American Diabetes Association recommend routine screening for "pre-diabetes" (a major public health problem), but we do not know how best to detect it. The United States is experiencing a dramatic rise in both type 2 diabetes and its antecedent, "pre-diabetes" (i.e., impaired glucose tolerance, IGT). Diabetes Prevention Program results show that progression from IGT to diabetes can be abated, but patients can only be directed to risk reduction programs if they are recognized; detecting IGT will be especially important for minority populations such as African Americans, who suffer disproportionately from diabetes. However, since we do not screen for IGT, many IGT patients progress to diabetes and already have complications and increased cardiovascular risk by the time they are finally diagnosed. Risk factor-based "predictive models" might identify individuals who should be screened to detect IGT, but approaches such as an **oral glucose tolerance test** (OGTT) may have limited applicability and are generally not used to screen for gestational diabetes, where the metabolic defect is similar to that in IGT. In this example, a viable research hypotheses might be this: A two-step screening by a one-hour oral glucose challenge test (GCT) followed, if abnormal, an OGTT will have good predictive ability to identify IGT, and will be superior to "predictive models" in both diagnostic efficiency and cost-effectiveness. The specific aims of this study would be formulated in this way: Specific Aims: (1) To validate the GCT as a reliable predictor of IGT, we will perform both the GCT and an OGTT in a large number of African Americans and Caucasians, with two objectives: (a) to identify cutoff levels that provide optimal test characteristics in both groups despite variation in prandial status or time of day; (b) to determine how predictive ability is modified by the presence of potential risk factors (e.g., age, ethnicity, family history, BMI, waist–hip ratio, dyslipidemia, hypertension, etc.). (2) To compare GCT screening to "predictive model" screening, we will evaluate both predictive ability and cost-effectiveness. Fulfilling the potential of the Diabetes Prevention Program (DPP) demands a highly generalizable, low-cost screening strategy, our multidisciplinary team will translate approaches proven beneficial for gestational diabetes into a cost-effective method to identify individuals who could benefit from programs to decrease progression from IGT to diabetes and reduce cardiovascular risk. In diabetes care, beginning management soon enough is a major problem, particularly for minorities that suffer disparities in health. By applying existing knowledge to disease control and prevention, achieving these Specific Aims is the critical first steps to solving this important problem.

Thesaurus Terms. In the course of composing a research proposal according to the structure of a formal grant application, the repetition of language phrasing can become tedious for the reviewer. Therefore, synonyms are often used to provide variety and to increase readability in the application. A good thesaurus is a valuable resource for this aspect of preparation. Here are some examples of similar terms that may be helpful: Diagnosis design/evaluation, diagnosis quality/standard, glucose tolerance test, noninsulin dependent diabetes mellitus, oral administration, pathologic process, prediabetic state, prognosis, rapid diagnosis, African American, Caucasian American, cost-effectiveness, diabetes mellitus genetics, disease/disorder prevention/control, disease/disorder proneness/risk, early diagnosis, gender difference, glucose metabolism, health disparity, obesity, clinical research, data collection methodology/evaluation, human subject.

---

4. *Unsupported assertions*. Another catalyst for reviewer annoyance is *unsupported assertions* that are authoritatively stated as fact but are not backed up with evidence or citations to the literature. The reviewer is left to guess: Is this contention the opinion of the investigators or is there unstated research support that the writer assumes the reviewers will know? The acronym A-S-K (Assumed Shared Knowledge), is one of the most frequent editorial "red flags." Always assume that the reviewer does not know what the investigator knows. This includes the use of acronyms, which should always be spelled out on first use.

5. *Surprises*. Reviewers react poorly to items that suddenly pop up in the later stages of a proposal. Consider a reviewer who has devoted three hours to diligently reading through a grant application and believes that (s)he has a firm grasp on the details of the protocol. Near the conclusion of the methods section, new and previously unmentioned ideas and techniques start to appear in a casual format. This may strike the reviewer as a sign that the investigators do not know what they want to do or may manage the project in a similarly ad-hoc manner.

6. *"Hide and seek" organizational structure*. Poorly organized information makes a grant proposal painful to read. Sometimes the flow (e.g., sequencing) of ideas in grant applications is so obtuse and disorganized that it almost seems intentional—as if the writer is challenging the reviewer: "Let's see if you can figure out the details of this project on your own."

When writing a grant application, assume that the following statements are true as reminders to write as clearly as possible:

- Most reviewers will not read an application completely, and many will only skim it.
- Some reviewers will only read the abstract and specific aims (project objectives) and

will make a decision about the merits of the grant based on these two sections (see part 2 of this chapter).

- Some reviewers will be only remotely familiar with the area of research proposed in the grant.
- No reviewer will understand the project as well as the investigator and/or writer.
- Some reviewers will misinterpret or simply forget key elements of the proposal.
- A grant writer will not be able to answer questions, provide missing details, or clarify misconceptions when the reviewers read the grant proposal or when the entire review committee meets to discuss it. The fate of a grant rests on the clarity of the story told in the grant application and the strength of the case built for the project.
- The final take-home message in relation to reviewers is this: a grant writer and/or investigator is competing for the reviewer's attention. Do not assume that the reviewer's attention is automatically captured. The reviewer's attention is captured by clear, compelling, and convincing writing.

Before leaving the reviewer's world, here are four closing recommendations for enhancing grantsmanship:

1. *Become a reviewer*. Grant-writing success will increase when the review process is carefully considered. As discussed, grant reviewing can be "more work for the already overworked," but reviewer feedback can be powerful learning tool for the applicant. There is no better way to see what works and what does not work than to review critiques of grant applications of various formats and quality, noting the characteristics of grants that are funded and those that are not.

2. *Heed the "fatal seven" red flags listed below*. Although the NIH periodically analyzes reasons for grant rejection and publishes them, the fatal red flags below have not substantially changed for many years.[4]

Several of these red flags evolve from problems in the conceptualization of the overall research design, use of inappropriate statistical techniques, or the application of scientific principles and methodology that are out-of-date or have been discredited. These issues are beyond the scope of this chapter, but few research grants will be approved for funding if the underlying scientific foundations are weak, even if the proposal is communicated with persuasive use of the three C's.

Seven Fatal Red Flags[5,6]

1. The proposed research is not unique, novel, or innovative. For example, the research plan addresses questions that have already been answered or are no longer of scientific interest.
2. The proposed project is not conceptually significant. Even if the protocol is successfully implemented, the results of the project will not produce a substantial finding that will enhance understanding of disease mechanisms or improve the public health.
3. The proposed methodology is not feasible; the study cannot be implemented given the resources of the institution.
4. The principle investigator lacks expertise or experience in the topic area.
5. Methods, equipment, and procedures are not state of the art.
6. The research design or statistical methods are not appropriate.
7. The proposal is not communicated clearly; for example, reviewers cannot understand the purpose of the project and the methodology after reading the synopsis (abstract) and specific aims (objectives).

---

3. *Investigator lacks expertise or experience (Red Flag Number 4).* Inexperience becomes a more fatal flaw as an investigator moves upward in the hierarchy of funding sources toward the NIH level. At the federal level and among the major foundations (e.g., Robert Wood Johnson, Pew, Macy, and Kellogg), review panels almost always fund the grant application with the most experienced principal investigator (PI) when choosing among several well-written applications that have equal scientific merit. Young investigators and other individuals who have considerable professional experience but a limited research track record, will benefit from being team oriented when preparing a research proposal. Reviewers expect partnerships and collaborations with individuals who have established records of publication and funding in critical areas of a research protocol. In particular, it is essential to have partners (e.g., co-investigators) who will be perceived by reviewers as subject and method experts in the research areas addressed in the grant. For example, if a proposal addresses juvenile arthritis, at least one of the coinvestigators needs to be an established investigator with 5–10 publications, and hopefully, previous funding, related to this disorder. Sometimes methods experts are useful collaborators as well (e.g., in genetic research). You may wish to consider mentioning the recruitment of collaborators skilled in novel or complex methods proposed as well.

4. *Use recommended resources.* The *Grant Application Writer's Handbook* (4th edition)[7] by Liane Reif-Lehrer is an outstanding resource; it focuses exclusively on writing grants in the biomedical sciences and contains many useful examples of effective writing strategies for the various components of a grant application. Although the examples in this work are geared toward NIH proposals, most of the principles and recommendations described by Reif-Lehrer apply to other

funding sources as well. Two other valuable resources are recommended here:

Bauer D. *The "How to" Grants Manual: Successful Grant Seeking Techniques for Obtaining Public and Private Grants*, 5th ed. Westport, CT: Praeger; 2003.[8]
Ogden T. *Research Proposals—A Guide to Success*, 3rd ed. San Diego: Academic Press; 2002.[9]

WRITING STRATEGIES FOR THE SIX MAJOR NARRATIVE SECTIONS OF RESEARCH GRANT APPLICATIONS

Figure 5–2 displays the six sections of a research grant application where the story of the proposed project is told. Reviewers read each of these sections seeking answers to specific questions that are indicated on the right side of the figure. The grant writer makes the answers to these questions as obvious and convincing as possible. For most applications, the first and most critical section, the abstract, is a stand-alone item that appears on the second or third page of the application package. Sometimes the abstract is called the project synopsis or project description. In the middle of the application package, often following the budget, are resumes of key personnel and several pages of information about institutional resources. Four sections are typically packaged together as the research plan: (1) specific aims (objectives or goals), (2) background and significance, (3) preliminary studies, and (4) research design and methods. The research plan is the central element of the proposal and typically uses 10–25 pages (or approximately 6000–15,000 words) in a proposal that is single-spaced with one-inch margins and typed in 12-point Times New Roman font. The sixth narrative component is the budget justification, which appears in the financial section of the proposal following the budget request. The justification for personnel and other expenditures is often written haphazardly as an afterthought. However, this is a substantial mistake because this section provides an opportunity to further convince reviewers of the

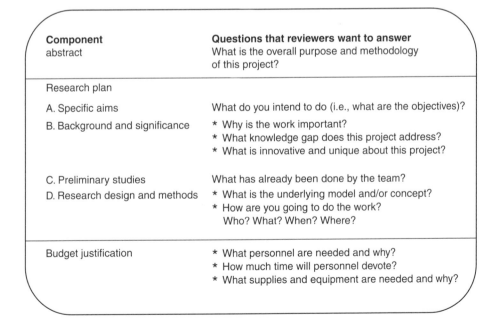

Figure 5–2 Principal narrative components of a research grant application.

expertise and credentials of the research team. The following sections of this chapter describe each of these sections in detail and what specifically grant writers need to address in each section to create a successful proposal. After reviewing writing goals and organizational strategies for each of these components, several red flags are included for each element. Finally, the terminology used to describe the narrative components of grant applications is linked to the Public Health Service Form 398 (PHS 398), which is the most commonly used application for federal grants. The PHS 398 application package and directions are available online at the NIH Forms and Applications website (**http://grants1.nih.gov/grants/forms.htm**).

Abstract

Development of the abstract is the single most important piece of writing involved in preparing a research grant application. Although abstracts are typically 200–400 words, allowable lengths vary depending on the grantor. Grant writers should massage the abstract carefully to make sure that every word counts and that every sentence clearly communicates information that reviewers need. Also, grant writers should enlist qualified colleagues to critique the abstract. These proofreaders/critics/experts should be vigorously quizzed to provide feedback and editing recommendations. A critical request when debriefing individuals who have read the abstract is: *Describe my project to me.* If the reader cannot coherently explain the details of the project, then the abstract needs more work. The abstract provides the critical first impression that will linger with reviewers while they read the rest of the proposal. Abstracts stimulate one of two reactions: (1) excitement or intrigue about the grant that leads to wanting to read more or (2) skepticism regarding the merits of the proposal that prejudices the rest of the proposal. The damage that can be caused by a sloppily written and unclear abstract cannot be overestimated. Thus, the abstract needs to contain the best writing of the entire proposal. Unfortunately, many abstracts with little thought at the end of the application preparation, literally in the final moments before the grant application is submitted.

The overall purpose of the abstract is to provide an executive summary of the entire research study. The abstract is often referred to as the "box," because the text appears within a prescribed space that literally limits the number of words that can be typed. What questions do reviewers want answered by the box? An informative abstract that helps reviewers do their job should provide answers to the six questions below. These questions should form the template for constructing an abstract and for allocating the limited number of words to the task.

1. What problem will be addressed, and in what population? The problem statement should identify an unknown, a phenomenon that is not understood, or something that has been problematic to accomplish.
2. What is the purpose of the project? What, specifically, is proposed?
3. What research question(s) will the project answer? OR What hypothesis will be tested?
4. What methods will be used to answer these questions or test the hypothesis?
5. What outcomes will be measured? (i.e., what data will be collected?)
6. What will be learned if the project is conducted? (i.e., what is the benefit?)

The abstract displayed in **Exhibit 5–6** is organized around and answers these six questions. This abstract also demonstrates two other desirable techniques: use of an "attack the gap" writing style, and directional headings that focus the reader's attention. Investigators are encouraged to use "gap" language in the sentences describing the problem. Gap language includes phrases such as "it is not known," "has not been investigated," "do not understand," and "no studies have evaluated." These phrases focus attention on the knowledge gap. The second sentence of the abstract contains a good example of an attention-grabbing gap statement: "Education is proposed as the key to asthma management, *but no studies have evaluated* the effectiveness of educational interventions for Hispanic children in outpatient settings." This abstract also

Exhibit 5–6 Example of Abstract for an Application Written in Response to an RFA

Problem: Hispanic children experience asthma with equal frequency as the general population but have greater morbidity. Education is proposed as the key to asthma management, but no studies have evaluated the effectiveness of educational interventions for Hispanic children in outpatient settings. **Purpose:** This study will evaluate an outpatient intervention for Hispanic children with asthma that includes physician and patient/family education. **Research questions:** (1) Will physician education improve medical management of Hispanic children with asthma in an outpatient clinic? (2) Will an educational intervention for Hispanic children with asthma and families decrease morbidity and improve quality of life? **Methods-physicians:** Prior to patient enrollment, pediatric residents will participate in an educational intervention including case conferences, workshops, role modeling by attending physicians, pocket cards depicting asthma management algorithms, convenient access to peak flow meters and spirometry, computer-based asthma management simulations, and asthma knowledge self-tests. **Methods-patients:** 160 Hispanic children with asthma, 6–15 years old, receiving care in a continuity clinic, will be enrolled. A research associate will interview parents and children separately using standardized questionnaires to obtain data about healthcare beliefs and behaviors, asthma knowledge and attitudes, functional morbidity, acculturation, and socio-demographics. A research nurse will perform spirometry on each subject. Medical records and school attendance logs will provide additional information. Patients will then be randomized into treatment and control groups. The treatment group will participate in the intervention to learn asthma self-management and to learn how to use inhalers, peak-flow meters, and how to perform peak-flow charting. Patients and/or parents will participate in four educational modules conducted by a bilingual nurse educator. Patients and/or parents will view videotapes that provide peer role modeling by showing Hispanic children performing asthma self-management tasks. Patients will review asthma management skills with a research nurse at appointments six, twelve, and twenty-four months following enrollment. **Physician outcomes:** The physician education outcomes will be measured by asthma knowledge tests, chart audits and computer-based patient simulations administered pre- and postintervention. **Patient outcomes:** Longitudinal data will be obtained from interviews, medical record reviews, and spirometry at the six-, twelve-, and twenty-four-month visits. Intervention and control groups will be compared for morbidity (e.g., ER visits, hospitalizations, school days missed), quality of life (Stein's Impact on Family Scale and Functional Status Measure), asthma knowledge and beliefs and pulmonary function (FEV_1). **Benefit:** This project will enhance knowledge of outpatient asthma education strategies for physicians and for patients and their families.

---

includes eye-catching headings (i.e., bold-font bullets) linked to the six questions. Bold headings, while not required, provide clear demarcations that guide reviewers through the text. Headings can be placed where they naturally fall in the text as demonstrated in **Exhibit 5–6**, or they can all be placed at the left margin.

As a rule of thumb, follow these assumptions and guidelines when writing abstracts.

Assumptions: The following pointers emphasize the essential aspects of a successful abstract:

- Assume that reviewers will *only* read this page.
- Assume that the proposal will be judged *only* on the information communicated in the abstract.
- Assume that reviewers will initially make an hasty judgment about the merits of the proposal based only on the abstract and will either read the rest of the proposal with enthusiasm or will skim it with a skeptical attitude.

Writing guidelines: The following suggestions outline the characteristics of winning abstracts and can help beginning grant writers avoid crucial mistakes.

- Do not waste words telling reviewers about things they already know, especially for RFAs and RFPs. Abstracts often contain articulate and thoughtful descriptions of problems that need to be explored or resolved, but these problem statements consume much of the text in the abstract box, leaving only a few sentences to briefly describe how the project will be conducted. Reviewers who are critiquing applications submitted in response to a solicitation already are well informed about the scope and severity of the problem; they want to read the details of the proposed study. Even with unsolicited proposals (i.e., those initiated by the investigator), grant writers tend to devote too many words to explaining the problem and too few words to describing the "plan of attack."
- Related to the previous guideline, at least fifty percent of the words in the abstract should describe the methods and outcomes as specifically as possible. As in almost all areas of science and research, "the devil is in the details," and reviewers want to be assured that an investigator is completely capable of undertaking the study proposed. Starting with the abstract and continuing throughout the research plan, the primary goal is to convince reviewers that the plan is well-conceived for implementing the project.
- Be specific, that is, clearly state the outcomes to be measured and name the measurement instruments that will be used to obtain the outcome data. For example, in the abstract in Exhibit 5–6, instead of using a global term such as "spirometry" to measure pulmonary function, the grant writer named a specific test, FEV_1. In the same abstract, the writer named a specific instrument to measure impact on family, Stein's

Impact on Family Scale, rather than using global language such as "functional status and family impact will be examined."
- Do not leave unanswered questions in the minds of reviewers. Avoid S-A-Ts that interrupt the flow of the study explanation at all costs. If a reviewer is confused after reading the abstract or annoyed by having to deliberate about unclear ideas, the opportunity for a positive first impression is lost. Intense critique and review of the abstract prior to submission by numerous qualified colleagues will help identify areas that need better clarity and more detail as well as impart confidence in the quality of the final application.
- Avoid detail drift between the abstract and the methods section. The details outlining "who, what, when, where, and how" should be precisely the same in the abstract as they are in the methods section. It is not uncommon for grant writers to make a flurry of tweaks to the methodology, often at the last minute before submission, while neglecting to modify the abstract in parallel. Although varying language and phrasing is important for readability, as stated previously, the primary hypotheses and/or research questions should be repeated verbatim throughout the proposal. It is not uncommon for grant writers to tweak the research questions each time they are written in the proposal. As a result, reviewers may perceive several versions of research questions, or other key statements, as they proceed through the grant, leaving an impression that the grant application is imprecise or disorganized. Therefore, maintaining key statements intact is an important aspect to review and consider.
- Allocate words wisely. Using single-spaced lines and 12-point Times New Roman font, roughly 380 words will fit in the current NIH abstract box. **Table 5–3** provides a guideline for allocating these words in abstracts written in response to an RFA and

Table 5–3 Template for Allocating Words in Abstracts for NIH Grant Applications

	Response to RFA		Unsolicited	
	%	Words	%	Words
Problem & purpose	15%	54	35%	126
Research questions	10%	36	0%	36
Methods & outcomes	70%	252	50%	180
Benefit	05%	18	05%	18
Total:	100%	360	100%	360

in abstracts for unsolicited proposals. For an RFA, the authors recommend using no more than fifteen percent of the total text, that is, 50–60 words conveyed in two or three sentences, to describe the problem and state the overall purpose of the project. In an unsolicited proposal, investigators need to do more case building when describing the problem and purpose, but it is recommend that no more than five sentences be allocated to this part of the abstract, that is, 125 words or thirty-five percent of the text. A research question or hypothesis (depending on the nature of the research) should be stated next using approximately ten percent of the abstract text. In an abstract written for an RFA response, seventy percent of the text should be devoted to detailing the methodology and outcomes. In an unsolicited proposal, the writer should allocate at least fifty percent of words to methodology and outcomes. The abstract displayed in Exhibit 5–6, which was written in response to an RFA, has the following word allocation: (1) problem and purpose (60 words, fifteen percent), (2) research questions (37 words, ten percent), (3) methods and outcomes (268 words, seventy percent), (4) benefit sentence (19 words, five percent).

The last sentence of the abstract should answer this question: What will be learned if this project is conducted, that is, what is the benefit? An ideal benefit statement directly addresses the gap identified at the beginning of the abstract. Even a brief 20-word sentence consumes five percent of the abstract and needs to contribute to the overall positive impact of the abstract. Benefit sentences often start with the phrase, "if successful." This phrase should be avoided because it could cause reviewers think that the project might not work. Instead, reviewers should be reminded of what can be learned if the research question is explored by beginning the benefit sentence with the words, "This project will enhance our knowledge of. . . ." The sentence should be concluded by describing what is not understood or not known (i.e., the knowledge gap that was articulated early in the abstract). A successful abstract often includes a sentence modeled after this 17-word example: This project will enhance the knowledge of strategies to provide prompt emergency care services in rural communities. The concluding benefit sentence in the abstract displayed in Exhibit 5–6 also follows this format.

Red Flags in an Abstract

In summary, the following red flags should be rigorously avoided in an abstract:

- The abstract fails to answer the six questions that reviewers want addressed.
- If responding to an RFA, the abstract "belabors the obvious" with too much background information about the problem that reviewers probably already know.
- Inadequate narrative is devoted to methodology (e.g., less than fifty percent of the words), so reviewers must guess about key "who, what, where, when and how" details.
- The abstract lacks of eye-directing headings within the text.

- The abstract suffers from detail drift; the description of "who, what, where, when and how" details and other key information in the abstract does not match the description of these details in the methods section of the proposal.

Specific Aims

In NIH grant applications, the statement of the project's objectives is known as the *specific aims,* or simply, "This is what we aim to do during this project." For some grantors, the term "goals" is used. The statement of the specific aims (or goals or objectives) for the project is section A of an NIH research grant application, that is, the first section of the research plan. The expectation for an application submitted to the NIH is that only one page will be used to communicate the specific aims, which has led to the common use of the term, "the aims page." Other non-NIH funding sources may use different terminology for this page, such as project goals and objectives, project purpose, or project outcomes, and other application formats may allow more or less space to communicate this information. No matter what terminology is used, the grant writer's goal is to answer this question clearly: *What will be done to answer the research questions or test the hypothesis in the proposed study?* Another way to say this is, what is going to be done to produce the data needed to answer the research question or test the hypothesis? One of the primary goals when writing the aims page is to establish a direct link between the aims and the research question. The specific aims may be thought of as the contractual agreement with the funding agency. The investigators takes on the problems and the funding agency supplies the financial support. Ultimately, the eventual evaluation of the success or failure of the project hinges on the degree to which each aim (task) is accomplished.

There are two strategies for writing specific aims. Which one is used may in large part depend on personal style, but it may also depend on the nature of the proposed research. One strategy for writing aim statements is specific and contains "what, how, and who" details within the text of the aim sentence. The other strategy is a more general statement of a goal. An aim written in the "what, how, and who" format includes information to help reviewers answer three questions:

1. What task will be performed to collect needed data?
2. How will this task be accomplished?
3. Who are the subjects (e.g., in what populations will this task be performed)?

Here is an example of a specific aim from a funded NIH grant written in the "what, how, and who" format, followed by a breakdown of the text into the three components.

Assess the impact of an evening home visit (EHV) program conducted by internal medicine resident–RN teams by comparing emergency department (ED) visits and hospitalizations twelve months prior to the intervention period among elderly patients enrolled and not enrolled in the EHV program.

1. What? . . . *Assess the impact of an evening home visit (EHV) program conducted by internal medicine resident—RN teams . . .*
2. How? . . . *by comparing ED visits and hospitalizations twelve months prior to the intervention period . . .*
3. Who? . . . *among elderly patients enrolled and not enrolled in EHV.*

An aim written in a more broadly stated "goal" format includes information that addresses two basic questions: (1) what is being evaluated, and (2) in what population? Here is an example of the same aim written in the goal format, followed by its breakdown into these two components:

Determine whether an evening home visit program by internal medicine resident–RN teams decreases ED visits and hospitalizations among home-bound elderly individuals.

1. What are you evaluating? . . . *Determine if an evening home visit program by resident—RN teams decreases ED visits and hospitalizations . . .*
2. In what population? . . . *among home-bound elderly individuals.*

One way to make the specific aims (or objectives) reviewer friendly is to use the active voice, which means that the first word of the aim statement is a verb that clearly communicates the task: calculate, develop, analyze, measure, perform, evaluate, compare, etc. Avoid vague language in aims statements such as "this projects seeks to understand mechanisms that influence . . . ," "learn about the interaction of . . . ," or "continue exploration of factors that predict . . ."

How should the specific aims section be organized? One format is displayed in the example in Exhibit 5–7. This section should start with an overview paragraph, labeled as the "project overview" by a bold-font heading consisting of approximately 80–100 words (four sentences) that serves as an "abstract of the abstract." The purpose of this mini-abstract is to emphasize the knowledge gap addressed by this project and the overall purpose of the study. Next, the research questions or hypotheses are stated with exactly the same words used in the abstract. A bold-font header and "white-space" before and after these statements further focuses attention to these statements. A bridging,

---

Exhibit 5–7 Example of Layout for the Specific Aims Page

A. SPECIFIC AIMS

A.1. Project Overview

Acute otitis media (AOM) is one of the most common indications for antibiotic prescriptions in the outpatient setting, but it is not known whether antibiotic therapy provides any advantage over nonpharmaceutical approaches. In Europe, an approach called watchful waiting is utilized instead of routine antibiotic therapy. Under watchful waiting, antibiotics are withheld unless symptoms persist for several days. It is unclear which approach is the most cost-effective. To explore this issue, we will perform a cost-effective analysis of watchful waiting versus antibiotic therapy.

[Four sentences; 83 words including a "gap" statement: "but it is not known"]

A.2. Research Questions

1. In children with acute otitis media, does watchful waiting in comparison to antibiotic treatment produce equivalent clinical outcomes at less cost?
2. What is the cost of antibiotic-resistant Streptococcus pneumoniae when AOM is routinely treated with antibiotics?

To investigate these research questions, we will complete the following tasks described in the specific aims below. [Bridge sentence]

A.3. Specific Aims

Aim #1: Develop a decision analysis model using efficacy-of-treatment probabilities from the AHRQ Evidence Report that outlines the management options and their range of outcomes for AOM if: (1) they are managed by watchful waiting, or (2) they are treated with antibiotics.

Aim #2: Calculate utilities from the Quality of Well-Being Index (QWB) and compute quality adjusted life years (QALYs) to produce outcomes for the decision analysis in AIM 1.

Aim #3: Perform a cost-utility analysis of watchful waiting compared to antibiotic treatment using the outcomes from the decision analysis model developed in AIM 1 and AIM 2 and cost-of-therapy estimates obtained from the literature.

Aim #4: Estimate costs of antibiotic-resistance S. pneumoniae attributable to antibiotic treatment for AOM. Repeat the cost-utility analysis of AIM 3 with this estimate to determine the effect of antibiotic-resistant S. pneumoniae on the cost-to-utility ratio.

---

or transitional, sentence links the research questions to the specific aims. A bridging sentence takes this form: *To investigate these research questions, we will complete the following tasks that are described in the specific aims.*

Using one of the two formats previously described, each of the specific aims should be stated as demonstrated in Exhibit 5–7 and in the list below by numbering each aim along the left margin with a distinct bold-font header, and each aim statement should begin with an action verb.

Aim # 1 Identify
Aim # 2 Categorize
Aim # 3 Evaluate

Most reviewers expect to read three or four aim statements. More than four aims may indicate that the investigators are overreaching their capacity or that the application is disorganized or lacks cohesion. The tasks communicated in the aims statements should flow logically from one to the other in a progressive fashion, with the first aim being the most essential and subsequent aims building upon the outcomes derived from accomplishment of the first aim.

One of the most important writing goals for the aims page is to ingrain three critical pieces of information the reviewer will need for the next several hours of reading: (1) the knowledge gap (e.g., the unknown), (2) the research questions, and (3) how data are going to produce what is needed to answer the research question or test the hypothesis (i.e., the specific aims). Taking the time to carefully lay out the aims page in the manner displayed in Exhibit 5–7 will help accomplish this goal and will also convey an important subliminal message to reviewers that the writer is organized and has a well-thought out research plan.

This chapter focuses on strategies to communicate the scientific plan with the three C's and is not intended to review research design. However, one critical element in the clarity component of the three C's overlaps with research design considerations: the research questions. The problem(s) may be stated as a *research question,* a *hypothesis,* or a *null hypothesis.* Regardless of the form, the problem to be investigated drives the overall study, and it must be stated with precision. Research questions that are vague and S-A-T-inducing rarely lead to positive outcomes. One strategy for writing clear and precise research questions, especially for studies that compare different approaches (e.g., controlled trials) is called the P-I-C-O format.[11] P-I-C-O (pronounced "pie-co") stands for the problem in a particular Population, Intervention, Comparison, and Outcome. The first research question in Exhibit 5–7 is stated in the P-I-C-O format: *In children with AOM, does watchful waiting in comparison to antibiotic treatment produce equivalent clinical outcomes at less cost?* The breakdown of this question into the P-I-C-O components appears in **Table 5–4**.

Red Flags in the Specific Aims Section

- Aims are not clearly linked to the hypothesis or research question. Reviewers cannot easily ascertain that the aims describe how data will be collected to answer the research question or test the hypothesis.
- Too many aims are presented; the project looks overly ambitious or poorly planned.
- Aims statements lack precision and are difficult to understand.

Table 5–4 P-I-C-O

Population/Problem	Intervention	Comparison	Outcome
In children with acute otitis media,	does watchful waiting	in comparison to antibiotic treatment	produce equivalent clinical outcomes at less cost?

- Aims do not start with action verbs that give the reviewer a clear sense of the task to be performed.
- Aims are not integrated with each other (e.g., the aims give the impression of a "grab-bag" of unrelated projects).
- The aims page does not start with a brief 100-word project overview or mini-abstract to remind reviewers of the knowledge gap and overall purpose of the project.

BACKGROUND AND SIGNIFICANCE

The primary goal in the background and significance section is to convince reviewers of the merits of the project. Grant writers want reviewers to become advocates for the project so they read the remainder of the proposal looking for reasons to approve it rather than reject it. Unfortunately, many grant writers see this section as merely the "literature review," which is a mistake. Truly, one of the purposes of the background component of this section is to trace the evolution of the problem and the corresponding research (which hopefully is both skimpy and inconclusive) that lays the groundwork for the current proposal. However, a second and more critical task is to provide the strongest case-building arguments in the background and significance section; this is the section where the compelling and convincing components of the three C's must impress the reviewer.

The directions for the PHS 398 package suggest that the background and significance section should be three pages long. What questions need to be answered in these three pages?

1. What knowledge *GAP* will this project address? What are the unknowns?
2. Why is this work important? Why does this knowledge gap need to be investigated now?
3. What is unique about the investigators' approach? What makes this project stand out from the others? Does the project *GRAB* the reviewers' attention and impel them to read further?

4. What is the deliverable? (i.e., what is the product or outcome?) What will the grantor and the scientific community *GET* as a consequence of funding this project?

Three words in the preceding list of reviewer's questions have been emphasized: GAP, GRAB, and GET. One strategy for writing the background and significance, especially the introductory paragraph, is to structure the narrative around the *Triple G formula:* First, focus reviewer's attention on an unknown (knowledge *gap*) and convince him/her that it is important and understudied; then *grab* the reviewer's interest with compelling data that provides a solid and convincing rationale for the research; and finally, describe tangible outcomes that will evolve from the project so the reviewer will know what the sponsor will *get* in exchange for financial support.

Conceptually, this writing strategy is illustrated in **Figure 5–3**. To use a marketing term, this is the "pitch" to the reviewers. For example, a project designed to develop strategies that minimize barriers to primary care services among a specific underserved population, begins by describing current healthcare practices and then identifies documented deficiencies in current practice and provides evidence of substandard healthcare outcomes. Next, the writer "attacks the gap" by clearly identifying an

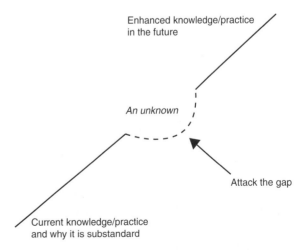

Enhanced knowledge/practice in the future

An unknown

Attack the gap

Current knowledge/practice and why it is substandard

Figure 5–3 Writing strategy for the background and significance section: the case-building "pitch" to reviewers.

unknown (i.e., a causal factor) related to the barriers that need to be investigated or describes a proposed mechanism for alleviating barriers that has not yet been evaluated. The background and significance section concludes by painting a picture of a potentially brighter future as a result of an enhanced understanding of underlying causal factors that inhibit access to healthcare services.

The first paragraph in the background and significance section is another of the most critical pieces of writing a grant writer contributes to a grant proposal. It is an excellent opportunity to build a strong case for the proposal and convince the reviewers to read this section carefully rather just skimming it. The Triple G formula can be used to construct a paragraph that outlines the project's approach to "attacking the gap." **Exhibit 5–8** demonstrates how to structure this paragraph. Each sentence of this paragraph is written to address one of the questions that reviewers want answered in the background and significance section. In the first sentence, the GAP sentence, the goal is to answer this question: What is the unknown? Several examples of lead-off gap sentences are presented in Exhibit 5–8 to demonstrate appropriate writing style. This first sentence should provide a definitive gap statement (see underlined text in Exhibit 5–8) and should be written in a succinct style. For example, an initial sentence in the background and significance section might be stated this way: Seventy percent of postmenopausal women at risk for osteoporotic fractures *are not diagnosed* despite availability of accurate screening tests. Or, The influence of cultural context upon the decision-making of urban low-income African American women about infant feeding *has not been studied.*

The second, third, and fourth sentences are the GRAB sentences. They are designed to answer the question: Why is it important to study this problem? These sentences outline the most compelling and convincing data that documents the societal and/or scientific consequence of allowing this problem to continue. The fifth and concluding sentence is the GET sentence, which answers the ultimate question: What will the grantor "get" from this application if it is funded? To illustrate this idea, the "get" sentence in **Exhibit 5–8** is linked to one of the gap sentences by the arrows. Ideally, the

---

Exhibit 5–8 Writing strategy for an "attack the gap" first paragraph in the background and significance section

First Sentence: GAP Sentence What is the unknown?

Several Examples

The etiology of Meniere's disease is not known.

Despite being one of the most detectable of cancers, the mortality rate for oral cancer is 53%. Strategies to increase early detection of have not been successful.

Seventy percent of postmenopausal women at risk for osteoporotic fractures are not diagnosed despite availability of accurate screening tests.

The influence of cultural context upon the decision-making of urban low-income African American women about infant feeding has not been studied.

Second to Fourth Sentences: G RAB Sentences Why is it important to study this problem?

Describe societal consequence: % households affected, morbidity and mortality, financial costs, resource consumption, missed school and work days, etc.

Fifth Sentence: GET Sentence What will reviewers "get" from this application?

This project will develop a testable, conceptual model of how low-income African American mothers in District of Columbia made infant feeding decisions. We will use qualitative methods and a collaborative partnership with the women in the community to develop this model.

relationship between the gap and the get is clearly established in the reviewers' minds as they read the remainder of the proposal.

The second paragraph in the background and significance section begins a discussion of the pertinent literature related to the knowledge gap addressed in this proposal. This is the classic literature review component of the grant application. A well-written paragraph here inserts a signpost that signals the transition between the opening approach to attacking the gap and the synopsis of the work of other investigators. This example of a signpost sentence sets the stage for the upcoming literature review and reinforces the fact that little is known about this particular topic:

> Our current understanding of the factors that influence infant feeding decisions among low-income African American mothers is based on only three cross-sectional studies conducted in the 1980s with small samples of subjects. These studies will be reviewed in the next section, followed by a discussion of questions that remain unanswered by these studies.

Strategic use of signpost sentences guides reviewers through the proposal, gives a sense of what is coming next, and addresses the tendency of reviewers to skim proposals. Another strategy toward this purpose is the insertion of full-sentence signpost headers that communicate the key concept (also known as the take-away message) of each paragraph. **Exhibit 5–9** displays the first page of a background and significance section and demonstrates the use of headings used to center the reviewer's attention. If reviewers remember only these signposts, they will retain the important messages about previous research pertinent to the problem. Exhibit 5–9 also illustrates another useful technique of communicating effectively with reviewers, the use of a table to summarize several key studies. **Table 5–5** in Exhibit 5–9 provides reviewers with a convenient encapsulated summary of previous studies indicating investigator name, date, research design, number and type of subjects, type of intervention, and outcomes. Strategically placed tables like this one are welcome visual pauses that send the message that the proposal is well organized.

The background and significance section should close with a strong "significance" paragraph

---

Exhibit 5–9 Strategies for Focusing the Reviewer, Including Use of Signpost Headers and Summary Tables

B. BACKGROUND AND SIGNIFICANCE

It is not known whether depression treatment leads to improved metabolic control in patients with diabetes. Major depressive disorder is present in at least twenty percent of diabetic patients and is associated with poor treatment adherence and an increased risk of diabetes complications. Cross-sectional studies have linked depression with poor glycemic control. No prospective studies have tested the effect of improved depressive symptoms on metabolic control. We will conduct a randomized, controlled trial to evaluate the metabolic results of treatment-related improvement of depression among adult patients with diabetes in primary care.

B.1. Depression Is Associated with Poor Diabetes Outcomes

One in three people with diabetes has depression at a level that impairs functioning and quality of life, adherence to medical treatment, and glycemic control.[1] Severity of depressive symptoms is associated with poorer diet and adherence to medication regimen, functional impairment, and higher healthcare costs in diabetic patients.[2] Depression increases the morbidity and mortality of cardiovascular disease,[3] the leading killer of patients with diabetes.

B.1.1. It is Not Known Whether Improvement in Depressive Symptoms Results in Better Diabetes Outcomes. Only three published studies have examined the association of depression improvement with glycemic control. No studies have evaluated outcomes of equivalent importance to cardiovascular risk in diabetes (blood pressure and lipids). The methodology and outcomes of these three studies are presented in Table 5–5.

Table 5–5 Summary of Interventions That Have Been Implemented to Improve Glycemic Control by Treating Depression

Study	Methods	Participants	Intervention	Outcomes
Lustman 1997	RCT	68 DM pts w/ new diagnosis of depression	Nortriptyline vs. placebo	At 8 weeks: Remission in 40% HbA1c unchanged despite hyperglycemic effect of nortriptyline
Lustman 2000	RCT	60 DM pts w/ new diagnosis of depression	Fluoxetine vs. placebo	At 8 weeks: Depression improvement 67% vs. 37% Remission 48% vs. 26% HbA1c better (trend)
Lustman 1998	RCT	51 referred DM-2 pts with depression	CBT (weekly × 10) vs. control [both groups got DM education]	At 6 months (n = 42): Remission 70% vs. 33% HbA1c −0.7% vs. +0.9% Responders vs. persistent: HbA1c −1.0% vs. +1.7%

labeled with a bold-font heading that alerts reviewers that this is the concluding paragraph. In many grant applications, the background and significance section simply ends, often with an inconclusive thud, when the grant writer runs out of literature to discuss. Instead, this section should end on a positive note by reminding reviewers of the knowledge gap and answering the critical question: What is unique and important about this project? **Exhibit 5–10** demonstrates how to structure the concluding paragraph for the background and

significance section of a grant application. Note how the grant writer reminds reviewers how little we know about the issue by using phrases such as: "no previous investigation has documented," "there have been only three studies," and "no studies have described."

As a concluding note, the selection and discussion of literature should reveal an acute awareness of current, cutting-edge research pertinent to the topic, as well as the investigator's knowledge of pivotal papers that are more than 5 years old. With

Exhibit 5–10 Project Significance

No previous investigation has documented the rates of hospice utilization by minority groups compared to non-Hispanic Caucasians in populations for which detailed social and demographic data are available. Only three studies, all involving small numbers of upper-middle-class African Americans, have investigated hospice utilization among minority populations. No studies have described hospice utilization patterns among Hispanic/Latinos, Native Americans or Asian Americans. No studies have compared the factors associated with end-of-life hospice care between non-Hispanic Caucasians and minorities. For example, what is the effect of racial concordance between provider and patient on hospice use? To address this lack of information about hospice decision-making among minority populations, we will analyze hospice use among the ethnically diverse urban populations in three cities and evaluate the effect of racial concordance between provider and patient on hospice use.

the exception of classic and comprehensive review articles, the articles described in the review should represent the most recent work available. Lack of recent citations gives the impression that the investigators are not current in their knowledge or are just recycling an old grant that has been submitted previously. Comprehensive reviews should be included where available rather than discussing scores of individual studies. Assume that reviewers are equally familiar with the literature, if not more so, and that they will notice key studies that have been omitted or poorly designed studies that have been included in the review.

Red Flags in the Background and Significance Section

- The proposal did not attack the gap, and the grant writer did not provide a convincing argument that an important knowledge gap exists.
- The background and significance did not begin with an "attack the gap" paragraph using the GAP, GRAB, GET format.
- Section titles were not used to focus the reviewer's attention.
- The section suffered from a lack of real familiarity with the literature; no selecting recent, pivotal and well-designed studies, and comprehensive reviews were cited rather than large numbers of individual articles.
- The concluding sentence was lackluster; it did not remind reviewers of the knowledge gap and why this project is unique.

PRELIMINARY STUDIES

The preliminary studies section of the application answers this question: What has been accomplished already by the investigator or his/her research team? In the background and significance section, what is known and more importantly what is *not known* about the problem was summarized by focusing primarily on the work of other investigators. In preliminary studies section, attention turns to the work produced by *the investigator and*

the research team. One question reviewers often ask during the review process is this: Are these investigators ready and able to conduct this project? Clear, convincing, and compelling descriptions of any preliminary studies or work can increase reviewer confidence that investigators have adequate experience with the techniques and equipment proposed, can design appropriate and well-run experiments, and can present the results in an objective manner. Reviewers want to be convinced that investigators possess these attributes. The grant writer must provide clear evidence that will make them comfortable with research skills.

What are the grant writer's goals when creating this section of the proposal? To facilitate reviewers in their task, concentrate on four writing goals:

1. Convince reviewers that the proposed hypothesis is valid and testable by showing preliminary data that naturally leads to the next question that will be answered.
2. Prove that the primary investigator has appropriate training and experience to conduct the project.
3. Demonstrate that a *team* (including coinvestigators and support staff) is capable of accomplishing project tasks.
4. Answer feasibility questions by presenting pilot data that indicates that the project can be completed successfully.

The directions for the PHS 398 application package recommend 6–8 pages for this section. However, new investigators, especially students, rarely have enough research background to fill more than a few pages. The space should be used as needed, not padded to use up the space. When presenting any data, it should be communicated in a professional manner using well designed tables and figures that are clearly labeled with a title that is cross referenced in the text. A one- to two-sentence legend should appear directly below the table that explains in clear language what information is displayed in the table. Within the text, the type of statistical analyses that were performed should be carefully described, the key results should be summarized. Reviewers cannot be expected to stare at tables and deduce the important implications without guidance from the text of the application. Only data that is directly relevant to the study proposed in the application should be presented. Above all, this section should be objective and candid; *do not overstate outcomes* or make unsupported claims. Reviewers react adversely to blatant attempts to prematurely "declare victory." Reviewers also respond negatively to proposals in which copies of several reprints have simply been placed in an appendix rather than creating a fully developed preliminary studies section that educates the reviewer about the work that formed the pathway to the current proposal.

One final suggestion that does not directly relate to writing the preliminary studies section may help build an impressive inventory of preliminary projects and a tangible track record of scholarship: Every effort should be made to publish, even in abstract form, all aspects of any the preliminary work. Any publication record is helpful. In academia and the world of research, publications are still the currency of the realm. In the upper echelons of the grant-writing world, it is too difficult to acquire funding without the expected quota of peer-reviewed publications. In many highly competitive disciplines, investigators are expected to meet quotas in high-impact journals. One publication in a certain highly respected and extremely selective journal may be worth five publications in lesser rated, second-tier periodical.

If the RFA or RFP or grant application requires a "studies" section, use a book-end structure to organize the section, A "tone-setting" overview paragraph begins the section. which is concluded with a paragraph that reiterates how the various preliminary projects lead naturally to the current project. The first paragraph of approximately 100 words (four sentences) should summarize the pilot studies and other pertinent past work of the entire team. Frequently, new investigators focus exclusively on their own work but fail to mention research conducted by collaborators on the proposal. The applicant's understanding of the teamwork aspect of research projects should be clearly conveyed. In the overview paragraph, identify past collaborations among members of the research team. The penultimate sentence in this overview paragraph should state that the experience gained from any preliminary studies and past collaborations will enhance the quality of currently proposed project. An example of a final sentence in this overview paragraph is displayed in **Exhibit 5–11**. The purpose of this final sentence is to act as a signpost that alerts the reviewer to the next element, that is, summaries of a specified number of prior studies that demonstrate the capacity and readiness of the research team to undertake the project proposed in the application.

As demonstrated in the example of the first page of a preliminary studies section in Exhibit 5–11, each pilot project should be clearly labeled with a

---

Exhibit 5–11 Example of Organizational Structure for the Preliminary Studies Section

C. PRELIMINARY STUDIES

Overview. Several preliminary investigations demonstrate the expertise of this interdisciplinary research team and its ability to carry out the proposed scope of work. The team is led by an experienced health sciences researcher and includes coinvestigators from informatics, oncology, family medicine, nursing, public health, health services, and journalism. The team has conducted research in five areas that are pertinent to the proposed study: (1) the role of the patient in healthcare decision making, variations in self-care and patient practice; (2) healthcare consumer guides and organizational performance reports in hospital care and managed care; (3) management of breast cancer and other chronic illnesses; (4) clinical oncology; and (5) patient and employer use of healthcare information. These studies are described below.

(continues)

Exhibit 5–11 *(Continued)*

C.1. Variations in Patient Practice (A. Smith, XYZ Foundation, 1995–1997)

This paper established the initial conceptual underpinnings of the theory that has guided our research on the role played by patients in their own health care, especially as it relates to chronic problems such as smoking and cancer and other areas in which the patient plays the primary role, such as prenatal care. The theory of patient practice variation is presented as the patient analogue to Wennberg's concept of physician practice variation and is applicable to the way breast cancer patients make decisions about their healthcare options.

Source: Smith A. Patient practice variation: A call for research. *Medical Care* 1993;31(5 Suppl):YS81–YS85.

C.2. Consumer Reports: Do They Make a Difference in Patient Care? (A. Smith, et al.)

This study, published in *JAMA*, is one of the few studies to evaluate the impact of consumer guides on the quality of patient care. It found that within one year of the Oregon obstetric report, of the hospitals that did not have a car-seat program, formal transfer agreements, or nurse educators for breastfeeding prior to the report, fifty percent instituted these services. Hospitals in competitive markets that did not offer one of these services at the time of the report were more likely to institute a service or were about twice as likely to consider improving service. Clinical outcome indicators, ultrasound rates, Caesarean delivery rates, and rates of vaginal delivery after Caesarean all improved in the expected directions.

Source: Smith A, Green B, Black M, Blue D. Consumer reports in healthcare: do they make a difference in patient care? *JAMA* 1997;278(19):1579–84.

C.3. Nature, Process, and Modes of Hospice Care Delivery (A. Smith, PI; ABC Trust, 1992)

This project evaluated the quality of care provided by hospices throughout the United States to determine the extent to which hospices were able to meet national standards established by the JCAHO hospice accreditation program and HCFA reimbursement participation conditions. Among other factors, this national evaluation investigated issues of patient self-determination. The study methods included on-site data collection as well as the fielding of survey instruments by mail. The study resulted in revised JCAHO hospice standards and HCFA requirements for hospice care.

Source: Blue D, Smith A, Green B. Do not resuscitate (DNR) policies in healthcare organizations with emphasis on hospice. *Proc Ann Meet Am Soc Clin Oncol.* 1987;6:263.

C.7. Summary of the Preliminary Studies Section

In summary, results from the Flagstaff medication compliance study (preliminary project 1), the UAHSC/IRGP study (preliminary project 2), and TAHEC study (preliminary project 3) will provide baseline information concerning patient morbidity and medical care problems prior to implementation of physician or patient interventions, and will help identify barriers to optimal care as well as barriers to effective education. Preliminary study 4 (Pima-Kino Community Hospital focus groups) provided information from the patient's and parent's or care provider's perspectives about issues and skills to emphasize in asthma education. These preliminary studies will help us design relevant educational programs for physicians and patients. Results from preliminary study 5, supported by the Southwest Asthma Foundation and UAHSC Institutional Research Grant Program, will produce questionnaires pilot-tested in Spanish and English with members of the target population. Each preliminary study is directly linked to a key component of the project proposed in this application and has provided our research team with valuable experience that will be used to implement our new initiative.

definitive title and described in one or two paragraphs as a distinct entity. As shown in the example, the PI for each study should be identified, as well as the source of funding. Below each description, a full citation to key publications that were generated by the project should be provided. A smaller 10-point font may be for these descriptions (if allowed by the grantor). Following the bookend format, this section should be concluded with a wrap-up summary paragraph of approximately 100–150 words that succinctly explains the key outcome of each preliminary study and "ends on a high note" by stating that the experience and knowledge gained in these pilot projects sets the stage for the proposed project. An example of a wrap-up paragraph for a preliminary studies section appears in Exhibit 5–11.

Red Flags in the Preliminary Studies Section

- The section did not employ a book-end writing structure.
- Preliminary studies were included that were not pertinent to the research question.
- Preliminary results were not presented or were not presented in an objective manner.
- The grant writer neglected to showcase the overall strength of the team.
- Reprints were appended without an explanation; preliminary studies were not adequately described.

RESEARCH METHODS

At any level of grant writing, the methods section constitutes the majority of the text. For an NIH grant application, as much as sixty percent of the 15,000–20,000 words in a fully developed 25-page research plan are discussed in the research section. What do reviewers want to learn when they read the methods section? The research methods section must address three questions:

1. At a conceptual level, how does the investigator propose to organize this project?

2. Why did the investigator decide to approach the project in this manner; that is, what is the underlying concept or model that is driving the design of this project?

3. What is the plan to do the work? The plan addresses the classic questions: Who? What? When? Where? and How? Failing to address these questions is likely to lead to an unsatisfactory review.

What are the goals of a grant writer when developing the methods section? Consider these five critical goals:

1. Demonstrate that the methodology is based on a recognized, sound, and appropriate model. In other words, what is the underlying framework for what is proposed to do? Why did the investigator decide to conduct the project this way?

2. Communicate the conceptualization of the project's experimental design. This is the opportunity to share unique insight into the problem and to show the sophistication of the approach.

3. Describe how experiments are designed to accomplish each specific aim.

4. Show the depth of planning by explaining the following:
   - The rationale for each experiment and/or study and/or procedure (i.e., why is it an appropriate test for the specific aim?)
   - The exact details of how each component is conducted, at the level of specificity found in a manuscript published in a high-caliber journal
   - How data will be analyzed
   - The plans for revising the study design, if needed, during the course of implementation

5. Help the reviewers link tests and analyses to hypotheses or research questions and specific aims.

All of these goals are important, but goal number 5 is particularly important because all study components must connect. The reviewers must be able to follow the research procedures and make sense of the work to be done. All too often, methods sections require substantial rereading, note writing, guessing, or even drawing diagrams just to determine the relationships between the research questions, specific aims, data collection measures (tests), and statistical analyses. The S-A-T rule certainly comes to mind here! Lack of coherent organization in the methods sections of grant proposals is a frequent and often fatal flaw. The grant writer should concentrate on making the reviewer's job easy. Lack connectivity across all elements of a grant application is fatal for the proposal. **Exhibit 5–12** illustrates the organizational structure and sequence recommended for this component of the proposal. As with other sections, employ a book-end structure that begins the section with a strong overview and concludes with a concise summary.

The overview of the entire project should comprise the initial two to three pages of the project so reviewers can understand how the whole project is constructed, including the rationale for the decisions about research design. The overview begins

---

Exhibit 5–12 Writing Outline for the Research Design and Methods Section

Overview of Project Design (2–3 pages)

The project design should contain the following elements:

1. One paragraph synopsis of the entire project (100–150 word mini-abstract)
2. Conceptual model (if appropriate, depending on study objectives and design)
3. Research questions and/or hypotheses
4. Table of the study design that summarizes the section (see Table 5–6)

Table 5–6 Example of a Study Design Summary Table

Aim # and Text	Outcomes Data to Be Collected	Measurement Methods	Methods of Statistical Analysis
Aim 1 [Type full text of the aim here]	Provider screening, identification and intervention	Chart abstraction Patient phone interviews	Fixed-effects logistic regression Chi-squared test
Aim 2	Patient, community, and expert viewpoints on patient outcome measures	Mini-conference proceedings	Conference report
Aim 3	Effects of domestic violence over time	Instruments that measure constructs of domestic violence severity, psychological sequelae, quality of life, and correlates of well being, and healthcare utilization	Logistic or linear regression
		Semi structured qualitative interviews	Thematic analysis
Aim 4	Cost categories for domestic violence	Patient self-report and data obtained from community agencies	Descriptive analysis

(continues)

Exhibit 5–12 *(Continued)*

Procedures and/or Methods to Accomplish Each Specific Aim (10 pages)

Table 5–7 Procedures and Methods to Accomplish Each Specific Aim

Aim	Interventions	Data to Be Collected	Data Collection Instruments	Statistical Analysis
Aim 1: Type full statement of the aim	Describe protocol	Describe types of data to be collected	Name instruments & methods used to collect data	Name statistical tests
Aim 2: full text	Protocol	Data	Instruments & methods	Name statistical tests
Aim 3: full text	Protocol	Data	Instruments & methods	Name statistical tests

5. Description of how the team plans to interpret the result. (½ page)
6. A "limitations" section (½ page)
7. A summary at the end of the section (½ page)

with a one-paragraph synopsis of the entire project (i.e., another mini-abstract) that reminds the sleepy reviewer of the knowledge gap, the research questions, and the key methodology that will be used to attack the gap. Depending on the nature of the research, it might be appropriate to include a graphic and describe the underlying conceptual model for the design of the study. More discussion of the reasons for using the specific conceptual model is presented later in this chapter. Next, the research questions and/or hypotheses are stated with exactly the same words used previously in the proposal. Table 5–6 is an example of a study design summary table. Tables like this one are invaluable to reviewers and send the message that the research team is organized and has assembled a well-orchestrated plan. A good design is the four-column table displayed in Table 5–6 with the columns labeled *aims, data to be collected, measurement methods and/or instruments,* and *statistical analyses.* The full aim statement should be presented verbatim in the left-hand column rather than relying on the reviewer to remember the wording of the aims. If the study includes an intervention, for example, two different types of training for experimental and control groups, a five-column table that lists an intervention or

protocol column inserted immediately to the right of the aims column may be advantageous (see **Table 5–7** in Exhibit 5–12).

After the overview, the bulk of the text of the methods section is devoted to presenting the exact details of how each specific aims will be accomplished. Distinct sections are created for each of specific aims. The most essential key to remember when writing this part of the methods section is this: *organize around the aims.* This section must clearly answer the "who, what, when, where, and how" questions for each aim that are pertinent to any review. All of these elements should be presented for each aim. These protocol descriptions should be similar in outline and detail to the methods sections that appear in published articles in a high-caliber research journals of the topical field. For each aim, the protocol description should include details about subject selection, inclusion and exclusion criteria, randomization (if applicable), location of subject activities, study duration, and other implementation items. All data that will be collected as outcome measures must be described. The instruments and methods used for acquiring this data must be described clearly and by name. Teams members that will do the data collection should be named, along with details regarding when, where, and how often. For each aim, data analysis should be discussed by naming specific statistical tests and methods of analysis. The statistical analysis component of the methods section is very important. Reviewers are very keen on data interpretation, and this section should be clear and specific. It is a good idea to recruit a statistician to the team and to work closely with this individual when developing all phases of the methods section, and especially the description of the analytical strategy.

After providing a complete game plan for each aim, the remaining text in the methods section should be devoted to three additional questions that reviewers will want answered:

1. How will the research team interpret (make sense) of the results that are obtained, that is, what is process for making decisions about the data and what it means?

2. What are some of the limitations in the study design or potential problems that may occur as the study protocol is implemented, and how will problems be handled if they emerge?

3. What is the timeline or work plan? What is the sequence and duration of the various activities that need to occur to complete the project? (An example of a work plan is illustrated in **Table 5–8.**)

A full paragraph should detail the projected timeline; a table displaying the work plan without accompanying explanatory text is insufficient. The discussion of limitations and potential pitfalls should be thorough; it is better to identify potential problems and discuss coping strategies than for reviewers to discover them and criticize the proposal for not being alert to certain potential glitches in the protocol. Experienced reviewers are aware

Table 5–8 Displaying a Project Work Plan

Project Activities	Pre-	Year 1						Year 2					
		Apr–May	Jun–Jul	Aug–Sep	Oct–Nov	Dec–Jan	Feb–Mar	Apr–May	Jun–Jul	Aug–Sep	Oct–Nov	Dec–Jan	Feb–Mar
Project organization	■												
MD training			■										
Nurse training			■										
Staff training			■										
Data collection procedures	■	■											
EC enrollment				■	■								
EC implementation				■	■	■							
Baseline data				■									
Outcome data						■	■						
Data analysis						■				■			
Write and submit								■				■	

that no protocol can be perfect and that successful project management requires ongoing tweaking. However, reviewers expect a candid discussion of concerns to demonstrate that all aspects of the study have been considered. Anticipate predictable pitfalls and present them. In the discussion of limitations, potential sources of data contamination (e.g., crosstalk among subjects in different study groups) should be identified, and methods of minimizing this contamination should be discussed.

The concluding paragraph in the methods section should be very similar to the concluding paragraph in the background and significance section. The goal in this paragraphis to remind the reviewer again why this project is needed and to emphasize what is unique about the strategy employed to study this research question.

Conceptual Models

Figure 5–4 is an example of a conceptual model for a grant that proposes to implement a training

intervention. Why would a grant writer want to create a graphic representation like Figure 5–4 and devote a paragraph of text to describing it? There are a number of reasons for including a model in the overview component of the methods section. The first two reasons in the next list make the project more clear to the reviewers, and the last three items primarily help investigators.

A rationale or framework for the structure of the study should be provided in the conceptual model that answers the question: "Why must the proposed study be conducted this way?" The underlying assumptions and reasoning that influenced project design need to be explained. The rationale for providing a conceptual model consists of five parts:

1. Help reviewers understand the background "context" for the project that influence the implementation of the project or the results that may be obtained
2. Help reviewers understand the underlying assumptions or theories for the interven-

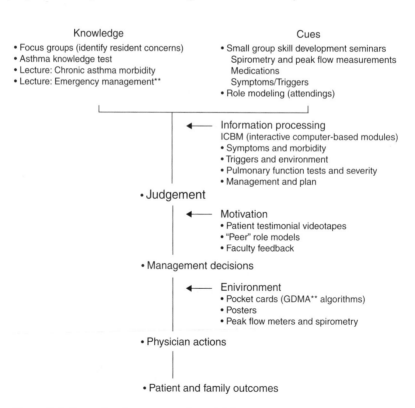

Figure 5–4 Example of a conceptual model for a training intervention educational model for physicians' curriculum.

tion that is proposed. For example, if the project involves efforts to change healthcare provider behaviors or to provide patient education, what is the investigator's basis for selecting this particular strategy?

3. Provide a classification or analysis system to categorize subject behaviors and actions
4. Provide a mechanism to interpret or explain the outcomes
5. Help explain or understand variability among subjects or treatments (i.e., provide a framework to help answer the question, why did we get these results?)

Bulletproofing

The methods section is a target-rich environment for reviewers who are eager to criticize. An important strategy for successful grantsmanship is to bulletproof the proposal as much as possible before it is submitted. After completing the methods section, the first paragraph should be reviewed for items that reviewers could possibly criticize in the plan. For each item a one-sentence "defense" (or rationale) for each of these potential criticisms should be crafted. As needed, these "bulletproofing sentences" can then be inserted into the text to justify or defend the methods chosen. Reviewers often reject proposals because they do not understand the reasoning or logic behind the investigators' decisions, not because they disagree with the methodology selected. Thus bulletproofing the review will also alert the grant writer to areas that are not well explained or to elements of the proposal that employ questionable methods. These areas need to be updated to enhance the proposal. Experienced reviewers expect an explanation of why an alternative approach was not used where options exist. An important part of bulletproofing is to strategically insert sentences that justify why method A versus method B or method C was used. This effort is well spent; these rationales for choosing particular methods convey a depth of thought and planning as well as a strong understanding of the topic and research field.

Bulletproofing also provided reviewers density of detail sufficient to evaluate key decision points.

Reviewers expect thorough explanations of all aspects of methodology where there are decision points, for example, decisions about how often to collect data and what instruments or equipment to use. Reviewers typically evaluate the research team's decisions in the following six areas; therefore, the narrative description of these items should be thorough and carefully reviewed.

1. Sequence, duration, frequency and redundancy of data collection (measurements)
2. Critical details for technical procedures such as exposure times, temperature, concentrations, equipment, and instruments
3. Subject sampling (recruitment strategies, inclusion and exclusion criteria, number of subjects, randomization process, strategies for dealing with subject attrition)
4. Statistical tests and analyses
5. Data management, that is, collection, entry, editing, storage, retrieval, access, and security
6. Sequencing of project activities throughout the proposed funding period

Subject sampling is an easy target for reviewers to attack. In particular, grant writers need to convince reviewers that there are an adequate numbers of subjects available to conduct the proposed statistical analyses. Most individuals who review research grants submitted to state and federal agencies and the major private foundations have been well educated about the concept of "power analysis" and will keenly look for a description of the statistical methods that were used to establish the sample size requirements needed to detect statistically significant differences among study groups. Again, a statistician is an invaluable team member in this important area.[11]

Support Letters

Finally, a note about support letters completes the methods section. A support letter is a notice of intention to *perform a service in support of a project*. Support letters must be included in the proposal from all individuals who are not part of the core team but who will perform critical tasks or who will provide services and consultations during the course of the project. For example, support letters should be obtained from administrators of clinical or laboratory facilities that will be used, from supervisors of support staff (e.g., research associates or laboratory technicians) who will have responsibilities in the protocol, and from consultants who will serve as advisors or will perform specified tasks such as conducting training or providing external evaluation. Many support letters are vaguely written votes of confidence (e.g., "great idea, hope you get funded, glad to help if you do") that provide little meaningful information about the role and tasks to be played by the individual who wrote the letter. To avoid cheerleading letters, a more proactive strategy is to draft a letter for the individual who will perform the service if the project is funded. These letters should be presented as drafts that encourage the recipients to make revisions as they like. Their final drafts should be printed on their institutions' letterhead, signed and returned to the investigator. Most consultants and other project support personnel rarely make changes and usually are glad that the task has been made simple for them.

Exhibit 5–12 provides an example of the format for a support letter. A one-page letter with three paragraphs is a good format. The first paragraph should read like the "attack the gap" paragraph of the background and significance section; it should identify the problem to be addressed by this proposal, describe a key outcome, and pledge support for the project. Appropriate phrase to consider is "This project addresses a significant gap in our knowledge of (fill in the blank)," and the word "innovative" should be worked into the text of the first paragraph. The second paragraph stipulates the specific tasks to be performed, when they will occur, and the duration or frequency of these tasks, and it indicates the nature of the compensation for these services. The grant writer should also alert reviewers to pertinent task-related experience of these contributors in the second paragraph (see **Exhibit 5–13**). The third paragraph is a recapitulation of the project that includes the critical nature of the knowledge gap, the research problem, and the likely benefits of this project.

Grant writers and/or PI's should be sure to obtain letters from individuals who will actually perform the designated services and from administrators who actually have control over facilities, personnel, and equipment. If the grant writer is the PI or project manager, the PI's immediate supervisor should also contribute a support letter that generally follows the format outlined above. However, in the middle paragraph the supervisor should pledge to allow "protected" time (e.g., thirty percent of time for two years) for the project activities indicated in the proposal and in the budget request. As discussed in the following section on budget issues, one of the biggest red flags for a reviewer is concern that the PI will not have enough protected time to accomplish project tasks and manage the project.

In conclusion, the methods section of the grant application is the final component of the overall research plan, which, for NIH and many other organizations that emulate the PHS 398 application format, consists of the specific aims page (also called project objectives), background and significance section, preliminary studies section, and research methodology section. **Exhibit 5–14** summarizes questions that reviewers consider regarding each component of the research plan and indicates key writing strategies.

Red Flags in the Methods Section

- The methods section neglects to present an initial overview and a concise conclusion.
- No model is proposed that serves as the logical framework for the project.
- The overall study design is not graphically displayed in a table.
- Linkages between aims, methods, data collection, and statistical analysis are not clear.
- Key decision points have not been explained and justified in adequate detail.
- The timeline is vague, unrealistic, or missing altogether.
- Alternative study designs are not discussed.
- Potential limitations and sources of data contamination have not been acknowledged or addressed. Coping strategies possible problems have not been considered or presented.

Exhibit 5–13 Example of a Support Letter Using the Three Paragraph Template

January 6, 1999

Jane R. Green, PhD
Associate Professor
Department of Respiratory Care
The University of Wyoming Health Science Center
Laramie, Wyoming

Dear Dr. Green,

[Paragraph 1: Identify Gap, Describe Key Outcome, Pledge Support]
I am pleased to write this letter in support of the Multidisciplinary Project in Health Promotion and confirm my willingness to contribute to the project as described in the second paragraph. This project addresses a significant gap in our knowledge of how best to prepare healthcare professionals for public service: does interdisciplinary training create health professionals who are more capable and willing to work in cross-disciplinary teams? Implementation of an integrated curricular experience for students in clinical laboratory science, respiratory care, occupational therapy and physician assistant studies will make interdisciplinary primary care more than an abstract concept in the minds of the students. The evaluation plan for the project will allow us to assess impact of this approach as these individuals begin their professional careers. For these reasons, I look forward to supporting this innovative project.

[Paragraph 2: Specify Tasks & Compensation, Describe]
Per our previous discussion, I will be pleased to contribute to this project by (1) conducting 16 hours of seminars annually for students on patient education strategies in years 1, 2, and 3, (2) conducting an annual retreat for the steering committee and core faculty in years 1, 2, and 3 of the project, and (3) serving on the project steering committee, which will meet monthly. I understand that this grant will assume ten percent of my base salary for all three years in exchange for these services. I have served as the educational consultant on interdisciplinary patient and provider education grants in the areas of asthma, altered pain perception, diabetes mellitus, oral health for HIV+ patients, renal failure, rheumatoid arthritis, and substance abuse.

[Paragraph 3: Describe Benefits]
This pilot project will help faculty evaluate the implementation logistics, attitudes toward cross-disciplinary training and effect on early career job selection, which will substantially increase our knowledge of interdisciplinary education strategies.

Sincerely,
Michael Blue, PhD
Educational Specialist

CC: Fred Brown, PhD
            Director, Division of Professional Development

Exhibit 5–14 Summary of Questions to Be Answered and Writing Strategies for Components of the Research Plan Based on PHS 398 Format Used by NIH

A. Specific Aims: What Do You Intend to Do?[1 page]

1. Start with a one-paragraph summary of the overall study; purpose, methods, expected outcomes.
2. Depending on the study design, state the research questions to be answered or the hypotheses to be tested.
3. State 3–4 specific aims that describe what the research team is going to do to produce data that will answer the research question or test the hypothesis.

B. Background and Significance: Why Is This Work Important? [2–3 pages]

1. Convince reviewers of project need and value.
   - Define the knowledge gap you will address in this project (Attack the Gap).
   - Build a convincing case for why this gap is important to study.

   Describe a compelling benefit: What will a better understanding of this knowledge gap allow us to do in the future?
2. Summarize theory and research outcomes leading to the present proposal.
3. Discuss the work of other investigators even-handedly, acknowledging important contributions that paved the way for the proposed investigation, and clearly identifying limitations in the knowledge base that represent unknowns or which have not been explored adequately.

C. Preliminary Studies: What Has Already Been Done by the Research Team? [3–6 pages]

1. Describe projects the team has completed that are directly related to this study and that set the stage (e.g., are logical preliminary steps) for the current proposal.
   - Describe the published findings; do not just append copies of articles.
   - Graphically display key preliminary data, but also explain these data in the narrative.

D. Research Design and Methods: How Are You Going to Do the Work? [up to 15 pages]

1. Begin the methods section with a project overview. Help the reviewer understand the overall approach by explaining the research questions and the design of the study.
2. Provide a table that graphically displays the overall study design (see Table 5–7).
3. If appropriate, describe and visualize the conceptual model that communicates the underlying logic of how you organized the research study.
4. Use the specific aims as the organizing structure for the remainder of the method section; organize information about each aim as displayed in Table 5–9.

Table 5–9 Aims Organized

Aim	Interventions	Data to Be Collected	Instruments	Statistical Analysis
Type full text of each aim	Describe protocol for each aim	Describe types of data to be collected	Name methods and instruments to collect data	Name statistical tests

WRITING THE BUDGET JUSTIFICATION

The art and science of writing budget requests is a grantsmanship skill of its own; a detailed exploration of the many facets of budget planning is beyond the scope of this chapter. Research activity is intertwined with governmental and institutional regulations that influence distribution of awards within institutions. At many health science centers, the manuals explaining the rules and regulations that govern the allocation of direct (the money received) and indirect (i.e., the money the institution gets for overhead, now identified as financial and administrative costs) are hundreds of pages long. The fine details of what budget items are allowable, or not, and under what conditions for state and federal grants are seemingly endless. Many of the textbooks on grant writing listed at the end of the chapter provide in-depth discussions of financial and project management issues, including "do" and "do not" examples. Reif-Lehrer[7] has useful recommendations for budgeting strategies as do Carlson et al. in the general resource list. The goal for this section of the chapter is to make the reader aware of a group of universal principles that apply to the budgets of all grants, whether the source of funding is a small local philanthropic foundation, a state agency, a major nonprofit organization or the NIH, and to present a template that can be used to write clear, compelling, and convincing justifications for personnel on a research project.

The planning and level of detail evident in the budget and the supporting narrative justification communicates much to reviewers about how you are likely to manage the project. Here are seven suggestions to help formulate a successful budget:

1. *"Size" the budget request appropriately.* As discussed earlier in the chapter, do the homework to determine the range of financial awards, average award, and typical project duration for the funding agency. If the organization's typical award is $50,000 for two years, do not request $180,000 for three years. This guideline particularly applies to foundations, but in reality, most federal agencies also have publicized award ranges for various types of grants or the size of the grant is predetermined, as in the case of RFAs.

2. *Present the sum of the parts.* For a research grant, create the overall budget by assembling the individual budgets needed to accomplish each specific aim. Everything that will be needed to accomplish the aim should be accounted for in the budget request: staff members' salaries, equipment purchase, lease and repair, facility rentals, maintenance and warranties, consumable supplies, communication costs, data management costs, transportation costs, stipends for patients, and so on.

3. *Follow the budget directions for the funding agency precisely.* If in doubt, place phone calls or emails to determine answers rather than guessing.

4. *Justify everything.* Do not assume that any expense item will be obvious to reviewers.

5. *Do not create a bargain (low-bid) budget* in the hope that a funding agency will award financial support because "they are getting a lot for a little." Experienced reviewers and grant program managers are skeptical of the low-bid approach because they know that a common reason for project failure is trying to do too with too little money and too little time.

6. *Confirm deadlines.* Everything should be checked well in advance of the deadline submission date by the institutions' grants management office if such an organization exists at the institution and/or by the accounting manager in the department.

7. *Create two budgets.* Budget A is the "wish list" support request that is submitted with the application. Budget A reflects the best estimate of the financial resources needed to conduct the project in an ideal situation. Budget B is the "we can live with this" budget. Budget B designates items that are negotiable and items that are essential. Some degree of budget negotiations occur after the award notification is received, and investigators

fare better during budget "whacking" if they know in advance what they willing to eliminate without compromising project viability. Investigators can be caught off guard when they receive an unexpected phone call from a grants program manager who says: "Good news. Our foundation has approved the project for your funding. Congratulations!. . . . But . . . we would like to reduce the budget by fifteen percent so we can fund one more deserving project."

Here are a few time-tested tips for standard budget items:

Personnel. At the level of NIH, major foundations, and state agencies, designating less than thirty percent time for the principle investigator will raise concern that the PI will be overextended with other responsibilities and will not have adequate time to attend to the day-to-day details of the project. For major projects with substantial budgets, funding agencies may expect the PI to devote at least fifty percent of their time to directing the project, particularly if the investigator is relatively inexperienced.

Equipment and supplies. Avoid requests for deluxe models of equipment (e.g., do not request funds for a Mercedes SUV when a Ford Explorer will probably be adequate). Justifications for deluxe items truly need to be clear, compelling, and convincing. Do not guess about costs. Obtain bids from vendors that indicate exact prices, and quote these bids in the budget justifications. Do not frontload the budget by requesting equipment and supplies (and personnel, too) in year one that will not be needed until year three. Frontloading leads reviewers to suspect that this equipment may be used for purposes other than activities associated with the grant.

Travel. At the state and federal level, do not exceed the allowable per-trip expenditures and the total number of trips per fiscal year that are stated in the budget directions. These guidelines change from time to time, so do not guess or assume. Carefully justify all travel requests, and in general, be parsimonious in requesting travel, especially for personnel who are not key contributors.

Renovation of facilities. In general, do not bother requesting funds for remodeling or construction of physical space.

Consultants. Clearly justify each consultant's role, tasks to be performed, time commitment, and compensation. Do not list several "big name" consultants in the budget who have ill-defined roles or vague tasks. Reviewers at all levels are sensitive to the padding strategy of enhancing the apparent star power of the research team by listing several noteworthy or famous people as either coinvestigators or consultants but who have token involvement in the project.

Coinvestigators. The same guidelines apply for coinvestigators as consultants. Each coinvestigator should be a participant because of a clear need for that individual's expertise and experience. However, coinvestigators who are listed on the budget page as nonsalaried contributors draw a red flag from reviewers. What control or accountability will exist in this situation? The time commitment for coinvestigator needs to be commensurate with that persons' assigned tasks. An individual listed at ten percent time for the project (i.e., four hours per week), but who is responsible for several major project activities is not likely to be successful in accomplishing these tasks unless sacrifices are made in other areas of responsibility, which may not be appreciated by other administrators in the organization.

WRITING JUSTIFICATIONS FOR PROJECT PERSONNEL

At some point during the critique of a grant application, all reviewers ask themselves this question: Does the team assembled for this project have the individual and collective expertise and experience to be successful? This question is often critical if a reviewer is "on the fence" about the overall merits of the proposal. One way to win over wavering reviewers or to secure the approval of a favorable reviewer is to write informative and convincing justifications for key project personnel. As mentioned earlier, grant writers often fail to communicate the strengths of the team members when preparing the narrative justification that accompanies the budget request. The template below provides a guide for writing personnel justifications that gives reviewers the information they need to understand an individual's role for the grant and his/her qualifications and experience. Using this template is another way to facilitate the task of reviewers, which, in this case, is to assess the capacity of the project team for the proposed work. **Exhibit 5–15** is an example of a personnel justification that was prepared using this template. As demonstrated in this example, at least half the text should be devoted to key tasks, supervision responsibilities, pertinent training, and prior work experiences.

- Name, degree, current title (e.g., Sandra Black, PhD; Associate Professor, Bioinformatics).
- Identify department, school, university.
- Percent time that will be devoted to the proposed project.
- Identify job title on this project (e.g., Director, Data Management).
- Describe key tasks this person will perform.

- Identify any supervision responsibilities that this person will have on the grant.
- Describe pertinent training and prior work experiences.

One troublesome area should be avoided when describing personnel in grant applications. It can be confusing and annoying to reviewers if the grant writer fails to use exactly the same job titles for project staff when their roles and assignments are described at various points in the proposal. For example, in one application a single person was variously described as the clinical nurse specialist, research nurse, research coordinator, nursing research manager, and project coordinator. In fact, all of these references were to the project manager (yet another title) listed on the budget page. Prior to writing the proposal, it is a good idea to make a list or diagram of all the players in the project and designate one clear title for each person that is used every time that individual's role is mentioned.

Billions of dollars are available to support projects; the job of a grant writer is to communicate the story of the project with clear, compelling, and convincing language. If done well, the reviewer's job is easy. Ultimately, with motivation and persistence, anyone can become a successful grant writer. Remember, there are two ways to make sure that a grant is not funded: (1) never submit a grant application, and (2) fail to resubmit the grant if at first you are not successful.

Exhibit 5–15 Example of A Personnel Justification

Archie Dennis, PhD, MPH is a Senior Associate in the Center for Health Professions Education at the UAHSC and is an associate professor at the University of Arizona School of Educational Policy and Research. He will devote ten percent of his time as co-investigator and physician education coordinator. He will play a major role in the development and evaluation of the physician education component, including the computer-based asthma knowledge pre- and posttests and Interactive Computer Based Modules (ICBMs), and will also assist with the patient education component, assuming major responsibility for design and production of the videotapes. Dr. Dennis will supervise the fifty-percent-time educational media specialist who will do software programming for the computer-based tests and patient management simulations in the physician education intervention. Dr. Dennis earned his PhD from Yankton State University in 1971. He has been a medical education specialist at the University of Washington Medical School (1971–1976), the University of Tennessee Medical School (1976–1985), and the University of Arizona Health Sciences Center since 1986, and he has served as a consultant to more than 100 universities. He has directed bilingual patient education programs for the American Dietetic Association, the American Heart Association, and the Tennessee Kidney Foundation.

CHAPTER SUMMARY

We have patterned this chapter around an NIH submission. Certainly, there are variations in requested content, format, length, etc, but we believe that the points made in the chapter will serve the reader well regardless of the type of grant sought.

FURTHER READING: RESOURCES ON WRITING GRANT APPLICATIONS

Web Resource for Proposal Writing

The Foundation Center's Proposal Writing Short Course, http://fdncenter.org/learn/shortcourse/prop1.html

Books

Barbato J, Furlich D. *Writing for a Good Cause: The Complete Guide to Crafting Proposals and Other Persuasive Pieces for Nonprofits.* New York: Simon & Schuster; 2000.

Bauer D. *The Teacher's Guide to Winning Grants.* San Francisco: Jossey-Bass; 1999.

Brewer E. *Finding Funding: Grantwriting and Project Management from Start to Finish.* Thousand Oaks, CA: Corwin Press; 1995.

Brown L, Brown M. *Demystifying Grant Seeking: What You Really Need to Do to Get Grants.* San Francisco: Jossey-Bass; 2001.

Browning B. *Grant Writing for Dummies.* New York: Hungry Minds; 2001.

Carlson M. *Winning Grants Step by Step: The Complete Workbook for Planning, Developing, and Writing Successful Proposals,* 2nd ed. San Francisco: Jossey-Bass; 2002.

Collins S, ed. *The Foundation Center's Guide to Winning Proposals.* New York: Foundation Center; 2003.

Fey D. *The Complete Book of Fund-Raising Writing.* Rosemont, NJ: Morris-Lee; 1995.

Gitlin L. *Successful Grant Writing: Strategies for Health and Human Service Professionals.* New York: Springer; 1996.

Karsh E, Fox A. *The Only Grant-Writing Book You'll Ever Need.* New York: Carrol & Graf; 2003.

Knowles C. *First-Time Grantwriter's Guide to Success.* Thousand Oaks, CA: Corwin Press; 2002.

New C, Quick J. *Grantseeker's Toolkit: A Comprehensive Guide to Finding Funding.* New York: John Wiley; 1998.

Leslie Ramsey L, Hale PD. *Winning Federal Grants: A Guide to the Government's Grant-Making Process.* Alexandria, VA: Capitol Publications, 1994.

Tremore J, Smith N. *The Everything Grant Writing Book.* Avon, MA: Adams Media Corp.; 2003.

REFERENCES

1. National Institutes of Health. Orientation handbook for members of scientific review groups. Division of Research Grants; Bethesda, MD: 1992b.
2. Miner LE, Miner JT. *Proposal Planning and Writing.* Westport, CT: Greenwood Press; 2003.
3. Reif-Lehrer L. *Grant Application Writer's Handbook,* 2nd ed. Boston: Jones & Bartlett; 1995.
4. Cuca JM, McLoughlin WJ. Why clinical research grant applications fare poorly in review and how to recover. *Cancer Invest.* 1987;5(1): 55–58.
5. Schwartz SM, Friedman ME. *A Guide to NIH Grant Programs.* New York: Oxford University Press; 1992.
6. Rush AJ, Gullion CM, Prein RF. A curbstone consult to applicants for National Institute of Mental Health grant support. *Psychopharm Bull.* 1996; 32(3): 311–320.
7. Reif-Lehrer L. *Grant application writer's handbook* (4th ed.). Sudbury, MA: Jones and Bartlett; 2005.
8. Bauer D. *The "How to" Grants Manual: Successful Grantseeking Techniques for Obtaining Public and Private Grants.* 4th ed. Phoenix: Oryx Press; 1999.
9. Ogden TE, Goldberg IA. *Research Proposals: A Guide to Success,* 2nd ed. New York: Raven Press; 1995.
10. Read P. *Foundation Fundamentals: A Guide for Grantseekers,* 3rd ed. New York: The Foundation Center; 1994.
11. Sackett DL. *Evidence Based Medicine. How to Practice and Teach EBM,* 2nd ed. Edinburgh: Churchill Livingstone; 2000.
12. Lipsey MW. *Design Sensitivity: Statistical Power for Experimental Design.* Newbury Park: Sage Publications; 1990.

GETTING STARTED

CHAPTER OVERVIEW

This chapter discusses the development and refinement of the research problem. Developing a research question, hypothesis, or null hypothesis is not automatic and sometimes is not easy. Identification of the research problem and defining it in terms that can be investigated, studied, and researched is a critical step in the research and scientific process. Sound methodology can only be developed when the research problem is well defined in a format that can be investigated. Defining the research problem and developing a research question, hypothesis, or null hypothesis requires effort and time. Students in healthcare professions must be able to define research projects by formulating a research question, hypothesis, or null hypothesis. The way the research problem is defined depends on how the problem is framed. This can present quite a challenge.

The Research Problem

Salah Ayachi, PhD, PA-C
J. Dennis Blessing, PhD, PA

INTRODUCTION

Research provides a systematic process for uncovering answers to clinical and other questions. Research also expands on current knowledge that can be applied to education, to clinical practice, and for the benefit of society. Although some problems may be evident, others are not as easily recognized or defined. When a problem or question is identified that requires study, that problem must be defined in a format that allows for successful study. To the novice this may be the most difficult step.[1]

So, how does a healthcare professional go about identifying the problem for research? The process involves more than just asking or writing down a question; it involves a mental exercise that requires moving stepwise from general to more specific concepts, thereby focusing on and defining the question as specifically as possible. This skill or mental exercise needs to be learned, developed, and honed, just like any other.

Why go through the mental exercise and invest time before beginning a research project? Because getting the right researchable question or statement will define the problem effectively and accurately (i.e., clarifies it), thus setting the tone for the entire exploratory process and subsequent work. Generally, healthcare professionals investigate problems that interest them or impacts their work and clinical care. Therefore any question in practice, specialty, or interest is worth researching.

Identifying the research problem is not always a simple task, because every problem has compounding factors that can interfere with what needs to be studied. This challenge is particularly true for those who are new to research. For many investigators, getting to the exact problem that needs to be studied is like looking through foggy glasses or a smudged windshield. Without a clear focus (that is, a well-defined research question) the process is confusing, frustrating, time consuming, and wasteful. In fact, failure to develop a clear, concise, and defined research problem can lead to unsuccessful research. Think of the research problem as the guiding light that points the investigator in the right direction. Until the fog has dissipated or the windshield has been cleaned, the view remains unclear.

THE PROCESS

How are topics selected? Generally, the topics of interest come from the environment, work, or interest in a particular subject or problem.[1] Sometimes literature creates a topic that needs further investigation; some research articles generate more questions than they answer. This provides healthcare professionals a chance to take a study a step further to answer some of those questions. For example, when a study indicates that one healthcare profession spends more time with patients than other healthcare professions, a natural follow-up question would be, "What component of care allows or causes that particular group of healthcare professionals to spend more time with patients?" Anyone interested in the subject recognizes that a research problem has been identified for further investigation.

Study replication can be an exciting adventure and may lead to confirmation of findings or perhaps new findings. Published work may lead an investigator to research a similar problem in a group or area not covered by the first study. Questions about study methodology or an author's conclusions can lead to new studies and research replication. Replication is a good way to determine whether findings are applicable in a different clinical setting or practice. Replication can confirm or repudiate study findings or redefine previous study results or conclusions.

In general, existing knowledge or prior experience in a specific field is necessary to discern what research needs to be done. Researchers must be sufficiently knowledgeable about what has been accomplished, where current knowledge stands, and where to go from there. A preliminary literature review and search is conducted to examine current information and to help further define the problem or research question. Otherwise, the problem will remain unclear as long as there is uncertainty about the nature of the issue or problem. Knowledge of previous research is key to developing a project that will truly explore a problem. New understanding or knowledge must be built on what has gone before. A research project that does not consider what has gone or been done before may repeat what has been done and add nothing to the fund of knowledge. Research done without knowledge of previous studies and existing data is, truly, an exercise in futility and a waste of time and effort. The research problem needs to be defined by both a literature search and what is already known.

WHAT CONSTITUTES A RESEARCH PROBLEM?

A research problem may be viewed as a situation that begs resolution or needs improvement, modification, or an answer. In other words, it is a situation that warrants examination and study,

---

Table 6–1 The Origin of Research Topics

- Work environment (clinical observations, problems, or challenges)
- Personal interest (medical condition of self, family member or acquaintance)
- Prior studies (journal articles or reports in medical and lay literature)
- Mentor or preceptor or teacher interest
- Literature review
- Studies by others
- Graduation requirements

whether for the purpose of doing things more effectively and efficiently or to validate observations made in the classroom, clinic, or other setting. Or the research problem could be something in which a healthcare professional is curious or interested.

An example of a research problem that is often studied in the healthcare professions is the identification of factors that determine patient satisfaction with care provided by the healthcare professional. This satisfaction might deal with a particular profession or satisfaction within a specific practice or setting. A similar and related problem of interest is the contrast among patient satisfaction with care provided by different types of providers. Another example of a research problem is identifying the factors that affect patient adherence to treatment regimens. These influences could be religious beliefs, cultural beliefs, and ethnic standards, socioeconomic factors, etc. These problems are interesting to others, both within and outside the healthcare environment. For the researcher, the results are the results. Results are accepted, even if they do not reflect what the investigator believes or thinks.

GETTING STARTED

One way to get started on a research endeavor is to take a few moments to list five problems or questions for which solutions or answers are needed. **Box 6–1** offers one way to prioritize the questions. Keep in mind that substantive research is not accomplished overnight. Research can be a lengthy process and has the potential to become tedious and frustrating. Investigators sometimes have to work to maintain enthusiasm for their research, but without continued enthusiasm, goals are not likely to be met.

HOW TO IDENTIFY A RESEARCH PROBLEM

Identifying the research problem is the first step in conducting research. It begins by asking, "What is the question to be answered?" It is a good idea to write down questions to begin the record keeping for a study. Every researcher must be able to manage problems, because having a large number of problems in a single study can hinder its success. Remember, "Keep it simple." It is best to identify a problem in its basic form and to do a thorough investigation rather than tackle a large number of problems. This aspect is analogous to a predator that only becomes successful after it has learned to identify and focus on the appropriate prey. A successful predator chases one prey, not the whole herd. Otherwise, the negative outcome of the chase is a foregone conclusion, and the predator is left hungry. The same is true for identifying research problems. One well-identified and well-defined problem is much better than a number of ill-defined or general problems. It is worth remembering that it is unlikely that an earth-shattering discovery will be made, but each investigation can add a small piece to the larger body of knowledge.

Box 6–1 Exercise: List five research problems of interest (see Table 6–1). Rank the degree of interest in each (most interesting = 5; least interesting = 1).

Problem	Rating
1. _____	_____
2. _____	_____
3. _____	_____
4. _____	_____
5. _____	_____

A healthcare professional determined to investigate a problem must be able to focus on what needs to be done to resolve the problem (or situation) at hand. To further define the problem, several useful questions can be posed along the following lines:

1. Given a problem, what can be done, or what approach should be taken to improve it?
2. What is known (what does the literature say) about the problem?
3. What is not known about the problem?
4. What information or data is needed to improve the situation?

Based on answers to these and other questions, the problem(s) should become better defined.

Consider the following as examples of a process for development of a problem and study:

Scenario 1. A respiratory therapist (RT) is keeping a log on patients who are on ventilators. She notes an unusual number of postoperative infections in patients needing postoperative ventilation. The RT discusses this observation with the chief of pulmonology. After perusing several patient charts, the two concur that the problem is real and decide that "someone should look into it" to determine the reason for these infections and ultimately minimize the number of cases of postoperative infections. In this case, determining the reason for the infections is the purpose of the study, and minimizing the number of postoperative infections is the goal of the study. Other reasons for performing the study include reducing morbidity and mortality, reducing the costs of care, and other equally important goals.

The RT and the pulmonologist then devote time deciding what to do (brainstorming), and they formulate questions to narrow the focus, determine the importance of the study, and decide the degree to which an investigation can be done. They consider, among others, the following questions:

a. What information needs to be gathered?
b. Where can the information be accessed?
c. Will the investigators rely solely on medical records or will they include survey data from patients, nursing staff, or others?
d. What, if any, consents need to be obtained from patients and the IRB?
e. Will the investigators recruit a consultant to help design the study or analyze the data? If so, whom?
f. Should the results be published and in what medium (i.e., how the information should be disseminated)?
g. What are the ethical issues and how will they be addressed?
h. Where can the investigators find financial support to perform the study?

Figure 6–1 is a schematic of the process of developing a hypothesis from an observation based on the scenario above.

Some examples of possible research questions for this particular scenario include the following:

a. Are there procedural differences between infected patients and noninfected patients?
b. Are there demographic differences between infected and noninfected patients?
c. Are there care differences between infected and noninfected patients?

Using the null-hypothesis format, these questions would be considered with regard to the following statements:

a. There are no procedural differences between infected and noninfected patients.
b. There are no demographic differences between infected and noninfected patients.
c. There are no care differences between infected and noninfected patients.

Using the hypothesis format, these questions would be considered with regard to the following statements:

a. There are procedural differences between infected and noninfected patients.
b. There are demographic differences between infected and noninfected patients.
c. There are care differences between infected and noninfected patients.

Which format should be used? Certainly, the research question is broad and can be used for al-

Observation: Astute RT notes an unusually high number of post-operative infections in a particular patient population.

Brainstorming: RT discusses observation with chief pulmonologist; they decide to "investigate" the situation. Questions are developed that need answers. Various factors are considered.

Review: Chart review provides data that, indeed, the incidence is above what is expected from similar cases involving other patient populations. Literature review also indicates the incidence is excessive.

Problem identification: RT and pulmonologist identify the problem to be researched and discuss the questions needed to be answered in order to discern the reason(s) for the infections.

Identification of the purpose and feasibility of the study: RT and pulmonologist consider the significance of the study and its outcome.

Identification of variables: Variables to consider are: patient related – age, type of surgical procedure, "population", gender, other.
Surgical team-related – prophylactic antibiotics, technique including maintenance of sterile field, surgical skills, other.

Hypothesis development: Hypothesis developed after review, and variables to study identified.

Start the study

Figure 6–1 Schematic diagram of developing a hypothesis from an observation.

most any study. However, the null-hypothesis and hypothesis formats are stronger in their specificity and better define the relationship between two or more variables. Hypotheses are predictive statements. Null hypotheses can be thought of as a "no difference" contention. Often hypotheses deal with probability. Null hypotheses deal with differences or change caused by some action or intervention. The choice of format can influence the approach

to the problem as well as the statistical analysis of data collected.

All variables need to be identified as a study design is developed. Statistical analyses will determine the answers to the research questions, indicate whether null hypotheses should be retained or rejected, or prove the hypotheses.

Scenario 2. A group of three students in a healthcare profession are required to identify a research problem and conduct a project as part of the curriculum. They choose to study the effectiveness of a new postoperative method for managing pain in surgical patients with herniated disks. They discuss the idea with their mentor, and they decide it is a worthwhile endeavor to determine whether the new method is "better" than the older methods. They discuss the following aspects of the study (suggested answers are given in parentheses):

   a. What information to gather (patient satisfaction, pain scales, etc.)
   b. Where to access the information (surgical practice)
   c. Whether to rely solely on subjective data (reported pain score) or to include objective data (type to be determined)
   d. What, if any, consents to obtain (patient and physician consent, approval from the IRB)
   e. Whether or not to recruit a consultant to help design the study or analyze the data after it is collected (perhaps a faculty member who is savvy in statistical methods)
   f. Whether the results should be published and in what medium (i.e., how the information should be disseminated)
   g. What the ethical issues are, and how to address them (patient consent, confidentiality, etc.)
   h. Where to find financial support to perform the study (could this be accomplished without incurring financial expenses?)

Research questions related to Scenario 2 include the following:

   a. How safe is the new method?
   b. What is the cost of the new method?

c. What are the morbidity and mortality rates of the new method (compared to older methods)?

d. What is the degree of patient satisfaction with the new method?

e. How many work days (days for patient return to normal activities) are saved using the new method (compared to established methods)?

As an exercise, the null hypothesis is used to develop the appropriate hypotheses:

a. There are no differences in patient satisfaction between new and older methods.

b. There are no differences in morbidity and mortality between patients undergoing the new vs. older methods of pain management.

c. There are no differences in outcomes between the two methods.

NARROWING THE FOCUS OF THE QUESTION

To achieve the focus necessary, investigators are systematic in their approach to honing and defining problems and questions. Generally, the research concept begins broad and becomes more specific.[2] Here is an example of one approach, and an outline form is provided in **Table 6–2**.

Problem statement. There is no information on how many people, trained and educated as healthcare professionals, never practice clinically following successful completion of a program.

Question (problem converted into a question that can be answered). How many health-

care professionals do not practice clinically following successful completion of an educational program?

Aim (or purpose) *of the research project.* To determine how many students in healthcare professions do not practice clinically following successful completion of their particular program?

Objective(s) (more specific than the aim). What the researcher is going to do to answer the question:

a. Collect information on the number of graduates in healthcare professions who do not practice clinically

b. Determine how many are males and how many are females

c. Determine the age distribution of these graduates

d. Determine how many practiced initially then stopped and how many never practiced

e. Identify the reasons provided for not practicing clinically

f. Determine whether the type of healthcare professional has any impact on the decisions not to practice

g. Determine the impact on the decision by personal, marital, financial or other reasons

Here is a second (reverse) approach using a different problem. A group of public health nurses are interested in the subject of hyaline membrane disease, but they are not quite sure what to study and/or research. Moving from general to the more specific, they take this approach:

1. Incidence of hyaline membrane disease (Too broad.)

2. Incidence of hyaline membrane disease in African American neonates (Better.)

3. Incidence of hyaline membrane disease in female African American neonates. (Even better.)

4. Incidence of hyaline membrane disease in female African American neonates born to teen mothers. (Getting more specific.)

Table 6–2 Going from Broad to Specific

- Problem statement
- Question (Problem converted into question that can be answered)
- Aim/Purpose
- Objective/s (what the researcher/s will do to answer the question)

Box 6–2 Exercise: Consider the top choice problem (from Scenario 1). Work from general to specific in the manner outlined above.

Problem statement:

_____

_____

Question:

_____

Aim/purpose:

_____

Objective/s:

a. _____

b. _____

c. _____

d. _____

e. _____

f. _____

g. _____

5. Incidence of hyaline membrane disease in female African American neonates born to teen mothers between 2000 and 2010. (Even more specific.)
6. Incidence of hyaline membrane disease in female African American neonates born to teen mothers between 2000 and 2010 in Bexar County. (Very specific.)

They have identified a research problem aimed at determining the incidence of hyaline membrane disease in a specific population. Is such a project feasible? Theoretically, yes it is. However, other issues have to be addressed and other factors must be considered, including costs and available resources, before the study can be successfully performed. As a cautionary point, if a study is too narrow in it subjects or demographics, difficulty extrapolating findings to the general population may occur. The final topic (number 6 above) may be an example of a focus that is too narrow.

SOURCES OF IDEAS FOR RESEARCH PROBLEMS

Some topics that are certainly in the realm of possibility for any healthcare professional to research or, at least, explore for a research project include the following:

1. The role of the healthcare professional in health promotion
2. Learning styles of students in the healthcare professions

3. Patient attitudes toward healthcare professionals
4. Cost-effectiveness of healthcare professionals
5. Best healthcare profession to provide a service
6. Attitudes of healthcare professionals toward specific patient populations (e.g., people with HIV/AIDS, minorities, gays and lesbians)
7. Impact of healthcare professionals on health care in medically underserved areas
8. Any type of clinical investigation
9. Does the degree level of the healthcare professional improve the quality of patient care (Do higher degreed professionals provide better care?)
10. Does research training in a program have an effect on practice?
11. The healthcare professional's niche in research
12. Differences in professional healthcare practice by site (e.g., hospital, clinic, nursing home, etc.)
13. Economic impact of a professional healthcare practice on a community
14. Professional healthcare malpractice and liability

Healthcare professionals, especially those new to research, may glean research ideas from various sources. These sources may include clinical practice (as in the scenario described earlier), literature review, interaction with other students in didactic and clinical settings, interactions with colleagues at meetings, interaction with supervisors, or published work where authors point out aspects that need to be explored further. Ideas can also be obtained from government, private and public organizations (e.g., requests for proposals, or RFPs) that seek information and data on or about a particular subject or point of interest. These types of requests are distributed by government agencies or private foundations and, often, are formulated by experts and specialty groups.[3]

Need for the Study

As alluded to previously, the need for studying a particular problem is determined by many factors such as the following:

1. Significance in medical, legal, and socioeconomic terms[3]
2. Whether or not the issue has already been addressed (i.e., its novelty)
3. Acuity or seriousness
4. Human, time, and financial costs
5. Contribution to knowledge

A survey of nurse researchers indicated that focus on "real-world concerns" and soundness of methodology are the criteria of greatest significance in research projects, and that focus on timely or current concerns was less important.[3] On the other hand, personal interest in a particular problem may be the most important driving force.

Must a Study Be Original?

Although some researchers view replication studies as less scholarly and less valuable than original studies (an attitude that is more pervasive in some disciplines than in others), the fact remains that there are many instances where replication may be both indicated and valuable. Some of the reasons studies are replicated include extending the generalizations of the findings, establishing credibility, reducing errors (types I and II), and providing support for developing theories.[4] For novice researchers who might find identifying research topics and problems confusing and overwhelming, replication studies may actually be a good place to begin their first efforts.

Stating the Research Question

A good research question is one that can be answered using observable data, includes the relationship between two or more variables, and is logical.[5] According to Sutherland et al.,[6] the three most frequently identified indices of the merit of a research question are potential impact, justification, and feasibility. These terms should be considered as research questions are developed. The questions should be posed in a straightforward way, regardless of structure or format. Only one variable per research question should be addressed, if possible. Questions should be developed to fully explore the problem being investigated. One question answered well with sound methodology is better than many questions not answered well.

There are three ways to frame the research subject/question/project:

Null hypothesis. A statement of no relationship or difference between two variables. Example: *There is no difference in outcomes between OMA patients treated with "watchful waiting" and those treated with antibiotics.*

Hypothesis. A statement of prediction/observation that can be evaluated, measured, or analyzed. Example: *OMA patients treated with antibiotics have better outcomes than patients treated with "watchful waiting."*

Research question. A question that needs to be answered through systematic testing/evaluation/analysis. Example: *Is there a difference in outcomes between otitis media patients treated with antibiotics versus watchful waiting?*

SUMMARY

The first step in any research effort is to identify the problem(s). Each problem is then put into a research question, hypothesis, or null-hypothesis format. These statements should be concise and should deal with only one variable or subject. Each statement must be in a form that allows investigation. In developing questions, a manageable num-

---

Exhibit 6–1 Pearls

1. Carry a pocket notebook or piece of paper and write down research ideas when they occur.
2. Define research problem in the simplest format.
3. Learn what is known or has been done about the problem or related issues.
4. Be able to define goals, objectives, and purposes.
5. Be able to describe the significance of research and why it can be the solution or part of the solution of the problem.
6. Be able to answer the questions of why a project is important to society, health care, and your profession?

---

ber of questions or variables should be adopted. Small steps are best; some helpful tips are listed in **Exhibit 6–1**.

REFERENCES

1. Bailey DM. *Research for the Health Professional—A Practical Guide,* 2nd ed. Philadelphia, PA: FA Davis Company; 1997:1–4.
2. Jenkins S, Price CJ, and Straker L: *The Researching Therapist: A Practical Guide to Planning, Performing and Communicating Research.* London: Churchill Livingstone; 1998:21–26.
3. Lindeman CA, Schantz D. The research question. *J Nursing Admin.* 1982;12(1):6–10.
4. Sutherland HJ, Meslin EM, Cunha DA, Till, JE. Judging clinical research questions: What criteria are used? *Soc Sci Med.* 1993;37(12):1427–1430.
5. Moody L, Vera H, Blanks C, Visscher M. Developing questions of substance for nursing science. *West J Nurs Res.* 1989; 11(4):393–404.
6. Beck CT. Replication studies for nursing research. *Image J Nurs Sch.* 1994 Fall; 26(3):191–194.

CHAPTER OVERVIEW

No research project begins in a vacuum. There is always something that has gone before. For any project to advance knowledge, what has occurred must be known and understood. A complete and expansive literature review and search is the key foundation to every research effort. This chapter provides an overview and guide to the literature review.

Review of the Literature

Linda Levy, MSW, MLS, AHIP

"Science is a way of thinking much more than it is a body of knowledge."

—Carl E. Sagan, PhD

INTRODUCTION

One of the most important steps in performing research is the review of the literature that has already been published on the study topic. The review should be as comprehensive as possible and should cover relevant journal articles, books or book chapters, and even dissertations, meeting presentations, government documents, resources, and pertinent personal communications like emails. The format of the review is determined by the objective of the research, so the literature review and a summary of the research may be the final product. More commonly, however, the literature review will be used to formulate a summary of what is known in a research area, the strengths and weaknesses of existing research, and a discussion of the purpose of the research in terms of what is yet unknown.

This chapter is designed as a guide through the systematic process of the literature review, including designing a research strategy, selecting the appropriate sources to search, performing effective and efficient searches, and critically analyzing search results.

A successful literature review should do the following:

1. Provide an overview of the available literature on the study topic
2. Help to determine what is known and what is not known about the study topic based on the relevance of the search results
3. Identify areas of controversy
4. Identify weaknesses in the existing research
5. Help to formulate questions requiring further research

A review may also provide tools for research such as instruments that have already been validated, studies that can be replicated, and data that can be useful for research design or correlation.

A review of the literature is typically a large and well-referenced section of a thesis, dissertation, or manuscript. The literature review should provide a solid basis for evaluating and understanding the depth and breadth of the research investigation and its significance. A good review also provides information with which the reader can contrast the results and conclusions of the current research with what was known about the problem(s) being investigated.

WHERE DO I START?

A previous chapter of this book discusses the importance of carefully determining a study topic or research question *before* beginning the literature review. What information is needed? It may help to consider the research question in the form of a sentence instead of just words. Taking the time to develop a well-written, carefully defined, and focused research question helps the researcher choose the best resources for the literature search and the most appropriate keywords to use during the search process. A focused research question also avoids wasting time as the search is performed.

For example, a research interest may involve the role of the physician assistant on the healthcare team. What does the researcher want to know specifically? Is there a particular interest in specialty practice area? For example, does the question relate to the acceptance of physician assistants by patients in general or patients of a specific age or ethic population? Is there an economic advantage to integrating physician assistants into the healthcare team for in-office or in-hospital practice? What is the job satisfaction of physician assistants who are part of healthcare teams? The more specific the topic of inquiry, the better the resulting review will be.

SELECTING RESOURCES

Once a research question has been defined, the resources needed for the literature review can be considered. Resources such as printed books can help to define terms, establish the state of the science or practice at the time the book was written, and possibly identify authorities in specific fields. Because the publication of printed books requires time, however, the information published in books may not be current.

While the literature review should include any resources that are relevant to the background of the research topic, the review normally focuses on resources that offer the most current primary information about original research. That information is usually published in scholarly, "peer-reviewed" professional journals, where research articles are reviewed and the research is critiqued by experts in the field before the articles are accepted for publication. (This process is sometimes called "refereeing.") Citations relevant to the research topic from peer-reviewed journals are generally found by searching an online bibliographic database of discipline-specific information rather than by searching an Internet search engine like Google. Information published in magazines and newspapers usually does not go through the same rigorous review process.

Most bibliographic databases are subject specific, meaning that the information within a database is focused on a specific area of knowledge. Research information and study results presented at professional conferences is also considered primary information. Although many bibliographic databases do not include conference proceedings, some research information may also be available through a database that includes meeting abstracts or specifically covers conference content. Conference content is sometimes included on the conference sponsor's site as well. Theses and dissertations provide another resource for research information, and some bibliographic databases do include citations to theses and dissertations. For example, **Proquest's Dissertations & Theses** database, which is available at many academic libraries, consists wholly of citations to dissertations and theses, and the full text of an article is often available.

Some databases are free to all, but access to the information in most professional-level databases depends upon a licensed subscription that is purchased by the library at an academic institution, an organization, or a hospital or healthcare facility. When a database is licensed, access is usually restricted to people who are affiliated with the purchasing organization. In some cases, the academic institution or organization allows unaffiliated people to use the database at their site.

Another helpful way to locate comprehensive information is by taking advantage of citation information included in many databases. This step can lead to experts in the research area of interest and reveal the bibliographies of articles (and other sources) that they consulted. Sometimes it is possible to determine who has cited these experts in subsequent publications. This method provides a means to track research progress. If the information is not included in the database, the bibliography of cited references will be available as part of the research article.

There are *many* different databases and other types of information resources. Talking to a librarian or to a professional in your field before starting a literature search can help determine what resources will be most appropriate for the research.

Once the best resources have been located, it is always wise to spend some time learning to use them effectively and efficiently, especially when online academic or professional databases are involved. Read (or listen to) the available tutorials, Q&A sections, and FAQs. Students and those associated with an academic institution or a hospital with a librarian on staff can take advantage of any database classes that are taught through the library. Hospital or academic librarians are excellent resources for additional help. Time spent deciding which resources are pertinent for the needs of the project and learning to use those resources well ultimately saves time and leads to a better literature review. Even the databases that are designed with "user-friendly" interfaces can usually be searched more easily and yield better results when the features like a "controlled vocabulary" or special search limits are used.

If the research question relates to a biomedical or social science topic, some online databases to consider for a literature search are described in the sections that follow. A single resource is usually not adequate for a comprehensive literature search.

MEDLINE®

MEDLINE is a very large database with records of journal articles dating back to 1948. MEDLINE provides links to biomedical information in professional journals in the subject areas of medicine, dentistry, nursing, allied health, veterinary medicine, and the biomedical sciences. MEDLINE, which is produced by the National Library of Medicine, is free to all through a user-friendly interface called **PubMed** (http://pubmed.gov). Many academic institutions also buy access to MEDLINE through proprietary interfaces like OvidSP or EBSCO.

How to Search?

The MEDLINE database has a very useful feature called a "controlled vocabulary." A controlled vocabulary is a carefully selected thesaurus or list of words and phrases that are used to describe subject concepts. Controlled vocabulary terms (often called "key words") are added as part of the article record before the record is added to the database. Assigning controlled-vocabulary key words is a way of uniformly indexing articles by subject. Taking advantage of a controlled vocabulary means that synonyms or other issues of natural language are avoided. The system can usually automatically determine the necessary key word based on the term or terms that have been entered. The controlled vocabulary of MEDLINE is called **MeSH** (Medical Subject Headings). Using our previous example of the role of physician assistants and patient care teams, the MeSH heading would be "physician assistants" and "patient care teams." MeSH terms can be combined with AND or OR to achieve precise results.

Whatever interface is selected to search MEDLINE, it will probably use MeSH to retrieve the most relevant citations for your research interest, even if that is not obvious. The tutorials or search guides associated with the interface are useful for learning more about using MeSH effectively.

For expert authors in the field, authors' names can be searched to retrieve articles published in the professional journals included in MEDLINE. For specific articles, the citation-matching feature can be used to retrieve it. Non-MeSH terms for concepts that are not included as part of the MeSH vocabulary can also be used in searches. Limits are available; searches may be limited to a specific range of year, by English or other language, by age groups, or by publication types.

How to Find the Articles?

Searching MEDLINE through PubMed yields some citations that have links to the full articles available for free or via "open access" in a separate database called **PubMed Central (PMC)**. Free and open-access articles are selected from a range of journals and are deposited there by publishers for free access. PMC also has the author-prepared manuscripts of articles published by National Institute of Health (NIH)-funded researchers in other journals not generally available through PMC. PMC can be searched directly at http://pubmedcentral.gov.

Access to articles published in most professional journals is not free. An academic library that subscribes to the journal can provide access to them, or articles may be ordered through interlibrary loan at a hospital library or public library.

CINAHL®

CINAHL (Cumulative Index to Nursing and Allied Health Literature) is a database that covers content in the subject areas of nursing and allied health.

CINAHL is available only through an interface with the database vendor EBSCO. Many academic libraries, hospitals, and even some public libraries purchase access to CINAHL. While MEDLINE includes only records of journals articles, CINAHL includes other formats such as dissertations, tests and evaluation instruments, and patient education materials.

How to Search?

Like MEDLINE, the CINAHL database includes a controlled vocabulary of subject headings. Depending on where CINAHL is used, the interface may be set to default to searching the CINAHL vocabulary. If that is not the case, the controlled vocabulary can be used to combine heading terms. The "Help" link on the CINAHL database is a useful tool, and librarians are invaluable resources as well. CINAHL can also be used to search by author or to access articles from a specific journal or articles of a specific publication type.

How Do I Find the Articles?

The basic CINAHL database includes very limited full-text information. At an academic or hospital library, the interface site may have purchased an expanded version of CINAHL that includes links to many full-text articles. Other full-text information may be accessible because the library provides links to articles in other subscription journals. If a particular article cannot be accessed, it may be possible to order it directly from the publisher or through interlibrary loan.

PSYCINFO®

PsycINFO, produced by the American Psychological Institute (APA), is a database that covers content in the areas of behavioral science and mental health. PsycINFO is available through database vendors such as EBSCO, OvidSP, or ProQuest at institutions that subscribe to the database. Individual subscriptions are also available through the APA.

How Do I Search?

PsycINFO also uses a controlled vocabulary of key words to help locate citations relevant to a search. The database can be searched by author, research area, or publication type.

How Do I Find the Articles?

Sites that support PsycINFO, such as an academic or hospital library, may have purchased an expanded version of the database that includes links to many full-text articles. Other full-text information may be accessible because the library provides links to articles in other subscribed journals. If a particular article cannot be accessed, it may be possible to order it directly from the publisher or through interlibrary loan.

GOOGLE SCHOLAR

Although we cautioned against using Google or another general Internet search engine to find information for research, Google Scholar (a subset of Google available at http://scholar.google.com) can be very helpful in finding scholarly literature across many disciplines and sources, including journal articles, abstracts, and theses. Retrieval is "ranked" based on where the full-text article was published, who wrote it, and how often and how recently it has been cited in other scholarly literature.

Google Scholar also includes records of dissertations since 2007. Searches retrieve basic metadata for each graduate work (e.g., title, author, abstract, keywords, etc.), and provide links to ProQuest for purchase or access.

How Do I Search?

Google Scholar has both a friendly "Google-like" option and an advanced feature, which increases the accuracy and effectiveness of the search. Although controlled vocabulary is not used in Google Scholar, the advanced feature supports the specification of words or phrases that must (or must not) appear in the article. Searches can be limited by author, source, date, and PDF format, and by broad subject area such as medicine, pharmacology, and veterinary science.

How to Find the Articles?

Some articles may be available free, depending on the source. Otherwise, a library that subscribes to the journal can provide access to specific articles, which may also be purchased from the publisher or ordered through interlibrary loan.

WEB OF SCIENCE®

Web of Science contains information gathered from thousands of scholarly journals in all areas of research. Web of Science is available only through access to the ISI Web of Knowledge[SM] set of database resources. Many if not most academic libraries subscribe to the Web of Knowledge.

How to Search?

Web of Science can be searched by subject topic using a word or phrase or by author; however, the strength of this resource is in searching for cited references: The citations include references cited by authors of the original articles. Once a relevant article is located through searches of MEDLINE or another database, cited reference search can find subsequent articles that cite this article.

How to Find the Articles?

Web of Science includes only citations to articles. Access to the full text of an article depends on the subscriptions purchased by the library or institution where the database is used. Articles from journals that are not available can sometimes be purchased from the publisher, or they can be ordered through interlibrary loan.

Other databases should be considered, depending on the subject of the search question. **Table 7–1** summarizes the information about the databases described here and also includes additional databases that could be useful for you.

Table 7–1 Summary of Databases

Database	Coverage	Free Access	Subscription Vendors	Citation Information (for tracking research)	Free Full-Text Articles
MEDLINE (www.pubmed.gov)	Medicine, nursing, allied health sciences, dentistry, biomedical sciences	Internet: PubMed interface; other Internet sites	OvidSP, EBSCO		Some through PubMED links to PubMed Central
CINAHL	Nursing, allied health sciences	No	EBSCO	Yes	Depends on subscription
PsycINFO	Psychology, psychiatry, social sciences	No	OvidSP, EBSCO, DIALOG, ProQuest		Depends on subscription
Google Scholar (scholar.google.com)	Scholarly literature	Google		Yes	Some
Web of Science	Science, medicine, social science	No	ISI of Knowledge	Yes	none
ERIC (www.eric.ed.gov)	Education	Internet: Education Resources Information Center (ERIC)	EBSCO		Some
SCOPUS	Science, medicine, social science	No	SciVerse	Yes	Depends on subscription
Digital Dissertation & Theses	Dissertation from American universities	No	Proquest, DIALOG		Available with subscription

DATABASE SEARCH HINTS

Databases can be searched in a variety of ways. For subject searching, a controlled vocabulary (if there is one) limits the search to information relevant to the research without worrying about issues of natural language, alternate terms, synonyms, etc. Searches for words or phrases can also be made even if the controlled vocabulary does not provide a satisfactory result or if there is no controlled vocabulary for the database being searched. Searching by author, journal title, publication type, research type, questionnaire, and many other indexed fields of the record, can also be productive, but the available fields vary among databases.

The best approach to searching for subject terms is to search for each term separately and then to search for them in combination. Subjects can be combined with an author's name; an author's name can be combined with a journal title; a word or phrase search can be combined with a questionnaire name, and so on. In most databases, at least two options for combining sets are available: OR or AND. When using OR, the retrieval from two (or more) sets is pooled. Thus the number of retrieved items is larger than any of the individual

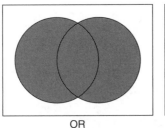 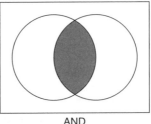

Figure 7–1 OR and AND operators.

sets. When using AND, the combined set containing each individual item must be present. Thus the number of retrieved items is smaller than any of the individual sets. Any number of search terms can be combined, but when using AND, the more items that are combined, the smaller the number of items retrieved.

The OR and AND operators are often illustrated using Venn diagrams, as shown in **Figure 7–1.**

RESULTS OF THE SEARCH

Methods for interpreting the information found through the literature search are described in detail in Chapter 19; however, some preliminary criteria should be considered as the search is performed. Questions to address might include the following:

1. Who is the author and what is the author's area of expertise?
2. What is the type of publication in which you found the information: a scholarly journal, a website, an academic textbook?
3. What is the date of publication: How current is the information?
4. Is the content of the material relevant to your research topic?
5. Are other authors citing this material? If so, how frequently?
6. If an article discusses previous research, how extensive was the research and how large was the research population?

Articles published in professional journals can include narrative review articles on a specific topic, case reports, cohort studies, clinical trial results, results of large randomized studies, and/or systematic reviews (i.e., literature reviews focused on a single question that try to identify, appraise, select and synthesize all high-quality research evidence relevant to that question). Sorting articles that have been retrieved by recognizing and evaluating differences in the process of conducting research help to determine the current state of research regarding the study question and to identify gaps in knowledge. Articles can be graphically represented by a pyramid (**Figure 7–2**) where the top of the pyramid represents articles that discuss types of research that are most time-consuming, objective, and clinically relevant.

CITATION TOOLS

Before citations are gathered, reference management tools should be consulted. These tools provide access to citations from database searches and to add additional references that may be accessed manually. Not only can citations be gathered in an easily accessible way and be used to keep track of the information that you have found, but citations may be organized into folders and the citations that have been saved may then be searched. When the research has been completed and the writing stage begins, the tool formats in-text citations and bibliography in the preferred output style, such as APA, MLA, or Vancouver. If the review is being written for publication, the management tools also "know" the formatting styles required by most professional journals; they accurately format the paper automatically. If the literature review itself and a

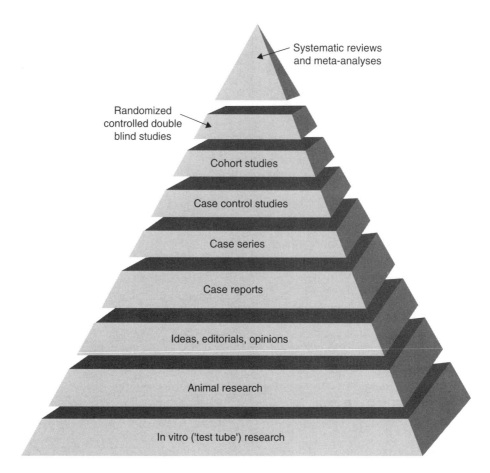

Systematic reviews
and meta-analyses

Randomized
controlled double
blind studies

Cohort studies

Case control studies

Case series

Case reports

Ideas, editorials, opinions

Animal research

In vitro ('test tube') research

Figure 7–2 The evidence pyramid.

summary of the research is to be the final product, citation tools can also produce a bibliography that is annotated.

Students or researchers at an academic institution may use the resources of their institution, such as management tools like RefWorks or Noodlebib that require a subscription. Software programs can also be installed on a personal computer. Available programs include Reference Manager (http://www.refman.com/) or EndNote (http://www.endnote.com/), both of which are powerful tools from Thomson Reuters. Because the software is personally proprietary, its use is not dependent on any institutional affiliation.

Some free Internet-based resources are also available. These include BibMe, RefBase, and Zotero. Some are completely free; others are free for basic use. When deciding which tool most closely fits the research need, considerations include ease of downloading citations or manual addition of citations into the resources as well as the process of adding in-text citations and formatting a bibliography in the required style. Free resources usually provide a basic set of reference styles, so for research that is to be published potentially, it may be worth investing in one of the software programs. Worthwhile reviews and comments by other users are available for many of these programs.

Some word-processing programs include a citation feature. Although these allow the addition of citations at the writing stage, citations cannot be stored for another use, nor are the features as powerful as those available through resources designed for this specific purpose.

WRITING THE LITERATURE REVIEW

Once all of the information is gathered, a literature review can be written as a summary of what is known (and not known) in the research topic area. This review is a discussion of previous research, not a list of references, so it is important to plan and organize the review carefully, whether it is organized chronologically or by research method or research trends. Literature reviews begin with a brief introduction summarizing the research question, the resources used for the literature review, and the search strategies. Then the results of the review are summarized. Be sure to discuss key points, reference quoted information, and include gaps in the existing research as well as areas of weakness or controversy. The reader should be made aware of the pertinent points of your research question and the research history on which they are built. Before the conclusion, readers should understand why answering this research question is important.

Additional hints for writing a good literature review are available on the Internet from writing centers at many academic institutions. Research in professional journals also provides valuable examples of literature reviews in terms of their content and how they are written.

> "Somewhere, something incredible is waiting to be known."
>
> —Carl E. Sagan, PhD

THE RESEARCH PROCESS—DESIGN

CHAPTER OVERVIEW

This chapter covers research design and methodology that become the "Methods" section of a research project. Choosing the right design adds validity, reliability, and strength to the results and conclusions. The best of projects can be derailed by errors in experimental design and weakened by a poor choice of research design, which guides the type of statistical analysis used in the study. Challenges to validity and reliability that may emerge at the peer-review stage must be considered when developing the methods for an investigation.

Methodology

Christopher E. Bork, PhD
Robert W. Jarski, PhD, PA-C
J. Glenn Forister, MS, PA-C

INTRODUCTION

Once the topic and specific research questions or hypotheses have been identified and the literature review has been completed and digested, the investigator must choose a method suitable for achieving the project's objective. This objective is stated as a hypothesis, a purpose statement, or a clear and specific research question. Additionally, the primary objective should be evaluated by this criterion: Is it important to medicine, the profession, or society? That is, will it be a significant contribution or addition to current available knowledge? Some journals refer to this as the "so what?" question. In many cases, authors are required to respond in writing to this question when submitting a manuscript for publication. Answering this question helps the investigator condense the meaning and value of the study. This question should be a guiding principle for all research endeavors.

The research methods should be driven by the research objective. When choosing a method, two mistakes may distract novice investigators. The first mistake often made is selecting a familiar method without first defining the research objective. The second most common mistake is planning to use data that are already available. Although convenient, this backward approach almost always leads to trivial information that is unlikely to significantly contribute to the project. The methods should generate data that achieve worthwhile objectives.

THE METHODS SECTION

The methods section describes how the research study was conducted. It should be sufficiently clear and detailed so that others can duplicate the study. The methods section includes descriptions of the following:

- Subjects
- Instrumentation used (including question-naires, when applicable)
- Procedures performed
- Analytic procedures used for evaluating and summarizing the data

Data analysis must be suited to the particulars of the study: the number of subject groups (e.g., two: an intervention and control group), the number of subjects within each group, and the procedures used for data collection (e.g., single or repeated measures). Generally, it is automatically assumed that every analysis involves a statistical method. Although this is often the case, some specific questions are better answered using a qualitative approach.

A Methods Scheme

Each study plan poses its own challenges. A system such as the one presented in **Table 8–1** is a useful tool for identifying some study options. First, the researcher must decide whether the approach will be analytic or descriptive by answering the question, "Is there a comparison between groups in this study?"

Table 8–1 Selected Research Designs

Name	Design	Statistical Test
One-shot case study	X O	None
One group pretest–posttest	O X O	Dependent or paired t test Wilcoxson matched pairs, signed ranks
Static group comparison	X O O	Independent t test Chi-squared Mann-Whitney U
Posttest only Control group	R X O R O	Independent t test or ANOVA Mann-Whitney U Kruskal-Wallis ANOVA
Nonequivalent control group	O X O O O	ANCOVA or ANOVA
Pretest–posttest control group	R O X O R O O	ANCOVA or ANOVA
Solomon four group	R O X O R O O R X O R O	ANCOVA or ANOVA
Counterbalanced	X1 O X2 O X3 O X2 O X3 O X1 O X3 O X1 O X2 O	ANOVA
Time series	O O O O X O O O O	ANOVA, trend analysis

X indicates experimental treatment or intervention; O, observation, measurement, or evaluation; R, randomization of a large number of subjects; nonequivalent group; ANOVA, analysis of variance; and ANCOVA, analysis of covariance.

UNDERSTANDING RESEARCH DESIGN

Controlling Bias

When designing research, the investigator must limit or control factors and biases that could potentially contaminate a study. As mentioned in previous chapters, all research starts with an idea or a problem. The research hypothesis is the investigator's expectation for the outcome or the solution to the problem. The objective of a research study is to prove or disprove the investigator's hunch.

When selecting a research design, the investigator must consider the expectation (i.e., the research hypothesis) and create a means of controlling biases that may result from this expectation. In other words, if an informed, objective observer must be able to conclude that the researcher's bias (or prior expectations) did not influence the result of the study. The investigator must design the research to eliminate bias, thus allowing the results of the study to truly represent the effect of the independent variable.

Other reasons for understanding research design include recognizing and minimizing the effect of threats to validity, both internal and external. In this chapter, the concepts of error and reliability, forms of validity, and a method of identifying and diagramming typical research designs will be discussed.

Error

All research involves measurement, and all measurements involve error. The common formula for a given measurement is

Observed measurement
$$= \text{true measurement} + \text{error}$$

As the concept of "error" decreases, the observed measurement begins to approximate the true measurement. In everyday life, errors in measurement are common. For example, anyone who has ever tried to cut a shelf to put inside a closet may be painfully aware of the formula for an observed measurement. If the observed measurement includes too great of an error, then the shelf will either be too large or too small and will not fit in the closet. Therefore, the error term can be either positive (too large) or negative (too small).

Types of Error

Error can be categorized into two forms, random and systematic. Random error consists of those errors that occur strictly because of chance; these errors are often thought of as "noise in the system." Small sample sizes tend to be more vulnerable to random error. For example, if five measurements are taken versus one measurement, the average of the five measurements is less likely to be incorrect or have a large error term. The carpenter's proverb of "measure twice, cut once" affirms the role of random errors. Systematic error can be thought of as a series of consistent biases affecting a measurement. Typical researcher errors may be related to poor technique, such as sloppiness, or to inappropriate protocols or research designs, inappropriate measures, or incorrect statistical applications. For example, if a researcher is using heart rate (beats per minute) as an indicator and calculates heart rate using 10-second readings in some cases and 15-second readings in others, then the error risk increases. The measuring technique introduces errors of inconsistency.

Similarly, if a researcher uses a survey to assess a clinical outcome, error may be introduced by several factors, including differences in verbal fluency among subjects or even the conditions under which the survey is completed. For instance, consider the differences in response to a telephone survey about practitioner satisfaction by an individual who has just experienced a two-hour traffic jam versus a responder who has just exercised and feels wonderful. Differences in their levels of stress may affect their responses.

By choosing appropriate measurements, using reliable techniques, and employing valid instruments to obtain measurements, a researcher can eliminate a substantial number of experimental errors in data collection. Reliability and validity are fundamental to obtaining appropriate and useful data.

Reliability

Reliability focuses on the consistency with which a measurement is taken. If a measurement lacks reliability, then the data obtained may be useless because of error. In other words, if substantial error exists in the measurements, then the researcher cannot know whether observed changes in the dependent variable are caused by manipulation of the independent variable or by poor measurement. Reliability is also of paramount importance to the professional in clinical practice. If a clinician does not gather reliable data, then there is no way of knowing whether apparent changes in the patient are the result of actual physiological changes or poor technique. In other words, the clinician will not know if progress is taking place as a result of treatment.

Forms of Reliability

There are three common forms of reliability: instrument reliability, intrarater reliability, and interrater reliability. Instrument reliability indicates the consistency of measurement by a particular instrument. For example, if a weighing scale has a worn spring, it may measure lighter weights accurately but heavier weights inaccurately. The method to improve instrument reliability is to consistently calibrate the instrument.

Intrarater reliability indicates the consistency with which an individual takes measurements. For example, does the healthcare provider measure blood pressure in the same way each and every time? If not, there is a strong possibility that the measurements will differ because of technique rather than differences in the patient. One method of improving intrarater reliability is to consistently follow an established protocol and to routinely check for consistency.

Interrater reliability indicates the consistency in measurements among individuals taking the measurements. If more than one individual is taking a measurement, there must be adequate assurances that any changes are caused by changes in the true measurement, rather than fluctuations in human error. The concept of interrater reliability is often ignored and has important ramifications for clinical research. Inattention to interrater reliability may obscure differences in the research outcome. If individuals collecting data do not perform the related tasks in the same way, the researchers will not be able to ascertain whether differences are caused by differences in the patient or differences in the way the measurement was performed (i.e., an error). In other words, if data are not gathered in a consistent or reliable manner, their accuracy is questionable and, therefore, the data may be useless.

The "two P rule"(Protocol and Practice)—applies when two or more individuals are taking measurements. Measurements should be taken using a standard protocol that has been practiced. Data collectors should also compare their measurements periodically; they may even wish to determine their consistency by performing one of the tests that assess interrater reliability, such as the kappa-statistic test. When reviewing any article that involves measurements, the reader should look for an assessment or other assurance that the data was gathered reliably.*

Validity

Another concept that must be considered regarding data and measurement in an investigation is validity. Validity indicates the usefulness or appropriateness of the data being gathered. In a practical sense, reliability and validity are related concepts. Reliability focuses on consistency of measurement, whereas validity focuses on the appropriateness of a given measurement. A simple illustration is a game of darts. Reliability can be viewed as the

---

*A discussion of the measures of reliability is beyond the scope of this text. Interested readers are advised to read the classic articles by Shrout and Fleiss and Bartko and Carpenter listed in the readings for this chapter found in Appendix C.

consistency of the pattern or spread of the darts. Validity can be thought of as ensuring that the darts are aimed at a dartboard. There are two principal types of validity: measurement or test validity, and design or experimental validity.

Measurement or Test Validity

Measurement or test validity answers the question: "Does the test or measure actually do what it is intended to do?" For this to occur, a given measurement should have a defined purpose and should relate to a given phenomenon (e.g., a clinician routinely takes a temperature because this vital sign can be an indication of an inflammatory process). For the purposes of this chapter, we will focus on some common forms of test validity.

The first form is face validity, which addresses the question, "Does the particular measurement or method appear to be appropriate?" This form of validity often relies on the opinion of experts. Most authorities consider face validity the weakest form of test and measurement validity. Another form is construct validity, which assesses the degree to which the measurement is based on theory. In the example of measuring body temperature, the construct that an inflammation involves heat provides modest construct validity. On the other hand, content validity asks whether the test is broad enough to address the scope of the content. For example, if students' knowledge of anatomy was being tested but they were only tested on the anatomy of the upper extremity, then that particular test would lack content validity. Finally, criterion validity is an indication of how well the test performs and whether it is useful when judged against a standard. There are generally two subcategories of criterion validity: predictive validity and concurrent validity. Predictive validity assesses whether and how well a test predicts a specific phenomenon or outcome. For example, how well does a positive straight leg raise accurately predict a lumbar disc protrusion? Concurrent validity asks whether the test performs as well as an accepted test. Generally, this category is used to validate a short or noninvasive version of a test. For example, concurrent validity would be used to establish the validity of a urine test, as opposed to a serum glucose test, to monitor diabetes mellitus. The next form of validity can be thought of as design or experimental validity.

Design or Experimental Validity

There are two forms of design or experimental validity: internal and external. Internal validity is concerned with limiting or controlling factors and events other than the independent variable, which may cause changes in the outcome, or dependent variable. These factors or events are known as threats to internal validity. External validity, on the other hand, is concerned with factors that may affect the generalizability of the conclusions drawn from the study. These factors are referred to as threats to external validity. The next section examines these two concepts.

THREATS TO INTERNAL VALIDITY

As mentioned, threats and concerns related to internal validity are unintended factors and conditions that can affect the results. For example, if an investigator is assessing the effects of two dietary regimens and does not take into account the subjects' levels of activity, then the internal validity of the study is threatened.

There are two broad categories of threats to internal validity: temporal or time-based effects, and measurement effects. Temporal or time-based effects consist of history, maturation, or attrition. History refers to effects on the dependent variable that are a result of the passage of time. For example, suppose an investigator is interested in a new topical ointment for the common cold sore caused by the herpes simplex virus. The researcher treats one group of patients with a new drug or topical ointment for seven days and obtains excellent results. However, cold sores from the herpes simplex virus are thought to be self-limiting anyway, with symptoms generally resolving in seven days. Therefore, the passage of time has obscured the effect or noneffect of the topical ointment. The next temporal effect or threat to internal validity is maturation. Maturation can be thought of as threats that happen by changes as a result of development. Suppose an individual suggests that a particular type of rehabilitative therapy improves the development of infants' motor skills. In this example, the individual contends that the therapy helps infants walk sooner. The effects of that therapy and potential changes in the infants' motor skills may not be the result of the type of therapy involved, but rather of the developmental process. Thus, the experiment may be flawed by threats to internal validity, specifically maturation.

The third temporal effect or threat to internal validity results from attrition. When subjects leave a study prematurely, the results may be distorted. Consider the consequences of a study involving a new drug for migraine headache sufferers. In this hypothetical study, one group of subjects receives the new drug, and their results are compared with another group of subjects who receive a placebo. The subjects will be seen every three weeks for a period of six months. Suppose subjects taking the new drug no longer experience migraine headaches, so they no longer come to their appointments. The only participants left in the study are those for whom the drug did not work. Therefore, when comparing the placebo to the experimental drug after six months, there is apparently no difference between the groups because the majority of participants who continue to have migraine headaches remained in the study. The subjects who were helped by the drug dropped out of the study, thereby effecting and possibly even distorting the results. Measurement effects are those threats to internal validity that result from an investigator trying to measure a phenomenon. The first threat is testing, especially when the test is repeated several times. Sometimes the actual act of performing a test on a patient affects the results of the study. Consider a hypothetical investigation in which the researcher is interested in the effect of a particular type of setting on function in individuals who have suffered a cerebral vascular accident. One of the measurements may be a functional test (e.g., how well the individual is able to dress without

help from others). In this example, the investigator decides to administer a pretest to determine the baseline time needed for an individual to self-dress. In this case, having the patient get dressed may help the patient discover new and better strategies for getting dressed, thus contaminating the results.

As a second example, consider an investigator who wishes to compare two forms of drug therapy on patients with cardiac problems. In this hypothetical study, the investigator chooses to use a step test (i.e., have the subjects step up and down repeatedly) and record the number of times subjects can continue until the heart rate reaches a predetermined maximum percentage. In this study, the patient's performance may be affected by the motor learning that takes place. In other words, the patient's coordination may improve just by virtue of a pretest using the step test. The next threat to internal validity is instrumentation. The type of instrumentation used may affect the results. Consider a study in which the investigator is interested in whether children with handwriting problems press their pencils harder on the paper. To measure the point pressure of the writing implement, the children are asked to use a pencil-type instrument containing a force transducer and a wire that leads to a recording device. The fact that the instrument represents an unnatural pencil may affect the results. Thus, the instrument itself is a threat to internal validity.

Another threat to internal validity is sampling. Sampling effects include the selection of subjects for a study according to some bias, whether recognized or not. If selected by virtue of a bias, the subjects are not representative of the population. For example, if subjects were surveyed in a study via a mail questionnaire that was sent only to residents in an affluent suburb, then the conclusions drawn from the results may be affected by the sample that was surveyed.

The final measurement effect that represents a threat to internal validity is statistical regression to the mean. Simply stated, this is the tendency for a group of outliers to move toward the mean (the average), not necessarily because of any difference in the subjects' characteristics, but because of the laws of probability. A classic example of statistical regression to the mean can be illustrated by what happened when students with developmental and learning challenges were mainstreamed into a classroom with so-called "normal" students. After a period of time, they were tested and their scores on a developmental and learning inventory improved. The researchers then hypothesized that, if scores improved by putting challenged students in a "normal" class, then perhaps putting "normal" students in a class with gifted students would bring the "normal" students' aptitudes up. However, when the students in the class were retested, the exceptional students appeared to do more poorly on the test. Did the exposure to "normal" students somehow contaminate these learners? The answer is no. What was happening was simply statistical regression to the mean. In both cases, the group that was being tested (the developmentally challenged and the gifted students) came from the ends of the distribution of test scores, that is, the highest and lowest scores. On the retest, their scores tended to migrate toward the mean or toward that typical score within a population. Therefore, investigations may be affected by statistical regression to the mean by utilizing subjects who may be considered outliers.

THREATS TO EXTERNAL VALIDITY

As previously mentioned, threats to external validity include factors and conditions that affect the ability to generalize the results of a study. Threats to external validity can be placed into two categories: threats related to the populations used, and those related to the environment in which the study takes place (i.e., environmental threats).

Population-Related Threats to External Validity

The first population-related threat to external validity concerns the subjects' accessibility to the study. When one performs a study, one usually studies

a portion of a given population—a sample. If the sample used in an experiment or investigation is substantially different from the population, then the ability to generalize the results to the population may be compromised. This threat may be of particular interest in clinical studies. In the majority of clinical studies, the subject generally has access to medical care and the ability to continue with treatment. Therefore, these subjects may not represent the entire population, which may include individuals who have compromised access to medical care.

The second threat to external validity in the population category is known as subject: treatment interaction. This threat can be described as the confounding effects of the subjects' attributes on the dependent variable. Because of genetic makeup, lifestyle, or other confounding variables, certain subjects react differently (i.e., either more positively or more negatively) to any given treatment. For example, some people are blessed with a metabolism that allows them to eat whatever they wish without gaining any weight. On the other hand, other people who follow the same diet may gain weight.

Environmental or Experiment-Related Threats to External Validity

One environmental or experiment-related threat to external validity is the description of the variables. If the variables used in a study are not described precisely and with sufficient detail, then it may be difficult for subsequent investigators to replicate the study or obtain the same results. For example, consider a new antihypertensive drug study where the control subjects receive "conventional therapy," but this is not specified in detail. A clinician may not be able to determine whether the new drug is preferable to current therapy if not enough detail is available to ascertain how similar the new drug therapy is to the control therapy. A second environmental threat takes place when there are multiple treatments involving test order. In some cases, when two treatments or two drugs are administered, one may potentiate the effects or affect the actions of the other. Failure to recognize the effect of treatment order or multiple treatments may hinder the practitioner's ability to apply the results of the study.

Named after a classic experiment by Elton Mayo, the Hawthorne effect is a threat to external validity. Mayo was looking at worker productivity at the Hawthorne Works plant located outside of Chicago. Mayo was interested in the effect of lighting on worker productivity. He explained to the workers that they would be in an experiment on productivity. Mayo then proceeded to increase the ambient lighting in the factory. As anticipated, productivity improved. In the next phase of his study, Mayo then dimmed the ambient lighting. Worker productivity increased again. Finally, Mayo raised the ambient lighting to the previous high-intensity level, and yet again productivity increased. Mayo concluded that the ambient lighting was unrelated to the workers' performance—rather, the fact that the workers knew they were being studied affected productivity. The Hawthorne effect is an effect on results caused by the subjects' knowing that they are participating in an experiment. Typically, subjects in clinical experiments have better compliance with treatment regimens than patients who are not participating in an experiment.

The Rosenthal effect refers to results caused by the involvement of the investigator in a study. The personal attributes, charisma, and abilities of the researcher can affect the results. For example, if an investigator is a charismatic practitioner, then patients may improve partially because of their belief in the clinician treating them. Other practitioners who attempt to obtain similar results are likely to be unsuccessful.

In every research study, the investigator must consider and try to control factors, conditions, and the effects of circumstances that threaten both internal and external validity. Similarly, professionals critically reading the literature must be aware of these threats to validity in order to determine the credibility of the conclusions and the applicability of the work in their practice. In many cases, the choice of research design affects the investigation's susceptibility to threats to validity.

TYPES OF STUDIES

Descriptive Studies

Descriptive studies generate data that are either numerical or nonnumerical. Nonnumerical information may be presented as verbal commentaries about subjects' clinical characteristics and behaviors, histologic slides, radiologic images, etc. For these data, descriptive methods from the subdiscipline of qualitative research are appropriate. For ethical and legal reasons, subjects' personal information must always be de-identified when qualitative findings are presented.

Similarly, numerical data on individual subjects are almost never presented in a research report. Numerical information is usually presented as statistical summaries such as averages and measures of variability. The mean, median, and mode are all measures of central tendency. The measure of variability most often used in medical literature is standard deviation. Occasionally, a range or standard error (SE, also called standard error of the mean, SEM) is used. When confidential information is not disclosed, numerical reports may be supported by exemplar, anecdotal, or model information that conveys valuable research or teaching lessons.

Analytic Studies

Analytic studies test for the following:

- Differences between groups (e.g., a group of patients receiving a drug compared to those receiving a placebo)
- Relationships among variables (e.g., the correlation between cholesterol levels and coronary artery occlusion)
- Both differences and relationships

The specific statistical test, as well as which data are analyzed by that test, are described in Chapter 14. A "true experiment" is a prospective design in which the researcher controls as many subject, treatment, and environmental variables as possible.

A cross-sectional study is a database of "snapshots" of subjects at one period. For example, childhood bone maturation may be studied by describing bone densities in a group of children ages 1, 3, 6, and 9 years old. A longitudinal approach would follow a group of 25 1-year-old children over the next eight years. If the researcher could control all or most variables over time, then a longitudinal study could also be experimental. However, it would be difficult to determine whether intervening variables had corrupted the design. Therefore, long-term experiments involving human subjects are rare.

When there is substantial risk to human subjects, it is not always possible to conduct a true experiment ethically. The risk may be caused by inducing the disease or condition being studied or by testing an experimental intervention or treatment. As an alternative, it may be possible to study a disease (e.g., cervical cancer) by identifying those who already have it and those who do not and then comparing the two groups for factors that might have been responsible for the disease (e.g., human papillomavirus exposure). This type of study is known as a case-control study design.

Another experimental approach is to identify people who have or do not have a particular risk factor (e.g., human papillomavirus exposure) and then examine the two groups over time to identify those who develop the disease or condition. This type of study is known as a cohort study design. Whether a cohort or case-control study design is used, a control or reference group is necessary. For example, if a newscast reports that all subjects in a group of heroin addicts have used marijuana, can we conclude that marijuana use leads to heroin addiction? If the heroin addicts were found to have consumed whole milk, can we conclude that whole milk leads to heroin addiction? A control or reference group composed of people who do not use heroin is likely to show that many have used marijuana or have consumed whole milk.

Prospective versus Retrospective Designs

Data collection for prospective studies is planned in advance. Prospective designs include true experiments and concurrent cohort studies. The concurrent cohort design involves subjects who do not have the disease in question but have a suspected risk

factor and are tested at a later time to determine whether the disease developed in them. In many cases, the prospective approach is the only way to obtain information about a new or recently discovered phenomenon, such as a previously unrecognized disorder or a newly developed technique.

True experiments attempt to gain strict control over the conditions of the study, including subject selection, instrument calibration, and the experimental environment. Compared to retrospective designs, prospective designs are credited with having better control of variables and a greater possibility of having valid and reliable standardized measurement methods. Disadvantages include cost (which may limit subject numbers) and the difficulty of extrapolating the results of strictly controlled methods to the clinical setting, where a similar level of control is not possible.

Retrospective studies examine data that already exists, including chart reviews and case-control studies. A retrospective approach may be the only ethical way to study the mechanisms of certain interventions. For example, thalidomide was widely prescribed outside the United States for nausea and vomiting during pregnancy, but it was later was found to cause developmental defects. Because the researcher may not know exactly how and under what circumstances the data was collected, it may be difficult to verify that retrospective data was collected properly. Collecting data retrospectively is usually inexpensive, and data are readily available in large quantities. A large N value (the total number of participants in a study) may be used to compensate for variability. Therefore, the value and usefulness of a study should not be based solely on whether the data was collected prospectively or retrospectively. The particular method of data collection should be evaluated on its own merit.

Uses of Statistics

Many skilled clinicians are skeptical or even fearful of statistics. They contend that "anything can be proved or disproved," and that readers are easily fooled. This is not true for those who have knowledge about research methods and the basic statistical principles presented in this chapter. Statistical information is common in medical literature. A few easy-to-learn concepts enable clinicians to become informed consumers of medical information. This ability is invaluable for interpreting study results in journal articles, conference presentations, and drug advertisements. Because we rely on scientific information throughout our professional careers to understand new information, a healthcare provider should be familiar with clinical research methods and basic statistical terminology.

Statistics are used primarily in three ways in medical literature. First, statistics are used to describe and summarize group information. Second, they allow us to infer or generalize sample results to the larger population, which is essential because it is impossible or impractical to measure each and every individual. Third, statistics test for significant relationships or differences between groups of subjects.

Types of Data

A datum (singular of data) is a unit of information about a subject. An example would be the total cholesterol value of 178 mg/dL on a subject participating in a lipid study. Data may be nonnumerical (nominal or ordinal, also referred to as nonparametric because of the statistical tests that can be legitimately performed on these types of data), or numerical (interval or ratio, also called parametric).

Nominal data are characteristic names that have no numerical value. Examples would be male or female, black or white, osteoarthritis or rheumatoid arthritis, smoker or nonsmoker. Ordinal data has characteristics that are comparative and can be ordered by rank. Examples are shorter or taller, less painful or more painful, darker or lighter, or an increased size of a palpable mass. Interval data have numerical values between units but no actual zero point. Examples include degrees centigrade and blood glucose (i.e., a patient could not have a body temperature or blood glucose value of zero). Ratio data have numerical values between units, and a zero value is possible. Examples include milligrams of alcohol per deciliter, basophils per cubic millimeter, and number of pack-years smoking history (number of packs smoked per day multiplied by the number of years smoked).

Like clinical data, numerical research data is preferred to nonnumerical data. For instance, in a study on smokers, knowing the number of pack-years (numerical data) provides better information than knowing only that a patient smokes (nonnumerical). The more powerful parametric statistical tests can be applied to numerical data.

Although it is not always possible to quantify data, data can be valuable in the descriptive, qualitative form. For example, a narrative about a radiograph of a hairline fracture with a detailed description of its important characteristics, landmarks, and possible origin may be more informative than just a report of a "hairline fracture: present or not present" on 100 films.

When it is not possible to use numerical data, nonparametric statistical tests (such as the Spearman's correlation or chi-squared) must be used. The application of parametric tests (e.g., Pearson's correlation or the t-test) to nonparametric data is a mistake because a falsely low P value (probability value) is likely to be fabricated (i.e., referred to as an alpha or type I error). A falsely high P value is likely to result when nonparametric tests are used for analyzing numerical (parametric) data. In this case, it is unlikely that a false hypothesis will be accepted, but consequentially a true one may be overlooked (i.e., a beta or type II error). This may occur especially when the calculated P value is close to the desired alpha level.

These classifications of numerical data are commonly used in most scientific articles. However, qualitative research methods also serve invaluable roles in some medical studies and are used as extensively in clinical research as in clinical problem solving.

Experimental Designs

An investigator must decide whether a qualitative or quantitative approach will more effectively address the research objective. A second decision is whether the study will involve retrospective data (e.g., clinical records) or prospective data (i.e., information that will be newly generated as part of the project). The implications of these decisions have been discussed earlier in this chapter.

If the investigator decides to use an experiment to answer the research question, then choosing the appropriate experimental design is imperative. In a project proposal, the investigator describes the methods to be used for analyzing the study's data. Many proposal guidelines suggest creating mock data that are likely to resemble the study's actual data. This process also helps the investigator plan for both computer needs and possibly consultation with a statistician or methodologist.

The selected research designs presented in Table 8–1 are likely to accommodate the needs of most investigators. Although experimental and epidemiological studies share some methodological similarities, epidemiologists have developed specialized techniques for the needs of their discipline. Some investigators may need to use advanced epidemiological techniques for their studies. In these cases, consulting an epidemiology textbook or an epidemiologist is appropriate. The statistical principles presented here apply to most experimental and epidemiological studies, whether prospective or retrospective. Familiarity with these principles should enable the clinician to converse knowledgeably with most clinical research methodologists and consultants.

Pre-Experimental, Experimental, and Quasi-Experimental Designs for Research

The purpose of this section is to provide the reader with a simple way to recognize common research designs and the associated threats to validity inherent in those designs. Most of the work conducted in this area can be attributed to Campbell and Stanley, who wrote the classic text Pre-Experimental, Experimental and Quasi-Experimental Designs for Research. They developed a shorthand method for diagramming research designs similar to the way that English grammar has been classically taught; by diagramming sentences, students learned to understand proper grammar and sentence construction. Similarly, individuals can more easily recognize a research design by diagramming it.

Campbell and Stanley and others have used certain conventions. For the purposes of this section, the following symbols are used:

1. An R represents randomization and indicates that a particular group was randomly selected or assigned.
2. An M indicates that the groups were matched.
3. An X (with or without a subscript) indicates a treatment.
4. An X0 indicates no treatment or, in some cases, the control condition.
5. An O indicates a measurement. If multiple measurements are taken, then subscripts, such as O1, O2, O3, and so forth, may be used.
6. A dashed line, indicates nonequivalency and denotes that the groups may be substantially different.

PRE-EXPERIMENTAL DESIGNS

The pre-experimental designs are the weakest of the research designs and are subject to many threats to internal and external validity. They are characterized by the lack of a control group, sensitivity to temporal threats to internal validity, and poor generalizability.

One-Shot Case Study

The first pre-experimental design, the one-shot case study, is diagrammed as follows:

$$XO$$

In this design, a treatment is given and a measurement is made. This particular design is typical of survey research. A group of respondents are identified based on one or more pre-existing criteria and are administered a questionnaire that is then measured. Another example of the one-shot case study is the typical high school or college classroom. The instructor assumes that the students have a certain level of baseline knowledge when they enter the class, but this baseline is not measured. The treatment consists of the exposure in the class, and the measurement is the student's performance in the class. If the students do well, then the instructor may conclude that it is because the students learned a great deal from the class. However, the instructor cannot justifiably arrive at that conclusion because the students' prior level of knowledge in the subject is unknown. This demonstrates how the one-shot case study is a weak design because of its vulnerability to both threats to internal and external validity.

Even with its limitations, the one-shot case study is useful for certain types of research, such as descriptive studies in which the investigator wishes to describe what currently exists. For example, most surveys can be characterized as one-shot case studies. Often the data they yield is very useful to clinicians and, therefore, is published in the medical literature. For example, Levine was interested in the clinical practice of lung transplantation and wanted to ascertain if there were wide differences among transplantation programs.[1] To describe the state of clinical practice, he surveyed 65 active lung transplantation programs. By requesting information on key areas of practice, such as lung preservation and post-transplantation care, he was able to conclude that there was substantial consensus as well as a few areas of variance among transplantation centers. The results could not be generalized to centers that did not respond. In addition, these studies do not have a long "shelf life" because a survey is most often a snapshot of a phenomenon at a specific time. However, the information could be considered valuable because lung transplantation centers may be able to determine if the practices at their center are consistent with those at other centers.

One Group Pretest–Posttest

Slightly more robust is the one group pretest–posttest design. In this particular design, subjects receive a pretest, the treatment, and a posttest or retest:

OXO

This design is characteristic of clinical practice in which a patient (or a group of patients) is evalu-

ated and diagnosed, a treatment is administered, and the patient (or a group) is then subsequently re-evaluated.

For example, a group of high school students is provided with education about alcohol abuse. The pretest and posttest may be a questionnaire on alcohol use. This design is particularly vulnerable to the temporal threats to internal validity, and therefore the investigator theoretically cannot conclude that the outcome was the result of treatment because the illness may have been self-limiting or the subject may simply have outgrown the problem as a result of development. In the case of high school students, changes in alcohol use may be related to the time of year and lack of parties where alcohol is served rather than to a result of alcohol abuse education.

Without the ability to compare the study group to a reference or control group, the effects of temporal threats to internal validity cannot be evaluated. Similarly, the results cannot be generalized because it is not known whether the patient (or group) is representative.

In a study on the effects of a five-day immersion leadership development experience on current and aspiring nursing leaders, Tourangeau et al. assessed and compared self-appraisals by participants and assessments by colleagues before and three months after the experience.[2] Although they concluded that "a concentrated leadership experience is effective in strengthening leadership behaviors," critical readers may point out several issues that challenge their conclusions. Because participants' colleagues assessed leadership behaviors before the experience and knew they would be completing another assessment later, they may have become more sensitive to observing leadership behaviors. In other words, some of the observed differences may be due to changes in the raters rather than the participants. The study could have addressed the concern about differences in the raters by having them also rate individuals who did not undergo the leadership program. Ideally, the raters would have been blind to the subjects' participation, or in other words, they would not know whether a person they were rating had or had not participated in the leadership development program. If changes in leadership were observed for individuals who had not participated in the program, then at least some of the observed change could possibly be attributed to the changes in the raters. This concern about the raters is further supported by the fact that the participants' self-report on leadership behaviors was not significantly different after the program. Finally, because the subjects were volunteers, those who felt they would benefit from the program may have self-selected to participate. Hence the subjects may not have been representative of aspiring nurse leaders.

Static Group Comparison

The third pre-experimental research design is entitled the static group comparison. In this design, a group that has received a treatment, or been exposed to a condition, is compared to a group that did not receive the treatment or was not exposed to the condition:

$$XO$$
$$-------$$
$$O$$

The dashed line indicates that these groups are not equivalent. This design, which attempts some form of control with the group that was not treated or exposed, is better than the previous designs. However, because the groups were not randomly assigned, it cannot be concluded that they are equivalent.

This design is commonly used in environmental or occupational epidemiological studies. For example, one may be interested in a group of people who are living in an area that might be contaminated with a carcinogenic agent. The investigator may hypothesize that living in this area may result in a greater incidence of certain types of cancers. People who live in the contaminated area are compared with similar people who live in an uncontaminated area. If there is a greater and statistically significant difference in the number of people with cancer in the contaminated area, then the researcher could conclude that the suspected carcinogen might be related. Please note that one cannot conclude causality from this type of design. Correlation and causation are different concepts.

Correlation helps to identify a relationship between variables, and the direction of that relationship.

The usefulness of the static group comparison is that it allows the study of variables that generally cannot be manipulated by the investigator. Legally and ethically, an investigator cannot require people to live in an area that is suspected to cause a disease or disability. On the other hand, if individuals choose to live in that area, then one can measure and analyze the effects and compare them to a similar group of individuals who live in a different "control" area.

An example of a static group comparison from the medical literature is a study by Lynch et al that compared residency choices by medical students who did or did not participate in an optional rural health awareness program.[3] One group of medical students participated in an enrichment initiative entitled the Rural Health Scholars Program (RHSP), which included both didactic and experiential learning focusing on practice in underserved and rural areas. The proportion of participants' that chose residencies in primary care, family medicine, community hospitals and known underserved areas were compared to their classmates who did not participate in the RHSP. While the results demonstrated that significantly more students who participated in the RHSP choose residencies in family medicine and community hospitals, the authors could not conclude that the RHSP was the "cause." Because the groups were nonequivalent, the possibility that medical students; self-selected participation in the RHSP because of a possible interest in a rural primary care setting could not be ruled out.

In summary, one of the major problems with a static group comparison occurs because the groups are nonequivalent. Therefore, there is always the possibility that some factor other than the treatment is causing the results.

EXPERIMENTAL DESIGNS

The next series of research designs are the true experimental designs. These studies are characterized by randomization of the subjects and a control group. Randomization does not mean that the groups are identical. Randomization works on the law of probability, which suggests that when a group is selected or subjects are assigned randomly, the traits, characteristics, and conditions that may affect the outcome (confounding variables) are distributed roughly equally among the groups, thus canceling out their effect.

Pretest, Posttest, Control Group Design

The first experimental design includes the pretest, posttest, and control group. In this design, subjects are randomly assigned to a group, pretested, given a treatment or not given a treatment, and then tested after exposure to the treatment or no treatment:

$$R \; O1 \; X0 \; O2$$

$$R \; O1 \; X1 \; O2$$

In this diagram, two groups are compared on a single variable with two conditions (X0 and X1), but more than two groups or conditions can be analyzed using this design. In addition, it is possible to examine more than one variable.

The pretest, posttest, control group design effectively rules out most threats to internal and external validity. Because it is the most rigorous design, the pretest, posttest, control group design is commonly accepted as the "gold standard" and is typically used in randomized clinical trials. It should be noted that, in clinical trials and other research involving human subjects, it is unethical and often illegal to withhold treatment. Thus the control group may be the group that receives the conventional treatment while the experimental group receives the new treatment. In other words, the conventional treatment is sometimes used as a control or the baseline.

In a study to examine whether fortified cereals actually increased subjects' blood levels of selected B vitamins, Tucker et al. compared a fortified cereal to a cereal that was not fortified in a sample of older adults.[4] Their approach was to measure blood levels of homocysteine (an amino acid), folic acid, B6, and B12 in subjects on two occasions to obtain baselines. According to the authors,

High homocysteine and low vitamin B concentrations have been linked to the risk of vascular disease, stroke and dementia[4(p805)]

After obtaining baseline measures, the subjects were randomly assigned to a group that ate either a cup of a fortified cereal daily or a cup of cereal that was not fortified. At 12 and 14 weeks the blood levels of homocysteine, folic acid, B6, and B12 were measured.[†]

Neither the subjects nor the investigators performing the tests knew whether a subject was consuming fortified cereal or not. When the group membership is unknown to the subject and the investigator (until the tests are concluded), the study is called a double-blind study. Both the subject and the investigator are "blind" to the treatment. Comparisons between the two groups revealed significant differences between them. Homocysteine levels were lower, while folic acid, B6, and B12 levels were higher in the group that ate the fortified cereal. Because of the rigorous design of the study, the authors concluded that eating a fortified cereal benefits older adults.[4] Because major threats to internal and external validity were controlled, the observed differences were due to the treatment. Therefore, the results may be generalized to similar groups of individuals, that is, eating a cereal fortified with B vitamins benefits older adults.

Posttest-Only Control Group Design

The second experimental design is termed the posttest-only control group design. The subjects

---

[†]The astute reader will undoubtedly observe that the example used is a slight variation from the classical pretest, posttest, control group design because the investigators used two baseline measurements and two posttest measurements, so the design was:

$$R \; O_1 \; O_2 \; X_{not\ fortified} \; O_3 \; O_4$$
$$R \; O_1 \; O_2 \; X_{fortified} \; O_3 \; O_4$$

Ordinarily one might also be concerned about pretest–posttest sensitization with multiple tests but in this study the dependent variable was blood levels of homocysteine, B6, B12 and folic acid, and it should not be affected by repeated testing.

are randomized, given a treatment, and then the results are measured and compared:

R X0 O

R X1 O

Typically, this type of design is used when a pretest is inappropriate or unavailable for other reasons. For example, an orthopedic group may be interested in the outcomes of a total hip replacement when using one particular appliance versus a second appliance. In this case, a pretest is inappropriate because patients who acquire total hip replacements generally lack substantial range of motion at the hip joint, often because of pain. In this example, the outcomes such as time to ambulation, pain, and range of motion may be appropriate to measure after the surgery. Because it is impossible to know the baseline or the pretest condition of the individuals, there might be some threats to internal validity based on pre-existing conditions. However, randomization minimizes these effects.

Gallo and Staskin investigated the effect of external cues on patient compliance in performing pelvic-floor exercises.[5] Because compliance is measured after a patient is educated about a treatment program, a pretest was not appropriate. In this study, 86 women with stress urinary incontinence were given a program on pelvic-floor exercises and then were randomly assigned to a group that either received an additional audio cassette or not. They were then subsequently evaluated for compliance to the pelvic-floor exercise program, and the results were compared. The women who received the audio cassette, labeled an external cue by the authors, demonstrated significantly better compliance than the group who only received instruction.[5] In this case, the robust experimental design, a posttest-only control group design, controlled major threats to internal and external validity, allowing the authors to conclude that external cues improve compliance for women with stress urinary incontinence.

Solomon Four-Group Design

The next experimental design is the Solomon four-group design. In this design, groups with and without pretests are exposed to one of two treatments and are subsequently tested after treatment:

R O1 X0 O2

R O1 X1 O2

R X0 O2

R X1 O2

The Solomon four-group design is actually a combination of the previous two designs: the pretest/posttest/control group design and the post-test-only/control group design. This particular design is useful because it allows an investigator to assess whether an effect occurs because of the pretest. On the other hand, this design requires twice as many subjects.

Danley et al. investigated the effect of a multimedia learning experience designed to prepare dental students and dentists to recognize and respond to domestic violence.[6] The investigators were interested in ensuring that observed changes in the subjects between the pretest and the posttest were not due to the fact that the subjects completed the pretest. When the subjects who completed the pretest (a multimedia learning experience) and the posttest were compared to subjects who completed the multimedia learning experience and the posttest, investigators found no significant differences between the groups. On the other hand, the two groups who completed the multimedia learning experience were more knowledgeable than the subjects in the control group.[6]

QUASI-EXPERIMENTAL DESIGNS

The final group of research designs is termed quasi-experimental designs. Although they are more rigorous than the pre-experimental designs, they are not as rigorous or as robust as the true experimental designs. Typically, they lack one or more of the characteristics that would make them true experimental designs. Generally, randomization or multiple measurements are lacking, thereby making testing effects a potential problem.

Nonequivalent Control Group Design

The nonequivalent control group design is similar to the pretest, posttest, control group design, but because the groups are not randomized, they must be considered nonequivalent:

$$O1 \quad X0 \quad O2$$

$$O1 \quad X1 \quad O2$$

An example of the use of this design is a hypothetical comparison of patient satisfaction with care from two clinics: one clinic hired a clinician 6 months previously (X1) and one clinic had no clinician (X0). Many ways in which the patients differ might affect the outcome, such as age, years seen by the provider, and so forth. Because the groups are nonequivalent, the results obtained from studies using this particular design must be viewed with caution; pre-existing conditions in the subjects may account for the changes after treatment.

Kristjansson et al. studied the effectiveness of a short-duration learning experience for teenagers that focused on preventing skin cancer.[7] Because the presentation was given in a classroom, they compared the classes that received the presentation to classes that did not. In this example, randomly assigning students would have made the study very complex and unmanageable. Although their results suggested that the short duration learning experience was successful, the fact that the groups were nonequivalent suggests that they should be viewed with caution. For instance, it is not known if one or more classes were comprised of students who were more concerned about their health, or more motivated to accept the content presented.

Separate Sample Pretest, Posttest Design

The separate sample pretest, posttest design is used when the investigators suspect that the pretest will significantly bias the posttest results:

$$O \quad X$$
$$----------$$
$$X \quad O$$

While measuring a change from pretest to posttest is appropriate when using a physical test such as blood level or heart rate, a pretest of a mental, psychological or performance variable often affects the posttest. For example, a pretest for manual dexterity may result in some motor learning that could affect subsequent performance. If the investigator was interested in evaluating the effect of a new treatment, the observed changes could be due to motor learning from the pretest. The separate sample pretest, posttest design addresses concerns about the pretest biasing the outcome.

Markert et al. used a separate pretest, posttest design to assess the knowledge acquired by professionals who attended continuing medical education (CME) programs.[8] The investigators noted in this article that pretesting and posttesting attendees was an inappropriate approach for assessing knowledge. They felt that a pretest would bias performance on a posttest. Given the observation that most medical professionals are bright individuals who are committed to learning, it seems logical that they would remember items from a pretest. Instead, Markert et al. randomly assigned attendees to either a pretest group, which they considered a "control" group, or a posttest only group, which they considered the "treatment" group. Upon comparing the groups, the "treatment" group demonstrated significantly more knowledge in selected topic areas.[8]

Time Series Design

A third quasi-experimental design is the time series design. In these designs, groups are compared to each other and there are multiple tests:

$$O1 \quad X0 \quad O2 \quad O3 \quad O4$$

$$O1 \quad X1 \quad O2 \quad O3 \quad O4$$

Because there are multiple measurements, one cannot conclude that changes or differences are not a result of sensitization or learning. In other words, the threat to validity of repeated testing is of concern, as well as the threat that groups may be nonequivalent.

In a study that compared nursing and medical interventions for skin care, Pokorny et al. examined differences in patients who developed pressure sores and those who did not.[9] Data was gathered on the day of admission, the day of surgery, and the following four days. Because the patients were admitted for cardiac surgery, it was anticipated that a subject would average six days in the hospital. The investigators in this study looked for differences in the daily nursing and medical interventions between patients who developed pressure sores and those who did not. For this study, the dependent variable (what was measured) consisted of the documented interventions, and specifically differences. The authors concluded that multiple assessments of skin condition by nurses were important in preventing pressure sores.[9] Because patients were not randomly assigned to groups that received standard or optimized skin assessment, differences in patients may have affected the results.

SUMMARY

The designs presented are by no means exhaustive of the pre-experimental, experimental, and quasi- experimental designs found in the literature. By recognizing the common designs, one can quickly focus on threats to validity. When designing a study, knowledge of common research designs may help avoid pitfalls. Although one can have a robust research design, failure to obtain reliable measurements using a valid instrument may render the conclusions of the study inaccurate or erroneous. Finally, reading research critically or performing research is a learning experience that generally requires a great deal of practice.

When evaluating the methods section of published research reports, this information should help clinicians to knowledgeably critique the methods used and evaluate the study's results before applying them to practice. For all clinicians, this information should help in interpreting new medical information presented in literature, professional conferences, and through other sources. Well-informed clinicians may be able to interpret and apply clinical information in new or better ways.

By definition, original research studies are unique. Applying the principles presented in this chapter should help beginning investigators select an effective research method for a planned research study and, when necessary, communicate effectively with methodological consultants.

REFERENCES

1. Levine SM. A survey of clinical practice of lung transplantation in North America. *Chest.* 2004;125:1–16.
2. Tourangeau AE, Lemonde M, Luba M, Dakers D, Alksnis C. Dakers D, Alksnis C. Evaluation of a leadership development intervention. *Nurs Leadersh (Toront).* 2003;16(3):91–104.
3. Lynch DC, Pathman DE, Teplin SE, Bernstein JD. Interim evaluation of the rural health scholars program. *Teach Learn MedM.* 2001;13:36–42.
4. Tucker KL, Olson B, Bakun P, Dallal GE, Selhub J, Rosenberg IH. Breakfast cereal fortified with folic acid, vitamin B-6 and vitamin B-12 increases vitamin concentrations and reduces homocysteine concentrations: a randomized trial. *Am J Clin Nutr.* 2004;79:805–811.
5. Gallo ML, Staskin DR. Cues to action: pelvic floor muscle exercise compliance in women with stress urinar incontinence. *Neurourol Urodyn.* 1997;16:167–177.
6. Danley D, Gansky SA, Chow D, Gerbert B. Preparing dental students to recognize and respond to domestic violence. *J Am Dent Assoc.* 2004;135;67–73.
7. Kristjansson K, Helgason R, Mansson-Brahme E, Widlund-Ivarson B, Ullen H. You and your skin: a short-duration presentation of skin cancer prevention for teenagers. *Health Ed Res.* 2003;18:88–97.
8. Markert RJ, O'Neill SC, Bhatia SC. Using a quasi-experimental research design to assess knowledge in continuing medical education programs. *J Cont Ed Health Prof.* 2003;23:157–162.
9. Pokorney ME, Koldjeski D, Swanson M. Skin care intervention for patients having cardiac surgery. *Am J Crit Care.* 2003; 12:535–544.

CHAPTER OVERVIEW

Clinical studies are invaluable to health care. This is where the laboratory research is translated to patient care. More healthcare practices are becoming involved with clinical research. Many healthcare providers are finding themselves involved with clinical research without having had much prior experience. This chapter provides an introduction to clinical research.

Clinical Investigations

J. Glenn Forister, MS, PA-C

THE CLINICAL RESEARCH PROCESS

Healthcare providers may be asked to participate in a clinical research study in the role of study coordinator. This request may come voluntarily, or the practice's administrators may mandate the role of designated study coordinator for the research project. Most clinical research studies are conducted in the same manner, whether it is a sponsored pharmaceutical, a medical-device study, or benchmark research from an academic institution. Whatever the setting, research processes are standard.

When conducting any type of clinical research, the most important aspects are (1) to ensure that the research participants have a complete understanding of the research study, and (2) to protect the participants at all times throughout the study. Specific guidelines, known as the *International Conference on Harmonisation of Technical Requirements for Registration of Pharmaceuticals for Human Use* (ICH) *Guidelines for Good Clinical Practices* (GCPs), maintains that every research participant will be completely informed of the study in which they are about to enter. Being completely informed means understanding the study expectations, potential risks and side effects, as well as how the research site and sponsor (and/or institution) will fully monitor their progress throughout the study. Because healthcare professionals of all types may be asked to assist with a research study in their practice (or even invited to be the study coordinator), the information in this chapter provide a general idea of what to expect when working with most clinical research studies.

Understanding the key personnel roles involved in a clinical research study is essential. A clinical research study will always identify a principal investigator, or PI. The PI is typically a physician who assumes total responsibility for the entire study. The PI is, therefore, responsible for the welfare of the study participants, that is, ensuring that study subjects have been properly informed, have given consent, and have met the study's inclusion and exclusion criteria. The PI also oversees any adverse events (AEs) and manages subsequent outcomes. The PI is also responsible for all of the personnel involved in the study: subinvestigators, study coordinator(s), medical technicians, practitioners, etc. The PI must ensure that each person involved is qualified to perform his or her designated role in the study. For instance, an inappropriate assignment of a study responsibility would have a medical assistant perform a physical exam on a research patient. Therefore, the role of the PI is a very serious responsibility. The PI always answers for any violations that occur at the research site or in the course of the study.

The PI may choose to designate a subinvestigator (sub-I) or coinvestigator, to help oversee the research study at the site. A sub-I is especially helpful when the research study is being conducted at several satellite clinic locations. The sub-I may be located at a different clinic than the PI and, therefore can assist in the follow-up of any research participants that are being seen at that particular clinic. Most sub-Is are physicians as well; however, other healthcare professionals or doctorly-trained researchers, such as PhDs or individuals with research degrees, can also serve in this role. Sub-Is typically hold some form of medical licensure, and this role involves responsibilities similar to those of the PI. However, the PI still retains the sole responsibility over the entire research study and research personnel, including the sub-Is.

The study coordinator is the central person in a research study and is highly involved in the research process. Most study coordinators are registered nurses. However, other healthcare professionals are being asked to assume the role of study coordinator in spite of their busy clinic schedules. The study coordinator's role is vital to the entire project. Most site personnel who are asked to be the study coordinator for a clinical research study are often surprised at the amount of work (or additional work) that this role entails. The study coordinator's primary responsibilities include the following:

- Recruiting study subjects for the study
- Explaining the research study to the patient and answering any questions
- Reviewing and obtaining the patient's informed consent
- Ensuring that all of the study entry procedures have been conducted
- Reviewing the study's inclusion/exclusion criteria with the PI and/or sub-I to verify the patient's eligibility
- Documenting the study visit information on the case report forms (CRFs), either transcribing the data onto paper CRFs or entering it electronically on e-CRFs
- Monitoring the patient's safety and well-being throughout the study by recording any adverse events, (AEs) unanticipated adverse events (UAEs), or serious adverse events (SAEs)
- Dispensing, tracking, and storing any study medication or investigational medical device
- Accommodating the sponsor's monitoring visits

If the site does not utilize separate personnel to oversee the regulatory documents (e.g., IRB submissions and approvals, continuing study renewals, UAE/SAE reporting, etc.), then the study coordinator will assume these responsibilities as well.

Another important role in a clinical research study is the clinical research associate (CRA), also known as the study monitor. The CRA is employed by the sponsor or the sponsor-delegated contract research organization, or the CRA is an employee of the academic institution. The CRA's primary duty is to conduct on-site visits, or "audits," to ensure that the research participants are eligible to participate in the study, are fully protected from harm, and that they are being treated with the utmost care. The CRA also ensures that the site is conducting the research study in compliance with the approved protocol, FDA Code of Federal Regulations, and IRB regulations by training the study personnel during the study start-up ("site initiation") phase. They also reinforce protocol training and regulatory guidance throughout the study. While on-site, the CRA will examine all of the research participants' medical records as it pertains to the study and review the study CRFs (either paper or electronic) to ensure all data have been captured correctly. The CRA works closely with the study coordinator to correct any data errors and to resolve any data queries during and after the visit. The CRA usually meets with the PI and/or sub-I to review any issues that were uncovered during the visit. Depending on the type of study and current study status, the CRA may visit a site as often as every four weeks to as rarely as once a year. CRA visits can add an additional layer of work and may seem incredibly burdensome for the study coordinator. However, these visits are completely necessary for the study participants' safety and well-being as well as the overall success of the study.

Written Consent

Once the research site has received IRB approval to begin the study, the site can begin screening and enrolling participants. The first step is to always obtain written informed consent from the patient prior to conducting any study-related procedures. Any designated study personnel can conduct the informed consent process with the potential participant. However, the person conducting the informed consent process must be properly trained in how to conduct the process, as well as be knowledgeable in every aspect of the protocol. The site is responsible per the ICH E6 Guidelines and FDA Code of Federal Regulations (21 CFR 50) for documenting the informed consent process in the patient's study file. The process entails (1) allowing the research participant adequate time to read and review the

informed consent, (2) discussing the study in detail with the patient, (3) allowing the patient to ask questions and answer any questions to their satisfaction, (4) witnessing the participant's signature/date by co-signing and dating the form, and (5) providing a copy of the informed consent form to the patient while filing the original version in the patient's study file. Additionally, most informed consent procedures include a separate informed consent form regarding the patient's rights that stem from the Health Insurance Portability and Accountability Act of 1996 (HIPAA). The HIPAA section or separate consent form requires the patient to provide his or her signature of approval for the release of medical records and information for the study sponsor or any regulatory agency auditing the study.

Meeting Inclusion and/or Exclusion Criteria

Once the patients' informed consent has been obtained, the study coordinator can then begin to "screen" each potential study participant, performing the baseline visit procedures to determine whether the patient meets the inclusion/exclusion criteria for the study. The FDA Code of Federal Regulations and the ICH Guidelines explicitly warn against "prequalifying" a patient for a research study (refer to 21 CFR 50 and ICH E6 Guidelines). A site cannot perform any study-related procedures on a potential research candidate prior to obtaining that participant's informed consent. For instance, if the study requires certain lab results or an EKG to be performed to determine eligibility, the research site cannot first draw STAT lab values or perform the EKG, to determine whether the results comply with the inclusion criteria, and subsequently enroll the patient in the study. Therefore, the site must obtain the patient's full written consent before determining eligibility. However, some research protocols will allow potential study subjects to be prescreened or prequalified to determine study eligibility. In this case, a designated "Pre-Screen Informed Consent Form," completely separate from the Informed Consent Form for the main portion of the study, is provided. This form must be approved by the IRB before being utilized with any potential patient. The Pre-Screen Informed Consent Form describes pre-screening procedures the patient will encounter in detail, and this form clearly states that the patient will be undergoing "pre-screening" for the study to determine eligibility. Whether pre-screening or screening, an emphasis must be placed on obtaining the patient's consent in writing. "Verbal" consent is not allowed in a clinical research study and would be in direct violation of the federal regulations.

Baseline Visit

Baseline visit procedures can vary greatly to determine whether a patient is eligible to participate in a study. Baseline visit procedures typically consist of a medical history, physical exam, and routine lab work. Depending on the study, baseline visit procedures can also consist of a variety of other diagnostic tests. The study coordinator may already have a good idea that the patient is likely to qualify to be enrolled in the study. However, the study coordinator must wait until all of the procedures have been performed and the results obtained to determine eligibility. Once all of the data is available, the next step is to determine whether the patient has met the inclusion and exclusion criteria. To be eligible to participate in a research study, a patient must meet *ALL* of the inclusion criteria and *NONE* of the exclusion criteria. If the patient meets just *one* of the exclusion criteria, then the patient is excluded from participating in the study.

During a monitoring visit, the CRA ensures that study subjects were properly enrolled in the study by verifying whether the patient met the inclusion/exclusion criteria. The CRA performs a detailed audit of the study subjects' medical records, paying close attention to the baseline visit procedures that were performed to determine eligibility. If the patient meets all of the inclusion criteria and none of the exclusion criteria, then the patient is determined eligible to participate in the study and, therefore, can continue forward to the next phase. However, if the study's entrance criteria are not met, then the patient is considered a "screen

failure" and is immediately withdrawn from further participation in the study. Properly determining study eligibility is as important as the informed consent process. The sponsor, IRB, and FDA always scrutinize these two processes because of the importance these processes place on the patient's direct health and safety. Research participants must be protected and well-informed of their study status at all times during a clinical study.

Randomization

After determining study eligibility, the next typical phase in a clinical research study is the "randomization" phase. The randomization phase determines which study participant will receive the investigational drug or device, and which participant will receive the "placebo" or "control." However, not all research studies involve a randomization phase. For instance, some medical device studies do not randomize the participants because the study plan is to have each participant receive some degree of exposure to the investigational medical device. In turn, these study subjects are often considered their own form of "control" (i.e., Did the device work for them or not?). With some research studies, the study design can become quite complex regarding the randomization scheme. The sponsor or research institution may want all of the research participants to be exposed to the product being investigated at some point in the study. Therefore, randomization "cross-over" schemes are often included in the protocol, where study subjects are randomized to either the placebo or active/investigational product group initially and then are crossed over to the opposite group after a certain period of time. From the study coordinator's perspective, ensuring that the randomization has been performed correctly for each patient is another crucial step in the research process.

Follow-up

Following the randomization phase—or baseline visit if no randomization is planned—the research participants usually begin the follow-up visits for the study. The follow-up visit procedures may appear very similar to the baseline visit procedures. The same lab work, x-rays, EKGs, physical exams, and patient questionnaires may be repeated to some extent during these follow-up visits. Once again, it is the study coordinator's job to ensure that all of the follow-up study visit procedures are being conducted. As the first person to receive and review these results, the study coordinator must also be vigilant about the study exam results and/or data generated from these visits. During the follow-up visits, any trends or discrepancies in the patients' results can be detected. For instance, if several of the research participants' lab results indicate that their liver enzymes are abnormally high and are becoming increasingly higher as the study progresses, then the study coordinator can alert the PI and sub-I(s) regarding this trend. Together, the research team can alert the sponsor or the research institution's medical advisor. Therefore, the study coordinator is the protective "watchdog" over the research participants' health and safety.

Adverse Events

The scenario mentioned above regarding the abnormally increasing liver enzymes is an example of an "adverse event" (AE). The amount and severity of AEs most often determine whether an investigational drug or device application will be submitted to the FDA for approval. Most pharmaceutical and medical device sponsors, as well as research institutions, require capture, report, and documentation of AEs to some extent in their research studies. The approved study protocol describes the extent to which AEs will be documented for that particular study. The ICH E6 Guidelines for Good Clinical Practice (and similarly Code of Federal Regulations 21 CFR 310.305) define an adverse event as

. . . any untoward medical occurrence in a patient or clinical investigation subject administered a pharmaceutical product and that does not necessarily have a causal relationship with this treatment. An AE can, therefore, be any unfavorable and unintended sign (including an abnormal laboratory finding), symp-

tom, or disease temporally associated with the use of a medicinal (investigational) product, whether or not related to the medicinal (investigational) product.

For example, if a patient returns for the three-month follow-up visit and reports to the study coordinator that they have had the flu for the past four days, this experience is considered an AE. Another type of AE that can occur in a research study is known as a serious adverse event (SAE). The ICH E6 Guidelines for Good Clinical Practice (and similarly Code of Federal Regulations 21 CFR 312.32) define an SAE as

. . . any untoward medical occurrence that at any dose:

- Results in death
- Is life threatening
- Requires inpatient hospitalization or prolongation of existing hospitalization
- Results in persistent or significant disability/incapacity
- Is a congenital anomaly/birth defect.

Serious adverse events must be reported immediately to the sponsor or research institution responsible for the study. The research site must report the SAE as soon as they become aware of the event, no longer than 24 hours from the time the event was initially registered. The sponsor or academic research institution will request that the research team obtain all available information surrounding the event (e.g., hospital records from admission to discharge or the death certificate). The process of collecting, documenting, and reporting AEs and SAEs is much more involved than this chapter covers. Generally, the sponsor review the data collection and reporting requirements in depth with the research site personnel during study start-up.

Study Termination

The final phase of a research study is study completion, or study termination. Research participants who completed all of the required follow-up visits are then dismissed from the study. The procedures for the exit visit can be as extensive as the baseline visit procedures. The research team wants to obtain as much data as possible during this visit, knowing that this visit is the last opportunity to collect any additional lab work, EKG's, x-rays, and/or patient questionnaires. Research subjects who have completed the study are rarely asked to come back and complete extra study visits to provide additional information. Study subjects can be withdrawn early, or undergo "early termination," from a research study. The protocol usually provides guidelines and/or potential reasons for a patient's early termination, or early withdrawal, from the study. The most common reason is the patient no longer wishes to continue participating in the study and, therefore, voluntarily withdraws consent. Other reasons why a patient may be early exited from a study include the following:

- Patient is unwilling or unable to cooperate with study visits or procedures
- Patient has experienced an AE or SAE
- Patient relocates to a different area from where the research is being conducted
- Patient is lost to follow-up (i.e., patient misses study visits and site is unable to contact the patient by phone, email, or certified mail)

IRBs most often want to know the reason(s) why a patient was withdrawn early from the study and, therefore, they require the research team to document this information in the study records. At first glance, a research team may feel that conducting a clinical research study appears to be rather easy. However, most clinicians have never participated in a clinical research project. Therefore, they may be unaware of the significant amount of extra time and effort required. A study adds additional demands and responsibilities to the clinic's normal operations. On the other hand, participating in a clinical research project, or being asked to fulfill a specific role in one, can be a rewarding experience. Becoming involved in a clinical research project, either as a PI, sub-I, or study coordinator, puts practitioners on the cutting edge of a new drug, device, or procedure that could ultimately make a difference in the lives of many patients.

PHASES OF CLINICAL RESEARCH

Clinical research is most often performed to determine the safety and efficacy of a new drug or medical device and/or a new indication for either. Conducting clinical research on a new drug or medical device is extremely expensive. Most pharmaceutical and medical device sponsors spend millions of dollars attempting to receive approval for a single drug or device. The process of developing a new drug or device, conducting clinical research trials, and submitting an application to the FDA, typically takes an approximately ten years, with most new drugs or devices never receiving FDA approval.

Clinical research trials involve four phases. Each phase is critical to the overall approval and success of a new drug or medical device. Furthermore, a clinical trial can be halted at any time and during any phase if too many adverse side effects or SAEs are occurring with the research participants.

Prior to phase I trials, preclinical studies are generally conducted on animals to determine whether the new drug or device will be effective. Phase I clinical trials are the initial studies performed to determine the metabolism and pharmacokinetics of a drug (or a device) in humans. Phase I clinical trials are, therefore, considered "first-in-human" research studies. These studies are conducted on a small number of healthy participants (20–100) for short period of time, usually for a few days to one month. Data regarding side-effects associated with increasing doses and evidence of investigational product effectiveness is collected. Phase I studies are used to determine the maximum safe dose that can be tolerated and establishes toxicity.

Once the maximum safe dosage of an investigational product has been determined, the next step in the research trial process is to conduct a phase II clinical trial. A phase II clinical trial is a randomized, controlled study conducted to evaluate the effectiveness and therapeutic range of a drug (or a device) for a particular indication in patients with the disease or condition, as well as to determine common side effects and risks. Phase II research studies are longer than phase I studies, typically lasting a few months to one year. During phase II, study participants are randomized to receive either the investigational product or a placebo. Phase II studies also involve a larger numbers of research participants (100–300).

After conducting phase II studies, sponsors generally have an established idea of the therapeutic range of the investigational product as well as the expected side effects. Sponsors then conduct phase III clinical trials to introduce the investigational product to a mass number of participants (1,000–3,000). Phase III studies are expansive clinical trials usually conducted nationally (and even internationally) across multiple research sites. Phase III studies are usually randomized, controlled trials comparing the investigational product to a placebo. These trials can also be "open-label" as well, with the research participants and research team aware of who is receiving the investigational product and who is not. Phase III trials are conducted to gather additional information on the overall benefits and/or risks of the product or device being investigated; they also provide a basis for product labeling. Sponsors prepare to submit their new drug or device application to the FDA for approval at the conclusion of the phase III trials.

If the sponsor receives FDA approval for the new drug or device, then a phase IV clinical trial can be conducted. Phase IV trials are "post-marketing" trials that can either be voluntarily conducted by the investigator or mandated by the FDA as a stipulation for the new drug or device approval. Either way, phase IV clinical trials are conducted to obtain an even greater amount of safety and efficacy data in a massive number of individuals (i.e., even more than phase II). During phase IV studies, the new drug or device is available to be marketed to the public. Phase IV studies can provide additional information regarding risks, benefits, and optimal use that perhaps did not appear during the phase III studies. Because of the large number of participants and amount of data generated, the FDA recommends that more sponsored research involve phase IV clinical trials.

SUMMARY

The overall goal of clinical research is to safely translate laboratory research into applied clinical interventions. The process must be transparent and follow the established national and international guidelines for conducting research on human subjects. It is therefore important that all parties understand the purpose and process of the investigation. Each of the steps from IRB protocol approval to the exit visit helps to maintain the integrity of the study and ultimately the results.

REFERENCES

1. Woodlin KE, Schneider JC. *The CRA's guide to monitoring clinical research.* Boston: Thomson Centerwatch; 2003.

Websites Mentioned in this Chapter

ICH E6 Guidelines website, http://www.ich.org/products/guidelines/efficacy/article/efficacy-guidelines.html. Accessed March 21, 2011.
21 CFR Part 50 website, http://www.accessdata.fda.gov/scripts/cdrh/cfdocs/cfcfr/CFRsearch.cfm?CFRPart=50. Accessed March 21, 2011.
21 CFR Part 310 Web site, http://www.access.gpo.gov/nara/cfr/waisidx _03/21cfr310_03.html. Accessed March, 21, 2011.
21 CFR Part 312 website, http://www.accessdata.fda.gov/scripts/cdrh/cfdocs/cfcfr/cfrsearch.cfm?cfrpart =312. Accessed March 21, 2011.

Survey Research

J. Dennis Blessing, PhD, PA

CHAPTER OVERVIEW

Surveys are one of the most commonly used methods to gather information and data in the world. Surveys are used to gather information as important as the U.S. Census to the kind of dishwashing soap we use, our favorite movie, of whom we plan to vote for in the next election. Surveys can reveal trends, attitudes, opinions, lifestyles, needs, expectations, knowledge/information, behaviors, demographics, etc.; the list of uses is infinite. Surveys can be used in almost every aspect of our lives, and health care is no exception. A large amount of data from any number of people on a wide variety of subjects and issues can be gathered using surveys. Several formats are used to deliver and conduct surveys; they can be long or short, simple or complex. They can use words or symbols, require written responses or simple choices, or collect quantitative or qualitative data. Despite its somewhat eclectic nature, survey research must still conform to the exacting requirements of design and methodology to have true value, meaning, and impact.

This chapter presents the basic concepts of survey research, including design, item construction, data analysis, and conducting the research. Emphasis is placed on designing items and developing concepts that are valid to survey research in health care. A short discussion of sample size is presented. The use of surveys in research and practice environments will be included.

INTRODUCTION

What Surveys Can and Cannot Do

Surveys are used to gather almost any type of information: information on demographics, opinions, preferences, expectations, knowledge, and outcomes. They can be conducted by mail (including email), in person, via telephone, and through the Internet. Survey samples can be very specific for selected individuals, less specific for groups of individuals, or more general for general population. Sample subjects can be defined by almost any characteristic. Samples can be randomized or assigned, stratified or open, well defined or ill defined, or a sample of convenience. As shown in **Table 10–1**, surveys have several advantages for data collection; they can be a relatively easy, inexpensive, fast, and consistent research tool.

As shown in **Table 10–2**, surveys can pose some disadvantages. One major disadvantage is difficulty in establishing causality.[1] Causality involves manipulating a variable and determining the effect on another variable. This is very difficult to do with a one-time survey. However, well-designed surveys can be effectively used as preintervention and postintervention assessment tools in experimental and quasi-experimental designs.

Other challenges associated with surveys revolve around reliability of respondent self-reporting, respondent interpretation of

Table 10–1 Some General Advantages of Surveys

Advantage	Reasoning
Costs	Relatively low cost, but depends on survey and methodology
Sample size	Can vary from small to extremely large; can be targeted
Issues	Can gather information on single or multiple issues or topics
Format	Can vary; mail, internet, interview, telephone
Impact	Can yield very influential results

survey items, extrapolation of results to a population, nonrespondent influence, and respondent bias. While these challenges to survey research cannot be completely avoided, good design and item construction should help to limit the impact and influence on outcomes of such problems.

Table 10–2 Some General Disadvantages of Surveys

Disadvantage	Reason
Respondent self report	There is no way to ensure individuals will respond to surveys or choose to participate.
Respondent interpretation	There is a risk that respondents will interpret survey items in a manner different from investigator intent.
Respondent bias	There is a risk that people who choose to respond may be different from the population being studied.
Extrapolation to nonresponders	Can the response of a few be extrapolated to the population? Can the data be generalized?
Item bias	Is there bias in the way an item is worded?

Types of Surveys

As shown in **Table 10–3**, surveys are delivered in different formats. The choice of delivery format (distribution) is part of the methodology and research design. Each format has advantages and disadvantages. The research purpose(s), study population, and sample size are factors that must be considered in the decision on the survey delivery. Surveys can be conducted by mail, telephone, internet, and interview.

Most of this chapter will concentrate on Web-based surveys and those delivered by mail. The construction of the survey itself in each case is very similar. Many Web-based surveys and paper surveys are delivered by email. Internet surveys are becoming the standard format for surveys, if not the standard. Telephone and interview surveys are briefly discussed.

Planning Is Key

Performing a survey investigation or study is more than thinking up some questions, putting them on paper, and sending them out. The meticulous planning required is just as important for surveys as for any other type of research effort. One of the first steps is to define what is to be achieved in the study. Not much can be accomplished beyond a literature review until the study goals are conceptualized and what is to be achieved and learned are defined. Once the goals and objectives of the project are defined, everything that follows will reflect the research effort. This planning generates the research questions, hypotheses, or null hypotheses.

Web-Based Surveys

Web-based surveys are likely the most common method used to gather data on healthcare professionals today. Typically, the survey is distributed by email notification that contains a URL for the survey. This format is rapidly becoming (or has become) the norm. Two key advantages to Web-based surveys are (1) that the sample size can be

Table 10–3 Comparison of Survey Methods

Characteristic	Mail	Telephone	Interview	Internet
Cost	Relatively low	Low to moderate, depends on local vs. long distance	Relatively high	Variable
Cost examples	Printing, postage	Telephone costs, personnel training, and expense to conduct interview	Personnel training and expense to conduct interview	Professional help with web design
Response rate	Potentially low	Dependent on willingness of subject to participate	Relatively high; only willing subjects are interviewed	Variable, but instant; respondents must have computer
Investigator time	Relatively limited	Requires training of interviewers and/or conduct of interviews	Requires training of interviewers and/or conduct of interviews	Relatively limited
Respondent time	Completed as convenient	Telephone time	Interview time	Completed as convenient
Study time	Relative long; must allow for mail and response times	Relatively short, but subject contact time may be long	Relatively short, but subject contact time may be long	Relatively short, dependent on subject time to respond
Anonymity	Survey form can be completely anonymous	Phone number is known	Person to person interaction	Web address can be identified
Sample size	Can be very large	Usually small to medium	Limited, usually small	Can be very large
Respondent bias	Respondent item interpretation	Interviewer influence by voice	Interviewer influence is high	Must be computer literate
Investigator bias	Generally very limited except for item construction	Voice influence; interpretation of survey items	Influence by voice, facial expression, body movement; interpretation of survey items	Generally very limited except for item construction
Other	Requires mailing lists	Multiple interviewers conducting survey	Multiple interviewers conducting survey	Computer access

large and dispersed and (2) that a large amount of data can be collected. Another advantage of Web-based surveys is that results can be downloaded to a database, eliminating data entry and its associated errors. Major limitations of email-distributed surveys are the potential for a low response rate and respondent misinterpretation of items. In ad-

dition, the target sample or population must have a computer. **Table 10–4** lists some of the positives and negatives of email surveys.

Response rates are a threat to any survey. Generally, response rates tend to be low, particularly when used without a well-defined target population or sample. Here are some helpful guidelines

Table 10–4 Aspects of Email Surveys

Aspect	Comment
Cost	Low; data entry may be costly
Personnel	Investigators only; requires no training of interviewers or field workers
Sample size	Can be very large; can be general or to a specific population set; can be geographically wide or distant from investigator; requires a name and email address
Response rates	Potentially low; a response rate greater than 30 percent is rare[1]
Data	Potential for quantity, but quality is limited by respondent interpretation of survey items; only survey item data can be collected
Bias	Relies on respondent interpretation of survey items; nonrespondent bias is high
Subjects	Not under pressure to respond; less intrusive than person-to-person contact

for surveys of health professionals, students, and educators.

1. An introductory statement (cover letter if using regular mail) should accompany the survey. A personal salutation should be used if the subject is known to the investigator. Otherwise Mr., Ms., Mrs., or a professional title such as Dr. should be used.
2. The survey instrument must be well designed in its content (items) and visually appealing.
3. A respondent should be able to complete the survey in a short period of time. The longer it takes to complete the survey, the less likely that it will be completed.
4. Some sort of inducement or gift may be included. However, this adds to the study expense, and there is no guarantee that response rate will be increased.[1]
5. A follow-up request may spur some respondents. An email reminder may suffice.

With regard to the form and format of an email survey, these additional suggestions may be helpful.

1. Begin with interesting questions.
2. Use graphics and various question-writing techniques to ease the task of reading and answering the questions.
3. Use capital or dark letters for readability.
4. Limit the length of the survey.
5. Send notices and reminders at carefully spaced times.

   - Notice by email that a survey is coming
   - Email with the survey attached
   - A reminder
   - A second reminder (optional)

6. If an identifier is used, explain that it is for recordkeeping only and that the respondent's confidentiality is protected.

Much literature on survey research is available. A literature or Web search or text purchase will help to develop and guide the survey research skills of the investigator.

Survey Introduction

The introduction to a survey is accomplished in two ways. First, the introductory information is presented on page 1 at the beginning of the survey. In addition, introductory information is included in the email or as a cover letter in conventional mail. Regardless of the manner of the introduction, certain basic points must be included. A well-worded, informative introduction (or cover letter) helps to increase the response rate. If the subject understands the purpose and need for their input or information, they are more likely to respond.[1]

The key points for an effective introduction or cover letter are summarized in **Table 10–5** and **Table 10–6**. A well-written and informative introduction or cover letter may induce subjects to participate by appealing to their sense of responsibility and the importance of their information or input. The statement or letter should be concise, well written, informative, and easy to understand, as exemplified in **Exhibit 10–1.** The level of wording, grammar, and writing style should fit

Table 10–5 Key Points for the Introductory Statement or Cover Letter

Key Point	Example
Who you are	Describe yourself and/or organization and/or business in the opening paragraph
Background for study	In our practice, we have been using an appointment system . . .
Purpose of the study	We want to learn . . .
What will be done with the data	The information you provide will help us to . . .
Why they were chosen	We are asking you to take part because . . .
Assurance of confidentiality	You do not have to identify yourself in any way . . . All information will be reported in aggregate. All responses will be coded for study purposes.
What respondents need to do	Please take a few minutes to complete the survey. Please follow the instructions for each question.
Who respondents can contact if they have questions	If you have any questions or concerns, please contact . . .
Approvals for the survey, if applicable	This study has been approved by the Institutional Review Board of . . .
Return deadlines	If possible, please return the survey by . . .
Statement of importance	The information you provide will be helpful in determining . . .
Acknowledge support	This study is supported by a grant from . . . This study is being conducted for ABC, Inc.
Statement of appreciation	We greatly appreciate your help in this matter and for taking the time to . . .
Closing	Sincerely, Your name, degree, titles
Signature	Co-investigators, degree, title

Table 10–6 Construction of a Hard Copy Cover Letter

Construction Point	Explanation
Limit to one page	The longer the letter is, the less likely it is to be read completely.
Use common block format with a readable font, e.g., Times New Roman, font 12.	Script, serif, calligraphy, etc. are hard to read.
White or beige or light gray paper, black print	Reading ease; visually pleasing
Common language	Readability and ease of understanding are key

the subjects to be surveyed. Unless you are dealing with highly educated professional people, the introduction statement (like newspapers) should target an audience with middle school reading ability.

Proofreading and editing are essential. It is a good idea to have individuals read and interpret the introduction who are not part of the investigation or who may be representative of the subject sample. One way to achieve this is to include the introductory statement in any prestudy evaluations or pretests of the survey instrument and pilot studies.

Follow-Up

Follow-up notices or reminders to complete and return surveys may aid to increase responses. A follow-up email, letter or postcard can be used. Be aware of

---

Exhibit 10–1 Example of an Introductory Statement from the Author's Research

---

Dear [Participant],

I invite you to participate in an survey on the importance of ranking health professions programs. You may access this survey by "clicking" on the URL below. You were selected to participate in this investigation by random selection from your professional organization's membership list. You do not have to identify yourself in any manner. Results will be reported in aggregate form. This is the first investigation on the opinion of health professionals on the ranking of educational programs. Your input will guide us in recommendations to the public and organizations. This investigation was approved as exempt by the IRB of State University. Please contact me at the address below if you have any questions.

Thank you,

J. D. Blessing

---

reminders of surveys that deal with sensitive or very private information. For example, an investigator is studying the rate of sexually transmitted diseases (STDs) in corporate executives who travel frequently. Any reminder must be private. Good wording for such a reminder is "This is to remind you to take a few minutes to complete and return the survey we recently sent you." In the follow-up, add or use language that will encourage a response, such as, "Your opinion is very valuable to us, and we want to include your input in our study." The wording of reminders should be general and neutral to encourage survey return or completion. Do not threaten or even appear to be negative. For example, do not say, "If you do not complete and return the survey, no one will care what you think or know about STDs."

A follow-up or reminder should have enough information for the recipient to identify the survey. Alternately, the survey (or link to the survey) can be re-sent with the survey reminder note. How many reminders to send and when to send them should be part of the decision making that is done in the methodology planning for the research project. While there are no hard-and-fast rules for follow-ups, 10 to 14 days is usually reasonable. Subsequent reminders can be sent at 4 weeks. More than two reminders is probably a waste of time.

Follow-up reminders can be done in several ways. One way is to send a reminder to everyone who was sent a survey. The other way is more economical if surveys have identification codes. If the survey is coded, the investigator can identify who has returned a survey and send follow-up reminders only to those subjects who have not responded. An explanation must be done for any codes that appear on a survey or a reminder. Subjects should be informed about what the number is and how it is used. Remember, if some type of code is used, the respondents are not anonymous, but their information is kept confidential. **Exhibit 10–2** is an example of a reminder message used by the author.

Internet Surveys

An obvious advantage of Internet surveys is that they can incorporate attractive photographs and illustrations in color that are difficult to reproduce in print. An Internet survey can be longer without increasing the costs of delivery. In fact, the cost of administering an Internet survey is the hosting fee and is not dependent on the amount of activity at the site. A number of commercial Internet companies design surveys and help with data collection. Typically, these sites are user-friendly and economical if the investigator does not have the time, skill, or tools to develop their own Internet surveys. Intuitively, it would seem that Internet surveys are more cost-efficient, but some analyses bring this into question.[3] However, Internet surveys are associated with certain advantages:

1. Data are immediately available when the respondent submits the survey.
2. Results can be loaded directly into a database for analysis.

Exhibit 10–2 Example of a Reminder via Email or Post

REMINDER

A few weeks ago you received a "Learning Assessment Survey" from me. It was distributed through your program via email. If you have not completed the survey, please take a few minutes to do so and hit the submit button. If you need the survey site, please contact me. The information you provide through this survey will be helpful to me in my study of how students learn and, hopefully, to education in the future.

Thank you for your time.

Dennis Blessing, State University
(123) 555-9876

---

3. High-quality graphics and great detail can be used.
4. Respondents can be "skipped to" appropriate items based on responses.
5. Statistical analysis is facilitated because data is in a format for analysis.

Of course, one significant disadvantage of Internet surveys is that respondents must have a computer. One 2002 report stated that 70 percent of adults have access to a computer.[4] One limiting factor is that computer owners tend to be younger adults (less than age 54). Therefore, a consideration in using the Internet in survey research is the demographics of the study population. Sampling may also be a problem because access to Internet addresses or some form of notification is required to facilitate subjects to "log on" to an Internet survey. Email may be one way to contact subjects and provide a URL to a survey, or subjects may have to be contacted by direct mail. Whether or not response rates are higher with Internet surveys is open to question, and evaluations of Internet survey responses are mixed.[3] The Internet and computer skills of the investigator may affect overall costs.

Telephone Surveys

Political parties and pollsters seem to love telephone surveys, particularly near election time. Interviewing by telephone can provide very timely information. **Table 10–7** presents some key aspects of telephone interviewing as a survey format.

Table 10–7 Aspects of Telephone Surveys

Aspect	Comment
Cost	Actual telephone costs, such as long distance Training costs of interviewers Interviewer time costs
Personnel	May require multiple interviewers Interviewers can telephone from one location Skilled interviewers get better and more complete responses
Sample size	Subjects must have a telephone Size determined by investigator and funding Can be large Can be geographically dispersed
Response rates	Vary, due to willingness of subjects Timing of call may influence willingness of respondent to participate
Data	Potential for moderate amount and quality of data based on number of subject willing to participate
Bias	Interviewer's manner, voice inflections, interpretation of survey items may influence subject responses
Time	Study can be conducted over a short period of time Responses are immediately available

One obvious limitation of this method is that subjects must have a telephone. Telephone interviews allow for some personal contact between the respondent and the interviewer while maintaining a moderate level of anonymity. This may be very valuable when dealing with sensitive or personal information. Speaking directly with a subject allows the interviewer (or investigator) to interpret survey items, to move through a survey based on responses, and to clarify responses. Cost may be a major factor in telephone surveys because interviewers often must be trained and paid. Telephone costs increase if long distance is needed or if a large number of subjects must be contacted. The "annoyance factor" must be considered. Individuals may not want to be called or to have their routines interrupted by the phone ringing. The length of time a respondent will be on the phone will influence their response. The longer the subject is on the phone, the more likely are to hang up.[1]

An investigator must also consider the type of responses that will be allowed in a telephone interview. Are subjects asked to respond to specific choices or are they allowed to respond in an unrestricted manner? Response recording must also be considered, particularly with open-ended questions. Quantifying open-ended responses may present some analysis difficulties.

Personal Interview Surveys

Person-to-person, face-to-face interviewing has a number of advantages and disadvantages (**Table 10–8**). Interviews must occur where people are (e.g., in the office, at the mall, hospital room, patient's home, etc.) or where they go (e.g., an office or clinic). Special sites can be utilized, but something must entice the subject/respondent to travel to a special site. If a special site is used for the survey, specific scheduled appointments for the interview may work best. Person-to-person interviewing requires that contact occur between the subject and the investigator or interviewer.

Unlike a telephone respondent, who can be influenced by the interviewer's voice, a personal interview respondent can be influenced by the physical

Table 10–8 Aspects of Personal Interviewer Surveys

Aspect	Comment
Cost	High; takes time and people
Personnel	Requires training
Sample size	Tends to be relatively small because of time needed to conduct interviews
Response rates	Can be high once respondents agree to be interviewed; face-to-face encounters may improve or facilitate response and allow for clarification of responses
Data	Varied, time may limit amount
Bias	Interviewer bias
Time	Training and interviews take time

being and bearing of the interviewer and the site of the interview. In addition to voice inflections, facial and body movements may influence responses. The interviewer's personality and animation has influence. For these reasons, interviewer training may need to be more exact and extensive, and supervision of interviewers may be required. Interviewer bias may be high. The time needed to train interviewers and the required time for interviews are always factors to consider in telephone and personal interviews, study methodology, and costs.

Interviews can be used to collect qualitative and quantitative data. They can allow for greater exploration of subject responses and can add detail that may help interpret or understand responses. Certainly, if a product is being investigated, subjects can see and handle the product. The types of allowed responses must be considered in a personal interview process. How responses are handled is something that should be planned for as part of the methodology. A decision on responses should not (cannot?) be made after data collection.

Survey Item Construction

Survey items must provide data that answer the research questions, hypotheses, or null-hypotheses.

Table 10–9 Definitions

Type	Definition	Example
Null-hypothesis[5]	A negatively worded statement about the relationship among or between variables. It does not necessarily mean or refer to zero or no difference, but provides a hypothesis that is "rejected" or "accepted."	There is no difference in 5-year myocardial infarct rates between angina patients treated with a CCB and those treated with a beta-blocker.
Hypothesis[5]	A statement about the relationship among or between variables. This statement may be a conjecture or prediction of a relationship or outcome.	Patients with angina who are treated with a CCB will have a lower number of myocardial infarctions after 5 years than patients treated with a beta-blockers.
Research Question	Similar to a hypothesis, but is constructed as a question.	Will angina patients treated with a CCB have less myocardial infarctions than patients treated with a beta-blocker?

Before any survey is constructed, much less applied, the purposes of the study must be defined. Generally, the best format for defining and guiding survey research is to use research question(s) or hypotheses as outlined in **Table 10–9**. This does not exclude use of null-hypotheses.

Without a well-developed and defined research question, hypothesis, or null-hypothesis, a well-designed survey cannot be developed. As a survey item is constructed, the investigator must ask, "How does the information or data gathered by this item help me answer my research question or hypothesis, or null-hypothesis?" If the survey item does not provide part of the answer to the research question, it is not needed.

Demographic Data

Surveys almost always collect some type of demographic data. In many instances, the demographic data provides the basis for comparison groups. Some common types of demographic data are age, gender, occupation, education, etc. For healthcare professionals, some types of demographic data are practice location, practice specialty, length of time in practice, number of patients seen, procedures performed, etc. Demographic data is the information that describes or characterizes the subject or sample or population in some way. Demographics often strengthen the extrapolation of a sample result to a population by demonstrating how similar the sample is to the population. Most demographic data comprise nominal data. In the past, demographic information was usually collected at the beginning of the survey, but there is no reason that it cannot be collected at the end. In an interview setting, it may be best to get to the heart of the survey first and save the routine demographics for the end.

Demographic survey items should be straightforward questions about the information sought. Here are some examples:

1. What is your gender?
2. What is your age?
3. What degree did you receive from your program?
4. What is your practice specialty?
5. How long have you been in practice?

When constructing these survey items, a direct response is probably better than using a range as a choice. An example is age. You may want to group respondents by age, but it is better to have each respondent give their exact age and then group the responses if that method fits the project needs. **Box 10–1** gives an example.

Box 10–1 Example: Age Demographic Questions

What is your age in years? _____

vs.

What is your age group in years?

A. 21–25

B. 26–30

C. 31–35

D. 36–40

E. >40

When collecting sensitive or private information, it may better to group responses. One example is the salary demographic. Respondents may be more willing to provide salary data in a range rather than their exact salary. This provides some degree of privacy. It may also be useful when respondents cannot recall information precisely, as shown in the example in **Box 10–2**.

Some points to remember when gathering demographic data are these:

1. Be specific with the statements or questions. Specify the unit of measure. For example, if time related information is sought, specify that time interval in weeks, days, months, or years.
2. When using ranges, make sure they do not overlap; this could lead to confusion. Using

---

Box 10–2 Example: Salary Question

What is your annual salary? _____

versus

What is your annual salary?

A. <$25,000

B. $25,000–49,999

C. $50,000–74,999

D. >$75,000

Box 10–3 Example: Unclear Salary Question

What is your annual salary?

A. $50,000 or less

B. $50,000–60,000

C. $60,000–70,000

D. $70,000–80,000

E. $80,000 or more

---

salary as an example, how can a respondent accurately answer the question shown in **Box 10–3**, when the options overlap?

3. Avoid asking for the same data in more than one statement or question.
4. Use short, to-the-point, but understandable statements or questions.
5. Ask only for information that is relevant to the study. The construct of a survey item should make clear to the respondent why a piece of data is needed for the investigation. Do not be overly invasive unless the data is key to the project.

The Survey Instrument

The heart of the survey consists of items that provide the data for the investigation. The construct of these items influences respondent rates, willingness to answer, and quality of the data for analysis. Survey items that provide unequivocal data help ensure reliability and validity. *Survey items must be short, clear, exact, understandable, and answerable.* Items must be designed to provide the data needed to answer the research questions, hypotheses, or null-hypotheses. An investigator must decide on a format for the survey items and questions. However, it is not unusual for surveys to include a variety of item formats.

First Things First

Developing survey items is a process that goes from very general to very specific. One way to start is to sit down and write down every possible question even remotely related to the investigation. This brainstorming approach helps develop a list of considerations for the survey. This list does not have to be neat, orderly, grammatically correct, or even very specific; it is the beginning of the critical thinking for the development and building of the survey. A brainstorming list is often very expansive and far longer than the final product. Team members and colleagues can provide valuable assistance at this stage. Seek consultation on ideas and specific points, if needed. Good research surveys are rarely the result of one person's efforts!

Once general thoughts have been recorded, the investigator can begin to edit, define, delete, combine, categorize, and develop the specific survey items. The process of refining the survey and its items is often a long process, always aimed toward improving the survey. While there is always room for improvement, at some point development has to stop and the survey must be finalized before it is administered. One question that may help decide when a survey is ready is, "Does each survey item reflect some aspect of the answer to the research question?"

Item Format

The format of survey items is dependent on the information sought. There are two basic forms of survey items: structured and unstructured (or open-ended).[1] Some examples of "open-ended" questions are listed in **Box 10–4**.

These types of questions may remind healthcare professionals of the essay questions that everyone hated in school. Open-ended questions certainly have value, but they may be difficult to quantify or interpret. Structured survey items allow the investigator to control responses to a large degree as well as define the responses as values that are more statistically useful to the study. The formats of structured survey items are varied; examples are presented in **Table 10–10**.

The choice of format depends on the data sought. When constructing the survey items and the possible responses to those survey items, it is important to state whether or not more than one option can be selected. This prevents misunderstanding by the respondents. **Box 10–5** provides an example using activities related to earning continuing education units (CEUs).

Generally, ranking is a more robust method for obtaining meaningful results.

Table 10–10 More Examples of Survey Item Formats[1,2,7]

Item format	Example
List responses	A checklist of responses or multiple choices
Semantic differential scale	A scale defined by its extremes, with a range between the extremes
Comparison scale	Choice between two or more items
Visual analogue scale	Indicates the intensity of a subjective experience along a continuum
Picture scale	Series of pictures/drawings indicate a response; may be useful for children or people who cannot read
Forced ranking	All items in a list are ranked
Ranking versus Rating	Usually ranks items with each ranking value only used once Rating values may be repeated for different items

---

Box 10–4 Example: Open-Ended Questions

1. What do you think are the benchmarks for a quality medical practice?

2. What do you do to stay up-to-date for your practice?

3. What is the best way to deal with non-compliant patients?

Box 10–5 Example: Wording Format

What activity do you prefer for earning CEUs?

(Check all that apply.)

A. _____ Formal lectures

B. _____ Hands-on exercises

C. _____ On-the-job experiences or consultations

D. _____ Patient/case studies

E. _____ Seminars/expert panels

versus

What activity do you most prefer for earning CEUs?

(Check only one.)

A. _____ Formal lectures

B. _____ Hands-on exercises

C. _____ On-the-job experiences or consultations

D. _____ Patient/case studies

E. _____ Seminars/expert panels

Specific wording can be used in the item stem, as shown in **Box 10–6**. (The items in **Box 10–5** could be worded in this manner.)

In developing survey items, an investigator must try to eliminate interpretation errors as much as possible. Ultimately, no investigator can guess how respondents will interpret what is written or asked. It may be clear to the investigator, but not to the subjects. A pilot test helps reduce interpretation errors.

Box 10–6 Example: Alternate Wording

Check all the activities you prefer for earning CEUs.

vs.

Check the one activity you most prefer for earning CEUs.

Rankings

The ranking of responses is valuable in many cases. An example using the above material may resemble the example presented in **Box 10–7**.

In this case, the investigator ensures that the ranking numbers (1–5) are defined and specifies whether or not all items should be ranked. This example could state "Rank in order of preference those items you use to earn CEUs: 1 = most preferred, 5 = least preferred. Do not rank items you do not use." This may be a long statement, but it clarifies both what data is sought and what the respondent is to do. In some instances, it may be desirable to rate some items with the same value. Two examples of the rating approach are given in **Box 10–8** and **Box 10–9**.

In some instances a two-level question may serve as a better construct, where respondents indicate "preferred" items, then "rank" their "preferred" choices.

Ranking or rating systems should always be defined clearly. Using the number "1" is a common format for the most preferred or highest value, but sometimes a reverse rating (e.g., 5 as the most preferred to 1 as the least preferred) may be useful or desired. The instructions to the respondents must be very clear. The item format must be completely consistent. If more than one item format is used, group similar format items together. Not only

---

Box 10–7 Example: Ranking

Rank each activity in the order of your preferences for earning CEUs.

(1 = most preferred, 5 = least preferred)

Rank all items.

A. _____ Formal lectures

B. _____ Hands-on exercises

C. _____ On-the-job experiences or consultations

D. _____ Patient/case studies

E. _____ Seminars/expert panels

Box 10–8 Example: Rating

Rate the value to you of each of the following CEU delivery formats.

(Rate all)

1 = Preferred, 2 = Acceptable, 3 = Not preferred

_____ A. Lecture

_____ B. Workshop

_____ C. Video

_____ D. Computer program

_____ E. Monographs

Box 10–10 The Likert Scale

1. Strongly agree

2. Agree

3. Neutral

4. Disagree

5. Strongly disagree

---

is this space-efficient, it will also help in survey presentation. It will also be less likely to confuse respondents.

The Likert and Verbal Frequency Scales

Verbal frequency scales are very common tools in survey research. One of the most common types of verbal frequency scales is the Likert Scale (pronounced Lick Ert). This is an "ordinal" scale used to gather information about respondent's opinions or positions on the subject under investiga-

tion. The true Likert Scale uses the values shown in **Box 10–10**.

The descriptors can be reversed where descriptor "1" is *strongly disagree* to "5" *strongly agree*. Remember, the number does not matter because this is "ordinal" data, not continuous data. However, these types of scales are often treated as interval data in large samples with normal distributions. Analysis by parametric tests may be misleading. A statistician should be consulted with regard to handling ordinal data as continuous data. Investigators sometimes use a scale similar to this one, but with different descriptors or an increase in the number of descriptors. In these cases, the scale should be termed a "Likert-like scale" or, more accurately, a "verbal frequency scale."[1] An example of a verbal frequency scale with regard to angiotensin-converting enzyme (ACE) inhibitors used for treatment of high blood pressure is given in **Box 10–11**.

Regardless of the descriptors used, verbal frequency scales are very powerful and popular

---

Box 10–9 Example: Alternate Ranking

Rank the value of each of the following CEU delivery formats.

Rank all items 1–5, with 1 being the most valuable to 5 being the least valuable.

_____ Lecture

_____ Workshop

_____ Video

_____ Computer program

_____ Monographs

Box 10–11 Example: Verbal Frequency Scale

How often are ACE inhibitors given as the first drug in hypertension therapy?

A. Always

B. Often

C. Occasionally

D. Infrequently

E. Never

Table 10–11 The Likert and Verbal Frequency Scales: Keys for Their Successful Use

---

Key

Be clear in the instructions.

Use direct statements.

Avoid redundancy.

Address one element in each item.

Group survey items in sets of 5–10.

Make sure that word responses are appropriate for the item statement or question and that scale responses are logical.

Allow for neutral responses if possible.

Use terms that are easily understood.

Be consistent in format as much as possible.

Avoid overlap of grouped responses, and make sure that response options are logical for the questions asked.

Have a survey pilot-tested or reviewed by expert.

Always proofread everything that is distributed to subjects.

Make it short and simple; the shorter the survey, the more likely that it will be completed.

Number the pages; 1 of 4, 2 of 4, etc.

Allow respondents to comment at the end of the survey.

---

research tools.[1] **Table 10-11** lists keys for using verbal frequency scales.

In items in a verbal frequency scale, asked the respondent to state his or her level of agreement to that item. However, a verbal frequency scale may indicate some responses other than agreement. Likert and other scales are generally used with a series of related survey items. Instructions for respondents should lead with a direction statement such as, "Indicate your level of agreement or disagreement to the following statements." **Box 10-12** is an example from the author's research.[6]

In addition, the instructions should ask respondents to respond to all survey items. Unanswered items lead to questions of validity, extrapolation, and analysis. Initially, investigators should make a plan to handle nonresponses in the analysis.

When constructing survey items, ensure that the statement can be answered by the scale used. Avoid redundancy. Also, each item should address only one idea or concept. An example of a conflicting statement is shown in **Box 10-13**.

This statement contains two separate components. A respondent may agree that ranking benefits society but disagree that ranking should be part of accreditation. Item clarity is a key to accurate responses and sound interpretation of results. When using verbal frequency scales, be sure that the choices reflect the responses that will provide the subject information needed by the project. Some examples of descriptors used in verbal frequency scales are given in **Box 10-14.**

For some surveys, choices of "Not Applicable," "Unsure," "No Answer," "Unknown," etc. may be needed. Also, in some instances more or less than five responses may be needed. Regardless, there must be consistency in the options presented. Items and their responses must provide adequate choices along a continuum for the subjects' responses. Consistency allow for appropriate analysis, which leads to more accurate conclusions.

Another key to developing survey items is that each item should have an equal number of positive and negative responses with a neutral response,

Box 10–12 Verbal Frequency Scale

For each of the following items concerning the ranking of programs, indicate your degree of agreement or disagreement using the Likert scale:

1. Strongly agree   2. Agree   3. Neutral   4. Disagree   5. Strongly Disagree

1. Physician assistant programs should be ranked.	5 4 3 2 1
2. Ranking programs will benefit society.	5 4 3 2 1
3. Ranking programs will help ensure the quality of PA education.	5 4 3 2 1
4. Only the top 25 ranked programs should be published.	5 4 3 2 1
5. The rankings of all programs should be published.	5 4 3 2 1
6. Program rank should be a component for accreditation.	5 4 3 2 1
7. Ranking creates ill will or loss of collegiality among programs.	5 4 3 2 1
8. Ranking creates unnecessary competition among programs.	5 4 3 2 1

if possible. This is not always necessary. For example, a neutral response would not be necessary to make a choice using the verbal frequency scale. This is called a "forced response." One risk of the "forced response" approach is that respondents, who are neutral, may not answer. Therefore, decisions must be made as to whether or not the risk of a respondent not answering the question is acceptable or whether a neutral or noncommittal response is acceptable. Another option is to have a choice such as "does not apply" or "no experience" or "no knowledge," etc.

Putting the Survey Together

Once the research question has been developed, the appropriate literature search has been completed, the methodology has been designed, and the survey items have been confirmed, the survey has to be to put together. An introduction should be first, followed by the survey. (Telephone and personal surveys also have these elements, but they are presented verbally.) For Web-based and paper surveys, a plain, easily read, black print on white background is probably best. If a colored background is desired, light beige or gray may be acceptable. The survey should be organized so that like items are grouped, particularly if some type of scale is used. Demographic questions, in the past, have been presented first, but recent trends have moved toward placing them at the end of the survey.

Assess the visual quality of the survey. Does it appear organized with well-defined borders,

Box 10–13 Example: Conflicting Statement

Ranking health professions programs will benefit society and should be part of accreditation decisions.

Box 10–14 Descriptors for Verbal Frequency Scale

Very Satisfied Satisfied Neutral Dissatisfied Very Dissatisfied

Very Good Good Neutral Poor Very Poor

Highly Positive Positive Neutral Negative Highly Negative

Excellent Good Fair Poor Very Poor

Very Important Important Somewhat Important Not Important

sections, etc.? Ensure that the method of submission is clear. The "submit" button for an Internet survey must be very apparent and visible. A decision must be made about whether respondents can to come in and out of the survey in multiple sessions. Proofread everything, and then have someone else proofread. It is difficult to proofread one's own work, particularly if the work as been repeatedly reviewed by its developer.

Pilot Testing the Survey

A pilot test is an excellent way to ensure that the survey is understandable and that the survey items get the information desired, but a large group of subjects is not needed. Ask pilot test subjects to evaluate the survey, that is, give feedback on their feelings, interpretations, and suggestions for improvement. The pilot-test group or a separate group can participate in a focus group for review, feedback, and critical comment. Do not take critical review personally, the review is an important step toward making the survey as perfect as possible. Make sure that appropriate institutional approval is obtained, if needed. Institutional Review Board or Research Ethics Committee approval must be obtained in writing and maintained in study files. If approval of an Institutional Review Board, Research Ethics Committee, etc. is required, do not conduct the survey until it is granted in writing. To do so, even if approval is forthcoming, would be an ethical violation. Once all of these small steps are completed, start the study.

When results begin to accumulate, work on the investigation regularly. The most efficacious way to proceed is to set aside a specific period each day for working on the project. Keep good records, protect confidentiality, do the follow-ups, and set a deadline after which no further data will be accepted. Data cannot continually be added indefinitely, and at some point, data analyses must start. Once analyses are completed, the conclusions can be drawn. REMEMBER: If the methodology is sound, the analyses are appropriate, confounding variables are controlled, and study biases minimized; the results are the results. As a researcher,

the search is truth, not "hoped for" outcomes. Ultimately, the most that the majority of research contributes is just one very small piece in the universe of knowledge.

How Many Subjects?

How many people (subjects) should be surveyed? This is a simple question, but it can be a tough one to answer. If the population of interest is small, survey the entire population. One good example of a fairly easy population to sample is a specific healthcare profession's educational programs. Another example might be all of the occupational therapists who work only in nursing homes in communities with a population of less than 5000. In these cases, the sample and the population are the same. In some instances, a convenience sample may be used. As the name implies, the sample subjects are convenient for the investigator to survey. One example is faculty members who survey students in their program or classes. These subjects are convenient. However, a convenience sample may *not* be representative of a population. In this example, students in a healthcare profession program may be demographically different from students in another program. A convenience sample presents problems with extrapolation to the larger population. Convenience samples are of very limited benefit.

An investigator wants the sample to represent the population to be studied. However, consideration of costs and logistics in setting the sample size must be part of the methodology. In other words, an investigator has to be able to afford the costs of the study and to handle the survey distribution and analysis. Remember, a larger number of respondents does not necessarily increase accuracy of the results; a good response rate from a smaller sample may be better. The survey instrument must be valid and reliable. The sample must represent the population. Small sample groups are more likely to be different from the population than large or multiple sample groups.[1]

Every investigator has to accept the fact that there is always a chance of error. There are some ways to try to control these inherent errors. First,

---

set a confidence level and a confidence interval. (See **Box 10-15**.)

The confidence level is usually set at 95 percent or 99 percent. This means that one can state with 95 percent or 99 percent confidence that the results are within the margin of error. The confidence interval is the margin of error, usually expressed as a range (e.g., 3–4). The size of the population must be known. With these pieces of information, the sample size can be calculated. Many statistical texts and Web sites have tools for determining sample size. Some statistical computer programs will do the job. If there is difficulty in determining sample size, consult a statistician.

What Statistics to Use?

Chapter 14 presents data analysis techniques and brief explanations. Again, it may be wise to consult a statistician to determine the best statistical tests to use for analysis of the results. Statistical tests can be bewildering, and most of us need help from an expert. However, make the analysis decisions part of the planning and methodology initially, not after the data is collected. Consult a statistician early in the planning. Demographic data can be presented as percentages and, if necessary, can be compared to known population data. This is a good way to demonstrate that the sample is similar to the population of interest.

Another key to successful survey strategies is to understand what the statistical tests mean and what they demonstrate. Use statistical tests that fit the data and meet the study needs. The questions about evaluating ordinal data with continuous data analysis is one of contention within the healthcare research community. Chapter 14 has flow charts that can help.

SUMMARY

Surveys can provide a wealth of useful information. Survey research requires the same attention to detail as any other part of any research project. The same process is used in survey research as with any other type of research. Survey and survey item construction are the keys to success.

REFERENCES

1. Alreck PL, Settle RB. *The Survey Research Handbook*, 2nd ed. Boston: Irwin McGraw-Hill, 1995.
2. Cui, Wei Wei (2003). Reducing error in mail surveys. *Practical Assessment, Research & Evaluation.* 8(18).
3. Sharp K. White papers: Public sector use of internet surveys and panels. http://global.networldalliance.com/downloads/white_papers/Public%20Sector.pdf Accessed September 12, 2011.
4. Rea LM, Parker RA. *Designing and Conduction Survey Research: A Comprehensive Guide*, 2nd ed. San Francisco: Jossey-Bass; 1997.
5. Fricker RD Jr, Schonlau M. Advantages and disadvantages of internet research surveys: Evidence from the literature. *Field Methods.* 2002;14(4):347–67.
6. Vogt WP. *Dictionary of Statistics and Methodology*, 2nd ed. Thousand Oaks: Sage Publications; 1999.
7. Blessing JD, Hooker RS, Jones PE, Rahr RR. An investigation of potential criteria for ranking physician assistant programs. *Persp Phys Asst Educ.* 2001;12(3):160–166.
8. Portney LG, Watkins MP. *Foundations of Clinical Research: Applications to Practice*, 2nd ed. Upper Saddle River, NJ: Prentice Hall Health, 2000.

CHAPTER OVERVIEW

This chapter covers clinical reviews. Clinical reviews are one of the most common types of articles found in medical and healthcare journals. Clinical reviews are also a common form of scholarship performed by students, and for some programs, they are the educational capstone. Clinical reviews summarize what is known, present new information or theories, and serve all healthcare professionals in a number of ways. Clinical reviews are a form of scholarship in which any clinician can participate.

The Clinical Review

Richard W. Dehn, MPA, PA-C
J. Dennis Blessing, PhD, PA

INTRODUCTION

Clinical reviews are a common form of scholarship in the health professions. The purpose of a clinical review is to share the knowledge and understanding of practicing clinicians, and ultimately, to improve the overall quality of how healthcare is delivered. Successful clinical reviews address clinical conditions that are encountered frequently or are of interest to healthcare providers. Often, clinical reviews emphasize diagnosis and treatment of commonly seen or important diseases or of particularly challenging clinical dilemmas. Typically, a clinical review takes the form of a written manuscript that is intended for publication. However, a clinical review can also be delivered as a formal presentation or multimedia production.

Unlike experimental or investigative research, clinical reviews do not seek to answer a specific research question; instead, they aim to educate the clinician concerning a specific aspect of practice. Sometimes clinical reviews are based on a specific clinical question. However, in the clinical review process, this question does not lead to an experimental or observational process, but instead provides a review of the relevant existing literature.

Clinical reviews can be divided into three subcategories:

1. General review of a clinical topic
2. Systematic review on a specific topic
3. Case or case series report

These types of clinical reviews differ primarily in the degree to which the source information is grounded in the literature.

THE GENERAL CLINICAL REVIEW ARTICLE

A successful general clinical review article addresses a common or particularly vexing problem of interest to a sizable number of practitioners.[1] Thus, narrow topics, or those of value only as a curiosity, are best avoided. Because many clinicians utilize the contents of clinical review articles as practice recommendations, authors should pay careful attention to factual accuracy and make efforts to avoid personal bias. The key to accuracy and quality is a well-referenced clinical review that contains the most recent data. The clinical review article is structured similarly to topics presented in a textbook, with defined sections that review basic facts and concepts relating to the topic or disease entity. Clinical review articles often are called "update articles" because their purpose is to bring the reader's practice knowledge and skills up to date in the topic area. General clinical review articles are often structured to contain the following sections:[2]

- *Introduction and background.* This section typically includes a definition of the disease, the historical background of the disease, and the disease prevalence. Here, the author tries to justify the importance of the topic to the practicing clinician as well as to pique interest. Thus, the beginning of clinical review should be written in a way that convinces the reader to invest the time and effort to read the rest of the article.
- *Review of anatomy, physiology, and pathophysiology.* This section should review the basic anatomy, physiology, and pathophysiology as it applies to understanding the disease presented. Additionally, this review provides information that encourage the reader to understand how clinical and physical findings, as well as other aspects of the topic, interrelate.

- *History and physical exam findings.* In this section, the signs and symptoms associated with the topic are reviewed. Risk factors and historical data commonly associated with the disease should also be included, as well as information that may facilitate the recognition and interpretation of pertinent physical findings. Any required physical examination techniques must be described and explained. Unique physical findings that allow differentiation of this particular disease or condition and that rule out competing diagnoses should also be discussed.
- *Laboratory and diagnostic testing.* This section includes the selection and interpretation of the most appropriate studies that aid in the recognition and management of the disease or problem. A full explanation of study indications, cost-effectiveness, as well as test sensitivity, specificity, and value to the assessment should be included.
- *Assessment and differential diagnosis.* This section covers the reasoning processes that lead to the correct diagnoses of the disease or condition. This section often includes a broad differential diagnostic list. The reasons for selecting the correct diagnoses over other possible diagnoses should be explained in this section. This section explains to the reader how to move to this important point from all that has come before.
- *Treatment and follow-up.* This section includes the prioritization of the medical interventions necessary for treatment and emphasizes the need for referral, consultation, hospital admission, necessary emergent/acute care, and the reasoning by which decisions are made. If appropriate, detailed descriptions of these actions should also be included. Well-accepted treatments are emphasized here, as well as potential complications, appropriate aftercare, pharmacotherapy, and drug-to-drug interactions. Finally, this section provides a follow-up plan and monitoring regimen that includes signs of relapse and treatment failure.

- *Prevention and patient education*. This section provides patient education and disease prevention guidelines. It explains the common screening tests for the condition, including the relative value of each test. In today's litigious society, patient education is a must and should be a part of the treatment plan for every disease condition.

THE SYSTEMATIC REVIEW OF THE LITERATURE

Systematic reviews can be defined as concise summaries of the best available evidence designed to address carefully defined clinical questions. Systematic reviews are a type of evidence-based medicine. The purpose of a systematic review is to summarize all available information on a specific clinical topic. This summary allows clinicians to make decisions based on more than one study.[4,5]

The systematic review is a product of the evidence-based medicine (EBM) philosophy. Many journals and websites dedicated to EBM offer systematic reviews. Systematic reviews are generally quantitative, meaning they are composed using a system devised to determine which data and publications are included in the review. Authors specify inclusion criteria, outcomes of interest, and criteria used for determining the quality and validity of individual articles chosen for review. Additionally, authors also indicate how the search for research articles was conducted, including what databases were used, and whether unpublished articles or those written in foreign languages were actively sought out and included. The overall quality of a systematic review is dependent on the effectiveness of the systematic search approach utilized to find the best data available.

Biases in systematic reviews are often inherent in the article selection system. One example is publication bias, where only data showing significance is published, while data demonstrating other conclusions is omitted, thereby resulting in the exclusion of unpublished data from the analysis. Another potential bias in systematic reviews is selection bias, where the selection criteria skewed the data selected. Multiple publications that magnify the impact of a single data set can also complicate systematic reviews. The most challenging part of composing a systematic review is finding data from different studies that are similar enough to be combined and analyzed without "comparing apples and oranges."

The systematic review process requires the author to exercise several unique skills:

- *The ability to search the literature*. A high-quality systematic review ideally requires that all data and information that exists on a specific clinical question be located and reviewed. Therefore, the author needs to be proficient in searching research databases. Proficient searching skills include a combination of general library science knowledge, competence in informatics, and practical skills in operating various search engines within numerous information databases. The best selection processes may include unpublished data. However, such data is often difficult to obtain or may not be known to the author.
- *Critical skills to accurately deconstruct and critique a research article*. This process requires a solid understanding of the research process: the principles of scientific study design, basic statistics, understanding common problems associated with clinical research, and realizing what conclusions can be derived (or not) from a particular study.
- *Statistical and data manipulation skills*. If the review is systematic and quantitative, the author uses sophisticated data skills to determine the quality of available data and how best to combine it. Advanced statistical analysis skills, including meta-analysis, are necessary to determine the best methods for combining and analyzing data sets.

Case or Case Series Reports

As the quantity and quality of experimental data have increased over time, the popularity and usefulness of the case or case series report has decreased. Clinicians have become more aware of potential biases produced by small sample sizes inherent in case series reports. However, the case or case series report always has an important role in alerting the healthcare community with regard to the treatment of new diseases, or in describing diseases so rare that traditional study designs cannot, for all practical purposes, be used to investigate them.[6] Case study and case series reports are presented in Chapter 18.

SUMMARY

Clinical reviews are ideal publication opportunities for many health professionals because the subject matter deals with clinically relevant material. Clinical reviews can be updates for the assessment and management of common conditions encountered in practice or for unusual conditions. Clinical reviews can be comprehensive literature reviews where disagreement exists. Almost all health professions' journals publish clinical reviews.

REFERENCES

1. American Family Physician Web site. Authors' guide. http://www.aafp.org/x13554.xml. Accessed April 25, 2011.
2. Journal of the American Academy of Physician Assistants Web site. *JAAPA* submission guidelines. http://www.jaapa.com/for-authors/section/507/. Accessed April 25, 2011.
3. Cook DJ, Mulrow CD, Haynes RB. Systematic reviews: Synthesis of best evidence for clinical decisions. *Ann Intern Med.* 1997;126(5):376–380.
4. Mulrow CD, Cook DJ, Davidoff F. Systematic reviews: Critical links in the great chain of evidence. *Ann Intern Med.* 1997;126(5):389–391.
5. Siwek J, Gourlay ML, Slawson DC, Shaughnessy AF. How to write an evidence-based clinical review article. *Am Fam Physician.* 2002;65:251–258.
6. Henley CE. Writing for publication. http://www. healthsciences.okstate.edu/college/fammed/faculty_development/writing_for_publication.pdf. Accessed April 25, 2011.

CHAPTER OVERVIEW

Qualitative research has been described as interpretive, constructive, naturalistic, or "real world." Rooted in social science, qualitative methods are now frequently used to inform practice and research in medical and healthcare science as well. This chapter explores indications for using a qualitative approach and describes the philosophy, methods, and analysis process of qualitative research.

Qualitative Research

Anita Duhl Glicken, MSW

INTRODUCTION

Rapid advances in medical technology, an increase in patient information and expectations, as well as the size and diversity of the healthcare system, all contribute to a new level of complexity in our healthcare system. As a result, there is no easy solution to improving the quality of patient care. The research that informs our thinking about this issue is, by necessity, multi-dimensional. Many of the questions we wish to answer are best explored through quantitative research. Quantitative research assists clinicians in identifying new approaches to care based on randomized controlled trials, case controlled, cohort studies, as well as experimental and quasi-experimental design. However, it is often difficult to translate these findings effectively to the clinical care setting. This difficulty is partially due to the fact that views regarding quality are also dependent upon the attitudes and skills of the professionals working in the healthcare system and patients who are the recipients of these treatments.

Qualitative research comprises a variety of methods that identify and address patient and provider preferences. Historically, qualitative methods have been seen as a way to enhance quantitative research. Medical researchers now recognize the unique contributions of qualitative designs in the development of contextually grounded, culturally sensitive research that informs clinical decision making. These methods are recognized for providing important independent outcomes that contribute to the effective implementation of new treatments. This chapter explores the role and function of qualitative research methods in medicine. At the end of this chapter, the reader will be able to do the following:

1. Identify indications for using a qualitative study design
2. Identify the methods, data, and goals of qualitative analysis
3. Describe the process of qualitative data analysis
4. Describe the use of an integrated approach to research methods, designs and purposes in health care research

PHILOSOPHY OF THE METHOD

As described in previous chapters, quantitative research is traditionally based on the belief that a single, objective reality exists. This reality is governed by a set of laws and can be examined in terms of fragmented parts (facts) that can be more completely understood with the accumulation of high-quality research. Quantitative research begins with an idea (usually stated as a hypothesis or null hypothesis) that is measured by generating data and then, by deduction, allows a conclusion to be drawn.

In contrast, the philosophy behind qualitative research states that although there may be an objective reality, individuals assign complex meanings to their perceived reality. Subsequent decisions are then based upon these subjective meanings and interpretations. Qualitative methods, therefore, attempt to make sense of and understand phenomena in terms of the meaning that individuals bring to the issue. Qualitative research is generative; it is designed to describe and explain the topic at hand. Data is collected (often through interviews and observations), and hypotheses are generated from this data through inductive reasoning. Due to this shift in philosophical perspective, qualitative research differs from quantitative methods in three ways: (1) the purpose of the research, (2) the use of the literature review and relationship between theory and data, and (3) the level of investigator involvement in the imposition of specific procedures and steps throughout the research process.

INDICATIONS FOR USING QUALITATIVE RESEARCH

Once a topic is identified, the literature search helps refine research questions. As explained in Chapter 7, there are many reasons to conduct a literature search. The most obvious reason is to explore the previous research that has been conducted on the topic. This helps the investigator clarify whether the current body of information is descriptive, explanatory, or predictive. In this way, the literature search reveals the level of knowledge related to the topic, thereby establishing a rationale for the investigator's study design. For example, when there is little or no existing information available about a particular topic, an exploratory descriptive study may be most appropriate. In the case of experimental design, the research question, testable hypotheses, and interventions are often refined based on reports from past studies. However, what if this is not the case? What if you find little or no research that is directly related to the study topic is available? This lack of background literature, which provides the foundation for any study, could be a strong indication that an exploratory, qualitative approach is warranted.

Studies that use qualitative methods are often the first step in a new area of inquiry. Using techniques such as semi-structured interviews, focus groups, and participant observations, researchers can identify previously unrecognized variables, clarify the role of the variables in a particular relationship, and construct experimental study designs. For example, in an attempt to improve the quality of health care provided to gay and lesbian adolescents, an initial study consisted of focus groups of recipients (subjects) used to uncover the variables that they perceived affected the quality of their health care. After the relationships of these variables were explored, an experimental study design ensued based on the information provided by the focus groups.

Qualitative methods can also be used to augment and enhance a study when they are used in conjunction with other methods. This mixed-methods strategy, which will be addressed in greater detail later in this chapter, is increasingly visible in healthcare research, particularly in studies that emphasize new treatment protocols. For example, in evaluating the impact of preventive interventions, valuable information is gained by asking participants what they did and did not find useful. Similarly, the reasons some chose not to participate or what obstacles led them to drop out of the intervention prior to completion can be explored and may provide additional useful information.

In summary, indications for using qualitative approaches include the following:

- Studying "real" phenomenon outside the laboratory setting, such as any field research or naturally occurring setting
- Conducting a needs assessment in the absence of existing literature (i.e., either the question has not been asked, or the problem is still poorly understood or is very complex)
- Evaluating an existing or proposed program; establishing accountability to the stakeholders, including patients or funders
- Strengthening quantitative research designs

RESEARCH TECHNIQUES

Three basic data collection techniques are used in qualitative research: observation, interviews, and document review. All of these techniques have several variations, suggesting the potential complexity of relatively simple strategies.

Observation

Patient behavior is a central element present in most healthcare settings. A natural technique is to observe what patients do and then describe, analyze, and interpret what has been observed. Rather than ask people about their feelings and attitudes and how these might affect their behavior; you actually record what they do in response to a situation. This direct method of observation is often used to complement other methodologies.

Investigators may find, for example, that questionnaire or interview responses do not reveal the whole picture because there is often a discrepancy between what people say that they have done, will do, and what they actually did or will do.

Observational methods vary in four distinct ways. First, in "classic" fieldwork, an individual that actually participates in the situation under study collects data. For example, an investigator interested in the barriers to healthcare delivery for a rural population might live in the rural community for an extended period of time. The investigator lives in the milieu of the subject, enabling him/her to simulate the subjective experience of the participants and to develop relationships with the informants.

Second, observation varies based on the length of time the researcher is involved. Some observations have been conducted for months, even years, while many recent qualitative studies rely on more brief exposures to the research context. Depending on the research questions to be answered, more limited observations and involvement can provide sufficient data. For example, a researcher conducting an observational study of patient utilization of health education reading materials in a clinic waiting room may collect sufficient data from a limited exposure across several days.

Third, observations may be conducted with or without the subject's awareness or permission. While covert observation is politically and ethically controversial, the nature of the data collected by observation is often greatly influenced by the degree to which the researcher informs participants on the nature of the project. The Hawthorne effect postulates that subjects are influenced by being observed. Finally, observation may also be limited to a specific area of inquiry, as in the example just cited, or it may be extended to include a more comprehensive view of the area under study.

Interview

The second data collection method is the interview, and there are several interview strategies. Interviews may range from casual to formal in style; individual interviews may also range from highly structured and directed to unstructured and undirected. Similarly, the investigator can utilize a number of strategies in conducting the interview that will affect the quantity and quality of the information obtained. Some examples of these strategies include the number and nature of the questions asked, recall strategies, active listening, and probes for content. The degree to which the investigator attempts to standardize the information obtained from all respondents also introduces a degree of variability. Most often, qualitative interviews are typically unstructured during exploratory phases of the project, and more standardized and formal interviews are applied during later stages of investigation.

The focus group style of interview is becoming an increasingly popular research technique. A focus group session is a discussion where a small number of people (usually 6 to 10) discuss a topic introduced by a moderator or facilitator. In this case, the researcher sets the agenda for the meeting and attempts to keep the group focused on the topic, often using a series of probes to be sure the key questions are covered. The session is typically very open. Group members may ask their own questions as well as comment on what someone else has said in addition to their own feelings or beliefs. There are some clear advantages to this method, including the generation of a much broader and richer exploration of the topic under study. As previously mentioned, focus groups are a good way to identify variables that may be used to study a specific topic. This is particularly true when there is little or no information available about that topic.

Document Review

The third data collection technique is document review. Generally, document review involves organizing and evaluating a body of existing information that will be combined with other data or utilized as a stand-alone data source. Documents can range from formal to informal. Objective reports, patient records, etc. represent formal documentation, whereas informal documentation may be gleaned from things like personal notes or calendar notes. Clearly, documents vary with

respect to their relationship to the research question. A patient record may have direct statements related to a research question, requiring little need for interpretation. Other comments expressed in less formal documents that are not directly related to the research question may require conceptual translation and may mandate a more critical attitude on the part of the investigator.

Data Management

Qualitative methods are iterative and inductive. Therefore, qualitative research requires continuous recording of data that is under constant review, especially when utilizing an interview or observational approach. Two processes that enable the constant recording of data are "field notes" and "trigger notes." Field notes are the researcher's specific thoughts or ideas about how the data might later be interpreted; they might even identify future strategies for data collection. During this type of data collection, the researcher records his/her subjective experience. "Field notes" are often as critical to the data analysis as the content of the interview itself and, therefore, demand organized strategies for management and control. As opposed to field notes, trigger notes are recorded during interview observations, which are later expanded into a more comprehensive record of the interaction. Trigger notes often include direct quotes.

Some researchers choose to use electronic means to capture an observation or interview. While this method has an obvious benefit in terms of reliability and completeness, capturing data electronically has limitations as well. For example, a video camera may only capture one angle or perspective. The setting where the video was recorded may also "influence" the experience as well. In addition, an audio transcript cannot capture the rich detail that occurs in the nonverbal interactions of participants. Audio and video recordings also generate volumes of raw data that may be difficult for the researcher to manage. Transcribing audio recordings can be extremely time consuming and expensive, often requiring the researcher to be selective about the data chosen for analysis.

Therefore, when deciding whether or not to capture data electronically, the researcher must develop a comprehensive plan and have an explicit approach to managing this type of data.

Data Analysis

The data analysis for qualitative studies can begin quite early, unlike quantitative studies, where the data collection must often be completed before the analysis process begins. Qualitative data analysis is very different from the analysis of quantitative data. Analyzing qualitative data is an iterative process of constant cycling and review of the data. Preliminary analysis consists of the dual process of segmenting the data and developing early concepts or categories that will later evolve into theoretical models.

Assuming the data has been recorded in an accessible way, the first step of analysis consists of segmenting the data. The researcher first reviews transcripts and memos of the observations or interviews to begin the coding process whereby initial categories and themes begin to evolve. During this work, the investigator identifies pieces of information, indicated by words or phrases that appear to represent a significant finding. It is important to note that the researcher's personal experience may heavily influence construction of these categories. For example, categories may come from clinical practice, existing theory, or may be generated from abstract concepts such as time or space. Categories may also be suggested by the participants' report of their experiences. These categories ultimately evolve and relate in ways that subsequently lead to the germination of potential interpretative theories.

The next step in the analysis process is reorganizing and re-sorting the information contained in the transcripts and researcher's notes into the categories or themes that have been generated. Data is often literally cut and pasted into different theme bins. Computer programs can also facilitate this process. The researcher then utilizes a process of "constant comparison" in sorting and re-categorizing the data. Once data has been categorized, the investigator begins to explore how the categories may link to each other, thereby formulating a theory. Discrepant cases and alternative explanations are also considered. Occasionally, a researcher will actually begin with a contextualizing approach. Rather than searching primarily for categories and contexts, the researcher will look for connections between the events, as in some types of linguistic analysis. The cyclical process of working with raw data and deriving new theories continues until the researcher feels the theory that has been developed adequately fits the data and conceptual framework.

As various theories emerge, additional literature is reviewed. New information is identified via the secondary literature search, which is then related to the data. As previously mentioned, this inductive method helps to formulate a theory by progressively developing the theory as the data analysis is being completed. A literature search may become more extensive toward the end of the project as the researcher seeks a broader understanding and application of the data. Generating a new theory or a different understanding of an established concept is the goal of qualitative inquiry.

VALIDITY

It is important to recognize that the definition of validity and reliability in the context of qualitative research has been grounded in a different philosophical paradigm. The debate surrounding the validity of qualitative research methods often overlooks this important distinction. Qualitative methodologies offer several safeguards to researchers.

Triangulation, as the term has been used in naturalistic inquiry, refers to a multiple-strategy approach. This approach combines different methods to reveal an additional "piece of the puzzle" or to uncover varied dimensions of the same phenomena. This approach is referred to as the "completeness function," where different methods are purposely chosen because each assesses a specific dimension of the problem under study. For example, a researcher might combine open-ended interviewing with direct observation or chart extraction to achieve a complete understanding of recovery issues associated with a cerebrovascular accident. Each data collection strategy provides a unique perspective of the total experience of recovery. Possibilities for triangulation are often limited by logistics and the range of options available for sources of data, as well as the methods available for researching a particular question.

An additional strategy or "validity check" has been referred to as "informant review." In this case, participants are asked to review and comment on various categories, themes, and conclusions drawn by the researchers. They provide feedback on whether or not the inferences the researcher has drawn matches their experience or understanding of the situation. Informant review may be initiated early in the data analysis process or later, when some theories or conclusions have been generated in a more comprehensive way. Interpreting this feedback is often problematic. Participants might offer valid criticisms of the interpretive theories, or they might provide new data with respect to the issue at hand. In addition, informants may be resistant to theories that are unsympathetic or critical of their experience. This type of feedback, however, is still recognized as an important component in validating the researcher's conclusions.

A third strategy is based on the researcher's use of their own critical appraisal skills throughout the process. The researcher should constantly be looking for alternative explanations in the data and systematically testing their theories for wrong interpretations. This involves monitoring data for discrepant information or negative cases that do not fit evolving theories.

Similarly, colleagues may be called upon to review the data analysis. In a general way, colleagues may offer their own speculations about the experiences or may be asked to review the categories and contexts that were generated for data analysis based on their limited experience with the project. More specifically, they might be asked to independently review the data and generate themes and contexts from their own perspective. Colleagues might also be provided with the categories generated by the researcher and portions of raw data and asked to do a separate analysis based on these categories. This attempt to demonstrate some degree of "inter-rater reliability" also may serve to inform the analysis process through clarification of existing categories and the generation of new ones.

Finally, the qualitative investigator is obligated to describe, often in rich detail, the process they used to collect, analyze, and interpret their data. In quantitative research, such descriptions are often truncated by the use of commonly understood terms such as "randomized controlled trials" or "simple linear regression." In qualitative analyses, it is often necessary to describe the process in greater detail, including information related to ensuring validity of the process through the use of triangulation, informant, or colleague review.

MIXED METHODOLOGY: COMBINING QUALITATIVE AND QUANTITATIVE METHODS

A debate continues in the medical literature as to whether qualitative and quantitative methods should be combined in an overall research strategy. This debate is partially due to the discordant philosophical approaches and assumptions inherent to both methods. However, proponents of using a mixed methodology argue that both approaches offer different tools designed to address different tasks. Some argue that both methods are necessary to do a thorough job of exploring the issue at hand.

This perspective has become more common in needs assessment and program evaluation studies, where the "triangulation" approach is very popular. Qualitative methods are now often used extensively in the hypothesis-generating phase of the research. A mix of qualitative and quantitative methods is then employed to test the hypothesis and to refine the methodology as the study progresses. Finally, a qualitative investigation is often utilized to help the investigator explain the findings of the quantitative research. When used in this way, qualitative methods complement and extend our understanding of quantitative findings. Quantitative studies that answer questions such as "how many" or "how much" can be complemented by qualitative explorations of "how—this result is related to the process" we are investigating. For example, quantitative studies may tell us how many children are given prescriptions for oral antibiotics and in what quantity, but qualitative studies might tell us how these antibiotics are administered by parents and the reasons they comply or do not comply with their healthcare provider's recommendations regarding treatment with antibiotics. Using a combination of methods requires a wide range of expertise and skills, and often requires a team approach to research design, data management, and analysis. Despite the potential problems of attempting to merge two disparate paradigms, there are many benefits to utilizing this type of synergistic approach.

SUMMARY

Mastering the art of qualitative research offers healthcare providers the additional benefit of improving clinical skills. The approach reinforces good clinical interviewing and problem solving through the use of attentive listening, open-ended questions, and an objective attitude. Qualitative interviewing in utilizing these skills, forces the investigator to revisit interview content and acquire an understanding from several perspectives. Clinical interviewers become more adept at uncovering themes and categories of information, which are then related to the broader patient context. This ability to "contextualize" data trains the student to see not only isolated facts and events, but also the process and relationship of these facts or events to each other. Skilled clinicians have been observed to use this process of "theory building" in making complex diagnosis and clinical decisions affecting their patient's treatment.

In medical research, the debate continues regarding the scientific legitimacy of qualitative methods. However, in light of the relative strengths and weaknesses of various research paradigms, researchers should focus their attention on strengthening project design by selecting methodologies that most accurately reflect the philosophy and scope of their inquiry. Qualitative methods offer an important approach that broadens our understanding, thereby enhancing our ability to improve the quality of patient care. Qualitative research requires new skills and perspectives beyond that of established quantitative efforts. In some ways, qualitative methods demand a rigor that surpasses that of quantitative research, as the methods are less defined and open to interpretation. Although data collection strategies and subsequent analysis appears straightforward, the three major strategies presented in this chapter illustrate the degree of complexity that this process often entails.

SUGGESTED READING

1. Agar MH: *The professional stranger: an informal introduction to ethnography,* 2nd ed. San Diego, Calif, 1996, Academic Press.
2. Berg, B: *Qualitative research methos for the social sciences,* 5th ed. Long Beach, Calif, 2004, Longman.
3. Denzin N: *Collecting and interpreting qualitative materials.* Thousand Oaks, Calif, 2008, Sage.
4. DePoy L, Gitlin L: *Introduction to research: Understanding and applying multiple strategies,* 4th ed. St Louis, MO, 2010, Elsevier.
5. Flick U, Von Kardoff E, Steinke I. editors: *A companion to qualitative research.* London, 2004, Sage Publications.
6. Glaser B; Strauss A: *The discovery of grounded theory: strategies for qualitative research.* New York, 1967, Aldine.
7. Glicken AD: Mentoring students in research: the literature review process. *Perspective on PA education.* 1997 Spring, Vol. VIII, No V.
8. Glicken AD: Qualitative methodology: enhanced instruction for Physician Assistant student. *Perspective on PA education.* 1999 Spring Vol. 10, No. 2:70-2
9. Neuman WL: *Social research methods: qualitative and quantitative approaches,* 5th ed. Boston, 2003, Allyn & Bacon.
10. Padgett D: *Qualitative methods in social work research.* Thousand Oaks, Calif, 2007, Sage.
11. Patton M: *Qualitative evaluation and research methods,* 3rd ed. Newbury Park, Calif, 2001, Sage.
12. Silverman D, Marvasti A: *Doing qualitative research: A practical handbook.* Thousand Oaks, Calif, 2008, Sage.
13. Straus S, Glasziou MB, Richardson, WS, Haynes B: *Evidence-based medicine: How to practice and teach it,* 4th ed. London, UK, 2011, Churchill Livingstone, Elsevier.
14. Wolcott HP: *Writing up qualitative research,* 3rd ed. Calif, 2009, Sage.

Community-Based Participatory Research

Scott D. Rhodes, PhD, MPH, CHES

CHAPTER OVERVIEW

Despite the strides that have been made in overall health status in the United States, not all communities are benefiting equally from current medical and health advances. In fact, many of the complex health problems that persist in the United States have proven to be ill-suited for traditional "outside expert" approaches to health research, health improvement, and intervention development and implementation.[1-8] To decrease the growing gaps in health status among vulnerable communities such as minority communities (e.g., racial/ethnic communities, sexual minorities) and economically disadvantaged communities, alternative approaches to medical and health research, health promotion, and disease prevention are being explored and promoted. Community-based participatory research (CBPR) is an approach to research designed to promote community and population health through the establishment and maintenance of community partnerships.[5,7-9] Rather than a researcher coming into a community with a preconceived notion of what is best for a community, a partnership approach to research involves and benefits lay community members, representatives from community-based organizations (CBOs), and medical and health researchers alike.

A partnership approach to medical and health research promotes health and well-being and aids in disease prevention because, among its strengths, it creates bridges between communities and researchers, incorporates local knowledge and local theory based on the lived experience of members of the communities involved, ensures the development of appropriate research design and methods, and lends itself to the development of culturally congruent measurement design and instrumentation. Partnerships enhance both the quality of data collected and the validity of findings and their interpretation.[2,4,5,8-13]

In this chapter the advantages and processes of CBPR are defined and described. A discussion of why CBPR is an appropriate approach to research is presented. Four research methods are introduced that describe how a CBPR approach may be applied and incorporated. Finally, a case study of the application of CBPR in a behavioral research study is presented.

INTRODUCTION

Community-Based Participatory Research Defined

Emerging evidence suggests that, through a process of partnership that includes lay community members, organizational representatives, and researchers, advances in health status and reductions in health disparities can occur as health promotion and disease prevention approaches, strategies, and efforts increase in authenticity.[5,9,14,15] Lay community members and organizational representatives participate in the research process to provide insight into knowledge generated, to guide the study and intervention design, to ensure the accuracy of measurement, and to support the interpretation of results. However, partnership is not easy; researchers must establish and maintain trusting, authentic co-learning partnerships with community members if partnerships are to function well and improvements in health are to occur within communities, especially within the most vulnerable communities.

CBPR is an approach that ensures community participation in research (**Box 13–1**). CBPR establishes structures for full and equal participation in research by community members (including those affected by the issue being studied), organizational representatives, and researchers to understand and improve community and population health and well-being through

Box 13–1 CBPR

CBPR is a collaborative research approach that is designed to ensure and structure participation by communities affected by the issue being studied, by representatives of organizations, and by researchers in all aspects of the research process from conception, study design and conduct, data analysis and interpretation, to the dissemination of findings.

multilevel action, including individual, group, community, policy, and social change.[5]

CBPR emphasizes co-learning and the reciprocal transfer of expertise, decision-making power, and the ownership of the processes and the products of research. This approach involves a strong partnership in which all parties (e.g., lay community members, organizational representatives, health department representatives, and researchers) participate and share control over *all* phases of the research process. These research phases typically include the following elements:

1. Identifying research questions
2. Assessing community strengths, assets, and challenges
3. Defining priorities
4. Developing research and data collection methodologies
5. Collecting and analyzing data
6. Interpreting findings
7. Disseminating findings
8. Applying the results to address community concerns through action or intervention

Although participation of the affected community in all research steps is critical to CBPR, another hallmark of CBPR is the translation of findings into action.[5] The accumulation of knowledge is important for the progression of science and understanding; however, the priority for most community members and organizational representatives is the application of findings to improve the health status of community members, including friends, neighbors, families,

consumers, patients, and clients. Furthermore, growing concern exists that the pendulum has swung too far toward "research for the sake of research sake" without the application of new knowledge to effect change to improve the health outcomes of populations and community members.[4,10,14]

CBPR relies on community participation to ensure that the research questions asked are important not only to the researcher for accumulation of knowledge but also to lay community members themselves. CBPR also helps to ensure that the methods used are reasonable and authentic to existing community structures and experiences and are as noninvasive as possible. Finally, the increased validity of findings from CBPR yield more effective actions and successful interventions to positively affect health and well-being because of the inherent insights that emerge from partnership. **Table 13–1** illustrates the advantages of using a CBPR approach, as summarized from the literature.

RESEARCH PARADIGMS

All research approaches, including the design of a study and the methods selected, reflect a specific research *paradigm*. Research paradigms are defined as a set of basic beliefs about the nature of reality that can be studied and understood.[16] These basic beliefs are accepted simply on faith, and, however well argued, their ultimate truth cannot be established with certainty. The *positivist* and *postpositivist* research paradigms, for example, hold that a single reality on how things really are and really work exists to be studied and understood. The *positivist* research paradigm posits that this single reality can be fully captured; this paradigm is reflected in *experimental* research designs and methods, which are used most often in the basic sciences. Whereas, the *postpositivist* research paradigm holds that this single reality can only be *approximated;* human knowledge is based not on absolute "truths" but rather upon human supposition. Post-positivism often is reflected in *quasi-experimental* research designs and methods, frequently used in the social and behavioral health sciences. Both experimental and quasi-experimental methods require objective

Table 13–1 Advantages of Community-Based Participatory Research

- Enhances data relevance, usefulness, and use
- Improves the quality and validity of the research by blending local knowledge and local theory based on the lived experiences of community members, expertise from organizational representatives, and scientific perspectives
- Recognizes the limitations of the concept of value-free science and encourages reflexive and critical thinking among all partners
- Recognizes that knowledge is power, and thus knowledge gained can be used by all partners to direct resources and influence policies that will benefit the community
- Reduces the separation of the individual from her/his culture and context
- Aims to increase health and wellbeing of communities involved, both directly through examining and addressing identified needs and indirectly through increasing power, control, and skills (e.g., capacity building)
- Joins partners with diverse skills, knowledge, expertise and perspectives to address health
- Strengthens the research, program, and problem-solving capacity of all partners
- Creates theory grounded in social experience, and creates better informed and more effective action guided by such theories
- Increases the possibility of overcoming the understandable distrust of research by communities
- Has the potential to bridge "cultural gaps"
- Involves communities that have been marginalized on the basis of, for example, race, ethnicity, class, gender, and/or sexual orientation in examining the impact of marginalization and attempting to reduce or eliminate it

detachment between researchers and participants so that any influence in either direction on what is being studied can be eliminated or reduced.

CBPR is often aligned with a *constructivist* research paradigm, which holds that multiple realities exist to be studied and understood.[16] Each reality is an intangible construction, rooted in people's experiences with everyday life and how they remember and make sense of them. Individual constructions of reality are assumed to be more or less "informed," rather than more or less "true," because they are always alterable. This means that, as researchers and participants encounter and consider different perspectives, they will alter their own views. The result is a *consensus construction of reality*[16] that is mutually formed by variations in preceding constructions (including those of the researchers) and that can move both participants and researchers toward communicating about action, intervention, and change.[17] The methods of constructivist research require researchers and participants to be interactively linked so that the consensus construction of reality is literally created as the study proceeds. Researchers using a CBPR approach are cast, therefore, in the dual roles of participant and facilitator.

COMMON RESEARCH METHODS

Successful use of CBPR relies on various partnership principles and values[6,18,19] that tend to include the following:

1. Expressing mutual respect and genuineness
2. Establishing and utilizing formal and informal partnership networks and structures
3. Committing to transparent processes and clear and open communication
4. Establishing roles, norms, and processes that evolve from the input and agreement of all partners
5. Agreeing on the values, goals, and objectives common among researchers and practitioners
6. Building upon each partner's strengths and assets
7. Offering continual feedback among members
8. Balancing power and shared resources
9. Sharing credit for the accomplishments of the partnership

10. Facing challenges together
11. Developing and using relationships and networks outside of the partnership
12. Incorporating existing environmental structures to address partnership focuses
13. Taking responsibility for the partnership and its actions
14. Disseminating conclusions and findings to research and clinical audiences, community members, and policy makers[5,6]

Often the researcher feels that she or he must make decisions on behalf of the community. This is a natural inclination given the influence of years spent in school, in training programs, and/or in the field. The researcher may be highly motivated to apply and use her or his resources for the benefit of the community. After all, the researcher is armed with more than intellectual resources alone. Training and experience in the reduction of bias and in the traditional approaches to increasing validity are coupled with the hope of increasing general application and perhaps financial resources or, at the minimum, increased access to financial resources, among other tools. Thus, the researcher may forget that community members and organizational representatives have perspectives that are key for inclusion during the research process.

It has been said that for community members "the textbook of life is living." With this axiom in mind, researchers must recognize that lay community members have perspectives that can greatly enhance all phases of the research process. Community members have firsthand knowledge of the health issue of concern. They can contribute to identifying and understanding the most salient health needs of their community in ways that give context to epidemiological data that in turn are used to build theory about local needs, challenges, and potential solutions that may not be easily understood by outsiders (e.g., researchers and other health professionals). Each of these points can strengthen research and intervention design through the interpretation of data and the evaluation and revision of intervention strategies.

Although their training and experiences may or may not have resulted from formal educational or training programs, organizational representatives who are on the "front lines" also have an understanding of the community that is not probably readily available or apparent to the researcher. These representatives know systems and may have a wealth of experiences providing services to community members on the front lines or at the "grassroots" level. However, their perspectives may lack detail, and they may miss insights that have not been well discovered or explored.

Many researchers might conclude that they themselves are on the front lines in their capacity as health professionals (e.g., clinicians, counselors, health educators, pharmacists, providers of medical and mental health services, therapists, and other service providers), yet they may truly know very little about the lived experiences of their patients or clients, especially the lives lived after patients or clients leave the office. To illustrate, having access to care and medications does not ensure that a patient will adhere to prescribed medication regimens for diabetes management. Patients and clients (and providers themselves) live in complex social contexts that cannot be easily understood or teased apart by outsiders. Thus, although organizational representatives (e.g., individuals from community agencies like the health department, community clinics, agencies, etc.) may have useful knowledge, experiences, and theories, their insight alone is insufficient.

FOUR QUALITATIVE STUDY DESIGNS

CBPR can be infused into any research methodology; however, the following section highlights four research methods and briefly describes how CBPR can be applied. These methods include *action-oriented community diagnosis* (AOCD), *focus groups, photo-voice,* and *in-depth interviews*. Although this discussion is not meant to be exhaustive, it is meant to serve as an initial "starting point" for researchers who want to explore the use of CBPR.

Action-Oriented Community Diagnosis (AOCD)

The purpose of action-oriented community diagnosis (AOCD) is to understand the health status, the collective dynamics and functions of relationships within a community, and the interactions between community members and broader structures that can impede or promote the conditions and skills required to assist community members in making decisions and taking action for social change and health-status improvement.[3] AOCD can be a critical first step in program planning, intervention, and evaluation because it provides the foundation for the following steps:

1. The establishment of baseline data from which objectives, intended outcomes, and measures of change can be derived
2. The selection of intervention methods and delivery that are most appropriate based on the community's structure, including formal and informal power dynamics and community assets and strengths
3. A collaborative relationship between professionals and communities, who can begin "closing the gap between what we do not know and what we ought to know."[3,20]

AOCD may serve as a process for *needs assessment,* but it actually goes beyond traditional interpretations of needs assessment. Whereas needs assessment is defined as a systematic examination and appraisal of the type, depth, and scope of needs for the purpose of setting priorities (**Box 13–2**), AOCD also identifies and explores community assets on which intervention

---

Box 13–2 Needs Assessment

Needs assessment is the systematic examination and appraisal of the type, depth, and scope of needs for the purpose of setting priorities. It is the process to identify and measure gaps between what is and what ought to be.

---

can be based. Philosophically true to CBPR, AOCD utilizes a *strengths-based approach* to research to identify both the needs and challenges faced by communities, and just as importantly, the assets and strengths within the community. To forego the identification of community assets and strengths is to use a *deficits-based approach* that may omit key information vital to understanding the community's reality and lived experience and the strengths and resources on which successful intervention strategies can be based.

Like all research methods that adhere to a CBPR approach, AOCD begins with the establishment of a working collaborative relationship with community members. Representatives from the community, CBOs, and researchers come together to determine a research plan. Typically existing community-specific data are reviewed. These data may include epidemiological data usually available from public health departments at the local or state levels as well as other reports and resources available from local CBOs such as faith-based service providers and other agencies.

A *windshield tour* of the community can be an important initial step in the AOCD process. If the community consists of a geographical location, a researcher will explore the community guided by community members to gain an appreciation of the community's geography, size, physical characteristics, and important community venues (e.g., a corner store where people gather or a house of worship). This windshield tour is meant to be an introduction to the community and its context through simple observation and community-member guidance and commentary. If the community is less geographically defined, such as a community of elderly shut-ins, for example, a windshield tour may include the agencies and organizations that visit and offer support to these community members. A windshield tour for a virtual community might include exploring the resources used by members of the community (e.g., chat rooms, list serves, bulletin boards, and news groups) as well as sites that are advertised on pop-up and pop-under screens.

After the windshield tour and throughout AOCD, researchers document their experiences using *field notes.* Frequently kept using various study methodologies and often informal, field notes document interesting or noteworthy details about the community, and, when combined with other data, they often prove to be important. Field notes may serve several purposes:

1. Provide the opportunity to document first impressions about a community
2. Assist the researcher to remember experiences encountered in the field
3. Record names of individuals and places that may prove key in the execution of the AOCD process
4. Document unusual characteristics within a community

Field notes also allow the researcher to track his or her own perspectives, impressions, feelings, and frustrations during the AOCD research process. Field notes can simply comprise reflective writings while the research "event," such as a windshield tour, is still fresh in the mind of the researcher. It is wise to keep field notes of all research efforts because field notes serve as a documentation source for decisions that affect the research process and subsequent data interpretation.

Because researchers tend to be very different from the communities they study, researchers need to gain an *emic* or insider's perspective on how people live and the issues facing the community.[3,21–24] An insider's perspective comprises privileged knowledge that only members of a particular community have. Outsiders can guess and hypothesize, but those assumptions are not purely objective and may not be accurate or complete. Because no researcher can completely remove her or himself from their research, emic data provides the researcher insight into the perspectives of community members. For example, a homeless individual understands aspects of the lived experience of homelessness better than any outsider. Members from a disabled community can provide insights that may not be understood or correctly interpreted by an outsider.

Furthermore, one's social position in a community affects the "truth" of the experience of community life. For example, all African American gay men do not share a "truth of experience"; in fact, among other influences, perception of truth is affected by person's position within the community. Thus, AOCD allows for distinctions and differences to emerge that may be lost through other approaches such as quantitative approaches that are designed to identify overarching generalities. However, these emerging distinctions and differences challenge researchers who must work with community members to merge varying, and perhaps contradictory, data and perspectives to make useful sense of findings.

Although emic information is important, a hallmark of ACOD, and in fact CBPR, is the trend toward change through some type of action or intervention. Such action may include a behavioral intervention to promote medication adherence, or a policy change to increase access to medical or health care, as examples. Such movement also requires an understanding of *etic* or outsider's perspectives. Outsiders, who usually comprise representatives from CBOs and other service providers such as those from the local public health department, and may include health professionals (e.g., clinicians, counselors, health educators, pharmacists, providers of medical and mental health services, therapists) and other researchers, provide perspectives on the health and well-being of communities that includes their access to resources, their community's strengths that in turn serve to support subsequent action or intervention. Like community members themselves, outsiders have a story to tell based on their experiences as well.

After reviewing and incorporating secondary or extant data, and collecting, analyzing, and interpreting emic and etic data in partnership with community members and organizational representatives, the researcher helps the community disseminate the findings. AOCD relies on a *community forum* to present to *influential advocates* the findings of a research process. This forum highlights issues, may propose solutions, and allows the community to dialogue with influential advocates who are supporters but who may also benefit from increased awareness and greater understanding of the situation. The community forum is an opportunity to initiate dialogue and to come together during a facilitated discussion to explore potential action or intervention.[6,25] Without the forum, AOCD merely explores root causes but does not move to improve the health status of the community. Dissemination of findings within the community and movement toward action are important steps in both AOCD and CBPR.

AOCD requires the involvement of both insiders and outsiders to ensure the collection of accurate (defined as reliable and valid) data and the most correct interpretation of these data. AOCD might include understanding both the emic and etic perspectives of uninsured families within a cultural and geographic community. This understanding may lead to action and, perhaps, policy changes that reduce barriers and/or increase access. For example, Latino men may have little access to public health department services if their local health department does not have translation capacity. Coming together during a forum educates providers on the ramifications of the deficiency and sparks new ideas and innovative approaches to solving problems. AOCD facilitates the materialization of solutions based on the compilation of realities that come from various perspectives. No one group or sector is responsible for change; rather, direction and change come from a negotiated process that includes multiple groups or sectors. The exchange of perspectives and ideas allows insiders and outsiders to see community health from fresh perspectives and builds partnerships that are stronger and can move forward in directions that positively affect health.

Often emic and etic perspectives are explored and interpreted through the use of qualitative methods. A CBPR partnership may choose to conduct focus groups, photo-voice interviews, or qualitative interviews; these methodologies also are outlined within this chapter and in Chapter 12. More quantitative methods may be less useful during the early stages of AOCD because they may not allow for sufficient flexibility and exploration of perspectives. However, they may provide important data in less exploratory or developmental

research. Moreover, researchers, and in fact community members and organizational representatives, often assume that CBPR requires the use of qualitative approaches. However, CBPR is useful during all phases of quantitative studies as well, including intervention outcome evaluation studies.[5,26–29]

FOCUS GROUPS

As a qualitative methodology, focus groups provide the opportunity to investigate participant responses and reactions related to an issue or topic more fully. They also allow new areas of inquiry to emerge. This methodology can reveal key nuances and perspectives that clinician researchers may not be able to foresee.[30] Briefly, focus groups usually are comprised of six to ten participants who are guided through a set of general, predetermined, open-ended questions outlined in a *focus-group moderator's guide*. The guide may be based on behavioral theory[24,30] or may allow for theory to explain phenomenon to be developed based on the findings, much like a *grounded theory* approach to research.[6,31] Either way, the guide should be agreed upon by the partners. Not only should the research objectives be mutually agreed upon, but the selection of focus groups as a methodology and the line of inquiry outlined in the guide should reflect the most meaningful approach and language, as agreed upon by the research partners.

After an introduction to the focus-group process (and, of course, giving informed consent to participate) as well as ground rules (e.g., speaking one at a time, respecting various opinions, maintaining confidentiality), the participants sit in an informal circle and respond to open-ended questions. Group interaction is an explicit component of this methodology. Instead of the researcher asking each person to respond to a question in turn, participants are encouraged to talk to one another, ask questions, exchange anecdotes, and comment on one another's experiences and perspectives.[6,24,30] The moderator must be skilled and experienced in soliciting discussion from all participants in a group, reminding participants that there are no wrong answers, affirming all opinions, and probing for detail. Probing for detail whether through examples, clarification, or further exploration is key to successful qualitative data collection, especially when using focus groups. In most cases, qualitative research requires the researcher to allow the design to emerge more fully during the project's evolution;[32] thus, all potential questions cannot be predicted. The moderator's guide is meant to serve as an outline, but the moderator must facilitate the discussion beyond what is written within the guide. The moderator may need to probe into a perspective to develop and understand it more fully. However, the moderator must be skilled at keeping the discussion "on track." If the discussion deviates from the purpose of the focus group, the moderator must be able to bring the discussion back to the purpose of the focus group.

Furthermore, besides a moderator, successful focus groups most often involve at least one *note taker* who documents participant speaking order, body language, and facial expression that cannot be captured by an audio recording. These details may provide important insight during the data analysis and interpretation phases. Because anonymity may be desired, names of participants may not be used. Rather, participants may be assigned numbers that are added to the focus-group transcript to track which participant is saying what. It may not be important to know the name of a participant; however, it may be important to attribute certain quotations to certain participants. Perhaps one participant has a certain perspective about a topic that she or he continues to reiterate. When analyzing the transcripts, it may be important to recognize this and "weigh" the findings accordingly.

The note taker also documents nonverbal communication. If a participant is noticeably uncomfortable with a discussion topic or the focus group discussion but does not assert her or his unease or disagreement, such observations should be noted by the note taker. Overall, the note taker is documenting what is going on during the focus group session that may be missed by the audio-recorder and by the moderator who is leading the session.

When applying a CBPR approach to focus-group research, the research question, the moderator's guide, and the recruitment methods must be developed and agreed upon by the research partners prior to beginning the study. Data analysis and interpretation should be completed in partnership and should allow community participation.[8]

PHOTOVOICE

Photovoice is a qualitative method of inquiry that has the following characteristics:

1. Enables participants to record and reflect on their personal and community strengths and concerns
2. Promotes critical dialogue and knowledge about personal and community issues through group discussions and photographs
3. Provides a forum for the presentation of the lived experience of participants through the images, language, and contexts defined by participants themselves.[25,33–37]

As a method closely aligned with CBPR, photovoice improves quality and validity of research by drawing on local knowledge, developing local theory, and progressing toward action. Perhaps one of the most participant-driven research methodologies, photovoice engages participants in the following step-by-step procedure:

1. Attending a training session to receive a disposable camera, and determine the topic for their first photo assignment
2. Recording through photography each photo assignment
3. Sharing and discussing their photographs from each photo-assignment during photo discussion sessions
4. Organizing a forum to present their photographic and thematic data to *influential advocates* (e.g., local policymakers, service providers, healthcare providers identified by participants as potential collaborators and advocates for change)
5. Creating plans of action[36]

Photo discussions typically begin with a review and discussion of themes that emerged from the analysis of previous sessions followed by a "show and tell" activity that allows each participant to share her or his photographs and explain how the photographs relate to the photo assignment. These discussions often follow a Paulo Freirian-based[38] model of root-cause questioning and discussion known by the acronym *SHOWED* (**Box 13–3**).[37,39,40] However, because SHOWED has proven to be unwieldy at times,[40] other guides or triggers are used. For example, a simpler approach has been effectively conducted using these questions: (1) What do you see? (2) How does this make you feel? (3) What do you think about this? and (4) What can we do?[37]

At the conclusion of each photo discussion, the group develops a new photo assignment by asking, "Given what we have learned so far, what should we explore next?"

The photo-discussion data are analyzed like other qualitative data, through exploring, formulating, and interpreting themes. The participants share these themes with local community leaders, service providers, and policy makers. These photographs serve as the medium through which issues are discussed to raise awareness among a core group of allies, mobilize these allies, and plan for change.

Box 13–3 SHOWED

SHOWED follows the following discussion outline:

What do you **s**ee here?

What is really **h**appening here?

How does this relate to **o**ur lives?

Why does this concern, situation, strength **e**xist?

How can we become **e**mpowered through our new understanding?

What can we **d**o?

The photovoice method transforms knowledge, or raised consciousness around issues and assets, into direct community action. Although a relatively new methodology, photo voice has been found to be a flexible method both in terms of the issues it has been employed to explore and address and the geographic and cultural diversity of groups in which it has been employed. It has been applied in partnership with a number of communities including Latino youth in the rural southeast,[40] Chinese women in the Yunnan Province, China,[41,42] homeless men and women in Michigan, USA,[42,43] heterosexual immigrant Latino men,[34,37] youth peer educators in Cape Town, South Africa,[44] urban lay health advisors,[10] and public health department leaders and constituents.[45]

IN-DEPTH INTERVIEWS

Individual in-depth interviews are another common data-collection methodology. Simply, these interviews are *unstructured, semi-structured,* or *structured* depending on the research goals. Unstructured interviews are characterized by questions that emerge during the interview process. The research partners may have general topic areas or categories, but the questions are asked as they are formulated in the natural course of the discussion, without predetermined wording of questions. This style is more conversational and increases the salience and relevance of questions. A problem with unstructured interviews is that different information is collected from different individuals based on different questions. Less systematic and comprehensive data collection results in data analysis challenges, so unstructured interviews may be most useful for initial exploration or case studies.

Semi-structured interviews, by definition, provide more structure for the interviewer. Topics and issues that are explored and discussed are specified in advance, often in outline form. Semistructured and structured interviews require an *interview guide* that gives structure to the interview process. When leading a semistructured interview, the interviewer often decides the order and sequence of the questions during the course of the interview. The interviewer may probe for details and develop questions (and their wording) during the interview process. Data collection using this approach is more systematic than an unstructured approach. Because semi-structured interviews remain conversational and situational, gaps in data can be explored and closed. However, important and salient topics may be inadvertently omitted as interviews proceed in directions that jeopardize their comparability among interviews.

Structured interviews are often well defined prior to the interview. The sequence and exact wording of questions are determined in advance. All interviewees are asked the same basic questions in the same order and manner. Structured interview questions may be *open-ended, closed,* or may comprise a combination of question types. Open-ended questions tend to provide more exploratory, developmental, and contextual data. Data from open-ended questions tend to be more descriptive. For example, an open-ended question that was asked of healthcare providers who worked in an undocumented Latino community was this: "If you could envision an answer to meeting the healthcare needs of the local Latino community, what would that vision be?" Answers were descriptive and complex, providing not only ideas about how to meet healthcare needs in the short- and long-term but also providing further information about what healthcare needs existed in this community and root-cause explanations and insight into the socio-political context pertaining to health.

Closed questions are characterized by response options that are *fixed.* Participants choose among a list of fixed responses. Here is an example of a closed question from a structured interview that was implemented among Latino men: "Some men report having sex with other men for a variety of reasons; have you ever heard of a male friend having sex, including oral or anal sex, with another man?" The response options were "yes," "no," and "refused to answer."

Closed response options simplify data collection and analysis because many questions can be asked in a shorter period of time, and responses can be easily aggregated and compared. The disadvantage,

however, is that participants must fit their experiences and feelings into predetermined categories. This may distort the true experiences and feelings of the participants.

Conventionally, interviews comprised of closed questions collect data on a topic by asking individuals questions to generate statistics on the group or groups within a community or population that those individuals represent. Closed-question interviews do not tend to be formative or exploratory; rather questions are asked about a variety of factors that influence, measure, or are affected by health. For example, population-based or community-wide, closed-question interviews may document and follow health status. Or, closed-question interviews may provide local data and a baseline for evaluation of intervention efforts. After a local CBPR research project has evolved and developed a research intervention to effect change (e.g., individual behavior change, community change, or policy change), interviews comparing baseline data to intervention implementation or post-intervention follow-up may provide information on how well the intervention is working.

When applying a CBPR approach to research, the research question, measurement method (e.g., interview, questionnaire), and items or questions to be included must be agreed on by the partnership prior to beginning the study. Furthermore, recruitment and administration must be decided. Basic questions that the CBPR partnership will want to answer as members prepare a study include the following:

1. How will participants be recruited?
2. What type of compensation will be provided?
3. Who will administer the interview or questionnaire?
4. Will interviewers be used or will the questionnaire be self-administered?

Researchers may think they know the best way to recruit interviewees and administer data collection procedures. However, community partners may contribute great insight that may increase recruitment and response rates as well as honesty in responses.[46,47] In fact, what seems scientifically sound to the researcher (e.g., reducing bias and threats to validity) may actually inhibit responses for a number of reasons (e.g., local or cultural bias).

QUALITATIVE AND QUANTITATIVE DATA ANALYSIS

Analyzing and interpreting any type of data set, whether qualitative or quantitative, using a CBPR approach is challenging. Ensuring the participation of all partners in the process can be daunting. Researchers may have access to a variety of data analysis software that community partners may not have the time or energy to learn and/or apply. Thus, creative ways to examine data may be necessary. During qualitative data analysis, community partners may review and provide perceptions on potential themes through their detailed reading and rereading of the transcripts separately. The researcher may choose to analyze the data using a software program to code and retrieve non-numeric data (e.g., Nvivo, ATLAS.ti, Ethnograph, or NUD*IST). Coming together, the research partners compare broad categories, resolve discrepancies, and begin the process of interpreting the findings through the development of themes. Themes based in qualitative data are most often directional. Themes can be described as potential assertions that can be tested later through subsequent research. Examples of themes developed using qualitative analysis include the following: (1) *Manhood is affirmed through sex.*[6] (2) *Undocumented Latinos felt that they have no right to access public health care.*[48] (3) *Familiar brand-name medicines are preferred by immigrants.*[49] Quotations are usually abstracted from the qualitative transcripts to illustrate the themes.

Quantitative data analysis poses similar challenges.[8] How can community members who lack quantitative data analysis skills or software training participate in this phase? Researchers should communicate and solicit feedback with the partners throughout the process, keeping the partners up to date on statistical approaches, decisions, and methodology rationales. Furthermore, researchers should not assume that CBPR partners do not want to be engaged in the analysis process.[8] After all, CBPR promotes knowledge gain and skill development on all sides. As mutual co-learners, the researcher is learning about the partners and the partners are learning as well; this learning may include building data analysis skills.

Because it may be difficult to ensure participation of community partners, getting a commitment from one, two, or three partnership members who are from the community may be key to the data analysis.[8] The entire CBPR partnership may not choose to participate in all phases of the research process but establishing guidelines that ensures community member representation in each phases of the process is key.

In this section only a few research methods were described. However, it is important to note that a researcher need not give up traditional research methods, but may infuse a CBPR approach into any research method.

INITIATING CBPR

Beginning the exciting work of CBPR requires a clear understanding of partnership principles and values, as outlined earlier in this chapter. Below, we outline some pivotal tasks in the researcher's effort to engage in CBPR.

Network, Network, Network

A first task in the CBPR process requires the development of a network with other individuals with similar areas of interest or concern. A relatively easy and helpful initial contact for a researcher may be the local public health department. Providers and educators within health departments around the country are likely to have connections with community agencies working with those affected by and committed to a variety of health concerns. A clinician, administrator, nutritionist, intern, health educator, and/or epidemiologist within the public health department might already be working with established local health coalitions or community groups. Dialoguing with these potential partners is a good, solid start in this process that is well worth the effort. A simple review of a public health department's Web site or a telephone call to the health department may offer initial guidance and access to contacts, and an informational interview with a health department staff member will begin the networking process essential throughout CBPR. As a researcher, "casting a wide net" facilitates networking contacts to identify overlapping health concerns and resources, including talent that may support the research process synergistically. Networking also initiates the establishment of trust that is key to success in CBPR.

The researcher must understand local communities and work through collaboration, not confrontation, with local *stakeholders*. Stakeholders typically are individuals who are affected by the health issue, who will be part of the research, and who will be affected by the research and subsequent changes. Stakeholders may include community members experiencing the problem, service providers, and community leaders, among others.

In addition to contacting and networking with a local public health department, making connections with those healthcare providers in the community who are working with individuals and community members affected by overlapping health and research priorities may provide access to potential CBPR partners. The researcher benefits from thinking broadly about those individuals providing care (e.g., counselors, exercise physiologists, mental health providers, nutritionists, physical therapists, etc.). Furthermore, becoming familiar with other local CBOs, community agencies, and service providers and making contact with representatives from a variety of organizations will yield helpful results. The researcher may find partnerships for CBPR within the local school system, clinical settings, clubs and service agencies, and/or retirement communities, just to name a few more possibilities.

Build Trust

After commonalities have been identified, the researcher begins a process of *trust building*. Trust building is especially important, as communities have often felt exploited as "living laboratories" for universities and medical centers. Communities are often inundated by research projects that test hypotheses, but these projects do not benefit the community itself through some type of action or intervention to improve and promote health and well-being. Communities may be apprehensive about committing to a CBPR partnership, and the researcher may have to overcome a history of research that may not have been initiated and conducted in a respectful manner.[50] A positive relationship is built by working hand in hand with community members. A researcher may choose to spend some initial time volunteering with a CBO and serving on local health coalitions. This level of commitment serves several purposes. First, it advances a genuine and mutually respectful relationship between the researcher and key community leaders whom the researcher may need and want to have on board as partners in the research. It also may open other doors for the researcher; the researcher may be unfamiliar with all the players and may use the opportunity to identify informal community leaders who may be committed to a health issue and may be interested in the research. Third, the role of participant observer allows the researcher the opportunity to understand a community's structure, decision-making processes, and levels of influence of certain members. Finally, community service allows community members to interact with the researcher in a setting that is not focused on any one agenda. By selecting the right place to volunteer and thus "be seen," the researcher may build community trust by association. If a CBO serving a Latino community is well respected by the local Latino community, for example, the researcher will gain more immediate community favor, and thus participation, by spending time there. Such volunteer work not only builds trust, but begins to offer emic and etic community perspectives to the researcher.

Building trust includes building relationships. Relationships between lay community members, organizational representatives, and researchers may involve informal "working" meetings that allow partners to get to know one another.

Community events such as street fairs, church gatherings, and forums as well as parties and celebrations are ideal places for lay community members, organizational representatives, and researchers to convene. These types of opportunities show commitment to the community and allow lay community members, organizational representatives, and researchers to know one another better. This improves trust and communication, which improves the research process.

Maintain Relationships

The key to building trust is *relationship maintenance*. Although it may be easy to feel that one has built trust, one must remember that partnerships cannot be taken for granted. When things are being done "behind the scenes," gaps in the research process may exist, and the researcher must be present within the community. For example, getting a research protocol approved by an institutional review board (IRB) or ethics committee may require a delay in the research process, but the researcher must touch base with CBPR partnership members to supply informal status reports. This is important because the researcher does not want to lose community interest, motivation, or momentum. Community members do not necessarily understand the confusing steps that universities, research institutions, and funders require. Time should be spent in dialogue explaining these steps and their rationales.

Negotiate Partnerships

Subsequent tasks in the CBPR process include bringing key community members and organizational representatives together. This may be easy if an existing community health coalition exists. The coalition can determine whether a health issue is of interest or not. If a health issue is not a focus yet data suggest that it contributes profoundly to morbidity and mortality in the community that the coalition serves or represents, the researcher has to walk a fine line between asserting what she or he perceives to be "important information" and staying true to the priorities of the community. Exploring community priorities and perspectives may yield important insight or even areas of overlap. It may require thinking creatively or "outside of the box." The researcher may provide data and increase awareness affirming her or his agenda, or she or he may decide that the community-prioritized agenda is important and an opportunity to build trust and relationships. Nothing can impede or destroy trust between a researcher and the community members and organizational representatives more than going into a community to "fix" something without asking community members their priorities. After all, community members are not inanimate objects to be "fixed," they are potential partners. CBPR requires the researcher to be flexible, and no place is this flexibility more evident than in adaptations related to community priorities. A researcher may be required to address other priorities as identified by the community in the spirit of the CBPR partnership.

However, the importance of linking community needs and priorities with researcher interests and skills cannot be ignored. Just as community priorities must be respected, researchers must be honest with communities about where their mutual interests and skills overlap or complement each other. Researchers should not adopt community priorities without regard to the epidemiologic data; in fact, community members and organizational representatives may rely on researchers to provide that epidemiologic data and thereby provide a context for their perspectives. Thus, education and negotiation among community members, organizational representatives, and researchers are warranted to establish priorities. Through iterative negotiation, these priorities become more informed. Without negotiation of priorities, it is unlikely that anyone will be effectively served or that community health will be enhanced.

The researcher may begin with a community-health coalition, or it may need to identify and build a network of community members and CBO representatives. Through this network, the foundation of a partnership may be established. Although growth may occur throughout, this network may evolve into a partnership through the hard work of those involved.

A CASE STUDY

HoMBReS: Hombres Manteniendo Bienestar y Relaciones Saludables

HoMBReS, an acronym for *Ho*mbres *M*anteniendo *B*ienestar y *Re*laciones *S*aludables (Men Maintaining Wellness and Healthy Relationships), was an intervention research project in rural North Carolina that was initiated through a partnership of lay community members, organizational representatives, and university health professionals and researchers.[5,8,15,24,26,34,37,48,51–54] A community health coalition known as Chatham Communities In Action (CCIA) was formed in 1991 as part of the N.C. Community-Based Public Health Initiative (CBPHI).[55,56] Because of the rapidly growing Latino community in North Carolina and their early success in diabetes prevention within the African American community, CCIA, with expanding Latino membership, chose to explore Latino health concerns within their local community. A subgroup of CCIA members met with university researchers to develop a plan to explore the health priorities of the Latino community.

The CBPR partnership, which initially was comprised of members of CCIA, convened first to determine how to further develop the CBPR partnership to include Latino representation. Local Latino-serving CBOs and interested individuals that were not involved with CCIA were invited to participate in the process. This inclusion required time to build trust and clarify goals. These added members included representatives from a local adult Latino soccer league, a local Latino *tienda* (grocery store), and a farm-worker advocacy group. The soccer league was a nine-county organization of more than 1600 Latino adult men. The league's president, along with various other interested league members, became involved in the CBPR partnership. The research partners continued to build trust through personal relationships, genuineness, respect, and "being there." CCIA representatives and the researcher shared many dinners while meeting with league representatives. Although CCIA had a history of working with the university, these relationships

could not be assumed or taken for granted. Building and maintaining trust and communication always plays a paramount role in CBPR.

The expanded CBPR partnership gained consensus on the research aims. This process involved answering two equally important questions. First, the research partners had to ask themselves two questions: "What do we want to know?" and "Why do we want to know it?" This distinction is important because a CBPR approach recognizes that knowledge for the sake of knowledge (i.e., the accumulation of scientific knowledge) is important, but the immediate application of knowledge to positively affect the health and well-being of the participating community is equally important. The researchers had many questions and theories they wanted to explore, but the partners kept the focus on the practical use of knowledge that would be gained.

In this study, members of the CBPR partnership chose to explore health concerns of Latino men primarily because the majority of Latinos who had recently arrived to the United States were male, especially in rural North Carolina. Partners had to come to agreement on the research and recruitment design and the roles and contributions of each of the CBPR partners. They decided to use focus groups to explore health priorities. Partners created, reviewed, revised, and approved the focus-group moderator's guide. The soccer league president recruited focus group participants, and two partnership members served as the focus group moderator and the note taker. The note taker was a university public health researcher who was proficient in Spanish. A Latino-serving CBO hosted the focus groups. Seven focus groups were completed.[8,24]

The first stage of data analysis involved members of a subgroup from the CBPR partnership; they sorted the focus group transcripts into broad content categories. After the initial sorting process was complete, the analysis team came together to compare broad categories and begin the process of interpreting the findings into conceptual domains. After themes were created, the themes were presented to members of the CBPR partnership and other community members, including soccer league members, for *number checking* and interpretation. This was done by writing themes on flip charts and presenting these draft themes to the CBPR partners and representatives from the soccer league to review, discuss, and revise. Several iterations of this process were completed.

Findings were disseminated through community and national presentations, report writing, and manuscript development. Because action is a key component of CBPR, the findings also were used for funding proposals and intervention design. All partners had equal access to the findings. For example, organizational representatives used preliminary findings for service grant and programmatic grant preparation, and community members used the findings to advocate for Latino men's health within the health department. It was through the initial focus groups that sexually transmitted disease (STD) and human immunodeficiency virus (HIV) infection were identified as priorities by members of the Latino soccer league as well as the potential use of the social network of the league to develop, implement, and evaluate a lay advisor as an intervention.[24]

The HoMBReS intervention study was funded by the Centers for Disease Control and Prevention (CDC). The goal of this CBPR study was to reduce the risk of STD/HIV infection among Latino men through the development, implementation, and evaluation of a lay health advisor intervention. Briefly, HoMBReS was a multi-year, quasi-experimental, research study with four interrelated objectives:

1. Develop and implement a lay health advisor intervention to reduce STD/HIV risk behaviors among members of the soccer league

2. Evaluate the efficacy of the intervention by comparing soccer league members in the intervention to those in the delayed-intervention comparison group using self-reported sexual risk behaviors and utilization of STD/HIV counseling, testing, and treatment services

3. Evaluate the changes experienced by the lay health advisors by being trained and serving as lay health advisors

4. Assess the feasibility of engaging a soccer league in implementing a lay health advisor intervention designed to reduce STD/HIV transmission among Latino men

The lay health advisors, known as *navegantes* (navigators), were trained to provide STD/HIV prevention education and prevention information and service and resource referral to their teammates. They served as (1) sources of STD/HIV information and referral, (2) opinion leaders to change risky behavioral norms resulting from culturally infused male gender socialization, and (3) community activists to work with organizations such as the local public health department to better address the needs and priorities of Latino men in culturally congruent approaches.

This project was successful in the recruitment and training of a strong cadre of *navegantes* because of the initial "buy in" of the Latino soccer league. Without their history of interest, support, and involvement, the idea for STD/HIV primary prevention and the use of team members as lay health advisors would not necessarily have been considered or possible. Had it been considered, the risks would have been higher because buy-in would not have been garnered. Less knowledge about whether men would want to participate in a 16-hour, theory-based training and what that training should include would have left more opportunity for misjudgment on the part of the researcher. Instead, the partnership approach ensured that fewer problems were incurred and that, when unavoidable roadblocks occurred, creative solutions with a higher potential for success were explored. In this way, more perspectives and options were identified.[15,51,54]

The HoMBReS intervention was found to successfully increase condom use and HIV testing. At a postintervention assessment, the intervention was found to have increased condom use and HIV testing among teammates in the intervention compared to their peers in the comparison control group.[26] Furthermore, the success of this initial study that was conducted in partnership with lay community members and organizational representatives led to further interventions. The CBPR partnership developed a multisession, small-group intervention designed to increase condom use and HIV testing among heterosexually active Latino men entitled *HoMBReS-2*, which, in pilot testing, was deemed efficacious.[28]

The partnership is currently testing two different interventions for Latino men who have sex with men (MSM). One intervention is a lay health advisor intervention entitled HOLA: *Hombres Ofreciendo Liderazgo y Apoyo* (Hello: Men Offering Leadership and Help). This intervention is based on the original *HoMBReS* intervention; however, rather than utilizing the social structure of the soccer league, it harnesses informal social networks of Latino MSMs. Lay health advisors, also known as *navegantes,* are trained to work with their friends to increase condom use and HIV testing. The second intervention is entitled *HOLA en Grupos,* a small-group intervention for Latino MSMs that is also designed to increase condom use and HIV testing.

Since the partners began their intervention research with immigrant Latino men, Latinas (e.g., girlfriends, wives, partners, sisters, and cousins of male participants) have stepped forward and asked representatives of the CBPR partnership for HIV prevention programming tailored to their needs and priorities. Based on extensive formative research, CBPR partners developed a culturally congruent intervention entitled *MuJEReS: Mujeres Juntas Estableciendo Relaciones Saludables* (Together Women Establishing Healthful Relations). The intervention, which is designed to reduce the disproportionate HIV burden among Latinas in the United States, trains Latina lay health advisors, known as *Comadres,* from the community to work within their existing informal social networks. Latinas chose the term *Comadre* because of its common use to mean a trusted friend or neighbor who can be relied upon for advice and assistance. Besides the formal and informal health advising in which *Comadres* engage, partners determined that each *Comadre* also holds six 60- to 90-minute group sessions with their social network members during intervention implementation. These group sessions include (1) hosting a *fiesta* (party) to inaugurate

the *Comadre*'s role as a resource within her social network; (2) learning and practicing correct condom use; (3) brainstorming and discussing ways to overcome communication barriers with sex partners; (4) brainstorming and discussing ways to overcome communication barriers with healthcare providers; (5) demystifying the HIV testing process through describing available testing options, delineating the process (e.g., eligibility, etc.), and illustrating challenges that will be faced and how they can be surmounted; and (6) exploring what it is like to be an immigrant Latina through facilitated dialogue designed to build positive self images and supportive relationships.

DISCUSSION

Ensuring the health of the public will require clinicians, health professionals, researchers, and others to join forces with lay community members and organizations of both community insiders and outsiders to generate new understandings of health status, explore health status predictors and measures, and uncover innovative ways to effect change in the health status within vulnerable communities.[2,57] Although this may seem logical, the process of partnership requires time to establish trusted relationships, create a research infrastructure, and develop a history of partnership. The investment of time to build these trusted relationships is essential for successful CBPR activities; however, this effort is well worth the expense in time, energy, and resources if true improvements in community health status are to occur.

Although no road map exists to conduct CBPR, it is important to note that individuals, including health professionals, researchers, and community members, who are unfamiliar with CBPR often confuse *community placed* with *community based.* Community-placed efforts simply imply that clinicians, health professionals, practitioners, and researchers leave the traditional institutions such as the university, hospital, or medical center and go into the community to do their work. However, community-based efforts involve more than going outside physical walls of these traditional institutions. CBPR requires partnering with communities and basing efforts in the reality and structures *preferred* by the community.

Health research through community partnership is a viable mechanism for health promotion and disease prevention[2,4,5,7,10-12] because CBPR improves the quality of research, increases community capacity, and advances positive health outcomes by doing the following:

1. Bringing community members into a study as partners, not just as *subjects*
2. Using the knowledge of the community to understand health problems, take appropriate action, and design meaningful interventions
3. Connecting community members directly with how research is done and how it is used
4. Providing immediate benefits from the results of the research to the community that participated in the study

CBPR can be infused into any research design. In this chapter, four methodologies were briefly presented and one case study was described. Researchers who are exploring the use of CBPR in their own research and practice should remember two important issues. First, key to using a CBPR approach is the inclusion of lay community members, CBO representatives, health department and other agency staff, and university personnel, including students and faculty researchers.[10] Together, these partners must share control over all phases of the research process, including community assessment, issue definition, development of research methodology, data collection and analysis, interpretation of data, dissemination of findings, and application of the results to address community concerns. CBPR recognizes that lay community members themselves are the experts in understanding and interpreting their own lives.

Second, inherent in CBPR is a commitment towards action or intervention. This action may be loosely defined, including community organization and mobilization; the development of new and authentic community member and agency partnerships with concrete tasks; and measurable plans for action with assigned responsibilities and defined time lines. The actions may be focused on immediate changes to improve health-related conditions, such as changes in a clinical practice protocol that increases adherence to an AIDS medication, policies that increase access to community mental health services, or even improved lighting on an outdoor neighborhood running/walking track to encourage exercise in the community. Furthermore, actions may be focused on long-term changes in social determinants of health, such as improved racial equality in administrative and political representation through community mobilization and organization.

SUMMARY

CBPR not only may be an effective tool to addressing the complex health problems facing vulnerable communities, but CBPR also is considered to be a just and democratic approach to research; as has been noted by community members, "Nothing about me, without me," implies that community members have a *right* to participate in all aspects of the research endeavor. Although CBPR is a challenging approach to research, CBPR offers the researcher the opportunity to participate in a co-learning process of sharing resources, knowledge, skills, and attributes to increase the quality and validity of research. Increased quality and validity thus yields more effective interventions and improved health outcomes.

REFERENCES

1. Centers for Disease Control and Prevention, Agency for Toxic Substances and Disease Registry Committee on Community Engagement. *Principles of Community Engagement.* Atlanta, GA: US Department of Health and Human Services; 1997.
2. Institute of Medicine. *Unequal Treatment: Confronting Racial and Ethnic Disparities in Health Care.* Washington, DC: National Academy Press; 2003.
3. Eng E, Moore KS, Rhodes SD, Griffith D, Allison L, Shirah K, Mebane E. Insiders and outsiders assess who is "the community": Participant observation, key informant interview, focus group interview, and community forum. In: Israel BA, Eng E, Schulz AJ, Parker E, eds. *Methods for Conducting Community-Based Participatory Research for Health.* San Francisco, CA: Jossey-Bass; 2005:77–100.

4. Minkler M, Wallerstein N. Introduction to community based participatory research. In: Minkler M, Wallerstein N, eds. *Community-Based Participatory Research for Health.* San Francisco, CA: Jossey-Bass; 2003:3–26.

5. Rhodes SD, Malow RM, Jolly C. Community-based participatory research: A new and not-so-new approach to HIV/AIDS prevention, care, and treatment. *AIDS Educ Prev.* Jun 2010;22(3):173–183.

6. Rhodes SD, Hergenrather KC, Vissman AT, Stowers J, Davis AB, Hannah A, Alonzo J, Marsiglia FF. Boys must be men, and men must have sex with women: A qualitative CBPR study to explore sexual risk among African American, Latino, and white gay men and MSM. *Am J Men's Health.* 2011; 5(2): 140–151.

7. Hergenrather KC, Rhodes SD. Community-based participatory research: Applications for research in health and disability. In: Knoll T, ed. *Focus on Disability: Trends in Research and Application.* Vol 2. New York, NY: Nova Science; 2008:59–87.

8. Cashman SB, Adeky S, Allen AJ, Corburn J, Israel BA, Montano J, Rafelito A, Rhodes SD, Swanston S, Wallerstein N, Eng E. The power and the promise: Working with communities to analyze data, interpret findings, and get to outcomes. *Am J Public Health.* 2008;98(8):1407–1417.

9. Viswanathan M, Eng E, Ammerman A, Gartlehner G, Lohr KN, Griffith D, Rhodes SD, Webb L, Sutton SF, Swinson T, Jackman A, Whitener L. *Community-Based Participatory Research: Assessing the Evidence.* Rockville, MD: Agency for Healthcare Research and Quality; July 2004:99.

10. Israel BA, Schulz AJ, Parker EA, Becker AB. Review of community-based research: Assessing partnership approaches to improve public health. *Annu Rev Public Health.* 1998;19:173–202.

11. Wallerstein N, Duran B. The conceptual, historical, and practice roots of community-based participatory research and related participatory traditions. In: Minkler M, Wallerstein N, eds. *Community-Based Participatory Research for Health.* San Francisco, CA: Jossey-Bass; 2003:27–52.

12. Wandersman A. Community science: Bridging the gap between science and practice with community-centered models. *Am J Community Psychol.* 2003;31-(3–4):227–242.

13. Eng E, Blanchard L. Action-oriented community diagnosis: A health education tool. *Int Q Community Health Educ.* 2007;26(2):141–158.

14. Eng E, Blanchard L. Action-oriented community diagnosis: A health education tool. *Int J Comm Health Educ.* 1991;11(2):93–110.

15. Eng E, Rhodes SD, Parker EA. Natural helper models to enhance a community's health and competence. In: DiClemente RJ, Crosby RA, Kegler MC, eds. *Emerging Theories in Health Promotion Practice and Research.* Vol 2. San Francisco, CA: Jossey-Bass; 2009:303–330.

16. Lincoln YS, Guba EG. Paradigmatic controversies, contradictions, and emerging confluences. In: Denzin NK, Lincoln YS, eds. *The Handbook of Qualitative Research.* 2 ed. Thousand Oaks: Sage; 2000:163–188.

17. Habermas J. *The Theory of Communicative Action.* Cambridge, MA: Polity Press; 1984.

18. Seifer SD. Building and sustaining community-institutional partnerships for prevention research: Findings from a national collaborative. *J Urban Health.* 2006;83(6):989–1003.

19. Seifer SD, Maurana CA. Developing and sustaining community-campus partnerships: Putting principles into practice. *Partnership Perspectives.* 2000;1(2):7–11.

20. Steuart GW. Planning and evaluation in health education. *Int J Health Educ.* 1969;2:65–76.

21. Cassel JC. The contribution of the social environment to host resistance: The Fourth Wade Hampton Frost Lecture. *Am J Epidemiol.* 1976;104:107–123.

22. Kauffman KS. The insider/outsider dilemma: Field experience of a white researcher "getting in" a poor black community. *Nurs Res.* 1994;43(3):179–183.

23. Steuart GW. Social and behavioral change strategies. In: Phillips HT, Gaylord SA, eds. *Aging and Public Health.* New York, NY: Springer; 1985.

24. Rhodes SD, Eng E, Hergenrather KC, Remnitz IM, Arceo R, Montano J, Alegria-Ortega J. Exploring Latino men's HIV risk using community-based participatory research. *Am J Health Behav.* 2007;31(2):146–158.

25. Rhodes SD, Hergenrather KC, Wilkin AM, Jolly C. Visions and voices: Indigent persons living with HIV in the southern United States use photovoice to create knowledge, develop partnerships, and take action. *Health Promot Pract.* 2008;9(2):159–169.

26. Rhodes SD, Hergenrather KC, Bloom FR, Leichliter JS, Montaño J. Outcomes from a community-based, participatory lay health advisor HIV/STD prevention intervention for recently arrived immigrant Latino men in rural North Carolina, USA. *AIDS Ed Prev.* 2009;21(Supplement 1):104–109.

27. Rhodes SD, McCoy TP, Hergenrather KC, Vissman AT, Wolfson M, Alonzo J, Bloom FR, Alegría-Ortega J, Eng E. Prevalence estimates of health risk behaviors of immigrant Latino men who have sex with men. *J Rural Health.* In press.

28. Rhodes SD, McCoy TP, Vissman AT, DiClemente RJ, Duck S, Hergenrather KC, Long Foley K, Alonzo J, Bloom FR, Eng E. A randomized controlled trial of a culturally congruent intervention to increase condom use and HIV testing among heterosexually active immigrant Latino men. *AIDS and Behavior*. In press.

29. Rhodes SD, Vissman AT, Stowers J, Miller C, McCoy TP, Hergenrather KC, Wilkin AM, Reece M, Bachmann LH, Ore A, Ross MW, Hendrix E, Eng E. A CBPR partnership increases HIV testing among MSM: Outcome findings from a pilot test of the CyBER/testing internet intervention. *Health Educ Behav*. 2011;38(3):311–320.

30. Rhodes SD, Hergenrather KC. Exploring hepatitis B vaccination acceptance among young men who have sex with men: Facilitators and barriers. *Prev Med*. 2002;35(2):128–134.

31. Glaser BG, Strauss AL. *The Discovery of Grounded Theory: Strategies for Qualitative Research*. Chicago, IL: Aldine; 1967.

32. Sandelowski M, Davis DH, Harris BG. Artful design: Writing the proposal for research in the naturalist paradigm. *Res Nurs Health*. 1989;12(2):77–84.

33. Wang C, Burris MA. Photovoice: Concept, methodology, and use for participatory needs assessment. *Health Educ Behav*. 1997;24(3):369–387.

34. Rhodes SD, Hergenrather KC. Recently arrived immigrant Latino men identify community approaches to promote HIV prevention. *Am J Public Health*. 2007;97(6):984–985.

35. Hergenrather KC, Rhodes SD, Clark G. Windows to work: Exploring employment-seeking behaviors of persons with HIV/AIDS through photovoice. *AIDS Educ Prev*. 2006;18(3):243–258.

36. Hergenrather KC, Rhodes SD, Cowan CA, Bardhoshi G, Pula S. Photovoice as community-based participatory research: A qualitative review. *Am J Health Behav*. 2009;33(6):686–698.

37. Rhodes SD, Hergenrather KC, Griffith D, Yee LJ, Zometa CS, Montaño J, Vissman AT. Sexual and alcohol use behaviours of Latino men in the southeastern USA. *Culture, Health & Sexuality*. 2009;11(1):17–34.

38. Freire P. *Pedagogy of the Oppressed*. New York, NY: Herder and Herder; 1970.

39. Shaffer R. *Beyond the Dispensary*. Nairobi, Kenya: Amref; 1983.

40. Streng JM, Rhodes SD, Ayala GX, Eng E, Arceo R, Phipps S. Realidad Latina: Latino adolescents, their school, and a university use photovoice to examine and address the influence of immigration. *J Interprof Care*. 2004;18(4):403–415.

41. Wang C, Burris MA, Ping XY. Chinese village women as visual anthropologists: A participatory approach to reaching policymakers. *Soc Sci Med*. 1996;42(10):1391–1400.

42. Wang CC, Yi WK, Tao ZW, Carovano K. Photovoice as a participatory health promotion strategy. *Health Promo Int*. 1998;13(1):75–86.

43. Killion CM, Wang CC. Linking African American mothers across life stage and station through photovoice. *J Health Care Poor Underserved*. 2000;11(3):310–325.

44. Moss T. Youth put their world on view. *Children First*. 1999;3(27):3–35.

45. Wang C, Burris MA. Photovoice: concept, methodology, and use for participatory needs assessment. *Health Educ Behav*. 1997;24(3):369–387.

46. Angell KL, Kreshka MA, McCoy R, Donnelly P, Turner-Cobb JM, Graddy K, Kraemer HC, Koopman C. Psychosocial intervention for rural women with breast cancer: The Sierra-Stanford Partnership. *J Gen Intern Med*. 2003;18(7):499–507.

47. Lauderdale DS, Kuohung V, Chang SL, Chin MH. Identifying older Chinese immigrants at high risk for osteoporosis. *J Gen Intern Med*. 2003;18(7):508–515.

48. Rhodes SD, Hergenrather KC, Wilkin A, Alegria-Ortega J, Montaño J. Preventing HIV infection among young immigrant Latino men: results from focus groups using community-based participatory research. *J Natl Med Assoc*. Apr 2006;98(4):564–573.

49. Vissman AT, Bloom FR, Leichliter JS, Bachmann LH, Montaño J, Topmiller M, Rhodes SD. Exploring the use of non-medical sources of prescription drugs among immigrant Latinos in the rural southeastern USA. *J Rural Health*. 2011;27:159–167.

50. Rhodes SD, Yee LJ, Hergenrather KC. Hepatitis A vaccination among young African American men who have sex with men in the deep south: psychosocial predictors. *J Natl Med Assoc*. 2003;95(4 Suppl):31S–36S.

51. Rhodes SD. Tuberculosis, sexually transmitted diseases, HIV, and other infections among farmworkers in the eastern United States. In: Arcury TA, Quandt SA, eds. *Latino Farmworkers in the Eastern United States: Health, Safety and Justice*. New York, NY: Springer; 2009:131–152.

52. Rhodes SD, Hergenrather KC, Montano J, Remnitz IM, Arceo R, Bloom FR, Leichliter JS, Bowden WP. Using community-based participatory research to develop an intervention to reduce HIV and STD infections among Latino men. *AIDS Educ Prev*. Oct 2006;18(5):375–389.

53. Rhodes SD, Hergenrather KC, Zometa C, Lindstrom K, Montaño J. Characteristics of immigrant Latino men who utilize formal healthcare services in rural North Carolina: Baseline findings from the *HoMBReS* Study. *J Nat Med Assoc*. 2008;100(10):1177–1185.

54. Vissman AT, Eng E, Aronson RE, Bloom FR, Leichliter JS, Montano J, Rhodes SD. What do men who serve as lay health advisors really do?: Immigrant Latino men share their experiences as *Navegantes* to prevent HIV. *AIDS Educ Prev.* 2009;21(3):220–232.

55. Margolis LH, Stevens R, Laraia B, Ammerman A. Harlan C, Dodds J, Eng E, Pollard, M. Educating students for community-based partnerships. *J Comm Prac.* 2000;7(4):21–34.

56. Parker EA, Eng E, Laraia B, Ammerman A, Dodds J, Margolis L, Cross A. Coalition building for prevention: Lessons learned from the North Carolina Community-Based Public Health Initiative. *J Public Health Manag Pract.* 1998;4(2):25–36.

57. Institute of Medicine. *The Future of Public Health.* Washington, DC: National Academy Press; 1988.

CBPR RESOURCES

Besides the references cited within this chapter, supplemental resources are listed below.

CBPR

- Cashman SB, Adeky S, Allen A, Corburn J, Israel BA, Montaño J, Rafelito A, Rhodes SD, Swanston S, Wallerstein N; Eng E. Analyzing and interpreting data with communities. In Minkler M & Wallerstein N, eds. *Community-Based Participatory Research for Health: From Process to Outcomes.* 2nd ed. San Francisco, CA: Jossey-Bass; 2008:285–302.

- Hergenrather KC, Rhodes SD. Community-based participatory research: Applications for research in health and disability. In Kroll T, ed. *Focus on Disability: Trends in Research and Application.* Vol. 2. New York, NY: Nova Science; 2008: 59–87.

- Leviton LC, Rhodes SD, Chang CS. Public health: Policy, practice, and perceptions. In Kovner AR & Knichman JR, eds. *Healthcare Delivery in the United States.* 9th ed. New York, NY: Springer; 2008:84–124.

- Minkler M, Wallerstein N, eds. Community-Based Participatory Research for Health, 1st ed. San Francisco: John Wiley and Sons; 2003.

- Eng E, Moore K, Rhodes SD, Griffith D, Allison L, Shirah K, Mebane E. Insiders and outsiders assess who is "the community": Participant observation, key informant interview, focus group interview, and community forum. In Israel BA, Eng E, Schulz AJ, & Parker EA, eds. *Methods for Conducting Community-Based Participatory Research for Health.* San Francisco, CA: Jossey-Bass; 2005:77–100.

- Agency for Healthcare Research and Quality Web site. http://www.ahrq.gov/clinic/evrptpdfs.htm#cbpr

- Campus-Community Partnerships for Health Web site. http://depts.washington.edu/ccph/

- Preventing Chronic Disease: Public Health Research, Practice and Policy Web site. http://www.cdc.gov/pcd/issues/2004/jan/03_0024.htm

- Building a Truly Engaged Community Through Participatory Research Web site. http://www.med.wright.edu/ra/re/2003/tindall.html

Photovoice

- Hergenrather KC, Rhodes SD, Clark G. Widows to work: Exploring employment seeking behaviors of persons with HIV/AIDS through photovoice. *AIDS Educ Prev.* 2006;18(3):243–258.

- Hergenrather KC, Rhodes SD, Cowan C, Bardhoshi G, Pula S. Photovoice in community-based participatory research: A qualitative review. *Am J Health Behav.* 2009;33(6):686–698.

- Rhodes SD. Visions and Voices—HIV in the 21st century: Indigent persons living with HIV/AIDS in the southern USA use photovoice to communicate meaning. *J Epidemiol Comm Health.* 2006;60(10):886.

- Rhodes SD, Hergenrather KC. Recently arrived immigrant Latino men identify community approaches to promote HIV prevention in the Southern USA. *Am J Public Health.* 2007;97(6): 984–985.

- Rhodes SD, Hergenrather KC, Griffith D, Yee LJ, Zometa CS, Montaño J, Vissman AT. Sexual and alcohol risk behaviours of immigrant Latino men in the southeastern USA. *Culture, Health & Sexuality.* 2009;11(1):17–34.

- Rhodes SD, Hergenrather KC, Wilkin A, Jolly C. Visions and voices: Indigent persons living with HIV in the Southern US use photovoice to create knowledge, develop partnerships, and take action. *Health Promotion Practice.* 2008;9(2):159–169.

- Streng JM, Rhodes SD, Ayala GX, Eng E, Arceo R, Phipps S. Realidad Latina: Latino adolescents, their school, and a university use photovoice to examine and address the influence of immigration. *J Interprofessional Care.* 2004;18(4):403–415.

- Wang C. Project: Photovoice involving homeless men and women of Washtenaw County, Michigan. *Health Educ Behav.* 1998; 25(1):9–10.

- Wang C. Using photovoice as a participatory assessment and issue selection tool. In: Minkler M, Wallerstein N. Community-Based Participatory Research for Health. San Francisco: Jossey-Bass; 2003:179–196.
- Wang C, Cash JL, Powers LS. Who knows the streets as well as the homeless? Promoting personal and community action through photovoice. *Health Promotion Practice.* 2000;1(1):81–89.

Health Disparities

- Institute of Medicine. Engaging the Public in the Clinical Research Enterprise: Clinical Research Roundtable Workshop Summary. Washington: The National Academies Press, 2003.

- Wallerstein N. Powerless, empowerment, and health: Implications for health promotion programs. *Am J Health Promo,* 1992;6:197–205.

Qualitative Research

- Patton M, ed. *Qualitative Research and Evaluation Methods,* 3rd ed. Thousand Oaks: Sage Publications; 2002.
- Miles M, Huberman AM. *Qualitative Data Analysis,* 2nd ed. Thousand Oaks: Sage Publications; 1994.
- Krueger RA, Casey MA. *Focus Groups: A Practical Guide for Applied Research,* 3rd ed. Thousand Oaks: Sage Publications; 2000.
- Morgan DL, Krueger RA. *The Focus Group Kit,* Vols 1–6. Thousand Oaks: Sage Publications; 1997.

THE RESEARCH PROCESS—OUTCOMES

CHAPTER OVERVIEW

For a very basic overview of data analysis and statistical tests, this chapter covers a few of the common statistical techniques in an effort to provide a first step in the use and understanding of statistics. A large number of books are available on statistics and statistical analysis, and every researcher should have at least one statistical analysis book as a reference. Decisions about data analysis must be made prior to data collection; data analysis planning is part of research methodology. Even those who are fairly confident and accomplished in the use and understanding of statistical tests benefit from consulting a statistician about the type of analysis that should be used in any investigation. Careful attention should be given to the type of research being conducted and the type of data produced by the investigation. Selection of the correct statistical tests results in proper data analysis and greater confidence in the conclusions drawn from the results of analysis. As a practicing healthcare professional, understanding data analysis is a key part of interpreting medical and research literature.

Data Analysis

Meredith A. Davison, PhD
Bruce R. Niebuhr, PhD
J. Glenn Forister, MS, PA-C

INTRODUCTION

Why should clinicians use statistics? Although some healthcare providers earn advanced degrees and engage in health-related research, most are practicing clinicians. All healthcare providers have been exposed to statistical analysis in their education. However, many providers may not see the relevance of statistics in their clinical practice. The basic use of statistics for any clinician is to assist in understanding research articles that help to formulate important decisions for their patients and practice. Healthcare providers are called upon every day to make decisions that are the most cost-efficient and least harmful, and/or that comprise the most appropriate treatment plan. These decisions are best made by understanding the medical literature. Frequently, this understanding requires a basic knowledge and appreciation of statistical analysis and inference.

Healthcare providers are not expected to be statisticians. Biostatistics is a specialty unto itself. As previously mentioned, consulting a biostatistician is essential for conducting a research study. Regardless of whether a healthcare practitioner ever participates in clinical research, critically analyzing the results of research studies in order to make decisions regarding clinical diagnoses and treatment is an important part of healthcare practice. The primary objectives in evaluating the data analysis of a research study are these:

1. Become familiar with the types of data produced in the study
2. Become familiar with the most common statistics in order to read a journal article and grasp its use of statistics and how the study's conclusions flow from the statistical analyses and results
3. Understand the rationale behind the selection of statistical analyses and how and how well specific analyses test the study's hypotheses

In the following chapter, we explore descriptive statistics, inferential statistics, and styles of results presentation, statistical reference texts, and computer software options. Mathematical and statistical formulas are used sparingly in this chapter. However, those involved in research may wish to conduct some data analyses to hone and develop their skills.

LEVELS OF MEASUREMENT

The first step in deciding on the appropriate type of statistical analysis is to determine the level of measurement that is to be used, as shown in **Table 14–1**. As a general rule of thumb, the higher the level of measurement, the more information can be ascertained from the data. The most basic level of measurement is the nominal. With this level of measurement, responses are divided into named groups or categories. For example, subjects might be asked to choose the group to which they belong: male or female. The subjects' choice allows the researcher to group subjects by category.

The nominal level of measurement limits the researcher in the type and number of statistical and mathematical analyses. Primarily, only descriptive analysis or summary can be used. This data enables the researcher to determine how many subjects fall into each category. In the example given, in a survey of 100 healthcare professionals, 39% were male and 61% were female.

Some common nominal data types are gender, race, religion, eye color, year in school, home

Table 14–1 Definitions of Data Types

Data Type	Definition	Example
Nominal data	Data that categorizes	Gender, eye color, race, PA class, practice specialty
Ordinal data	Data defined by an ordering, but the distance between the choices or values is not defined	Likert scales, preference scales, rankings
Continuous data	Data with numeric values, two types: interval and ratio.	Numbers
A. Interval data	Data with a defined interval between the values, but with by no true zero (0) value	Ambient F° temperature. "0" does not indicate a total lack of temperature. It is a value on a scale. The temperature interval difference between +61° and +62° is the same as the interval difference between −61° and −62°
B. Ratio data	Data with an absolute zero (0) value, where "0" means there is a total absence of what is being measured.	Visual acuity, range of motion, height, weight, blood pressure, blood alcohol level

state, etc. Consider nominal data as information that helps to categorize something or someone.

Ordinal measurement provides an ordering (sometimes ranking) between variables. However, the distance between each variable is not defined. For example, research subjects may be asked to indicate their degree of agreement or disagreement with a series of statements. There is no defined distance between "Agree" and "Strongly Agree" or between "Neutral" and "Disagree." One of the most common forms of ordinal measurement is the Likert scale. The traditional use of the Likert scale is to provide the subject with a statement and ask for the level of agreement or disagreement with that statement. The true Likert scale is a five-point scale with the following terms:

Strongly Agree   Agree   Neutral   Disagree   Strongly Disagree

While offering greater possibilities for a more in-depth analysis than nominal measurement, ordinal measurement has limitations with regard to statistical analysis. For instance, several types of ordinal scales exist as well as different ways to construct them. Many ordinal scales are referred to as verbal frequency scales. Ranking is also a form of ordinal scale. Numbers are often used for the responses to ordinal measurements. Whether these numbers can be analyzed using statistical tests for ratio or interval data is debatable. A statistician can help determine the best method of analysis when utilizing ordinal measurements.

The most sophisticated statistical analyses involve two higher levels of measurement, ratio and interval. Ratio measurement differs from interval measurement in that the ratio measurement has an absolute zero. With both of these measurements, there is an ordering of the points, but the distance between each point on the scale is exactly the same. For example, research participants might be asked for the specific number of years since graduating college. A year is a well-defined and understood time interval, with the difference between any consecutive points the same. That is, the difference between 4 years and 5 years is the same as between 65 years and 66 years. A meaningful zero value would exist; therefore, this measurement is a ratio.

One example of an interval scale is ambient temperature. There is a zero value, but the presence of a zero value does not mean total absence of the variable being studied. For example, zero degrees Fahrenheit (0°F) does not mean the total absence of heat because you can have negative temperatures. Therefore, zero in this case is just one value on the scale. Continuous data, such as ratio and interval measurements, offer the researcher the option of utilizing the highest level of analytical operations. Continuous data also provide the researcher with the possibility of using inferential statistics to determine the significance of differences and/or associations between groups and variables.

The four levels of measurement, as well as the appropriate types of statistical analyses to be used with each level, are illustrated in **Figure 14–1**. Keep in mind that the terms parametric (normal) and nonparametric describe the distribution of the subjects or variables. Also, continuous data always has a normal distribution.

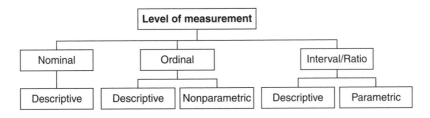

Figure 14–1 Level of measurement.

DESCRIPTIVE STATISTICS

A study may yield a large amount of raw data that is organized and summarized by descriptive statistical methods. Summarizing the data is the essential first step in understanding the results. Then the researcher uses various inferential methods to help test the hypotheses of the study. Description statistics are those processes or analyses that "describe" the sample.

When summarizing data using descriptive methods, the key concepts are *measures of central tendency* and *measures of variability*. In common parlance, measures of central tendency are averages. The most commonly used measures are the **mean**, **median**, and **mode**. The mean is the sum of the scores divided by the total number of scores. The mean can only be calculated for interval or ratio variables. The median is the midpoint of a sequence of ordered variables or the point where half the values are above and half are below. Medians can be calculated for ordinal, interval, or ratio variables. The mode is most frequently occurring value. The mode can be determined for variables that are nominal, ordinal, and interval or ratio.

To illustrate the measures of central tendency, consider the following hypothetical data set: The lengths of stay in the cardiac care unit for seven patients following an acute myocardial infarction were 3, 12, 5, 7, 5, 8, and 9 days, respectively. When performing the statistical calculation for this data set, the data is sorted first from the lowest to the highest numerical value: 3, 5, 5, 7, 8, 9, 12.

> The mode (most frequently occurring score) is 5.
> The median (midpoint of the ordered scores) is 7.
> The mean (sum of the scores divided by the total number of scores) is 7 [3 + 5 + 5 + 7 + 8 + 9 + 12 = 49 / 7 = 7].

By itself, measures of central tendency can give a misleading view of the data. For example, suppose that the lengths of stay for a second group of five patients were 7, 7, 7, 7, and 7 days, respectively. Similar to the first data set, the mean of this data set is 7. What differs, however, is the variability of the data. In the first group, the length of stay varies from 3 to 12 days. In the second group, everyone had the same length of stay: 7 days.

The three measures of variability most commonly reported in biomedical research are the *range, standard deviation,* and *standard error* of the mean. The range, which is the simplest measure, is the difference between the highest and lowest scores. In the first example, the range is $12 - 3 = 9$. The range provides an easy "rough cut" of the variability, yet it is of limited value because it does not include all of the data in the computation. As a point of interest, the range of the second example is zero $(7 - 7 = 0)$; this outcome is a statistical anomaly.

The standard deviation (SD) is the key descriptive statistic used to report variability. Mathematically, it is the square root of the variance. The variance is the sum of the squared differences between each score and the mean, divided by the number of scores minus one. The formula for SD is

$\Sigma(X - M)^2/(n - 1)$, where X = each score, M = the mean, n = the total number of scores in the sample.

To determine the SD for the first example data set provided, the square root of the following equation is calculated using the following equation:

$$[(3 - 7)^2 + (5 - 7)^2 + (5 - 7)^2 + (7 - 7)^2 + (8 - 7)^2 + (9 - 7)^2 + (12 - 7)^2]/(7 - 1)$$

This result is the square root of 9, or 3. The SD for this sample data set, therefore, is 3 days. The SD is the most commonly reported measure of variability.

The standard error of the mean (SEM) is another descriptive statistic. The SEM is the SD divided by the square root of *n,* and it represents an estimate of the population SD. In previous example, the SEM is 1.1 (calculated by dividing 3 by the square root of 7).

Although computation of such basic statistics can be performed with a statistical calculator, using computer software such as Microsoft® Excel® or SPSS® is preferred. The chosen software facilitates computation as well as data management. Additionally, utilizing statistical software minimizes the opportunity for computational error.

INFERENTIAL STATISTICS

Following a descriptive review of the data and determining the level of measurement, the researcher again asks the original question, "What is the hypothesis?" Most research studies are either looking for a relationship between two or more variables or for a difference between the variables. In the study described here, we might be interested in determining whether there is a relationship between a patient's age and the days that they spent in the hospital following MI. In this case, we would probably perform a correlation analysis to determine the potential relationship between these variables. Conversely, if we had hypothesized that the length of stay in the hospital cardiac care unit was shorter in patients who had HMO insurance compared to patients with PPO insurance, we would analyze the difference between patients with PPO insurance and patients with HMO insurance. The length of stay in days would be the variable analyzed.

Inferential statistics are the tools used to draw inferences about the results, particularly to test the hypotheses of a study. A researcher studying a problem usually formulates a hypothesis, such as "Aspirin reduces the incidence of colon cancer" or "Problem-based learning produces better clinicians than conventional instruction." Statistical inference, however, is based on testing a null hypothesis. The null forms for the hypotheses given here are "Aspirin has no effect on the incidence of colon cancer" and "There is no difference in the effectiveness of clinicians trained/educated by problem-based learning and conventional instruction." Therefore, the researcher needs to consider how problem(s) are stated as the study is developed.

In statistical hypothesis testing, the researcher and statistician select a significance level, called alpha (α). By convention, the α level is set at .05 or .01 and is reported without a zero in front of the decimal point ($\alpha < .05$). Remember, the α level is set by the investigator and can be some other level than the one indicated. However, selecting a value greater than .05 should be done with good reason. When the data are analyzed, the statistical test yields a "p" value, the probability that the observed result could occur by chance if the null hypothesis is true. (The p value is also reported without a zero in front of the decimal point.) If $p < \alpha$, then the researcher rejects the null hypothesis. If $p > \alpha$, then the researcher retains (does not reject) the null hypothesis. If the researcher rejects the null hypothesis, then the researcher is saying that the opposite of the null hypothesis is true. If the researcher retains the null hypothesis, then the researcher is stating that the null hypothesis is true.

Selecting which statistical tests to use is the big question. There are literally hundreds of tests. We cannot even begin to provide information on all of them, or the situations in which they would be used. A decision tree depicting the most common statistical tests is provided in **Figures 14–2** and **14–3** as reference guide for choosing which test(s)

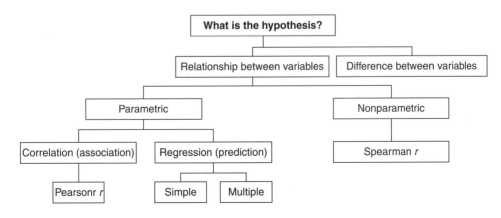

Figure 14–2 What is the hypothesis?

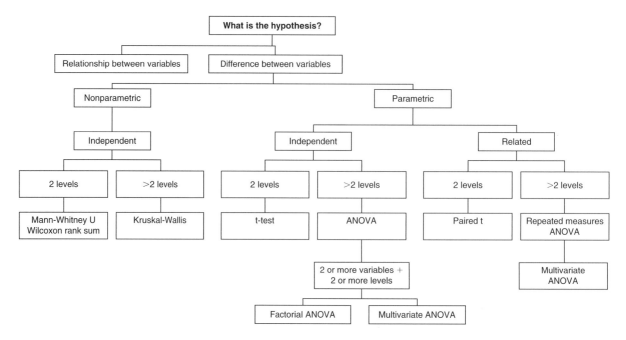

Figure 14–3 What is the hypothesis?

HYPOTHESIS TESTING: NOMINAL DATA

Much medical data is nominal. For instance, one patient has a diagnosis of breast cancer; another patient has a second myocardial infarction. Epidemiological studies also yield nominal data; a patient did or did not get the disease. In a study about smoking, the null hypothesis might state, "Smokers are not more likely to have asthma." For this study, with smoking or not smoking as the variables, an appropriate statistical test would be the chi-squared (χ^2) test. (We realize that asthma is a multi-factorial disease.) The χ^2 test is simply a way to determine whether an event has occurred more frequently than it would be expected to occur by chance. The observed χ^2 value is compared to the probability of the event occurring by chance. For example, if the χ^2 value is greater than 3, the probability is < .05, then the researcher can reject the

null hypothesis, concluding that there is sufficient evidence that asthma occurs more commonly in individuals who have a history of smoking cigarettes.

Epidemiological studies use nominal data to produce incidence and prevalence rates. For example, a study is conducted finding that cigarette smokers are seven times as likely to develop lung cancer or heart disease as those who never smoked. In other words, the relative risk for smokers is 7. Is this risk statistically significant? In this example, a confidence interval is used to test the null hypothesis, which indicates the relative risk = 1 (no added risk of smoking). If the researchers set $\alpha = .05$, then they use a confidence interval of 95 percent. Confidence intervals are reported as percentages. In this case, the confidence interval is found by calculating $[(1 - .05) \times 100\%]$ to give 95 percent. The 95 percent confidence interval for this example is 3.5. This means that the researcher can be 95 percent confident that the actual relative risk is between 3.5 and 10.5 (7 ± 3.5). Because the 95 percent confidence interval does not include the relative risk value of 1, the result is significant at the .05 level. Therefore, the researcher rejects the null hypothesis and concludes that smoking increases the risk of lung cancer or heart disease.

ANALYSIS OF CONTINUOUS DATA: MEASURES OF ASSOCIATION

Determining the association or relationship between two continuous variables (interval or ratio) is a common statistical problem. For instance, what is the relationship between a woman's age and hemoglobin level? What is the relationship between blood sugar level and weight in those who are obese? The measures of association most commonly used are subsumed under the general labels of correlation and regression.

Suppose a clinical educator is concerned about the reliability of an examination on interpreting electrocardiogram (ECG) tracings. Ten students are given the test on Monday, and then are given a parallel test on Tuesday. The exam scores are then correlated. Because the student scores are an interval/ratio variable, the Pearson product moment correlation technique can be used. The result of the statistical manipulation is an "r" value. This is the correlation coefficient. Values of the correlation coefficient (r) vary between -1 (a perfect negative correlation) and $+1$ (a perfect positive correlation). An r value of zero indicates a lack of relationship. The scores on the two days are graphed in **Figure 14–4**.

An experienced researcher/statistician would view Figure 14–4 and interpret the correlation as moderate to strong (based on the clustering of the points about a straight line) and as positive (i.e., as Monday's scores increase, so do Tuesday's). The correlation in this example is computed as $r = .88$. Is the result statistically significant? The null hypothesis of no relationship between the two tests results (variable) or ($r = 0$) is tested at the .05 level of significance. The observed p value is less than .05. The researcher rejects the null hypothesis that there is no relationship and concludes that there is a significant correlation between the two administrations of the EKG exam, supporting its overall reliability.

Multivariate regression techniques in which relationships among many variables can be examined simultaneously go beyond the simple two-variable correlation. Regression is based upon the concept of predicting one variable from another and assigning a probability to these predictions. Complex multisite clinical trials and epidemiological studies are increasingly being conducted utilizing these methods, including discriminant function analysis, factor analysis, path analysis, and logistic regression. In addition, nonparametric correlation techniques exist for ordinal and ranked data. Discussion of these methods, however, is beyond the scope of this book.

ANALYSIS OF INTERVAL/RATIO DATA: COMPARISONS OF GROUPS

The most powerful statistical tests are those that use interval and ratio data from well-designed studies. Ordinal data are often treated as if they are interval data and then are subjected to such tests. A decision as to whether this is acceptable is best left to the statistician. Even if an ordinal value is assigned a "number" value, the distance between the ordinal values is not defined. A technique known as Rausch analysis can be used with ordinal data, but it is beyond the scope of this basic introduction to completely discuss it in this book.

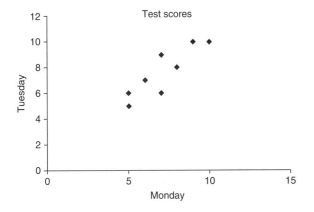

Figure 14–4 Test scores.

An example of an appropriate use for analyzing the difference between groups is a research study involving a new antihypertensive drug that is tested against a placebo. Fifty patients are randomized to either treatment or control. After a course of treatment, the diastolic blood pressure (DBP) is measured. The appropriate statistic to test the null hypothesis is the t-test (sometimes referred to as the Student t-test). The researchers set the α level at .05. Statistical analysis produces a t value. Is this case, $t = 6.4$. Using t tables yields a p value less than .05, so the researcher rejects the null hypothesis and concludes that the new drug significantly reduces diastolic blood pressure.

The t-test (or student t-test) is perhaps the most commonly used parametric test. It allows for a comparison of the means of two groups. (A paired t-test allows for comparison of the same group at two different times). The t-test is actually a special case of a general set of methods collectively known as analysis of variance (ANOVA). Data from complex designs can be analyzed with ANOVA because multiple independent variables, multiple dependent variables, and many subgroups can be tested within a single ANOVA model.

The following example illustrates how to use only one independent variable and one dependent variable. Imagine that a study aims to test the efficacy of over-the-counter pain remedies for nonmigraine headache pain. A total of 25 patients are randomly assigned to one of five drugs in a double-blind manner. The patients are asked to rate their headache pain on a 0–10 scale (where 0 is no pain and 10 is excruciating pain). The null hypothesis is "There is no difference in pain ratings between pain medications." The α level is .05. After one month, the results are compiled and summarized. The researcher then performs an ANOVA test that produces an "F" ratio. The F value is reported with its associated degrees of freedom that are based on the number comparison groups and the number of subjects. If the F yielded a score that had a p value $< .05$, then the researcher rejects the null hypothesis that there

are no significant differences among the drugs. However, what drugs are different from the others? Several multiple comparison procedures are available. However, a biostatistician can assist in selecting the most appropriate test for the analysis. (F values are found in tables produced with most statistical texts.)

META-ANALYSIS

Many evidence-based medicine studies and literature reviews rely on meta-analysis to simultaneously analyze a large number of research studies and determine a conclusion. Meta-analysis can be defined as a process of using statistical integration of the results of several studies to reach an independent conclusion. Meta-analysis is not a singular statistical test or procedure but rather a generalized conceptual approach. The steps to completing an overview are as follows:

1. Define the hypothesis.
2. Collect the "units of measurement," that is, the research studies that have been done on the defined topic.
3. Convert the statistics to common values (e.g., z scores, r values, etc.).
4. Compute the measures of central tendency, variability, and prediction from the accumulated data measures.
5. Determine whether the hypothesis is supported.

Meta-analysis has several advantages. It is precise, rigorous, and quantifies decision making about a question. It is also more objective than traditional literature reviews. In a meta-analysis, the inclusion criteria accounts for the incorporation of multiple related studies, which limits bias, thereby limiting any biases. Additionally, a meta-analysis is replicable, at least in theory. Any reviewer should be able to reach the same conclusion if the same criteria are applied to the same studies. However, disadvantages do exist when conducting a meta-analysis. Because a variety of studies combine different measures of the same variables and statistical techniques in different settings, information about individual differences in the various studies may become lost. Sample size effect may be an issue as well, particularly if some studies have large sample sizes and some have small sample sizes. Chapter 19 discusses evidence-based medicine and presents additional information on meta-analysis.

CHOOSING A STATISTICAL TEST

When choosing a statistical test, the best option is to consult a statistician. However, a general guideline to *some* statistical testing is detailed here. Choosing the right statistical procedures to test the results of data collection can be a major challenge. Most researchers begin by asking the question: "What statistics do I need to make sense of my results"?

The statistical tests that are performed should be the most appropriate for the purposes of the study objectives. Primarily, data is analyzed to summarize it, to identify relationships, and to identify significant differences while controlling confounding variables for all three of these purposes. The results of data analysis allow the researcher to extrapolate his or her findings to a population or group within a population. The choice of statistical tests should be optimal for the type of data to be analyzed and should meet the purposes of that analysis.

Step One

Before selecting statistical tests, a researcher must determine what kind of data is being collected: continuous, ordinal, or nominal.

1. *Continuous data* are unlimited values that are equally spaced along a continuum. They are numbers or values of some sort that have a defined interval or ratio. Examples of continuous data are blood glucose levels, weight, cholesterol levels, weeks, years, or months, IQ scores, mathematic value, etc. These data are numbers.
2. *Ordinal data* are those values that have some type of order but no defined spacing between categories. Examples of ordinal data are the approximate time of day that a person takes their medications: on arising, before breakfast, before lunch, mid-afternoon, with supper, at bedtime. Likert scale descriptors are ordinal: strongly agree, agree, neutral, disagree, strongly disagree. There is order but no defined interval.
3. *Nominal data* are categoric designations; there is no order to the categories. Examples of nominal data are marital status, gender, race, profession, church, year of college graduation, and so forth. Often these descriptive terms define a category.

Investigations can involve all three or only one type of data. The choice of statistical analysis depends on the type of data collected and how the data are compared.

Step Two

Once the type of data required has been determined, the researcher must decide whether the data is parametric or nonparametric.

1. Parametric analyses assume that a normal or near-normal distribution exists. For continuous data, a normal or near-normal distribution is always assumed.
2. Nonparametric analyses do not assume a normal distribution exists. Nonparametric analyses can be done on data with a normal distribution, but they are not as powerful as parametric tests. Nonparametric tests are typically used for ordinal and nominal data. Continuous data can be converted to nominal or ordinal form. An example would be grouping ages into age ranges.

Step Three

The researcher carefully considers the relationships of the data. Are the results "paired" or "matched?"

1. Result data is considered "paired" if the same sample is measured after some intervention (e.g., a treatment of some type).
2. "Matched" samples are those in which the characteristics of the experimental group are "matched" as closely as possible to a control group.

Step Four

The number and type of variables plays a part in the choice of tests: one, two, or more than two (multiple), independent or dependent. There may be no independent variables, one independent variable, or multiple independent variables. Statistical tests are for each dependent variable. There may be more than one dependent variable for each independent variable, but multiple measurements are for each dependent variable only.

Step Five

What is the researcher trying to explain?

1. The relationship between variables

OR

2. The difference between variables

Different tests are used to examine these relationships and differences. (Remember, both can be performed in the same study.)

STATISTICAL TESTS

The following statistical tests are the most commonly used in research. These descriptions are designed to provide a starting point and basic concept for the reader to develop an idea of what tests are and should be used. Many more statistical tests are available, and the choice of tests depends on study design and types of data.

Descriptive statistics: The four trends of the sample are mean, mode, median, and range. They are used to describe a sample and sometimes to demonstrate how a sample may reflect a population, if that population's measures of central tendencies (descriptive statistics) are known.

_t_-test: Tests the difference between two group's means; can be one-tailed or two-tailed; can be used with paired or unpaired samples. Sometimes called the Student _t_-test.

Analysis of variance (ANOVA): Tests the differences among the means of three or more groups for one or more variables.

Analysis of Covariance (ANCOVA): A variant of ANOVA that allows adjusting for extraneous, additional, or undesired variables.

Cochran's Q: Compares proportions between three or more matched groups.

Multiple Analysis of Variance (MANOVA): A variant of ANOVA that allows for study of multiple dependent variables. If MANOVA results are significant, ANOVA must be done for each variable.

Duncan Range Test: A test used after ANOVA to identify means that differ significantly from one another.

Kendall's Rank-Correlation: A test of the linear relationship between two ordinal or continuous variables.

Kruskal-Wallis Test: A nonparametric test for significance when using two independent samples. It is comparable to ANOVA, but for rank ordered data.

Mann-Whitney Test: Sometimes called the Mann-Whitney _U_-test; it is the nonparametric equivalent of a _t_-test. Used with ordinal data for two groups.

Multiple Regression Analysis: Any statistical method that evaluates the results of more than one independent variable on a single dependent variable.

Newman-Keuls Test: Tests for significance in multiple post-hoc comparisons.

Pearson's β^2 Test: A test of categorical data for goodness of fit or comparisons of observations.

Pearson's Product Moment Test: A test of the strength of the linear relationship between two interval or ratio (continuous) variables.

Regression Analysis: A method of predicting dependent variable variability by one or more independent variables. Most commonly used are simple linear regression and multiple linear regression.

Spearman Rho: A test that demonstrates the degree of relationship between two ordinal variables that may not have normal distribution.

Tukey Test: A test to identify significantly different groups after ANOVA.

Wilcoxon Rank Sum Test: A test of significance for two paired, ordinal data samples.

Tests that can be used with continuous data:

Descriptive statistics
t-test
ANOVA
ANCOVA
MANOVA
Duncan Range Test
Kendall's Rank Correlation
Pearson's Product Moment Test
Regression Analysis
Multiple Regression Analysis
Tukey Test

Tests that can be used with ordinal data:

Descriptive statistics
Cochran's Q
Kendall's Rank Correlation
Kruskal-Wallis Test
Mann-Whitney *U*-Test
Pearson's χ^2 Test
Spearman's rho
Wilcoxon Ranked Sum Test

What Test to Use?

The choice of the right statistical test can add power to study findings and provide strong support for outcomes and conclusions. Because so many tests (many more than the ones listed here) are available, much confusion reigns in the realms of statistical analysis, especially for novice investigators. Many investigators use the tests that are most familiar to them, that is, tests they have used in the past. Understanding what a statistical test can and cannot do is very valuable, but using only one or a few familiar tests for all data analysis can create research limitations.

The number of dependent and independent variables influences the choice of tests more than the category of the data (i.e., nominal, ordinal, continuous). Each *dependent variable* is tested separately, resulting in one big question for the researcher: What do I want to do, summarize, explore relationships, or test for significance of difference?

PRESENTATION OF RESULTS

Results of a study are presented in the body of the text, tables, figures, and/or charts. Examples of these methods have been included in this chapter. A general rule to follow is that extensive results are most easily comprehended when presented in graphical form (e.g., figure or chart) and least comprehended when written into the body of the text. Tables provide the middle ground. A second general rule is that tables and figures do not stand alone and must be referred to and described in the body of the text. [See Chapter 5 for more information.]

SUMMARY

In this chapter, we presented a short overview of some of the most common types of statistics used in biomedical and educational research. Healthcare professional participating in research projects need to understand the rationale behind the biostatistician's selection of statistical analyses and how those analyses test the study's hypotheses. The chapter and bibliography also provide the basis to perform selected data analyses.

This is one way to categorize some useful tests.

To summarize data:	Descriptive statistics
To examine the frequency relationship of ONE variable to a theoretical distribution:	Chi-squared test for goodness of fit
To examine the frequency relationship of TWO variables to each other:	Chi-squared test for association
To examine the measured relationship between two variables:	
For ordinal data:	Spearman's rho test
For continuous data:	Pearson's correlation coefficient
To examine the measured relationship of multiple variables:	Multiple Regression test
To examine the significance of difference between groups:	
For one group:	t-test
For two independent groups:	
Ordinal data:	Mann-Whitney U test
Continuous data:	Independent samples t-test
For two related groups:	
Ordinal data:	Wilcoxon matched pairs test
Continuous data:	Paired samples *t*-test
For multiple independent groups:	
One independent variable:	One-way ANOVA
Multiple independent groups:	MANOVA
For multiple related groups:	Repeated measures ANOVA

RECOMMENDED RESOURCES

Lang TA, Secic M. *How to report statistics in medicine: Annotated guidelines for authors, editors, and resources.* 2nd ed. Philadelphia, PA: American College of Physicians; 2006.

Norman GR, Streiner DL. *PDQ statistics,* 3rd ed. Philadelphia, PA: B.C. Decker, Inc.; 2003.

Dawson B, Trapp R. *Basic and clinical biostatistics,* 4th ed. New York, NY: Lange Medical Books-McGraw-Hill, 2004.

Creswell, *Research design: Qualitative, quantitative, and mixed methods approaches,* Thousand Oaks, CA: Sage Publications; 2009.

Cohen P, Cohen J, West SG, Aiken LS. *Applied multiple regression/correlation analysis for the behavioral sciences.* 3rd ed Mahwah, NJ: Lawrence Erlbaum; 2002.

Glantz, SA. *Primer of biostatistics,* 6th ed. New York, NY: McGraw-Hill, 2005.

Glantz SA, Slinker BK. *Primer of applied regression and analysis of variance,* 2nd ed. New York, NY; 2000.

Harris R. *ANOVA: An analysis of variance primer.* Itasca, IL: FE Peacock; 1994.

Harris M, Taylor G. *Medical and health science statistics made easy.* 2nd ed. Sudbury: Jones and Bartlett; 2009.

Jekel, J, Katz, D, Elmore, J, Wild, D. *Epidemiology, biostatistics, and preventive medicine.* 3rd ed. Philadelphia, PA: Saunders Elsevier, 2007.

FURTHER RESOURCES

Computer Software

Software for statistical analysis is categorized as (1) General purpose data analysis programs with statistical application; (2) complete statistical packages; and (3) special-purpose software for specific applications. All the software listed here are for personal computers running Microsoft® Windows® 98/2007/XP or Apple Macintosh operating systems.

General Purpose Data Analysis Software

Microsoft Excel®. Part of Microsoft Office®, general purpose software includes several statistical tools.

Third-party statistical add-ons are available at www.microsoft.com

Complete Statistical Packages

Stata. StataCorp, LP, College Station, TX. A comprehensive package with excellent graphing capabilities. Website: http://stata.com/

SAS. SAS, Inc., Cary, NC. A comprehensive and powerful package. Website: www.sas.com

SPSS. SPSS, Inc., Chicago, IL. A comprehensive and powerful package
Website: www.spss.com

Specialized Software

Mathcad. Mathcad, Inc., Cambridge, MA. Calculation software, not only for statistics. Website: www.mathsoft.com

SigmaPlot. SPSS, Inc., Chicago, IL. Primarily a graphing package, it includes extensive analysis tools. Website: www.spss.com

Design-Expert. Stat-Ease, Inc. Software set up and analyzes experimental designs. Website: www.statease.com

Websites

These sites are particularly useful to faculty and students in teaching and learning statistics.

StatLib. A system for distributing statistical software, data sets, and information. Archives of statistical routines and data sets. Maintained at Carnegie-Mellon University. Website: http://lib.stat.cmu.edu/

Rice Virtual Lab in Statistics. Excellent simulations and demonstrations. Maintained at Rice University. Website: http://www.ruf .rice.edu/~lane/rvls.html

CHAPTER OVERVIEW

This chapter discusses the results of data analysis. For most manuscripts, the results section is the shortest and most graphically displayed. It is important that findings, and particularly key findings, be presented clearly in a logical fashion. The results section should consist of the "facts and only the facts." Graphs and charts are useful methods for presenting results. The Results section (sometimes referred to as the Findings section) is an important part of a research report; key findings and outcomes of the study are reported here, and this is where the author indicates whether or not the hypotheses (null hypotheses or research questions) were supported or rejected. All preceding sections of a research report are designed to build up the reader's anticipation for what is shared in the Results section. Additionally, findings in the Results section should be consistent and correlate well with the preceding Materials and Methods (or Methodology) section.

The Results Section

Anthony A. Miller, MEd, PA-C
J. Dennis Blessing, PhD, PA

INTRODUCTION

The Results section should present only key findings related to the research question, *without* the author's conclusions regarding the meaning and importance of the data, which follows in the Discussion section. The Results section is typically one of the shortest sections of the research report, and it should be written clearly and succinctly, generally in past tense for experimental or quasi-experimental studies and in the present tense for descriptive studies. For ethical reasons, all of the key findings should be reported, not just those supporting the hypotheses. Information about or descriptions of what was done belong in the preceding Materials and Methods section and should not be included in the Results section.

The reported results must be consistent with the methodology and data analysis. Investigators must be careful to refrain from including any conclusions or opinions in the Results section. Anything other than the "facts" could bias a reader's interpretation. The Results section should be neutral in every aspect, allowing readers to form their own conclusions.

However, it is helpful if the Results section demonstrates the outcomes clearly. For example, reporting that the systolic blood pressure *decreased* on average 10 mmHg after administration of agent X is more clear than reporting that the mean systolic blood pressure was 120 mmHg after administration of agent X.

Ultimately, the Results section is the "meat" of the research report. The results are the items that provide the basis for all that follows and, most importantly, for the interpretation of meaning. The Results section represents "the major scientific contribution of your study."[1] A common beginners' mistake is reporting raw data rather than summarizing findings. The author's primary task in the Results section is to provide a picture of the data for the reader. The following excerpts provide an example of a poorly written segment in the Results section and a contrasting improved segment.

Facts Without Interpretation

The mean resting pulse rate for the 10 control subjects was 74 ± 4 (SD) compared to the 12 athletes with a mean resting pulse rate of 66 ± 5 beats per minute.

Improved

The mean resting pulse rate was 11% lower in the 12 athletes than the 10 control subjects 66 ± 5 (SD) vs. 74 ± 4 beats per minute, $p < 0.05$.

Note that the magnitude of the difference (11%) is reported as well as the probability value indicating that the difference was statistically significant. The first example is ambiguous and leaves it to the reader to determine the meaning of the data, whereas in the second example the author makes clear to the reader what is important about the data.

THE RESULTS SECTION

The Results section usually begins with a description or profile of the subjects and includes relevant demographics so that the reader has a good understanding of how representative the sample was compared to the population. Numbers, percentages, and central tendency statistics should be used to describe the study sample. An example of this section might read: "Fifty-two percent (n = 78) of the healthcare professionals responded to the survey. Twenty questionnaires were returned 'unforwardable.' Of the respondents, 33 were male and 45 were female. The average age was 34 years (SD = ±6.5)."

After describing the sample used in the study, the researcher reports the results of the statistical analysis with sufficient detail to permit the reader to determine that appropriate analyses were conducted and that the hypotheses were supported or were not. For descriptive research, frequencies, ranges, and measures of central tendency should be reported. For experimental or quasi-experimental research, the inferential or associational statistics should include the test statistic, the direction, and the level of probability. Confidence intervals and size effects should be reported, adding strength to decisions regarding statistical significance.[2-5]

The word "significant" in the discussions of data must be used carefully. "Significant" means "statistically significant" or "clinically significant" when written in the healthcare literature. Some authors see events or numbers of subjects affected as significant because of the event, intervention, treatment, or effect. In the Results section of the manuscript, something is significant only if the result is statistically significant according to the numerical data analysis.

In addition to reporting significance related to hypothesis testing, sufficient information about the statistical test must be provided to allow the reader to understand that the appropriate test was chosen and the preferred method for reporting the statistical test was used.[6] This may be particularly important if a novel approach to analysis was used or if the procedure is considered controversial. It may be appropriate to include such descriptions in the Methodology section. Always assume that readers have a working knowledge of statistics and research design.

Finally, the hypotheses that were supported should be indicated in the Results section, and they should be clearly linked to the null hypotheses or research questions or to alternate hypotheses where such an explanation is appropriate. At this point, the reason why the hypotheses were or were not supported are given; the data should speak for itself.

Tables and Figures

For the sake of clarity and brevity, tables and figures are often used to show research results. Because many researchers use commercially available software for data analysis, the construction of tables and figures are often preliminarily produced by the software program before the author begins writing the text of the Results section. Tables and figures are particularly useful for readers when numerical results are reported. Avoid the temptation of making the topic sentence (first sentence of the paragraph) a reference to a table or figure. For example, "Table 15-1 presents the means and standard deviations for the control and experimental groups." This is an inappropriate topic sentence and provides no useful information. A better example is "The experimental group showed a 10% improvement in scores over the control group (**Table 15-1**)."

Many commercial programs (e.g., Microsoft® Excel®, Harvard Graphics®, SPSS®) make it fairly easy to create tables and graphs, often without having to reinput data. Because tables and figures are more expensive to reproduce (compared to the body of the text), it is important to use only those graphic elements that are most important to the primary findings. If a large number of numbers, statistics, or other results need to be presented, a well-organized, consolidated table is ideal. Use tables, graphs, and figures wisely.

Tables are used to organize, condense, and list numerical data. Examples include tables that describe the study sample (example shown in Table 15-1), compare groups (example shown in **Table 15-2**), or show correlations (example shown in **Table 15-3**). The types of analyses performed on the research data dictate the format for display in a table. For qualitative or nonexperimental studies, tables are sometimes used to summarize or compare textual information (example shown in **Table 15-4**). For experimental studies, tables like Table 15-1 are used primarily to demonstrate that the independent variables for the control group and experimental group are not significantly different.

Tables should be clear enough to stand alone without explanation in the text. Although tables can be helpful for the organization and display of important findings, they can be confusing if they are not used and/or constructed appropriately. All relevant information for the type of statistic reported (e.g., test statistic, degrees of freedom, probability value, direction, etc. in the case of inferential statistics) must be included. Because readers tend to make comparisons first horizontally from left to right, primary comparisons in tables should be shown horizontally.[7] **Table 15-5** lists additional general guidelines for the use and construction of tables, and **Figure 15-1** shows the elements of a typical table.

Graphs, charts, pictures (including radiographs), computer-generated images, diagrams, flowcharts drawings, etc are considered figures. The variety of types of graphs includes line graphs (example shown in **Figure 15-2**), scatter graphs, histograms (example shown in **Figure 15-3**), bar graphs (example shown in **Figure 15-4**), and pie charts.*

Table 15-1 Demographic Profile for PA Class of 1999 ($N = 20$)

	Mean	Median	Low–high	SD
Age	28.10	26.50	23–44	5.44
Previous healthcare experience (months)	21.95	20.50	12–60	10.97
High school GPA	3.09	3.00	2.25–3.90	0.42
Undergraduate GPA	3.36	3.32	3.00–3.90	0.31

Note. GPA = grade point average.

Table 15–2 Comparison of Job Profiles for PA Classes of 1997 and 1999[*]

Demographic Characteristic	Class of 1997 (n = 12)		Class of 1999 (n = 18)	
	Frequency	Percent	Frequency	Percent
Specialty				
Family Medicine	6	50	6	33
Pediatrics	1	8	4	22
General Internal Medicine	1	8	0	0
Emergency Medicine	3	25	2	11
General Surgery	1	8	3	17
Other	0	0	2	11
Location				
Urban	5	42	8	44
Suburban	5	42	7	39
Rural	2	17	2	11
Practice type				
Solo	1	8	5	28
Group	4	33	7	39
Hospital	5	42	5	28
Other	2	16	0	0
Unknown	0	0	1	5

[*]Note. Because of rounding, percentages may not all total 100.

Table 15–3 Intercorrelations Between Educational Outcomes for PA Students (N = 50)

	HS GPA	College GPA	Basic science GPA	Clinical GPA	Packrat exam	PANCE
High school GPA	—	.77**	.54*	.36	.12	.11
College GPA		—	.79*	.23	.34*	.17
Basic science GPA			—	.22	.27	.21
Clinical GPA				—	.56*	.62*
Packrat exam					—	.81**
PANCE						—

Note. GPA = grade point average; *p < .05. **p < .01. PANCE = Physician Assistant National Certifying Exam.

Table 15–4 Comparisons of Common Cardiac Murmurs

Diagnosis	Location	Timing	Pitch	Quality
Aortic stenosis	Second right inter-costal space, sternal border	Midsystolic	Medium	Coarse
Aortic regurgitation	Base, patient seated and leaning forward	Early diastolic	High	Blowing
Mitral stenosis	Apex, patient in left lateral decubitus position	Diastolic	Low	Rumble
Mitral regurgitation	Apex	Holosystolic	High	Blowing

Adapted from Seidel HM, Benedict G, Dains JE, Ball JW. *Mosby's Guide to Physical Examination*, 4th ed. St. Louis, MO: Mosby-Year Book; 1998:467–471.

Table 15–5 Guidelines for the Construction of Tables

1. Choose a clear and specific table title so that there is no confusion about the contents.

2. Number tables consecutively using Arabic numbers from the beginning of the report and label them accordingly.

3. Use subheadings for the columns and rows. Format cells so the data are clear and easy to read; often alignment on decimals is preferred.

4. Limit your information to include only material related to your descriptive title. For example, do not mix sample demographics with inferential statistics.

5. Do not explain your table in the text; it should speak for itself. However, the table must be first identified in the text (e.g., Table 1).

6. Use table formats that are consistent and that conform to the publisher's guidelines. However, table formats should be consistent within the report. Check with the publisher in advance or consult the "Instructions to Authors" to determine whether tables and figures should be submitted separately or incorporated within the text.

7. Avoid excessive lines. Generally, vertical lines for columns are not needed, but there should be sufficient space between the columns so the table is easy to read. In addition, tables should be limited to one page.

8. Be sure to include appropriate units of measure (e.g., mg/dl).

Adapted from Wiersma W. *Research Methods in Education: An Introduction*, 7th ed. Needham Heights, MA: Allyn and Bacon; 2000: 393–94.

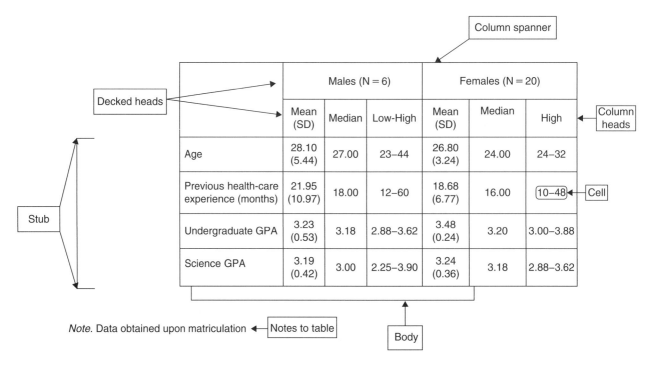

	Males (N = 6)			Females (N = 20)		
	Mean (SD)	Median	Low-High	Mean (SD)	Median	High
Age	28.10 (5.44)	27.00	23–44	26.80 (3.24)	24.00	24–32
Previous health-care experience (months)	21.95 (10.97)	18.00	12–60	18.68 (6.77)	16.00	10–48
Undergraduate GPA	3.23 (0.53)	3.18	2.88–3.62	3.48 (0.24)	3.20	3.00–3.88
Science GPA	3.19 (0.42)	3.00	2.25–3.90	3.24 (0.36)	3.18	2.88–3.62

Note. Data obtained upon matriculation

Figure 15–1 Table construction elements.

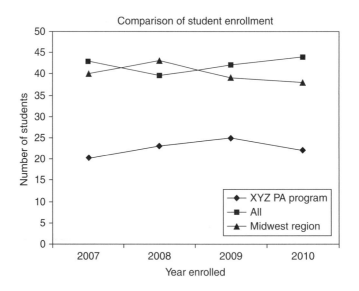

Figure 15–2 Example of a line graph.

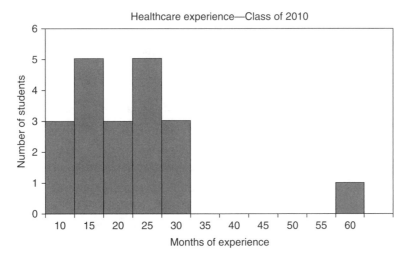

Figure 15–3 Example of a histograph.

Many journals have specific directions for the construction and display of tables, graphs, and figures. When submitting work for publication, be sure to follow the journal's "Instructions for Authors." Editors do not want to spend time correcting such items, and failure to follow instructions may result in rejection of the manuscript.

Generally speaking, polygons and histograms are used to plot frequency distributions. Bar graphs are different from histograms in that the columns are separated and are best used to show comparisons for two or more groups when the independent variables are categorical. When developing graphs (particularly bar graphs), care must be taken to ensure that proportions of the width and height provide an accurate display of the data and are not misleading because of dimensions of the graph. Line graphs are used to show the relationship between two quantitative variables.[8] The intersection of the x- and y-axes in the lower left-hand corner is

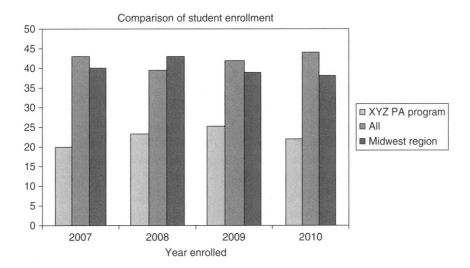

Figure 15–4 Example of a line graph.

Table 15–6 General Guidelines for Developing Graphs

1. Be sure the graph is labeled as a figure and has a self-explanatory title.

2. Select the proper type of graph based upon the data, statistical analysis, and clearest presentation to the reader.

3. Refer to figures in the text and number them consecutively. (Tables and Figures are numbered separately).

4. Be sure that there is enough spacing for ease of interpretation and that the grid is scaled proportionately.

5. Check spelling (including caption) and ensure data were entered and plotted correctly.

6. Ensure there is sufficient contrast or pattern difference to clearly separate segments of pie chart or bars on the bar chart. Avoid 3D or other special effects.

7. Check with the publisher for guidance on overall size, font size, resolution, and style specifications.

8. Include legends if necessary and define abbreviations.

9. Update permission from copyright holder for reproductions or adaptations from other sources. Be sure that the source is noted.

10. For photographs and other illustrations, be sure to mark "TOP" so the publisher has the proper orientation for typesetting and layout. In addition, be sure these items are labeled and identified with your name and article title in case they are separated from the manuscript. [*Note:* This may not be necessary if the graphic is imbedded in the manuscript.]

---

typically zero (0). If there is discontinuity in an axis, it should be represented by a pair of diagonal lines (-//-) to show the missing portion. The dependent variable is generally plotted on the vertical (y) axis.

Many software programs create graphs using color, but most journals reproduce the graphs in black and white. Therefore it is important to ensure that sufficient contrast exists between adjacent bars. Also keep in mind that, although certain other features (e.g., three-dimensional bar graphs) available with commercial software may enhance the appearance of the report for a PowerPoint® presentation, the graphs may not reproduce well when the size is decreased and colors are converted to black and white. The American Medical Association recommends a shading contrast of at least 30 percent.[7] In addition to using shading to distinguish bars or pie chart sections, many commercial programs allow different patterns such as cross-hatching. Pie charts are used to show percentages or proportions of different quantities (e.g., types of students in a cohort) and are used to display results of descriptive research. **Table 15–6**

provides a quick review of general guidelines for the construction of graphs.

When presenting results in a paragraph or graphically, double- and triple-check numbers and data for accuracy. Make sure that graphs present your results accurately and clearly. An inadvertent mistake in one number could make readers cautious about all results. More than one error will probably make them ignore everything, even if the conclusions and interpretations are correct.

A big advantage in using figures and tables is that a large amount of data can be presented in a relatively small print space.[10] The number of printed pages is important to publishers. Well-designed figures and tables can display a lot of data in a digestible manner as well as enhance the appearance of a manuscript.

SUMMARY

The Results section of the report is used for presenting the results of the statistical analyses. It should be clearly written in a concise format. Tables, graphs, and other figures help present data in a way that makes the results easily read, readily understood, and that invites interpretation. The Results section also provides the basis for a decision on the rejection or retention of null hypotheses and/or whether research questions were supported or answered. The Results section is free of author (or any other) bias. Think of this section as the place for the presentation of facts of the research results.

*Note that all data portrayed in the tables and figures for this chapter are fictitious and are not intended to represent any actual research study or source. Readers should consult the "Instructions for Authors" in journals to which they intend to submit manuscripts for specific guidelines and requirements.

REFERENCES

1. Hofmann AH. *Scientific Writing and Communication: Papers, Proposals and Presentations.* New York: Oxford University Press; 2010: 265.
2. Gehlbach SH. *Interpreting the Medical Literature,* 5th ed. New York: McGraw-Hill; 2006: 157–59.
3. Sterne JA, Smith GD. Shifting the evidence—What's wrong with significance tests? *BMJ.* 2001;322: 226–31.
4. Zeiger M. *Essentials of Writing Biomedical Research Papers,* 2nd ed. New York: McGraw-Hill; 2000: 156.
5. Wilkinson L, Task Force on Statistical Inference. Statistical methods in psychology journals: Guidelines and explanations. *Am Psychol.* 1999;54(8): 594–604.
6. Creswell JW. *Educational Research: Planning, Conducting, and Evaluating Quantitative and Qualitative Research.* Boston, MA: Pearson; 2012.
7. American Medical Association. *AMA Manual of Style: A Guide for Authors and Editors,* 10th ed. New York: Oxford University Press; 2007: 84.
8. American Psychological Association. *Publication Manual of the American Psychological Association,* 6th ed. Washington, DC; American Psychological Association; 2010: 151.
9. Bailey DM. *Research for the Health Professional: A Practical Guide,* 2nd ed. Philadelphia, PA: Davis; 1997: 193.
10. Suskie L. Summarizing and analyzing assessment results. In: Suskie L, *Assessing Student Learning: A Common Sense Guide,* 2nd ed. San Francisco, CA: Jossey-Bass; 2009.

CHAPTER OVERVIEW

The discussion section of a manuscript is where the author/investigator is allowed to state interpretations, conclusions, and opinions about the project and the results. Here the investigator can provide answers to the questions posed in the introduction. Of all the sections of a thesis, dissertation, or manuscript for publication, this chapter most reflects the author's ability to synthesize experimental results. This is the place where opinions, views, and meaning are presented.[1]

A number of subsections can comprise this section, or different titles for this section may be used, such as summary, conclusions, implications, interpretations, recommendations, plus a closing. The subtitles' and subsections' names depend on the type of work being produced, as well as local and publication requirements. The author also has some discretion on what subsections to include in the discussion section. This section should center on the importance of the results and their application in patient care, education, or the healthcare professions.[1]

The Discussion Section

Richard R. Rahr, EdD, PA-C

J. Dennis Blessing, PhD, PA

INTRODUCTION

The traditional discussion section of a research report covers the following areas: implications, limitations, discussion, bias considerations, recommendations, and conclusions. A review of several other "how-to" research books would reveal that similar descriptor terms, such as summary, interpretation, and analysis are used in the discussion section. Even the order of the subsections varies. This chapter focuses on the terms most commonly used in the research literature. However, local requirements or publication requirements may differ.[2]

THE IMPLICATIONS SUBSECTION

In the implications section, the author explores the meaning of the research results. This is author's opportunity to think critically about the results, draw conclusions, or make inferences. For example, what changes are indicated in clinical practice or in education, based on the research findings? What do the results mean to health care and society? Even if there were no statistically significant findings related to the research study's hypotheses or questions, the research effort may still have meaning. One inference from statistically nonsignificant results may be that current practice is supported by the data and results. The recommendations for such studies might well be to make no changes and to continue with the current best knowledge. If the investigation yielded significant results, then an author may take the opportunity to discuss why and what that means in light of what is known. If there are significant findings that have strong implications in practice or in the fund of knowledge, a new approach to the problem or a change in practice may be recommended. Remember, major changes in healthcare practice and theory are seldom based on a single study unless it is a very large, well-designed, and carefully controlled investigation. Meta-analysis, which is the integration and evaluation of several or many independent research studies, is now considered one of the highest levels of research sophistication, particularly for evidenced-based practice. Even in evidence-based analysis, however, questions are often raised that require further investigation.[1]

The implications of the study may point out the potential value of a finding or the need for replication or modifications in a subsequent study to strengthen the research results or findings. When an investigator believes the results have important implications; those results should be stated in positive terms. Rational arguments based on data and analyses, particularly when contradicting accepted dogma or theory, must be presented clearly.

Here is an example of an implication: Study antibiotic X increased the effective cure rate for osteomyelitis by 25 percent over the currently available drug treatment. If antibiotic X were without any major side effects, then it would certainly be recommended for the treatment of osteomyelitis. If an investigator found that giving antibiotic X with the addition of daily treatments in the hyperbaric chamber made no significant difference in the overall treatment outcomes, then the recommendation would be that the additional treatment not be used in tandem. The investigator must explicitly state the implications for clinical treatment based on the findings.

Statistical analysis meaning and limitations should be considered when stating the implications of the investigation. Here is an example: If the Pearson product moment statistical test is used to measure a variable, and the analysis results in a significant correlation of $r = .70$; then this would seem to be a good correlation. However, if further analysis using the coefficient of determination r with a second statistical analysis called the r^2 (the coefficient of determination), then $r^2 = .49$. This second statistic accounts for only 49 percent of the correlation variance. The fact that 51 percent of the research study variance is not explained should cause a conservative interpretation of the implications and recommendation decisions. The discussion must make sense of the statistical analysis and the results.

Ultimately, the implications subsection is where the author makes the case for the study and its results. Avoid mixing in information or data that does not belong in the subsection. The best critical thinking skills should be used to form the implications with awareness of the current literature in relation to the study results. This is one reason why the methodology is so important. Well-designed and sound methodology allows strong support for the implications. Implications, regardless type or nature, should have practical and clinical significance and should be clearly supported by the research findings.

THE LIMITATIONS SUBSECTION

The limitations subsection of the discussion section is of utmost importance. Addressing the study's weaknesses (or limits) must be included in the presentation of the research. Problems or limitations should be recognized and pointed out by the researcher so that the overall value of the study can be considered. This explanation may allow those limitations to be avoided if the study is replicated. The researcher may realize, in retrospect, that there were flaws in the methodology.

All studies have limitations. Putting these limitations in front of the reader gives credence to the conclusions and the investigator's understanding of the study. If an investigator realizes the study limitations, then the conclusions consider those limitations. Recognizing and stating the limitations of the work ultimately strengthens the work and its impact.[1]

Authors should clearly state to whom and in what situations the research study's findings or outcomes can be generalized and applied. This is where limitations become important. How well did the sample participants represent the population? The researcher may have inadvertently attracted or recruited only a certain subgroup of the intended population. For example, even though the researcher sought to have a representative sample of both men and women of various age groups, perhaps only women within a certain age range were willing to participate in the study. The findings and conclusions must take this limitation into consideration. Also, can the data from such a study be generalized to the general population? For some investigations, a pilot study may reveal some of these problems (limitations) and help guide the methodology. However, a well-designed, meticulous study usually has few limitations.

The limitations subsection should also discuss the randomness of the sample selection and the potential for error in the sampling. Having an experienced researcher as a guide and mentor can assist any investigator in developing a study that is as strong as possible within the ever-present constraints of a practice or educational setting. Consideration must be given to whether an intervening variable or research effect (e.g., the Hawthorne effect) could be responsible for the results.[2]

If limitations are identified or recognized in a research project, investigators must be honest and forthright about those limitations. Such forthrightness gives the researcher, the research project, and its outcomes greater credibility and potential for acceptance. If readers are informed of limitations, other researchers can attempt to avoid these limitations in similar, future studies.

THE DISCUSSION SUBSECTION

The discussion subsection of the discussion section is an informative section used to meld together the research report, the interpretation of the results, their implications, and the study's limitations into an objective presentation. In previous parts of the research report there is no room (or justification) for the author's subjective thoughts and insights. The discussion subsection is refreshing in that it allows and encourages authors to give their view of the impact and importance of the research outcomes. This is the author's opportunity to place the study in the ongoing conversation and context of the current literature. The author can interject subjectivity based on previous clinical and research experiences and wisdom (expert opinion). How did the significance or nonsignificance of the data relate to the conceptual framework of the literature that was reviewed? This is where the author gets to answer that question, in their opinion, based on the investigation.

In this subsection, readers expect to be apprised of some practical application of the research findings. The author demonstrated his or her research knowledge and wisdom here. A clinical example could be the matching of patients with providers of the same gender. Is the effectiveness of the encounter perceived to be better by patients? By providers? Again, a number of other factors can influence these perceptions. In the discussion subsection, all of these factors can be explored in light of the research findings.

In the discussion subsection, the author may want to discuss the characteristics of survey tools, limitations, generalizations, statistical methods, and bias considerations of the research project. Ultimately, this part of the report is used to discuss, critically, the evaluation of the research outcomes and their impact. In some formats, the discussion section is the last subsection of the chapter.[1]

THE RECOMMENDATIONS SUBSECTION

The recommendations subsection of the discussion section usually states the author's ideas on the future research requirements based on the outcomes of the current study. For example, an author often includes the suggestion to expand the existing research by adding more subjects to the current research plan or to conduct "next step" studies. Other recommendations may include developing a new research design, using a new data collection instrument, or addressing the gaps or weaknesses in the study. Recommendations may include making the study a double-blind crossover model, adding a control group, or suggesting that an outside independent investigator repeat the same study to determine if the results can be replicated may also be mentioned. The overall purpose of the recommendations subsection is to alert the reader that additional questions need to be asked and answered. The author should avoid providing so many recommendations that the most important ones are obscured. As elsewhere, the author should strive for relevance, clarity, and brevity in this subsection.[1,2]

THE CONCLUSIONS SUBSECTION

This is usually the last section of the paper, and it is generally brief. The conclusions subsection of the discussion section should begin with a brief restatement of the aim(s) of the study and the major research question (s) or hypotheses. Following that, the author should state the major findings of the study, using a format that can be easily followed. Here is an example: "This study demonstrated that patients who are treated for chronic severe pain with analgesic medication administered 'around the clock' rather than on a PRN schedule had a higher level of functional status. Based on this finding a major implication might be to change the treatment protocol to a regular schedule rather than PRN medication administration for patients with chronic severe pain." Clearly stated implications for practice, when backed by sound research findings, help to build evidence-based practice and improve the care of patients.

A high-quality contrast and comparison of the results with the relevant underlying literature is expected. For example, the author can point out that the same or similar research findings have been reported. The author may wish to restate the strong and weak points of the research study; however, redundancy should be avoided unless a point is restated purposefully. The conclusions subsection also provides the author the opportunity to share personal opinions and experiences that highlight and emphasize the impact of the research study. This should be done carefully, however, and these comments by the author must be clearly related to the current study and should not merely be the author's "general opinion." The overall practical value of the information presented in research studies is important in the context of healthcare practice.[2]

Table 16–1 Key Criteria for the Discussion Section

Clearly state what the research findings contribute to the understanding of the defined problem or question.
Be specific about implications for practice or society.
Describe how the findings fit into the present body of knowledge.
State how the findings support, enhance, or contrast with prior research findings.
If the findings are novel or in contrast to accepted norms, strong support is needed for the interpretations.

Table 16–2 Pitfalls to Avoid in the Discussion Section

Drawing conclusions or formulating implications that cannot be clearly supported by the research findings.

Providing so many recommendations for further study that the most important recommendations are lost.

Having an apologetic tone when describing limitations or study design weaknesses. Be matter of fact.

The conclusions subsection is much like a "closing" abstract, but with a bit more detail than is allowed in the abstract section. It should provide a complete but concise overview of the research study while bringing the discussion section to a close. In summary, **Table 16–1** presents key elements that the discussion section should ensure, while **Table 16–2** provides reminders of pitfalls to avoid in this section.[2]

Additional Readings

1. Bailey DM. *Research for the health professional: A practical guide,* 2nd ed. Philadelphia, PA: F. A. Davis;1991–1997.
2. Jenkins S, Price CJ, Straker L. *The researching therapist: A practical guide to planning, performing and communicating research.* New York: Churchill Livingston; 1998.
3. Publication Manual of the American Psychological Association, 6th ed. Washington, DC: American Psychological Association; 2009.

CHAPTER OVERVIEW

This chapter reviews common documentation styles used in scholarly and professional writing that apply to thesis, dissertation, and research paper writing. It also examines the process for documenting references using footnotes and the proper construction of bibliographies. Copyright law and fair use doctrine is discussed to provide a basis for the importance of assigning proper credit to sources used in the construction of the research paper. Finally, the chapter considers how the Internet can assist in finding source material for research projects.

References

Christine Gaspard, MSLS
Katherine A. Prentice, MSIS
Eric Willman, MSIS
Albert Simon, DHS, PA

CHOOSING A WRITING STYLE

Although a variety of styles and formats may be used for writing a research paper, most colleges, universities, and publishers dictate a style that must be followed for constructing a paper (e.g., the layout, bibliography, citation style, etc.). Particular departments or schools within universities often have their own specific style requirements. Many style manuals are available and before choosing one, the manuscript requirements should be investigated. Although you may have heard of (or used) the Turabian or Modern Language Association (MLA) styles, we focus here on the styles more commonly used within the healthcare professions. These include the *AMA Manual of Style* (AMA)[1], *The Chicago Manual of Style* (CMS)[2], the *Uniform Requirements for Manuscripts Submitted to Biomedical Journals,* also known as Vancouver Style, and the *Publication Manual of the American Psychological Association* (APA)[3]. It is important to recognize that some publications may publish their own style manuals with additional requirements. These requirements provided by the journal can be found in the "Information for Authors" or the "Instructions to Authors" guidelines usually provided on the publisher's website.

The APA, Chicago, and Vancouver styles are most often employed for writing undergraduate research papers and theses at the graduate level. Dissertation styles may follow one of these or other specific institutional guidelines. It is common for research works and dissertations to be published in the style of professional or academic journals within that discipline.

Each of these four styles has unique features. The differences that exist in reference styles relate to how the various details (e.g., author's name, etc.) are formatted or which elements are used. For example, APA does not use endnotes or footnotes, whereas AMA, Vancouver and Chicago do. Beyond these comparisons, there are variations in indentations, punctuation, and format among the four styles. The requirements may appear trivial, but publication and departmental requirements are generally very strict, and manuscripts may be turned down or graded poorly if the style rules are not followed.

The following examples illustrate the differences between these styles. These sample citations show a book by more than one author and a journal article by more than one author.

AMA

Hooker RS, Cawley JF, Asprey DP. *Physician assistants: Policy and practice.* 3rd ed. Philadelphia, PA: F. A. Davis Co.; 2010.

Bloomer RJ, Falvo MJ, Schilling BK, Smith WA. Prior exercise and antioxidant supplementation: Effect on oxidative stress and muscle injury. *J Int Soc Sports Nutr.* 2007; 4:9.

APA

Hooker, R. S., Cawley, J. F., & Asprey, D. P. (2010). *Physician assistants: Policy and practice* (3rd ed.). Philadelphia, PA: F. A. Davis Co.

Bloomer, R. J., Falvo, M. J., Schilling, B. K., & Smith, W. A. (2007). Prior exercise and antioxidant supplementation: Effect on oxidative stress and muscle injury. *Journal of the International Society of Sports Nutrition, 4,* 9. doi:10. 1186/1550-2783-4-9

Vancouver

1. Hooker RS, Cawley JF, Asprey DP. Physician assistants: policy and practice. 3rd ed. Philadelphia: F. A. Davis Co.; 2010.

2. Bloomer RJ, Falvo MJ, Schilling BK, Smith WA. Prior exercise and antioxidant supplementation: Effect on oxidative stress and muscle injury. J Int Soc Sports Nutr 2007; Oct 3;4:9.

Chicago

Hooker, Roderick S., James F. Cawley, and David P. Asprey. *Physician Assistants: Policy and Practice.* 3rd ed. Philadelphia: F. A. Davis Co., 2010.

Bloomer, R. J., M. J. Falvo, B. K. Schilling, and W. A. Smith. "Prior Exercise and Antioxidant Supplementation: Effect on Oxidative Stress and Muscle Injury." *Journal of the International Society of Sports Nutrition* 4, no. 9, (2007).

It is important to follow the style exactly. Writers are advised to consult the appropriate style guides to ensure that proper citation format is followed. Selection of style is largely a matter of convention, tradition, preference, or assignment guidelines.

The APA style is widely used in the social sciences and nursing fields. It offers a format that encompasses parenthetical citations within the text that contain the author's name, year of publication, and page number (when used for direct quotes). A reference list is arranged alphabetically at the end of the paper.

The Vancouver style is one name for the reference style of the *Uniform Requirements for Manuscripts Submitted to Biomedical Journals,* which is widely used in medicine and the healthcare sciences. Vancouver uses an "author-number" citation system from the American National Standards Institute style adopted in the National Library of Medicine's (NLM) *Citing Medicine.* The Vancouver style published in *Citing Medicine* is not published in a printed book, but it is available online.[4]

The Chicago style is popular with magazines and some other nonscholarly publications. When following the Chicago format, footnote or endnote documentation is used. In this style, the notes are placed on a separate sheet at the end of the document in the order they are cited in the text (i.e., as endnotes) or they are listed numerically at the bottom of each page of text (i.e., as footnotes).

Each style manual contains a comprehensive guide to the documentation of sources and other technical details of publication. These guides can be purchased at bookstores, but many are also available at university and public libraries. Detailed information about most styles is also available on the Web. While purchasing the style guide is often easiest, sometimes using a secondary or abridged version can meet a researcher's writing needs. For the APA and Chicago styles, a helpful source is the Purdue Online Writing Lab (or OWL) website "Research and Citation Resources."[5] This site provides detailed assistance for writers and includes examples of citations from different sources. Because the Vancouver style is freely available on the Web, the e-book should serve as the "go to" resource. Remember that synopses provide quick reference for general guidance and are helpful in many situations, but the amount and scope of information they contain may be limited.

DOCUMENTING SOURCES USING REFERENCES AND BIBLIOGRAPHIES

During the research phase, the investigator begins to synthesize his or her thoughts with data, facts, and opinions from research material. All information found in a literature search and other background detail represents the original work of other authors. Whether quoted directly or paraphrased, the use of background sources must be acknowledged with proper documentation. Any background information not known as "general knowledge" in the field should be documented with citations within the text and in a bibliography using the required style. The process of documentation involves creating and sharing a list of all the sources used in the production of your paper. The exact page numbers where the information is found are often required, so good recordkeeping is an advantage when performing a literature search.

Documentation is provided in two major ways:

1. Providing specific documentation either on each page or at the end of a chapter or section, by the use of in-text citations (i.e., author and date, footnotes, or endnotes).

2. Listing the sources of information used by constructing a bibliography. The bibliography (or reference list) is usually found at the end of the manuscript.

Using Footnotes, Endnotes, and Author-date Styles

Footnotes and endnotes are parts of a numbered reference style that places the citation number at the end of the relevant content and the bibliographic details at the end of the page, chapter, or paper. Footnotes appear at the bottom of each page. Endnotes may appear at the end of each chapter or at the end of a book (often divided by chapters). Depending on the style that is chosen (e.g., APA), the references may be displayed in parentheses, as author-date citations, or as numbered designators that correspond to a reference list at the end of a text.

Bibliographies

Scholarly writing requires the use of a bibliography, that is, a list of works consulted and referenced during background research. Some styles also suggest including all reference materials consulted whether or not they were actually used in the paper. Particularly for dissertation writing, the functional meaning of bibliography encompasses all works available on the subject. For example, some academic departments or thesis committees may prefer terms such as "selected bibliography," "references," or "works cited." The style guide should be consulted for the correct term to use in your research paper.

The bibliography generally follows the endnotes section of the paper (if an endnotes section is used) and is traditionally arranged alphabetically by author unless the style requires a numbered list (AMA). There will be slight differences in bibliographic format depending on the style used. Be sure to consult the specific style guidelines to determine the proper format.

By reviewing your bibliography or reference list, the reader can obtain a sense of the depth and caliber of the research. Clues to research quality include the type of works cited, the dates of publication, and appropriateness of referenced material. Accurate bibliographies promote scholarly communication by providing readers the information to locate and use the listed works as primary sources themselves.

Two additional variations should be considered when preparing a bibliography. The first is an annotated bibliography, which allows authors' comments to be included with any or all of the listings. The second is to group the entries by source type. In this method, the list is divided into primary and secondary, then published and unpublished sources. Within each category, entries are listed alphabetically. Remember, primary sources are original works such as a book or letter, but careful consideration of each item is required to determine status as primary or secondary sources. Secondary sources interpret or analyze content from other sources. Secondary sources can be in many forms, including articles, case studies, or books.

Bibliographies prepared by other authors can also be useful in conducting background research. Preliminary research produces a collection of articles that contain bibliographies that relate to your research question as well as stand-alone bibliography publications. It is acceptable to use these citations as leads to additional information, but be careful to locate the sources to validate the appropriateness of each entry. It is improper to simply copy the citation list in another article into a bibliography.

COPYRIGHTED MATERIAL, FAIR USE PROVISIONS, PUBLIC DOMAIN AND PLAGIARISM

Standards of academic conduct require the acknowledgment of all material used in the production of a scholarly work, whether the material was formally copyrighted or not. The copyright status of an item is not actually relevant when preparing your research paper. All materials should be cited, whether under copyright or in the public domain.

The Copyright Act is a comprehensive law that deals with the use of copyrighted material. Under this law, copyrighted material may be used without the permission of the copyright holder for certain specific uses.[6] Although permission from authors of copyrighted materials may be required under certain circumstances, the concept of "fair use" provides for limited use of copyrighted materials. Materials outside of copyright fall within the "public domain" and can also be used without permission, but they must be acknowledged. Generally, the public domain includes material for which the copyright has expired. It is safest to err on the side of caution—assume that all materials are under copyright when preparing research papers or preparing educational materials.

In educational settings, fair use is understood to cover an array of situations that allow the use of copyrighted material without written permission. However, fair use is a gray area within the law where only guidelines exist, and many instances of disagreement still occur. Under the fair use umbrella, research, teaching, and news reporting are included. Consideration of fair use standards can protect writers and instructors from not only plagiarism but also violating copyright laws. Copyright violation penalties can be very high, up to $150,000 for each willful act of violation, but even unintentional violations, can result in fines.[7] A helpful guide to the fair use doctrine is provided online by the University of Texas System.[8]

To learn more about copyright, the University of Texas System provides an entire web tutorial on copyright. The "Crash Course in Copyright" tutorial provides examples from a number of situations and is an important source for writers.[8] Copyright rules tend to change regularly, and legal interpretation sometimes varies by institution.

Certain works, such as those in the public domain, cannot receive the protection of copyright law. The public domain includes facts and other works that lack originality; the clearest example is the telephone book. Government publications are considered to be in the public domain. There are additional examples of public domain detailed at the "Copyright Term and the Public Domain in the United States" from Cornell University.[9] Remember, all works, even public domain items, must be cited in the reference list.

If uncertainty exists concerning whether a work is in the public domain or is copyright protected, legal counsel should be sought prior to publication so that infringement of copyright can be avoided. If a work that is not in the public domain is reused in the course of a study, it is necessary to obtain permission from the author and possibly publishing companies. Such use may require that a royalty fee for the right to use that property is paid. The Copyright Clearance Center (http://www.copyright.com/) is one broker of license fees that can assist with the copyright permission process.

According to the United States Copyright Office, Circular 1 copyright is automatically applied to all works (including computer software and programs) produced after 1978.[10] Some writers prefer extra protection. Writers may choose to have their work registered with the U.S. Copyright Office. Payment and registration paperwork is required when applying for formal copyright. For more information and to find forms online, visit the U.S. Copyright office website (http://www.copyright.gov/).

EVALUATING SOURCES

For most research questions, the problem is not finding enough material, but rather how to determine which sources to utilize. Writers need to evaluate the selected sources for appropriateness and authority. Before the resources are used, they can be assessed by considering the questions below:

- Is the source authoritative?
- Who are the authors of the source, and are they experts in the field?
- Does the academic community regard the authors as credible?
- Does the article represent current theories or trends?
- When was it published?
- Where was the article published?
- Did the work undergo a rigorous peer-review process?

The peer-review process used by some journals is a stringent process of article review before publication. When considering the authority of a pub-

lication, it is important to remember that within a peer-reviewed journal, not every item is peer-reviewed. Peer-review provides additional confidence that the article contains valid arguments and conclusions that result from sound methodology. The use of articles from peer-reviewed sources may carry additional weight and add value to the writing.

In today's web-based world, all sources should be carefully evaluated. Freely available web pages may not have received the benefit of peer review; they may have been posted by an individual to state an opinion. By considering the questions just listed and carefully evaluating the resources selected, many credibility and validity issues can be avoided.

FINDING REFERENCES USING ELECTRONIC AND INTERNET-BASED SOURCES

Although the following discussion was presented in Chapter 7, it is important to consider how the Web can be used effectively in scholarly research. In the recent past, most research was done using only physical library materials. However, most researchers now begin the search for information using online databases and search engines. Although online sources have not completely supplanted printed material, no comprehensive research process would be complete without searching both electronic and print sources.

Printed material can be stored in a variety of formats. Many academic and public libraries maintain material in a variety of digital or other technological formats. In addition to digital storage, microfilm and microfiche are still found in many libraries and are still used to provide access to older articles.

Traditional search engines use servers networked together via WAN (Wide Area Network) connections. Each individual server is part of WAN, which in turn acts as a networking mechanism allowing the information from around the world to be accessed from any device that can make the online connection. Each search engine uses a different method to find and show results from web pages. Search engines do not usually provide search results from library catalogs and other library resources. Therefore, it is important to find other tools that can access library-provided content. Concurrent searching of multiple library catalogs is available through search engines such as WorldCat®, which allow access to thousands of library catalogs with one search and also find nearby locations of desired materials.

Some online search tools, such as PubMed for biomedical literature, are tailored to specific subjects. PubMed can be accessed through the National Library of Medicine website (http://www.pubmed.gov). A popular web search engine for a variety of scientific topics is Scirus (http://www.scirus.com/). Scirus searches not only journal articles but also open courseware, preprint server material, patents, and institutional repositories. Depending on the area of research, it is wise to become familiar with a variety of search tools, because no single search engine can be considered comprehensive or complete.

Each search tool works differently, it is important to be flexible with search terms and search methods. Keywords, controlled vocabulary, algorithmic relevancy ranking, and good old-fashioned luck all affect your results. Using a variety of subject headings, keywords, and phrases with Boolean operators AND, OR, NOT to conduct a comprehensive search can improve results. Although some search tools can correct spelling mistakes, they cannot be relied upon to correct every problem. Misspellings can derail the most well-intentioned search strategies.

As documented in Chapter 7, libraries may subscribe to additional proprietary online databases (e.g., CINAHL®, Micromedex®, DIALOG® , Ovid, UpToDate®) to find specific content. These subscription search tools are able to narrow down a search term with progressively specific search terms to increase the relevancy of the results. Among the wide variety of library databases, some cater to the general market, and others are discipline specific. Web-search tools such as Google Scholar™ (http://scholar.google.com/) complement results found in library databases. Unlike traditional Google, Google Scholar™ limits search results to scholarly materials that are more likely to be useful in scientific research and writing.

Web tools can also be leveraged for research projects. Free tools from Google Docs™ (https://docs.google.com), Skype™ (http://www.skype.com), Windows Live™ (http://explore.live.com/), Twitter™ (http://twitter.com), and Wolfram|Alpha™ (http://wolframalpha.com) offer content, video conferencing, survey tools, online storage, online collaboration, and more. Subscription services also offer survey tools and video conferencing, but costs vary and should be compared prior to purchase.

Above all, it is important to remember that sources must be cited accurately. Sources should always be evaluated, and only accurate and high-quality content should be included in a serious research project. Using a variety of tools and conducting comprehensive and effective searches give researchers confidence in their results.

SUMMARY

No matter what type of research paper is being produced, the specific style guidelines must be followed meticulously. Bibliography and reference information must be accurate and attributed properly. Original sources that are cited must have actually been read. Avoid plagiarism and double-check details. Good documentation can only serve to strengthen a research paper overall as well as contribute to the validity of its parts, including the literature review, methods, results, and conclusions.

REFERENCES

1. Iverson C, American Medical Association. *AMA manual of style: A guide for authors and editors.* 10th ed. New York: Oxford University Press; 2007.
2. University of Chicago Press. *The Chicago manual of style.* 15th ed. Chicago: University of Chicago Press; 2003.
3. American Psychological Association. *Publication manual of the American Psychological Association.* 6th ed. Washington, DC: American Psychological Association; 2010.
4. Patrias K, Wendling DL, United States, Dept. of Health and Human Services, National Library of Medicine (U.S.). *Citing medicine the NLM style guide for authors,*

editors, and publishers. 2nd ed. Washington, DC: National Library of Medicine; 2007. http://www.nlm.nih.gov/citingmedicine. Accessed April 26, 2011.

5. Purdue University Writing Lab. The Purdue online writing lab (OWL). http://owl.english.purdue.edu/. Accessed April 26, 2011.

6. Library of Congress, Copyright Office. Copyright Law of the United States of America and Related Laws Contained in Title 17 of the United States Code. 2011. http://purl.access.gpo.gov/GPO/LPS440. Accessed April 26, 2011.

7. Library of Congress, Copyright Office. Reproduction of Copyrighted Works by Educators and Librarians. 2011. http://www.loc.gov/copyright/circs/circ92.pdf. Accessed April 26, 2011.

8. Harper G, University of Texas System, Office of General Counsel. Crash Course in Copyright. http://copyright.lib.utexas.edu. Accessed April 26, 2011.

9. Hirtle PB. Copyright Term and the Public Domain in the United States. http://www.copyright.cornell.edu/training/Hirtle%5FPublic%5FDomain.htm. Accessed April 26, 2011.

10. Library of Congress, Copyright Office. Copyright Basics. http://purl.access.gpo.gov/GPO/LPS4981. Accessed April 26, 2011.

Websites mentioned in this chapter

Copyright Clearance Center, http://www.copyright.com
Google Docs™, https://docs.google.com
Google Scholar™, http://scholar.google.com
PubMed, http://www.pubmed.gov
Scirus, http://www.scirus.com
Skype™, http://www.skype.com
Twitter™, http://twitter.com
U.S. Copyright Office, http://www.copyright.gov
Windows Live™, http://explore.live.com
Wolfram|Alpha™, http://wolframalpha.com
WorldCat.org®, http://www.worldcat.org

Uses for Your Research

CHAPTER OVERVIEW

Being a healthcare professional brings a sense of obligation, as clinicians and teachers, to contribute to the existing body of research knowledge. This applies to clinical practitioners, students, and faculty in a wide range of healthcare disciplines. The development of skills in writing, formal presentation, and publishing are essential tools for healthcare professionals as they progress through and develop their careers. Such skills facilitate expansion of multiple career options and further existing knowledge within the professions.

Skills and techniques related to research methods, report writing, and publishing are among the topics explored in this book and should be part of the educational preparation of all healthcare professionals. In education in the healthcare professions, scholarly work is an increasingly common requirement for graduation. In this chapter, which builds on material formally presented throughout this book, the essential components of a research paper are reviewed in general and the process of writing research papers generated by the various health professions is addressed. Presentations and posters are discussed.

The process by which research papers are transformed into research publications in the biomedical literature is also discussed. Additionally, the expansion of clinical investigations and the involvement of more practicing clinicians in the research process requires practitioners to develop publication and presentation skills.

Writing and Publishing in the Health Professions

James F. Cawley, MPH, PA-C

"A good paper has a definite structure, makes its point, and then shuts up."
—Steven Locke, Former Editor, British Medical Journal

"Begin at the beginning," the King said, gravely, "and go on till you come to the end, then stop."
——From Alice in Wonderland, by Lewis Carroll

"Let thy words be few."
—Ecclesiastes 5:2

INTRODUCTION

Since the 1600s, thinking and writing have largely been classified into two types: literary and scientific. The literary style has been associated with fiction, rhetoric, and subjectivity, whereas the scientific style has been steeped in fact, plain language, and objectivity. Through the centuries, this division of style increased as the body of scientific knowledge grew; barbs were increasingly exchanged between the two camps of thinkers and writers. By the mid-1800s literature and science often stood as two distinct domains, particularly in their respective written work. Although dissension and distance remain between these two broad fields, numerous examples of crossovers have shed light on scientific truths drawing from both domains. During the twentieth century, medical thinking and writing and the expression of medical knowledge have been reflected in the evolution of scientific writing.

Every healthcare professional and student should be able to communicate through writing. Effective writing in general and writing for publication are skills to be learned. Scientific writing has its styles and processes. Generally, short, effective sentences with a subject and predicate are better than long, multi-comma sentences. Learn to write good declarative statements in active voice.

STYLE MANUALS

Many resources are available that facilitate the process of preparing research for acceptance as an education capstone and for publication. **Table 18–1**

represents a variety of resources that can enhance this process. Additional style manual information can be found in the Appendices.

Before selecting a particular style manual as a guide, review the journals that offer publishing opportunities pertinent to the research field. The style requirements of the publishing resource (journals or books) must be followed stringently. For most peer-reviewed biomedical publications, two distinct resources offer the most frequently required formatting and guideline protocols. These are the *AMA Manual of Style,*[1] and the *Uniform Requirements for Manuscripts Submitted to Biomedical Journals.*[2]

The *AMA Manual of Style* includes five sections of in-depth instruction on topics including preparing

Table 18–1 Style Manuals

Title	Edition	Author or Publisher	Year
American Medical Association Manual of Style	10th	Williams & Wilkins, Baltimore, MD	2007
The Chicago Manual of Style	15th	University of Chicago Press, Chicago, IL	2003
Council of Biology Editors Style Manual	6th	Council of Biology Editors, Bethesda, MD	1994
A Manual of Style	29th	U.S. Government Printing Office, Washington, D.C.	2000
Modern Language Association Style Manual and Guide to Scholarly Publishing	2nd	Modern Language Association, New York, NY	1998
Publication Manual of the American Psychological Association	5th	American Psychological Association, Washington, D.C.	2001
Strunk W Jr. & White EB: The Elements of Style	4th	Allyn & Bacon, New York, NY	2000
Turabian KL: A Manual for Writers of Term Papers, Theses, and Dissertations	6th	The University of Chicago Press, Chicago, IL	1996
International Committee of Medical Journal Editors: Guide to Uniform Requirements for Manuscripts Submitted to Biomedical Journals		Available at http://jama.ama-assn.org/info/avinst_req.html	1997
National Library of Medicine Recommended Format for Bibliographic Citation		U.S. Public Health Service, Department of Health and Human Services	1991
National Library of Medicine Recommended Format for Bibliographic Citation Supplement: Internet Formats		U.S. Public Health Service, Department of Health and Human Services	2001
Scientific Style and Format: The CBE Manual for Authors, Editors, and Publishers	6th	Huth, EJ	1994

an article for publication, style, terminology, measurement and quantitation, and technical detail. The International Committee of Medical Journal Editors online documents describe in depth a range of ethical considerations, publishing and editorial issues, manuscript preparation, and reference formatting and usage guidelines. Together, these two resources offer the most commonly used guidelines and requirements for publishing in the peer-reviewed biomedical literature. However, it is always important to consult the "Instructions to Authors" section of any publisher to whom a manuscript is submitted as they may include other resources, and preferences vary from journal to journal. There is no substitute for consulting the "Information for Authors," which is published by all journals. It is the responsibility of author to submit manuscripts in the required style of target journals. Failure to follow prescribed style is likely to result in rejection of the manuscript.

WRITING

All students in healthcare professions should know how to structure a research paper and how to modify it into a publishable article. There are differences between a thesis or dissertation and a published paper. The skills needed to write for publication are also important to the seasoned clinician who has observed an interesting clinical case and seeks to make a contribution to the literature by "writing it up" for publication.

The proper culmination of any scientific research effort in a formal educational setting is the production of a written document reflecting the work that was completed. Since the beginning of time, recording one's work in a formal style has been and remains the hallmark of scholarly activities.

Scientific papers are the vital currency of academic endeavors and knowledge dissemination. The quality and timeliness of information and its presentation in scholarly papers are determinants of major decision points in central collegiate activities: assignment of student grades, student advancement and graduation, faculty appointment and advancement, tenure decisions, perceptions of

professional leadership, national academic reputations, and more. Publishing in prestigious journals with regularity is the expected and rewarded activity in most academic healthcare centers. However, of all faculty teaching in U.S. colleges and universities, only a small proportion publish regularly.

A healthcare profession's vitality, relevance, and intellectual pedigree are reflected in its literature.[3] When judged by that standard, some of the health professions may be viewed as underachieving. Many believe there is a critical and ongoing need for the healthcare professions to improve contributions to both the general biomedical literature and a specific healthcare profession's literature. One way to obtain this goal is to foster student research and writing with the hope (and aim) of those skills carrying forward into clinical practice.

For the faculty members and students of healthcare professions, writing ability and familiarity with publishing in the realm of healthcare science are essential professional skills. These skills, which are critical for success, can be learned by students, perfected by faculty, and appreciated by readers, both professional and lay. Beyond the academic setting, this process can pose a challenge for health professionals. **Table 18–2** provides a list of facts and myths about medical writing that are helpful to the clinician interested in research. Diana Hacker and Barbara Fister have composed a helpful Web site that includes examples of papers written in four commonly referenced style manual formats (http://www.dianahacker.com/resdoc/). Additionally, many style manuals now have quick reference links on the Internet, and California State University of Los Angeles offers a useful site as a point of departure (http://www.calstatela.edu/library/styleman.htm).

RESEARCH PAPERS

In the healthcare field, as in most other fields, good scientific research papers are the most common form of expression of a scientific finding. Research papers have a clear, well-defined structure. The logical sequence of the research paper's sections (i.e., Introduction or Problem, Review of Literature,

Table 18–2 Medical Writing Facts and Myths

Myth: "I'm a care provider, not a writer."

Fact: Writing is not a career but a necessary skill for medical professionals.

Myth: "I don't have any talent for writing. I've always been bad at it."

Fact: Writing is a skill, not a talent. Medical professionals should learn to write effectively.

Myth: "Writing has nothing to do with science."

Fact: Effective medical writing requires the same qualities found in scientific thought: logic, clarity, organization, and precision.

Myth: "If a piece of writing gets published, it's a good piece of writing."

Fact: Many published medical papers are badly written.

Myth: "Until I have my ideas clearly organized in my head, I shouldn't start writing."

Fact: The best way to clarify thinking is to start writing. Research shows that the act of writing helps clarify and organize thinking and generate ideas.

Myth: "I'll never be eligible for promotion or tenure unless I get a terminal degree. Why should I bother publishing if it won't help my career?"

Fact: Publishing papers in respected peer-reviewed journals has substantial academic value and generates far more career enhancing opportunities than having a terminal degree and not publishing.

Adapted from St. James D. *Writing and speaking for excellence: A brief guide for the medical professional.* Boston, MA: Jones and Bartlett; 1997: 13.

Methods, Results, and Discussion) is generally accepted as the gold standard of the classic research paper structure. This format requires the author(s) to address a given topic answering four basic questions:

1. What is the issue?
2. What methods have been used to investigate the issue?
3. What was found?
4. What are the implications of the findings?

Research papers take several forms, but generally the best form begins by posing a question or identifying a problem. The question may address the need for further research on an issue, propose a new hypothesis, or justify further analysis. The conventional format and approach used in research papers is derived from what Huth calls the concept of critical argument.[4] This idea holds that research papers must convey information in such a way that the reader is convinced that the research paper's findings are well considered and ultimately valid.

Critical argument describes text that is coherent and consists of a series of reasons, statements, or facts intended to support or establish a point of view. This tone is "critical" in the sense that it carefully scrutinizes the source of the text's assertions. The "critical argument" is the heart of research writing.

Prose Revision

Research articles published in the biomedical literature typically present new and original information on topics relevant to the primary readership. The accepted scientific standard is that the investigators have applied reasonable standards of methodological rigor and have presented their findings in an accurate, concise, and clearly stated fashion. To create an accurate, concise, and clearly stated manuscript, a great deal of review and revision of the manuscript is required. A well-intended statement of purpose may not be what the reader understands. Rarely is a first draft of a manuscript accepted for publication. After a paper has been written it must be reviewed, revised, and reread a number of times. A first step toward the revision of a manuscript is to revise for larger segments of content, such as missing or unnecessary information, or erroneous/misplaced content or sequence. The next step is to focus on prose, including sentence length, paragraph length, clauses, phrases, modifiers, and word choices. In revising prose, a seasoned writer seeks to develop fluency. Fluent prose runs along as the reader expects it to run. The reader is not jarred by defects that interrupt the line of thought. Short, simple sentences and structure are best. Once the initial revisions have been made, two people should review the manuscript. One person should be knowledgeable of the subject and scientific writing. The other person should be a general reader. Suggestions gleaned from these reviewers can be used to revise the manuscript again.

Reference Lists

Proper citation of sources of information used in a paper as references is critical. Two reference citation styles are commonly used in academic and biomedical circles. The Vancouver style is a distinctive academic reference citation method where the authors and year of publication are cited in the text as they are used. At the end of the paper, these references are listed alphabetically by first author's last name. The Vancouver style cites the author(s) and year as they appear in text, followed by an alphabetized list of full references. This format is typical for graduate school research papers.

The reference citation style used in most medical and health professions journals is the style of the *Uniform Requirements for Manuscripts Submitted to the Biomedical Journals,* as developed by the International Committee of Medical Journal Editors[3] and later the Council of Biology Editors.[4] This reference format for a journal article takes the following form:

Author(s). Title. Journal. Year;Volume:Pages. Here is an example:

Hanson RL, Pettitt DJ, Bennett PH, et al. Familial relationships between obesity and NIDDM. Diabetes. 1995;44:418–422.

Consistency is one of the most important aspects of reference citation in an academic paper. Reference citation style and policies are typically included in the "Information for Authors" section published in journals. References cited should include only those documents that are readily available. You, as author, should have access to every reference, either electronically or in hard copy. A good dictum to remember is "If you can't put your hands on it, don't cite it."

Special formats and/or requirements exist for monographs, government publications, informal documents, Internet sources, and personal communications. Here are some additional points about references:

- Recent literature sources are now available on the Internet on PubMed.
- Textbook citations should be rare.
- Garbled, incomplete, or nonfunctional references, particularly internet citation, will disturb your readers (and editors).
- Citation from Internet sources such as Wikipedia, DrKoop, WebMD, Medscape, etc., are *not* acceptable.
- References from subscription services (e.g., MDConsult, UpToDate, etc.) are generally not acceptable.

References drawn from Internet sources and used in an academic paper have created an ongoing controversy on the frontier of scientific communication. Internet sources are becoming a leading category of reference information used by authors in presenting a paper or defending a thesis. Internet sources allow authors to obtain information that should be accurate and current. For example, in a paper on the topic of healthcare professionals in surgery, an essential "factoid" included in the first paragraph of this paper might be the current number of providers working in a particular field of surgery. In the past published information would have been consulted to obtain that information, which would be, by its very nature, dated. Presently, consulting an Internet source is more likely to yield the most current data available.

Citation of Internet Sources

The value of Internet references applies to many, but not all, online sources. Some Internet sources are unreliable and have questionable credibility. It is now common practice to include Internet references in peer-reviewed medical and healthcare literature. Internet reference sources can and should be permitted with the following ground rules:

1. The Internet source is not a personal Internet site (e.g., an individual home page).
2. Any person can readily access the Internet site and obtain the same information cited by the author.
3. The citation contains as much specific information as possible.
4. The date of access is always included.

The following examples of Internet citations are from the American Medical Association's *AMA Manual of Style: A Guide for Authors and Editors,* 9th ed., p. 45.

1. Rosenthal S, Chen R, Hadler S. The safety of acellular pertussis vaccine [abstract]. *Arch Pediatr Adoles Med* [serial online]. 1996; 150:457–460. http://www.ama-assn. org/sci-pubs/journals/archive/ajdc/vol_150/ no_5/abstract/htm. Accessed November 10, 1996.
2. Gostin LO. Drug use and HIV/AIDS [JAMA HIV/AIDS Web site]. June 1, 1996. http:// www.ama-assn.org/special/hiv/ethics. Accessed June 26, 1997.

Additional care must be taken to insure that information or texts acquired from Internet sources are properly acknowledged. According to Glass and Flanagin, there are four types of plagiarism:

1. *Direct plagiarism:* Verbatim lifting of passages without enclosing the borrowed material in quotation marks and crediting the original author.
2. *Mosaic:* Borrowing the ideas and opinions from an original source and a few verbatim words or phrases without crediting the origi-

nal author. In this case, the plagiarist intertwines his or her own ideas and opinions with those of the original author, creating a "confused, plagiarized mass."
3. *Paraphrase:* Restating a phrase or passage, providing the same meaning but in a different form without attribution to the original author.
4. *Insufficient acknowledgment:* Noting the original source of only part of what is borrowed or failing to cite the source material in such a way that a reader will know what is original and what is borrowed.[5]

A key rule is to provide any and all information that is needed to allow the reader to go to the same Internet site and review the same information cited by the author. This cardinal rule also applies to published reference sources. The second rule is completeness; follow a sequence of author(s) (individual[s] or organization), work title, site, latest date, Web address, pages (if applicable), and any other specifics that allow the reader to access the site. If a reader is unable to verify citations in an article, doubts about the validity of your efforts may arise.

Electronic Journals

The number of electronic journals in the medical and health literature is increasing. There are three forms of e-journals:

Type 1 e-journals are completely electronic with no regular print version.
Type 2 e-journals are titled the same both in the print and electronic versions, but each publishes some unique content.
Type 3 e-journals with both print and electronic versions publish the same content (Weller, 2002).

A number of e-journals are listed among MEDLINE titles. Although editor's statements on editorial peer review are similar in the three different types of e-journals, there are differences in number and type of materials included.

APPROACHES TO PUBLICATION

A potential writer, such as a new graduate from a healthcare profession program, an experienced clinician or a faculty member, may take a wide range of approaches toward entering the world of the published. For many clinicians, the first effort at publication may be somewhat easier and have a greater chance at success if a manuscript other than an original research article is submitted. As publication efforts progress, the alternative options may be considered. Beginning with something other than an original research manuscript publication offers a new author experience in dealing with journals, editors, and the review process. A good place to start is sending query letters to the publishing editors of journals you wish to consider as potential targets.

A query letter is an appropriate method for determining interest in a research paper, commentary, or opinion article among the biomedical editors. Responses to a one-page query letter can be used to gauge the interest of a particular journal in publishing an article on a certain topic. Addressed to the editors of one or more potential target journals, a query letter should pique the editor's interest by asking, "Would you consider a submission on [your topic here]?" Avoid forcing the editor to make an immediate decision; recognize that no editor will commit to a publication decision before seeing the final manuscript and obtaining at least one other review. However, if they are not interested in your topic, you and the journal can save a lot of time and effort by establishing this up front. Query letters should be sent to a number of target journals. However, a manuscript should only be submitted to one journal at a time. If a manuscript is turned down for publication, it can be submitted to another journal.

BEST CHOICES FOR NEW WRITERS

To become familiar with the process of manuscript submission and peer review, it may help to "start small" and consider beginning with case reports, review articles, book reviews, or letters to the editor. They are listed in the descending order of their perceived value and importance in peer-reviewed publications, but all are good starting points for less-experienced writers. Each of the categories has different content and requirements, but the rigor of preparation is typically less than that required for an original research article. These options are described in more detail in the following section. On the opposite end of the spectrum, editorials, book chapter authorship, and textbook editor roles are typically reserved for subject matter experts and invited senior academicians.

Original Articles

In terms of academic currency, original articles are typically valued more highly according to the importance of their content, their relevance for promotion and tenure of the author, and establishing the author's reputation within a profession. Original articles are not required to be data-driven clinical projects of "bench science" or laboratory origin. They may instead reflect policy analysis, utilization patterns, cost–benefit analyses, and a host of other relevant topics that contribute to advancing the knowledge base of the healthcare professions. The key is that they are original pieces of work that represent original investigation or approach.

Clinical Review Articles

The clinical review is one of the most common types of papers that appear in healthcare literature. This reflects, in large part, the need for practicing clinicians to obtain an easy-to-read, concise summary of a particular health condition or disease. Review articles cite current theory and clinical practice for specific diseases and conditions, but they do not consist of original research on the disease or condition conducted by the author(s). Typical section headings of a clinical review article include Introduction, Etiology, Pathophysiology, Clinical Manifestations, Diagnostic Imaging/Laboratory Findings, Diagnosis, Treatment, Prognosis, and Health Promotion/ Disease Prevention, and Recommendations.[6]

Systematic Reviews

A more sophisticated research paper format is the systematic review, in which a far-reaching survey of the existing literature on a given topic is performed, analyzed, and presented. Systematic reviews essentially comprise a detailed literature review of all retrievable studies on a given topic; they attempt to identify, appraise, select, and synthesize all available high-quality research evidence relevant to that question. Systematic reviews often use statistical methods (meta-analyses) to combine results of the eligible studies, or they may score the levels of evidence depending on the methodology used when they pool similar data from a number of studies. Systematic reviews are more extensive and transparent than traditional literature reviews and depend heavily on current bibliographic retrieval services, (e.g., Pub Med) as critical sources.

Case Reports

Case reports, once a "staple of the menu of clinical literature," and for that matter the format of many academic teaching exercises and presentations, remain an important type of paper appearing in biomedical journals.[2] Case reports are typically detailed, illustrated clinical descriptions of individual occurrences of disease. Over the past 20 years, however, case reports have become less frequent in biomedical literature and tend to convey little new information. Biomedical journals usually publish clinical research trials, but case reports may provide important information. Those that merit publication include case histories that are unique, or nearly unique, and cases of a new disease or an unexpected association (such as an outlier case or one with unexpected therapeutic events). They may represent notable early clinical observations that herald new diseases. Case studies are common in the healthcare literature and offer practicing clinicians an opportunity to share interesting and informative cases.

Editorials

The editorial section of journals is often the most revealing and, occasionally, the most controversial section of the journal. At times, an editorial in a major biomedical journal is an invited comment on a paper appearing in the same issue. Editors may choose to invite subject experts to compare and contrast their opinions with the paper and other related studies. Articles that have the potential for substantial impact on a disease or society are often complemented with an invited editorial, as are articles that endorse a significant departure from the traditional method of treating a disease or condition. Editorials can be personal opinion pieces that address issues and controversy in society, medicine, and the profession. Editorials sometimes present minority opinions on professional trends and directions. Editorials can be submitted by anyone, but journals may have policies that govern what can be addressed in an editorial. Generally, the editor of the journal makes the decision on whether to publish an editorial or not.

Position Papers: A Variant of the Editorial

Many highly respected journals are owned by professional societies, and these often contain official statements and position papers produced by the organization. Some journals choose to publish occasional "point–counterpoint" position papers on controversial topics. Although such articles typically do not contribute new data to an issue, the questions they pose often result in the development of new studies or new ways to approach an ill-defined issue. Position papers may attempt to influence readers, members, or those outside of the profession or professional society.

Position papers sometimes deal with therapeutic or clinical issues. They are usually the result of reviews by experts who then recommend a course of action. It is common for standards of care to emerge from such positions or expert opinion.

Book Reviews

Book reviews are common departmental features of biomedical journals. In some journals, particularly those in the field of the history of medicine, book reviews comprise a large portion of the content. An effective and engaging book review begins when the reviewer, ideally an individual well versed in the field that the book addresses, begins by asking the following questions: Is this book needed? Does it add a new perspective to the topic? Is it a helpful addition to the clinician's library? Reviews of books are commissioned by the editor or the department editor and are thus usually invited publications. Book reviews may or may not count as "significant publications" by institutional promotion and tenure committees. However, doing a book review is a valid publishing opportunity and a good exercise for aspiring researchers and authors.

Letters to the Editor

For readers, the well-written, informed, pointed response to a previously appearing article can be among the most interesting sections of a journal. Letters to the editor often include frank challenges to published findings. The real and personal risk of publishing any work in a peer-reviewed journal is that writers open themselves for public and professional criticism and occasional humiliation when their work is challenged or refuted by experts on the topic. For other writers and aspiring authors, however, a letter to the editor may represent an entry channel to publication and further contributions. If they appear in a major medical journal, letters to the editor count as a "major publication" as indexed in Index Medicus. Letters to the editor should directly address a recently published paper and/or provide new information. Letters are usually limited to 500 words or less, and journals typically restrict the number of times letters to the editor by a given author can be published. Typically, if a published work is challenged or commented upon in some way, the original author is allowed a counter response.

Abstracts and Posters

Excellent opportunities to present research in a peer-reviewed forum are abstracts and poster presentations. National meetings of healthcare professional organizations typically offer an excellent opportunity for poster and abstract presentations. For example, in the physician assistant profession, the American Academy of Physician Assistants (AAPA) Clinical and Professional Poster Session is conducted every year at the annual physician assistant conference. AAPA's Clinical and Scientific Affairs Council sponsors the session and coordinates the submission and peer-review process. The following section is from the AAPA website (http://www.aapa.org/clinissues/PosterSession.htm, used by permission), and is an excellent resource for abstract and poster development and presentation:

Frequently Asked Questions

Q. What is a poster?

A. A poster is a method commonly used to present research in the biomedical sciences; it is actually a bulletin board that displays one or several large pieces of paper. A poster provides an opportunity to publish a very short article and discuss it with your peers at a conference. It is a static, visual medium used to communicate ideas and messages. When research is presented on a poster, the content of the poster should be focused on generating active discussion of the research. A great poster is readable, legible, well organized, and succinct. The Science and Engineering Library at the State University of New York at Buffalo has excellent web resources to help you create an effective poster (http://ublib.buffalo.edu/libraries/units/sel/bio/posters.html).

Q. Does it have to be original research?

A. No, although original research is the sine qua non for poster presentations, other types of research or scholarly activity are welcome. Appropriate research results from a survey, an interventional study, a secondary data analysis, an epidemiologic study, a cost–benefit analysis, an evaluation of a diagnostic test, or something else. Interesting case studies, patient vignettes, and innovative practice techniques are also welcomed. Posters that have been presented at other professional meetings within the past 12 months are typically eligible for submission. Students are strongly encouraged to present research done in the program. Faculty are encouraged to present their educational research, innovative curricular designs, or case studies.

Q. Is the process very competitive?

A. There is no competition to get your abstracts approved per se. In most cases, if the guidelines are followed and quality work is presented, the abstract is accepted. In general, originality of work, adequacy of data, and clarity of expression are the determining factors for selection. Specific selection criteria vary for each category as listed below.

- Original research
  - Is the purpose or the objective clearly stated? Is the scope of topic too broad or too narrow?
  - Is the description of the materials and methods understandable? Are the data collection and experimental technique adequate for the study?
  - Are the analytical procedures used adequately described? Is the research design appropriate for the data collected and the subject of the study?
  - Are the results presented in sufficient detail to support the conclusions? Do they follow from the data and analysis?
  - Is the conclusion clear and the interpretation sound?
  - Is the information presented important? Are there practical implications of the information? Is the information new? Is the research original?
- Clinical report or case study
  - Is the information presented clearly and understandably?
  - Is the information presented applicable?
  - Is the information clinically important, relevant, and significant?
- Previously presented poster
  - Is the information appropriate?

- Does it satisfy the criteria previously given for original research?
- Educational research or interventions
  - Is the abstract thoughtful, organized, and clear?
  - Is an innovative method presented that is original and effective?
  - Are measurable outcomes presented?
  - Does the project impact special populations?
  - Does the project have value to other health professions' educators and their professions?

Q. Do you have an example of what a poster looks like?

A. The University of North Carolina provides an example of the principles of poster design and summarizes the abstract review process at http://gradschool.unc.edu/student/postertips.html.

Posters

The poster display board is 8 feet wide by 4 feet tall with a 1-inch metal border. The background material is a neutral-color cloth. **Figure 18–1** demonstrates the look of a classic original research poster. The top banner should include the title, author names, and their affiliations. The poster should read from top left to bottom right. The title should be legible from 8 feet away and the remaining words from 4 or 5 feet away.

Look at Figure 18–1 for examples. Keep in mind these important tips:

- Keep it simple.
  - Present only enough information to support your conclusions.
  - Eight poster panels is the maximum for effective presentation.
- Use graphs, charts, and figures to emphasize the key points; less text is better.
  - A good ratio is 20% text, 40% graphics and 40% open space.
  - Don't use all capital letters; they are much harder to read.
- Above all, be clear, concise, and organized.

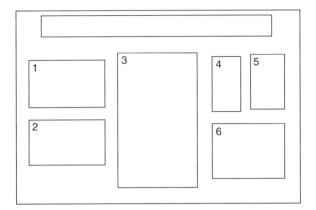 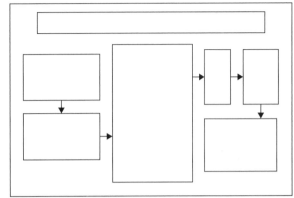

Figure 18–1 Example of poster formats.

ELEMENTS OF THE RESEARCH PAPER

Tables

Tables are an essential component, really the hallmark, of the Results section. As ideal vehicles for summaries of numerical and categorical data, tables are often far better than text for conveying this type of information. A table typically includes columns, rows, fields, titles, footnotes, and display trends. A table should stand alone and be readily understood without referring to the text, and each table should present at least one key result. Collectively, tables contain the vital findings of the investigation or study and represent the essence of an original research paper.

Effective tables should be constructed with a purpose in mind. Use of mutually exclusive categories is desirable, and the number of rows and columns should be kept to the minimum needed to convey the results. The use of several small tables is more effective than one large, complex table. Tables should be referred to in the text of your manuscript and placed within the text near that reference.

Illustrations and Figures

Illustrations or figures provide features central to the research paper: evidence, efficiency, and emphasis. The quality typically required for publication suggests that illustrations are best when prepared by professional graphic artists. Illustration examples include radiographs, ECG strips, and photomicrographs. Illustrations must have a descriptive legend. As with tables, figures and illustrations should be referred to in the text at the appropriate point.

Titles

The title of a research study in any form is important, particularly when it is published. The title may be the reason people are attracted to your work and introduces to readers what has been published. Basically, there are two types of titles: indicative (what the paper addresses) or informative (describes briefly the paper's specific message). The title should be accurate, succinct, and effective. As clinicians must triage through a voluminous and growing number of biomedical journal articles to determine which ones should be read; the first (and usually only) part read by most readers is the title. Word selection for the title is, perhaps, one of the most critical parts of the paper because it is the principal determining factor in the reader's decision to read the paper. The title should arouse enough curiosity that the article is further examined. Creating a catchy title is an editorial art form.

In the review and/or editing process, authors should not be disappointed or defensive if the title submitted with the manuscript is changed (i.e., it is often changed substantially). Editors are experienced at determining what title best catches the readership's eye for their particular journal.

ORAL PRESENTATIONS

Many professional meetings provide opportunities for participants to orally present their research. A common method is a 10-minute presentation followed by a 5-minute question-and-answer session. This is an excellent opportunity to present work in progress or the results of a finished project or study. The most frequently used product for digital presentation of data is Microsoft® PowerPoint.® Numerous self-paced PowerPoint training courses are available from Microsoft online (http://office.microsoft.com). Additionally, entering "PowerPoint presentations" on Internet search engines results in more than a million hits on sites that offer additional instruction or assistance.

Becoming a good speaker and presenter requires experience, effort, and practice. A beginning speaker only has effort and practice at hand. The experience comes from making oral presentations. A first-time speaker or presenter can expect to be nervous. As audience size grows, so do the levels of anxiety. These are normal responses and feelings, and even veteran speakers get "butterflies" from time to time. Two key ways to overcome initial fears are (1) to know your material and (2) to practice, practice, and practice some more. Two common traps plague all presenters. The first is reading the visual presentation. This pitfall should be avoided carefully. If all a presenter does is read a visual presentation, there is no need for an oral presentation. There are very few audiences that cannot read. In general, use notes or key words to guide the delivery of material. The second common mistake that many first time speakers make is that they have practiced to the point of reciting a memorized piece of work. Never recite. Good speakers retain some spontaneity and emotion in their voices, and they talk to the audience. Humor can add a lot to a presentation, but it must be appropriate for the audience, the material, and the speaker.

The last key aspect of being a good speaker and presenter is to respect the time frame allowed for your presentation. Practice helps frame a time period, but it is never the same as being in front of an audience. It is better to end a presentation a bit early than to run over the allotted time. One way to avoid running over is to allow some time for questions at the end of a presentation. In some venues, directions specify the allowance of a set time period for questions. Generally, 5 minutes is a reasonable time for questions. Much depends on the length and subject matter of your presentation. A plus point for always allowing time for questions is that if you run a few minutes long in presentation, the only thing lost is the question period. If you are short of your allowed time, it gives you a longer period to field questions.

Becoming a good presenter requires work. The more experience a presenter has, the less effort and practice necessary to do the presentation itself. Beginning presenters and speakers may benefit from participating in formats and venues that have short 10–15 minute periods or panels and co-presentations. Opportunities that involve small audience opportunities are also conducive to gaining needed experience.

GRADUATE PROJECTS/ PAPERS IN THE HEALTHCARE PROFESSIONS

During the 1990s, as more educational programs on healthcare professions either began by, or converted to, awarding master's degrees, and later clinical doctoral degrees, theses or dissertation requirements became more common. A final graduate paper typically requires extensive modification, usually specifically tailored reduction in length, to be a suitable candidate for peer-reviewed publication. The academic format needs to be modified to fit the format required by a specific journal. Editors and editorial board members are expert at determining whether a master's thesis or doctoral dissertation has been reworked to fit the specifications of a specific journal. Adding early publications to one's resume is likely to enhance employment opportunities and professional advancement. Some healthcare professions' publications do not accept manuscripts from students as a matter of policy, due to the high overall rejection rate of unsolicited manuscripts. If a graduate project is worthy of consideration for publication, then a query letter should be sent to either a member of the editorial board or the editor of a target journal.

Acquiring their guidance in advance can increase the chances for publication.

Writing the Paper

Huth (1994) proposed a writing system that utilizes a process in which one writes a first draft, places it aside for a couple of days, re-reads it, and then begins the second draft (rewrite). This iterative–reiterative process is continued until the paper is finished.[6] Authors should consider sharing the paper with a friend who has critical writing and editing skills. Colleagues with content expertise should also be consulted. It may take as many as 20 or more drafts and rewrites until a final product is achieved. Quality is the aim and a great deal of effort is needed.

Working with Editors

Writers and editors have historically shared an uneasy alliance. According to Arthur Plotnik in *The Elements of Editing,* editors are foot soldiers in the eternal war between raw talent and the people who process that talent.[7] As long as writers write primarily to advance themselves and editors edit to satisfy readers, there will never be a lasting peace. Writers know their particular subject; editors know their audience. A well-known truism is that knowledge of the subject does not necessarily translate into good writing, and good writing does not necessarily correlate with good editing. The editor may determine that a writer's style does not correlate with the journal's requirements or quality standards. Embrace the editorial review process. All writers need a good editor's touch.

When conflicts of interest arise in the editing process, the readership, not the writer, receives first consideration. This is where the writer must have thick skin. Some of the writing is always changed in the editorial process. Manuscript content is the writer's province, but the form is the editor's specialty. Many manuscripts must be revised a number of times. Each revision is reviewed, and the changes that are made to meet required or recommended improvements may need further work. Like other biomedical journals, journals in the health professions are typically expensive to operate, and editors are required to make the most efficient use of their printed pages. **Figure 18–2** shows the stages of publication.

BASIC STEPS IN PUBLICATION

How is the right journal chosen as a target for a manuscript's publication? Different journals feature different types of formats: original reports, special articles, short papers, editorials (usually invited), clinical notes, and letters to the editor. Initially the format of the paper should consider the choice of venue and format. If this decision is difficult or problematic, one of the journal's editors or editorial board members may provide clarification. Is the topic of the proposed paper within the journal's scope? Is the topic represented frequently or only rarely? Does the target journal offer the best match of audience with your topic? What formats does the journal accept? Determine who cares about the message of your paper. Is it best suited for a clinical specialty journal or a general medical journal? Is it best suited for clinicians, educators, researchers, or all of these groups?

Duties of a Potential Author

Based on the topic of the paper, several journals may be publishing candidates. Begin with the most recently published issue of a target journal and carefully read each back issue for, at least, the past year, then review the last few years' publications. Ensure that an article on the same topic has not recently been published. If it has, determine whether the paper merely rehashes existing information or adds new information. In assessing the suitability of a paper for a particular journal, these guidelines should be followed:

1. Read the journal's "Statement of Editorial Purpose."
2. Review the journal's editorial board membership.
3. Consult the annually published list of peer reviewers.

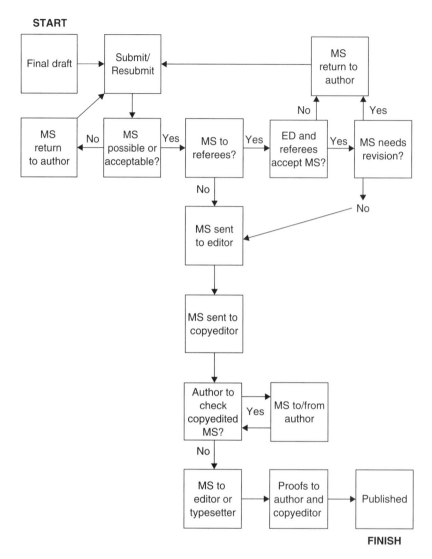

Figure 18–2 Manuscript process.

4. Read the journal's most recent "Information for Authors" statement.
5. Evaluate the journal's publishing style regarding article format and requirements for tables, charts, abstracts, footnotes, citations, and references.

As a result of performing these tasks, the author can determine in advance whether the project fits a specific journal or if it needs to be modified in certain ways. Have the relevant work of leaders, members of the journal's editorial board, and peer reviewers been reviewed and cited? This aspect of writing is often referred to as "chanting the names of the ancestors." At least one editorial board member and one or more peer reviewers review each provisionally accepted manuscript. If their relevant work is not cited, the paper may be deemed incomplete.

Communicate with the Connected

Dialogue with editors, editorial board members, peer reviewers, or subject matter experts on the research topic is extremely helpful in the publishing process. After a target journal has been chosen, send a proposed outline of the manuscript to determine preliminary interest. Getting from the "unsolicited" to the "solicited" side of the journal's editors is a challenging but worthwhile task to pursue. These are the "connected" people in the publishing realm.

Request Reprints of Previously Published Articles

Every peer-reviewed journal lists the contact person (usually the first author) for article reprints. One way to begin a relationship with professionals is to review their body of work and write a letter stating how much you enjoyed his or her work, combined with a few cogent observations. This individual may end up reviewing your manuscript, or may eventually become a collaborator.

Requirements and Resources for Writers

Writers must develop a "thick skin" to persevere through the paper's revision, possible or repeated rejection, and the eventual publishing process. Writers must be meticulous in their work.

Students in healthcare professions attempting to meet graduate-degree paper requirements must have access to biomedical literature databases (such as the National Library of Medicine's "Grateful Med" at www.Igm.nlm.nih.gov). Basic requirements include access to medical literature databases, preferably accessible electronically via online Internet service providers. Academic reference librarians can be wonderful friends; they can make the literature review and reference retrieval process much less intimidating. Writing also requires uninterrupted time, with ready access to reference and resource material, including reference documents, a personal computer, and other favorite writing aids. Time for writing must be scheduled on a regular and predictable basis. Close the door if necessary, or write from home if that option exists.

The Peer-Review Process

To evaluate the accuracy of submitted manuscripts, most reputable biomedical journals employ the peer-review process. This process typically involves sending the manuscripts to two or three individuals, selected by the editor, who are in a position to judge the value of the work. In more selective journals, only a few submissions ever make it to the peer-review process. These journals often have full-time editorial positions that are filled by healthcare professionals (e.g., physicians and other clinicians) who have developed skills in medical writing and editing. This is the case at journals such as the *New England Journal of Medicine,* the *Journal of the American Medical Association,* the *Annals of Surgery,* and the *Annals of Internal Medicine,* among many others.

On receipt, most reputable journals conduct an initial internal review of the manuscript. The editor or an associate editor reads the manuscript and determines its eligibility for peer review. If it is determined to be a candidate for publication, the manuscript is then sent to peer reviewers from various related fields. Often, peer reviewers are editorial board members and/or editorial consultants who perform these services for the journal on a regular basis.

The peer-review process is regarded as an extension of the basic principles of science and scholarship. Peer review has existed for more than 200 years and has achieved nearly universal application for assessing research reports before publication. Peer review is considered a critical quality control. Yet despite this widespread utilization, the process has been shown to have flaws, and relatively little is known with regard to the quality and utility of the information that this eventually published.[8,9]

Blinded Review

Journals vary in their policies with regard to "masking" the names and affiliations of authors. Most, but not all, biomedical journals mask the identities of authors. A question regarding the value of the peer-review process is the potential of a reviewer being familiar with the author's identity, which creates bias. In several disciplines, only a few investigators are involved in a particular field of research, and the identities of authors may be easily recognized by peers. This is the "Achilles' heel" of the peer-review process that has led some journals to adopt the policy of unblinded review.

The Publishing Decision

Possible outcomes of the peer-review process include the following:

1. Acceptance
2. Minor revisions required
3. Major revisions required
4. Outright rejection

The response from the editor typically consists of a cover letter summarizing the reviewers' comments, recommendations, and the blinded reviewers' evaluation sheets. Always pay close attention to recommended suggestions, changes, or critiques. Address all concerns expressed by the reviewers, including data inconsistencies and errors, even if you disagree with them. It is not unusual for authors to disagree with peer reviewers. When the case is well made by the author to retain the original version, the section of the manuscript in question may remain unchanged. Rejection letters with a copy of the submitted manuscript should be reviewed and saved. Some rejection letters are carefully worded invitations to resubmit. Rejection is part of the process. All successful authors have a history of rejection, and none should take it personally. The manuscript may be resubmitted after completing all of the required revisions and addressing all of the concerns of the editor and reviewers.

Submitting the Final Manuscript

Assuming that the final version of the manuscript meets all publishing requirements, the packet is then sent to the journal, including the requisite number of manuscript copies. Be aware that journal requirements may vary on specific format of the title page (e.g., for instance, whether or not an abstract is required as part of the manuscript). The final packet should also be accompanied by a cover letter that summarizes the basic rationale for the paper. The cover letter must also include an author

attestation statement that "the paper, nor its essential substance" is not presently under consideration by another journal and has not appeared elsewhere (e.g., in another journal). This statement must be fully acknowledged and signed by all authors indicating that the work is their own and has not been published or submitted elsewhere.

Authors must follow precisely the "Instructions to Authors" of the particular journal to which they are submitting. The final draft submission should be flawless. This becomes very important when work is submitted to a journal in which there is significant competition for space. If an editor must choose between two manuscripts of relatively equal importance, then the one that requires the least amount of corrective action from the editorial staff is more likely to be accepted.

The next step is the receipt of the page proofs. Be prepared for a rapid turnaround requirement; as few as 24 hours is not unusual. This requires an author to drop everything to address the proofs and return them for final typesetting.

Realize that the copyright protection is assigned to the journal that accepts the work; in reality, it is no longer the author's paper. If some of the data must eventually be included in another manuscript (e.g., a published table), permission must be secured from the publisher, regardless of authorship.

Conflicts of Interest, Disclosures, and Institutional Review Board (IRB) Approval

It is standard operating procedure for peer-reviewed healthcare professions journals to include requirements for full disclosure on any real or perceived conflict of interest with the manuscript content, affiliated sponsors and organizations, or coauthors. This also includes disclosure of any investment or financial interest or funding associated with any product or organization referred to in the manuscript. Additionally, federal law requires that any research involving human subjects be reviewed and approved by a designated and approved institutional or regional Institutional Review Board (IRB) prior to commencing any research. It is not fully appreciated within the health professions' communities that this includes ALL human subject research, regardless of whether or not the project includes federal funding. Any research including medical and administrative record data, leftover tissues, health services research, survey, behavioral, and biomedical or any other healthcare research is included in this requirement. Even if the research seems likely to be exempt from IRB approval (e.g., an anonymous survey that is optional to complete) evidence of an IRB-approved exemption must be acquired for biomedical journals to consider the work for publication. Many uninformed researchers have been frustrated when they completed a project and discovered after-the-fact that IRB approval was necessary, rendering their research unacceptable for publication. This standard applies to research in all healthcare professions.

Authorship

The corresponding and/or first author must carefully select coauthors as the research or project ideas are developed. Adding colleagues or friends who contribute little to the work is inappropriate and serves to alienate the coauthors who perform the work. A coauthor should have generated at least part of the intellectual content of the paper as well as had a part in writing the paper, including reviewing it for possible revision or revising its intellectual content. A coauthor should be able to publicly defend all of the content of the paper in the scientific community.

Before a researcher agrees to collaborate, it is wise to know the work habits, reliability, and temperaments of potential coauthors. Are they committed to deadlines? Do they return calls and provide information in a timely manner? Do they do what they say they will do? All of these issues matter when it comes to coauthoring manuscripts. The more coauthors included, the more difficult it becomes to reach consensus about and satisfaction with the paper. It is important to agree up front about work responsibilities and authorship order. The overall responsibility of the manuscript always rests with the first author.

Assignment and determination of authorship on papers submitted to biomedical journals has undergone significant evolution in recent years. Now a greater sense of accountability for the intellectual contributions of authors and what types of contributions merit authorship is the norm. Authorship of a paper submitted to a biomedical journal indicates that the individual has invested substantial intellectual effort in the conceptualization and writing of the manuscript. To qualify as an author, an individual should fulfill the following criteria:[10]

- Participated in the work sufficiently to take public responsibility for all or part of the content
- Made substantial contributions to the intellectual content of the paper in one or more of the following categories:
  - Conception and design
  - Acquisition of data
  - Analysis and interpretation of data
  - Drafting of the manuscript
  - Critical revision of the manuscript for substantive intellectual content
  - Statistical analysis
  - Obtaining funding
  - Administrative, technical, or material support

Today, the most reputable medical journals require authors to sign a form attesting to their input into the paper and verifying their qualification for authorship designation.

Group authorship sometimes presents problems, particularly with citations. Group authorship is the listing of the name of a group in place of the names of individual authors. Modified group authorship, in which individual names are listed followed by the name of the group, is also used. Group authorship is most often used by investigators associated with studies involving many investigators (e.g., multicenter clinical trials or genomics) because it allows investigators to share credit equally. PubMed is the National Library of Medicine's (NLM'S) bibliographic database, with citations dating back to 1966. The NLM has not included group authors in the MEDLINE author field; rather, the group name has been included as an add-on to the title. NLM now lists group authors under a separate "collective name" field. The Science Citation Index (SCI) is a scientific and biomedical bibliographic database used to track citations to individual articles. Instead of listing the research group in the author field in its source listing, SCI lists either all individual names in the group or the writing committee members' names in the order they are listed in the article.

SOME CHALLENGES FOR HEALTH PROFESSIONS PUBLICATIONS

Over the past 40 years, the healthcare professions have seen journals come and go and, in the main, have had difficulty in gaining recognition beyond their professional readership. Part of the problem is the very specialized interest of clinicians for, primarily, clinical review type articles. Most clinicians are employed full-time and therefore do not have the time nor direct incentive to write and publish medical articles. Those that do, primarily educators, are relatively small in number and tend to write on educational and curricular topics and not on clinical matters. The primary audience for health professions journals is clinicians who seek material of a clinical nature that will help them to remain current on advancements in medical care and make them more effective in serving their patients.

Thus, many healthcare professionals who might otherwise seek to write and publish are forced to compete with physicians and other biomedical scientists in the biomedical world who are academics, clinical researchers, or basic science researchers, and have the resources and incentives to write and publish. Healthcare professionals are usually not trained to be writers and/or scholars but instead are prepared to be clinicians. Most are in no position to produce original biomedical studies and research products sought by journals. As a result, the healthcare professions literature has tended to focus primarily on concise and current clinical review articles, that is, papers that summarize a specific clinical problem and outline recommended

management. While this focus tends to serve the needs of the primary audience, it does not contain original research material. As a consequence, journals specific to the healthcare professions fail to have a readership beyond their own profession. This may change as more students gain research experience as a component of their education, as more health professions educators become involved with research, and as more and more clinicians participate in research as part of their practice.

Medical Journals

Many healthcare professionals—both clinicians as well as academics commonly publish papers in biomedical journals. Those in the nonphysician healthcare professions (PAs, NPs, CNMs, PTs, etc.) at times publish in journals that aimed primarily toward physician audiences. They include the major general medical journals such as the *New England Journal of Medicine,* the *Journal of the American Medical Association, The Lancet,* and the *British Medical Journal,* as well as leading specialty journals such as the *Annals of Internal Medicine, American Family Physician,* and *Annals of Surgery.*

The modern medical publishing business is an intensely competitive enterprise. Virtually all biomedical journals are basically dependent on their sponsors (professional societies and commercial publishers) for their viability. The business operations of these ventures in turn depend, most of the time, exclusively on advertising revenue. This fact of life (that biomedical publications depend on revenues from advertisers) requires editors and editorial boards to balance scientific direction and standards and journal content with the requirements of those who are "paying the freight" in the operation of the publication.

The vast numbers of publications in biomedicine are essentially businesses. Publishing medical journals is an expensive venture. Publishers of various biomedical journals comprise the following:

1. Professional organizations that sponsor and produce a journal identified as their official journal
2. Proprietary publishing firms

3. Philanthropic organizations, including journals such as Health Affairs, a health policy resource subsidized by Project Hope, or the Milbank Memorial Fund Quarterly

MANUSCRIPT FLAWS THAT PREVENT PUBLICATION

Authors fall prey to several pitfalls in the preparation and submission of manuscripts to biomedical journals (**Table 18–3**). Editors and reviewers are always looking for reasons to be skeptical regarding the worthiness of a manuscript for publication. Although the reasons for rejections are extensive, the author should bear in mind the following common scenarios:

1. The topic is inappropriate for a specific journal. The manuscript is a sound piece of investigation, description, or opinion and is presented in a suitable format, but the topic is not quite appropriate for the particular journal. In some cases, these papers may represent previously rejected or recycled manuscripts that the author(s) did not bother to reconfigure in the required format for that journal.

Table 18–3 Reasons for Manuscript Rejection

Excessive use of philosophy
Loose organizational style
Material not sufficiently important
Information not easily generalized
Methods used unclear
Results described unclear
Statistics used incorrectly
Sample size inadequate
Conclusions unwarranted
Results not compared with similar studies
Inadequate period of observation, use, or evaluation of method
Inadequate review of the literature

Adapted from Geyman JP, Bass MJ. Communication of results of research. *J Fam Prac.* 1978;7(1):120.

2. The use of imperfect style and "crazy-quilt" fonts. A manuscript containing imperfect style that has differing sections with differing fonts and font sizes indicates that it may be a "cut-and-paste" effort, one that is basically recycling the work of others or an uncoordinated collaboration among authors that has not been properly edited. Manuscripts with these types of sloppy narrative reveal inattention to detail and a nonsystematic structure. Editors regard such papers as a waste of time if it appears that the authors have not put forth the proper effort to prepare the manuscript to specifications.

3. "Cut-and-paste" citations were used. Cut-and-paste citations lifted verbatim from reference sources are ill advised. If a citation is not physically available, then do not quote it. Do not be surprised if editors or reviewers ask for verification, particularly if the citation looks suspicious. If this verification falls short, it raises questions of plagiarism, and the paper will be summarily rejected.

4. Tables and/or text were used without permission. Give credit where credit is due. If you a table from someone else's work is copied or modified for use, acknowledge the source. The required permission may need to be presented to the publisher.

5. Errors in mathematical calculations occurred (bad math). Be aware that the journal will calculate any math included in the manuscript, such as percentages in a table. It is always recommended that authors double-check their data, including the math included in tables.

6. The same material was used to publish several articles. Editors are well acquainted with the tendency of authors to partition their work into "least publishable units," a phenomenon also known as "salami science." In this case, a data set is split into smaller subsets, each with a narrow focus, in an effort to publish as many papers as possible from one core data set. Examples

include submitting single-center reports from multicenter studies and short-duration reports from long-duration studies. The dangers of repetitive publication of the same material are many. An old or recycled paper must be sufficiently updated or have new data added to justify publication.

7. Citation or reference inaccuracies were found. Authors are obligated to double-check the accuracy of all citations within their work. Citation error is a serious problem in biomedical publications. One study of peer-reviewed surgical journals found a 48 percent citation error rate, casting doubt in many cases that original reference sources were reviewed by the authors.[9]

ON WRITING AND PUBLISHING

Writing is difficult and time-consuming work. Authors must fundamentally calculate the questions of "Why write a paper if it does not stand a reasonable chance of being published?" and "What do I have to say?" Dr. John Billings, founder of the National Library of Medicine, espoused four primary rules for the aspiring author:

1. Have something to say.
2. Say it.
3. Stop as soon as you have said it.
4. Give the paper a proper title.

Strive to Write Clearly

Clear thinking leads to clear writing. George Orwell said, "Good prose is like a window pane; that is, what you have to say should not be obscured by how you say it." Prose is bad when readers need to stop and look at it again to understand its message. The central message of a book written by a long-time editor of *JAMA* was embodied in its title, *Why Not Say It Clearly?*.[11] Interestingly, this book appeared during a time when biomedical writing was criticized by, among others, Michael Crichton (a well-known author and film and television producer), who was then a recent medical school graduate, as being deliberately "obfuscatory." Writing clearly means using words with the greatest degree of accuracy in transmitting what you wish to communicate to others.

A STEP-BY-STEP APPROACH TO PUBLISHING A MANUSCRIPT

The essential steps in the process of publishing a paper in the biomedical literature are as follows:

1. Determine the central message of the paper.
2. Decide whether the paper is worth writing or not.
3. Identify the appropriate audience for the paper.
4. Select the target journal.
5. Search the literature.
6. Determine authorship and an expected timetable.
7. Assemble the sources and materials needed to write the paper.
8. Develop a structure for the paper; make a detailed outline.
9. Write the first draft conforming it to the journal's requirements for manuscripts.
10. Revise the first draft and cycle through several more drafts; add appropriate tables, graphs, and illustrations.
11. Finalize the manuscript; complete all sections.
12. Obtain comments and critiques from selected "personal consultants."
13. Submit the article to the selected journal in the required format; include a formal cover letter with the appropriate disclaimer.
14. Promptly respond and revise the manuscript as indicated in the editor's communication; respond to all authors' queries.
15. Resubmit the corrected manuscript; proof the final typescript; assign copyright.

SUMMARY

After deciding to attempt to publish the paper that resulted from a research study, several key steps should be considered. These include making sure that the paper is a quality effort and that the writing is clear and concise. Authors must make a careful selection of the journal or journals that may be interested in the type of work that has been produced. The editor may be contacted about his or her interests. The "Instructions to the Author" should be followed explicitly. If the journal is interested, cooperate on revisions and suggestions for the paper. This process takes time and patience, sometimes up to 1 year. There may be many reasons for the rejection of a submission; rejection is not personal. In fact, for those who seek to publish often, rejection is part of life. Remember that the work has value in the experience gained in the process of scientific inquiry. If research is an ongoing part of a healthcare professional's life, publication success will eventually occur with perseverance.

REFERENCES

1. American Medical Association. *AMA Manual of Style: A Guide for Authors and Editors,* 10th ed. Chicago, IL: Oxford University Press; 2007. Accessed at: http://www.amamanualofstyle.com/oso/public/index.html. Accessed [ ].
2. International Committee of Medical Journal Editors. Guide to Uniform Requirements for Manuscripts Submitted to Biomedical Journals. 1997. Accessed at: http://jama.ama-assn.org/info/avinst_req.html. Accessed [ ].
3. Kole, LA, Currey R. Writing to be published—Why and how (and when). *J Am Acad Phys* Assist. 1999;12(3):92, 93, 96.
4. Huth EJ. *How to Write and Publish Papers in the Medical Sciences,* 2nd ed. Baltimore, MD: Williams and Wilkins; 1990.
5. Glass RM, Flanigan A. Communication, biomedical II. Scientific publication. In: Reich WT, ed. *Encyclopedia of Bioethics,* 2nd ed. New York: Macmillan; 1995; American Medical Association. *AMA Manual of Style: A Guide for Authors and Editors,* 9th ed. Baltimore, MD: Lippincott Williams & Wilkins; 1998.
6. Huth EJ. *Scientific Style and Format: The Council of Biology Editors Manual for Authors, Editors, and Publishers,* 6th ed. Cambridge, England: Council of Biology Editors; 1994.
7. Plotnick, A. *The Elements of Editing: A Modern Guide for Editors and Journalists.* New York: MacMillan; 1982.
8. Wagner E, Jefferson T. *The Shortcomings of Peer Review.* West Sussex, UK: Lear Publishing; 2001;14:257–263.
9. Lock S. *A Difficult Balance: Editorial Peer Review in Medicine.* London, England: Nuffield Provincial Hospitals Trust; 1985.
10. Journal of the American Medical Association Authorship Responsibility, Financial Disclosure, Copyright Transfer and Acknowledgment Statement.
11. King L. *Why Not Say It Clearly?* Boston, MA: Little, Brown; 1978.

Interpreting the Literature

CHAPTER OVERVIEW

More than two million biomedical articles are published in medical, health, and professional journals each year.[1] For most clinicians, wading through even a small number of journals or articles can be daunting, yet in 2010 almost 700,000 citations were indexed in Medline®.[2] The challenge is not only to stay abreast of current changes in practice but also to be able to meet the expectations of the informed healthcare consumer. Never has so much information been available to so many people. Patients appear in the office or clinical area with information such as news releases, newspaper and television reports, Internet information, and more. Sometimes patients have been apprised of information on new advances that have not appeared in the medical and healthcare literature. In a profit-driven system, information is frequently delivered about the benefits of new advances in medications, procedures, and treatments without disclosing the downsides.

Healthcare professionals must be able to interpret the scientific and medical literature quickly and completely to meet the challenge of applying new information and meeting the needs of eager patients. For centuries, textbooks were a reliable source of information. By the middle of the twentieth century, their slow revisions and lag time from completion to distribution meant they were never up to date. Today the role of textbooks is to provide a good foundation, but current literature is the key to modern practice. Reading journals remains a source of current information for many clinicians. However, even print journals have some delay in the source to provider pipeline. In the twenty-first century, the speed and access capabilities of the Internet provide resources unavailable to previous generations of healthcare providers. Information is posted quickly and efficiently, and is accessible to all.

Ultimately, an important question for every clinician is "What is important to my patients and my practice?" Answering that question is the key to providing contemporary and effective care. Part of the answer lies in developing skills that critically examine the literature to answer those questions. This chapter is designed to provide some guidelines to the process of interpreting the literature. This chapter is an introduction to interpretation. Entire books have been written on the subject. Professional growth and experience are undoubtedly aided by cultivating the ability to interpret the literature.

J. Dennis Blessing, PhD, PA

J. Glenn Forister, MS, PA-C

In no affairs of more prejudice, pro or con, do we deduce inferences with entire certainty, even from the most simple data.
—The Narrative of A. Gordon Pym, by E. A. Poe

Questioning: The beginning of genius without which no progress would flow
—Anonymous

INTRODUCTION

Interpreting medical literature is a process of integrating, synthesizing, and summarizing information obtained from different sources into a recommendation for application in practice. The intent is to apply the best knowledge available to make the best choice for the circumstances encountered in clinical practice. Summaries of this information, known as integrative literature, comes in many forms: systematic reviews, overviews, meta-analyses, practice guidelines, decision analyses, and cost-effectiveness analyses. The concept of evidence-based medicine is expanding, and the extraction of evidence from the literature into practice, while logical, presents some challenges. Busy clinicians must develop skills that allow them to become critical consumers of select literature and decide what applies to their patients. This process comprises "The application of the best available evidence to patient care."[2] As skills in interpreting the literature are developed, it is important to remember that patient care is at the heart of the procedure. Being patient-centered enhances the implementation of correct patient-care decisions.

Literature interpretation is a skill that must be learned, practiced, and applied. As more health-care research articles are reviewed, the results can sometimes be confusing, conflicting, and confounding. Given the advent of evidence-based medicine, systematic reviews, and meta-analyses, it is no wonder that clinicians often become more confused by the literature rather than enlightened. Clinicians must develop interpretation skills over time. If the literature is not continually read and effectively analyzed, clinical practices will become stale and even possibly incorrect.

The more immersed in research healthcare practitioners are, the greater their ability to synthesize and utilize the literature. However, becoming an expert in interpreting the medical literature takes years of experience as well as a broad understanding of processes, statistical designs, and analyses. This chapter helps begin a solid foundation and reference point from which an understanding of medical literature can be built.

To conduct a research project, the researcher must have some understanding of what the research problem is (*see* Chapter 6: The Research Problem) and what has occurred in the area of interest (*see* Chapter 7: Review of the Literature). This particularly pertains to obtaining the maximum benefit from the literature search. For example, healthcare students may wonder if they are entering a profession that will be the right career for them in the long run. The problem is that they do not know much about this subject and may not be sure where to go for the answers. The answer to this question can be researched as the degree of "satisfaction." That is, is the chosen profession a satisfying one? If someone is entering a profession where job satisfaction is low and attrition is high, then the profession's practitioners are not well served. Reviewing the literature on job satisfaction can help a student determine whether a chosen profession is satisfying to others who are on the same path.

The literature search is often a quest for theory building. It also helps to discover what research has been done and how it could be done better or differently. The scholar's research should say something new or validate existing work, while it connects with research that already has been reported. Literature provides a basis for a foundation in theory and topics of concern. How the literature is interpreted influences the overall research process. Understanding how to interpret the literature helps the practitioner develop a knowledge base as well as the ability to make the case for a new investigation. Information regarding the literature search performed prior to the practitioner project or scientific investigation is presented in Chapter 7.

Interpretation of the literature takes on greater importance when it involves the care of others. Misinterpretations can lead to significant errors in healthcare practice. This chapter is based on several resources[3,4] and the authors' experience to provide a general guide for how to interpret the medical literature.

INTERPRETING THE LITERATURE

First Things First

The first step to literature interpretation is to read enough background information on the subject. Understand as many aspects as possible of the issue that is being studied. Most healthcare professionals and students have developed some literature interpretation skills by reading or studying various resources in their fields. A rudimentary step in literature interpretation is to understand certain terms used in research (e.g., percentages, means, validity, limitations, probability, subjects, and population). Most of these terms are found in the glossary of this book or in other chapters. Recognizing the meaning and significance of research terms becomes easier as the ability to interpret the literature progresses. Furthermore, incorporating such terms in the context of research also becomes easier as experience is gained from understanding the literature. One useful suggestion is to *never* let a term go undefined while reviewing the literature, especially if the material is important to the clinician's own research projects, clinical practice, or patient care. Another suggestion is to develop a bibliography of useful references. Historically, many researchers have simply made copies of important articles and kept them in their file cabinets. Because so many articles are retrievable, storing electronic word documents on a computer hard drive may be all that is needed. Many journal articles are now available online and can be quickly accessed.

The Scientific Method

Understanding the literature can be a challenge because the research field is dynamic and fueled by new technology. The principles of the scientific method are integral to the literature process (searching and interpreting) because an emphasis is placed on gaining knowledge from the rigorous process of systematic observation, analysis, and reasoning.

Schematically, all concepts must pass through the scientific method corridor. This process adds value and becomes part of one's fundamental knowledge. Therefore, the literature search must include and incorporate scientific observation and data collection. The formal process of acquiring scientific knowledge, whether through reviewing the literature or recording observations, must be conducted in a logical and reproducible manner. In essence, this means that any competent clinician could replicate the literature search and reach the same conclusions. A researcher incorporates the scientific method into his project by defining each step as follows:

1. Problem: a precise statement of what knowledge was sought and why it was sought.
2. Question: a single sentence that asks a question related to the problem.
3. Method: the plan of how the research was done and how the knowledge was gained.
4. Results: unequivocal statements of the knowledge that was gained.
5. Interpretation: application of the knowledge gained.

How the results of this process are interpreted is key to understanding how the results will be utilized to provide better care for patients. Recognizing the steps of sound scientific investigation, as well as applying scientific concepts, will help the clinician interpret the results in a more meaningful manner.

Questions to Ask (and Answer)

Whether interpreting the literature for application in practice or gathering data for a research project, part of the task and challenge of reviewing literature is to assess what has been published on the topic of interest. **Table 19–1** outlines a set of questions to be asked and answered before making any assumption about the literature.

Ultimately, this method of literature inquiry or evaluation eventually becomes second nature as it is practiced. Writing down answers to these

---

Table 19–1 Questions to Ask and Answer

1. What is the source (journal) of the article?
2. Was the publication peer reviewed?
3. Who are the authors and what are their affiliations?
4. What is the main subject of the study?
5. What was the problem(s) investigated?
6. What is the purpose or rationale for the study?
7. Who or what constituted the sample or population?
8. What was the design of the study?
9. What are the statistical analyses used?
10. What are the results?
11. Are the results clear?
12. Did the results answer the identified questions?
13. Do the results seem valid?
14. Are the interpretations (conclusions) of the results consistent with design and analysis?
15. Are the results consistent with findings from similar studies?
16. What do the results mean to medicine and health care and you and your patients?
17. Can the results be applied to your research or clinical practice?

---

questions while evaluating an article reinforces the steps toward becoming a critical evaluator of literature. New questions may emerge as well during this process.

Although many of these questions are self-explanatory, additional clarification may be needed to ensure that thought processes are consistent and clear. While reviewing various information sources, new thoughts on evaluating the literature tend to emerge. Such thoughts and concepts precipitate the development of individual research style and process. Only through scrutiny, analysis, and replication can consumers of the literature ask the right questions, challenge the answers, and find answers to more questions. The scientific process and the information that results from that process are then validated. This process defines the cumulative development of scientific knowledge.

The Questions

1. *What is the source (journal) of the article?*
   The reputation of a source can be as important as a citation. Journals that tend to have the highest subscription rate typically have a higher degree of prestige. Generally, the top journals in a specific discipline are most often cited due to their solid reputation in the medical community. For clinical articles, these include the *Journal of the American Medical Association* (JAMA), *The New England Journal of Medicine, Lancet,* etc. However, other lesser-known journals also publish high-quality work. Each journal is ranked according to citation rates. Although lower-ranked journals can publish sound scientific articles and higher ranked journals can publish articles of poor quality, the ranking system is a helpful measure of quality.[3] Each publisher has a set of standards related to manuscript acceptance. Journals with high submission rates and low acceptance rates are often considered stronger sources than those with low submission rates and high acceptance rates. In addition, a journal's impact factor can be an important metric when comparing the relative value of a journal title within its field. The Journal Citation Reports® at ISI Web of Knowledge[SM] is a database that can be utilized to research this information.

2. *Was the publication peer reviewed?*
   Peer review is a process of manuscript critique by someone familiar with the same body of literature that the author is submitting. Since the 1950s, the majority of scientific manuscripts submitted for publication undergo a peer-review process. This type of review is intended to critically evaluate a manuscript so the reader is offered some confidence that the resulting publication has been scrutinized for soundness, valid results, and conclusions that fit the findings. Journals are ranked by their scientific merit and readership. Readership often rests on the journal's ability to bring new and important information that can be confidently accepted. However, not every article in a "peer reviewed" journal is necessarily subjected to the peer review process. Many journals have "special sections" or "features" that have a different manner of review or oversight. An article can be in a "peer reviewed" journal, but undergo a different process than peer review.

3. *Who are the authors and what are their affiliations?*
   The reputation of the author(s) can be important, particularly for controversial findings. Experts in a particular field may know many of the contributors to their body of literature. For the person just entering a field of study, time is needed to familiarize him or herself with subjects and the important names. To help feel confident about the literature you are reviewing, you may have to do some homework on the reporting media and the authors, particularly if the literature concerns important discoveries or contributions. You may recognize the work of some authors and the reputation they bring to the literature. On the other hand, a note of

caution is needed before accepting every finding regardless of the source or author.

The author's affiliation (who they work for or where) can have some influence in the consideration of a reported study. Certain institutions and universities tend to be centers of excellence in particular areas of science and learning. These institutions tend to attract a body of scientists and writers expanding work in a specific area. Being aware of this aspect of the research helps the reader understand the authors' perspective and what may have influenced their work environment. It also helps the reader to understand why the investigators are studying these particular problems in the first place.

4. *What problem(s) were investigated?*
The answer to this question should be self-evident from the text. The research problem is the issue or topic of focus. For example, perhaps a healthcare professional knows little about the career patterns of female EMT-Paramedics. The problem presented is the difficulty in predicting how long various types of EMT-Ps will remain in the workforce. Healthcare economists and labor experts need to address these questions for the purpose of education or implementation of health policies. The research question is always a narrower aspect of the research problem. The hypothesis is a method of addressing a research question. Research questions and hypotheses should be clearly stated and linked to the problems being investigated. Also, any assumptions made by the investigators should be assessed. Assumptions can confound and influence the study and report.

5. *What (or who) is the main subject of the study?*
The answer to this question may be the same, or similar to, the problem investigated. Depending on the type of investigation, the main subject could be different from the problem. For example, in a study

of student test-taking performance, the subjects of the study are the students. However, the problem investigated could be how the students study for tests, how they act during tests, and/or what they remember after the test. In health care, the subject of a research study could be cholesterol, but the problem investigated could be cholesterol's response to some intervention.

6. *What is the purpose or rationale for the study?*
This question is the "why" of the study. Why was it done? What purpose did it serve? Was it an important problem? In research, many questions can be asked. However, for research literature to be valid, the questions should serve a useful purpose with sound rationale for its undertaking.

7. *Who or what constituted the sample or population?*
Sample size is often critical for population research. Who or what was studied and how many were in the sample or sub-samples studied should be clear. It is important to understand this aspect of the study, especially in terms of applying the results in a healthcare setting or with patients. The number of subjects studied can affect outcomes: too small a number may not be representative or may miss a pertinent factor; too large a number may minimize some important or key findings. To extrapolate data and apply it outside a study, the characteristics of the sample must be evident and comparable to the population from which the sample is selected. However, what may be true for one group of individuals may not be true for another, so results should always be considered cautiously.

8. *What was the design of the study?*
Often the design of the study is critical to the outcome. The methods should be described in enough detail to allow the reader to make conclusions about the results and applications. Each type of study design are susceptible to its limitations, threats to validity,

threats to statistical analysis, and threats to conclusions. Even the fundamentally sound "randomized assignment, double-blind" studies have limitations. Clinicians should become familiar with the limitations of the various types of studies and look for biases in study design, because these flaws may affect conclusions and interpretation of the results.

9. *What statistical analyses are used?*
    Were the appropriate data analyses performed for the data type and study design? A statistics book is a very useful resource, it may also be a good idea to consult a statistician. Statistics can be confusing, and even experienced researchers make mistakes. Observe closely how the data were analyzed. Do the data and statistical analyses make sense? Sometimes reviewing the statistics may be helpful in understanding the results and conclusions.

10. *What are the results?*
    The results should be reported as unambiguously as possible. Two researchers undertaking the same study should report their findings in similar ways without any subjective interpretation. Determine whether the results of the study seem consistent with the study design and the analyses used. Do the data make sense and are the results consistent with current knowledge? Analysis results that indicate extremes should be examined closely.

11. *Are the results clear?*
    Do the results have meaning to the intent of the study? Are they understandable? Are they consistent with the methods and analyses proposed? When results are not clear, then either the study was conducted in a confusing manner, or the statistical methods used may simply be unfamiliar to the reader.

12. *Did the results answer the identified questions?*
    The results may not be expected, but that does not necessarily mean they are wrong.

If the methodological process was conducted correctly, then the results should stand alone, and the majority of readers should draw similar conclusions. Results should answer the questions posed earlier in the study. While the answers often lead to more questions, the primary research questions should be addressed in the results section.

13. *Do the results seem valid?*
    Validity is at the heart of most studies. Validity is defined as making common sense and being persuasive to the reader. The major categories of validity are internal and external validity. If a research study has been performed correctly without errors, then the study is considered to be internally valid. If the study represents the realities found in the general population, then it is considered externally valid. The various threats to validity are covered in Chapter 18.

    Face validity simply means that the results of a study can be taken at "face value." Because of vagueness and subjectivity, psychometricians abandoned this concept a long time ago. However, when reading an article, one may get a sense that something does not seem right, especially if the reader is very knowledgeable about the topic. This represents a problem with face validity.

    Construct validity assesses the degree to which the measure relates to other variables as expected within a system or theory. In contrast, content validity is the extent to which the method of measurement includes all of the major elements relevant to the construct being measured.

14. *Are the interpretations (conclusions) of the results consistent with the study design and analysis?*
    Here, the authors of the article make the correct conclusion about the data. However, this area can be open to personal bias and misinterpretation. The reader, therefore,

has to determine whether the conclusions are consistent with the type of information that the study design and analysis should yield compared to the results presented.

15. *Are the results consistent with findings from similar studies?*

Before reading a research article, one should have a sense of the problem either from previous literature reviews or from one's own clinical experience. Studies that deviate greatly from what is already known should be examined and with caution. However, this deviation does not mean the study is wrong. Occasionally, new discoveries emerge from unexpected or unanticipated results.

16. *What do the results mean to medicine and health care, and you and your patients?*

This question may be the most important one the clinician can ask. What do these results mean to your practice and to the people for whom you provide care? For medicine and health care, it is important to examine the validity of an intervention to make sure it is applicable to the patient population. The risks and benefits of an intervention study should be clearly understood, as well as what the results mean to the overall patients' well-being.

EVIDENCE-BASED MEDICINE: A NEW WAY OF LOOKING AT THE MEDICAL LITERATURE

A general assumption has developed that if something claims to be "evidence-based," it is the guiding light for practice. However, the key to evidenced-based medicine is the applicability to patient care. The evidence-based concept does not replace clinical experience and/or expertise. Evidence-based research should bridge the gap between rigorous research and clinical investigations for the clinician, and ultimately for the patients' benefit. Evidence-based outcomes can come from research studies (the more rigorous, the better) or from the synthesis of existing data and outcomes (e.g., meta-analysis). Regardless, the "evidence" must still be interpreted or evaluated as it relates to the needs of patients.

Friedland et al.[4] has developed a straightforward approach to evaluating evidenced-based medicine. This five-step approach is presented in **Table 19–2**.

While this is a concise approach, it does not eliminate the need to ask and answer the previous questions presented by the authors. The table outlines a process that is a part of a larger evaluation and interpretation scheme of medical literature.

When evaluating evidenced-based literature, two statistical calculations can be very useful when

Table 19–2 A 5-Step Study Guide for EMB

Step 1	Do I want to evaluate the study?	Is it interesting, novel, relevant?
Step 2	What are the research question, study design, study findings?	What are the populations studied, variables, study design, results, outcomes, findings, and/or conclusions?
Step 3	Are the findings believable?	Do the subjects and variable represent the research question? Are the findings attributable to chance, biases, or confounding variables? Are the findings believable in the context of existing knowledge?
Step 4	What are the important findings?	Are the findings clinically relevant?
Step 5	Will the study help my patients?	Are the subjects similar to my patients? Are the interventions applicable to my patients? Will the findings/outcomes result in an overall benefit for my patients?

Adapted from Friedland.[4]

interpreting the results from a randomized, controlled trial of a new therapy. These two calculations are the number needed to treat (NNT) and the 95 percent confidence interval (CI). Each of these calculations is used for different types of data. Remember, it is important to be aware of the type of data reported by the literature being reviewed.

The NNT calculation is used when the article being reviewed has categorical results (e.g., improved vs. unimproved) and two groups (e.g., treatment and control). The NNT is intuitive and helps clinicians communicate the expected outcome of a selected therapy. The 95 percent CI calculation is used to compare the means (i.e., the central tendency) and standard deviations (i.e., variability) of a continuous measure (e.g., blood pressure) between two sample groups (e.g., treatment and control). The 95 percent CI determines the potential range of possible values present in the overall population based upon the sampling scheme used in the study. Sometimes the CIs that are calculated overlap. This overlap is an indication that the treatment studied may be no different than the placebo or control treatment when it is used in a population larger than the study's sample.

To calculate the NNT, some basic rates are first calculated and applied as shown in the formulas in **Table 19–3**. Here are the steps:

1. Calculate the experimental event rate (EER).
2. Calculate the control event rate (CER).
3. Calculate the absolute risk reduction (ARR).
4. Express the ARR as a proportion and divide into 1.

The NNT to produce the intended clinical outcome can then be assessed. Be aware that the formula changes depending upon the type of outcome that is being measured (i.e., a reduction in bad events or an increase in good events).

Many papers include the 95 percent CI of the mean in the publication. When it is not given, it is important to perform a quick calculation. To calculate the 95 percent CI for a mean when using a continuous measure, the mean, standard deviation, and the number of subjects must be known for each group. If any of this information is missing or

Table 19–3 Calculating Event Rates, Absolute Risk Reduction, and Number-Needed-to-Treat

	Control	Experimental
Event	a	b
No event	c	d
Totals	a+c	b+d
Event rate	Control event rate CER = a/(a+c)	Experimental event rate EER = b/(b+d)

Measure	The Experiment Reduces Bad Event	The Experiment Increases Good Event
Relative risk reduction	(CER-EER)/CER	(EER-CER)/CER
Absolute risk reduction	CER-EER	EER-CER
Number needed to treat	1/ARR	1/ARR

if the outcome measure does not contain continuous data, then the calculation cannot be performed (**Figures 19–1 and 19–2**).

Here are the steps:

1. Calculate the standard error (i.e., the standard deviation divided by the square root of the number of subjects in the sample).
2. Determine the constant from a table if the number of subjects is < 60, otherwise use the constant 1.96.
3. Multiply the constant (usually 1.96) times the standard error from step 1.
4. Add the result from step 3 to the mean of the sample to get the upper confidence limit.
5. Subtract the result from step 3 from the mean to get the lower confidence limit.
6. Perform these steps for both the control and experimental group to see if the limits from each group overlap.

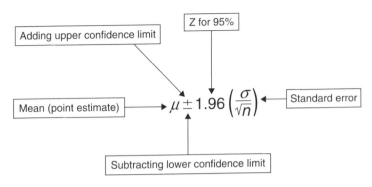

Figure 19-1 Formula of 95 percent CI of sample mean for n > 60.

If the confidence limits overlap, then no difference in the treatments are likely to occur when they are administered to a larger target population.

The last consideration in the interpretation of evidence-based literature is the level of evidence (**Table 19–4**). When studies are analyzed for best evidence, a rating system is used. This evidence rating can be a guide for clinicians regarding the strength of the evidence and its source.

In addition to the evidence-level rating, qualifiers are also used to describe the source of the evidence (**Table 19–5**).

Another presentation format for evidence-based medicine is the POEM™ or Patient Oriented Evidence that Matters. The POEM is a commercially available format in which the evidenced-based medical literature is reviewed and summarized.[5] The intent of the POEM format is to present evidence-based results in a concise and easily readable way that is applicable in clinical practice. A number of journals have a POEM section or a POEM feature. These types of summaries are very helpful, but for those interventions or outcomes that affect patients, the original work should always be reviewed.

A GENERAL APPROACH TO READING THE LITERATURE

Asking all the right questions, going through all these steps, and reading as much as possible are still very time consuming. Many resources are available that can be easily accessed. Still, the amount of information available is overwhelming. With more than two million biomedical publications per year,[1] developing an approach to reviewing the current medical literature is an important professional skill. However, no single approach works in

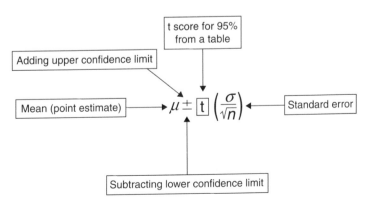

Figure 19-2 Formula for 95 % CI of Small Sample

Table 19–4 Levels of Evidence[6]

Level	Description
A	High-quality evidence that considers all important outcomes: randomized controlled trials (RCT), well-done systematic reviews of randomized controlled trials, meta-analysis systematic reviews using comprehensive search strategies
B	Well-designed, nonrandomized clinical trials: systematic reviews of studies other than RCTs with appropriate search strategies and well-substantiated conclusions, lower-quality RCTs, cohort studies, case-control studies with nonbiased subject selection and consistent findings, quality retrospective studies, certain uncontrolled studies, well-designed epidemiologic studies with compelling findings
C	Consensus or expert opinion

every situation. A general approach follows, but it may be modified in many ways.

1. Identify the journals that are pertinent to the specialty of interest.
2. Develop a strategy for reviewing those journals.
3. Set aside a specific time each week when journals can be reviewed. (Allow ample

Table 19–5 Level of Evidence Modifiers[6]

Modifier	Description
1	Nonrandomized clinical trial
2	Systematic review of nonrandomized clinical trial
3	Lower quality of randomized clinical trial
4	Clinical cohort study
5	Case control study
6	Retrospective study
7	Uncontrolled study
8	Epidemiologic study

uninterrupted time for the reading and review.)
4. Identify those articles of interest by their title or by reading their abstracts.
5. Make a quick review of the tables and figures.
6. Make a decision to read the article.
7. Apply the techniques for interpreting the article.
8. Apply the results to your practice.

SUMMARY

Interpreting the literature involves synthesizing information obtained from different medical, healthcare, and scientific studies and integrating pertinent outcomes into the healthcare practice and patient care. Healthcare professionals must develop a sound process for reviewing and evaluating medical literature. Skilled interpretation of the medical literature incorporates up-to-date information that benefits a practice and its patients. Professionals who fail to stay abreast of the medical literature are less competent practitioners. As evidence-based analyses increase, so does the pressure for practice trends to follow that evidence. However, evidence must be balanced with clinical experience and expertise to support the highest likelihood of improved patient outcomes.

REFERENCES

1. Arndt KA. Information excess in medicine: Overview, relevance to dermatology, and strategies for coping. *Arch Dermatol.* 1992;128(9):1249–1256.
2. National Institutes of Health. Key Medline Indicators. Website. http://www.nlm.nih.gov/bsd/bsd_key.html. Accessed Oct. 13, 2011.
3. Sackett DL, Richardson WS, Rosenberg, Haynes RB. *Evidence-Based Medicine: How to Practice and Teach EBM.* New York: Churchill Livingstone; 1997.
4. Friedland DB, Go AS, Davoren JB, Sblipak MG, Bent SW, Subak LL, Mendelson T. *Evidence-Based Medicine: A Framework for Clinical Practice.* New York: Lange Medical Books/McGraw-Hill; 1998:145–246.
5. InfoPOEMs Web site. http://www.infopoems.com. Accessed June 20, 2011.
6. Siwek J, Gourley ML, Slawson DC, Shaughnessy AF. How to write an evidence-based clinical review article. *Am Fam Physician.* 2002 Jan 15;65(2):251–258.

APPENDICES

Glossary

a posteriori—By observation of facts or results (literally "after").

a priori—By reasoning from self-evident facts (literally "before").

absolute value—The value of a number regardless of its sign.

abstract—The summary of a study in clear and concise terms. Usually limited to 100 to 250 words.

abstract thinking—Thinking oriented toward the development of an idea without application to, or association with, a particular instance, independent of time and space. Abstract thinkers tend to look for meaning, patterns, relationships, and philosophical implications.

accessible population—Portion of the target population or group to which the researcher has reasonable access.

accidental sampling—A method of sampling in which subjects are included in the study because they happen to be in the right place at the right time. One method of obtaining subjects for a study is to enter all available subjects coming into a room until the desired sample size is reached (also known as *convenience* sampling).

accuracy—The extent to which a scale correctly represents the amount or classification of a variable.

across-method triangulation—Combining research methods or strategies from two or more research traditions in the same study.

alpha (α)—Level of significance or cutoff point used to determine whether the samples being tested are members of the same population or of different populations. Alpha is commonly set at .05, .01, or .001.

analysis of covariance (ANCOVA)—A method of removing pretreatment variations (as measured by the control variable) from the post-treatment means (criterion variable) before testing the significance of the post-treatment differences among the groups. Analysis of covariance provides a basis for ruling out pretreatment differences when the interest is in testing post-treatment differences.

analysis of variance (ANOVA)—A statistical method that tests the difference between two or more means when studying groups. Independent variables are nominal (categorical) and dependent variables are interval values.

Asks whether the squared variation of the case scores around their treatment means (*within*) is greater than the squared variation of the means themselves around the grand mean (*between*). These two totals are expressed as a ratio. Comparison of variances reflects different sources of variability, that is, *within* vs. *between*.

analysis of variance, one-way (See **ANOVA**)—Only one independent variable is manipulated.

anonymity—Condition in which subjects' identities cannot be linked to their individual responses.

applied research—Research designed to answer practical questions.

area probability sample—A form of multistage *cluster sample* in which geographical areas, such as census blocks or tracts, serve as the first-stage sampling unit. Units selected in the first stage of sampling (e.g., all the households on a selected block) are listed and such lists are then subsampled.

associated key words—A set of words used as identifiers of the topic area.

associative relationship—A connection between variables or concepts that exist together in the real world so that when one variable changes the other variable also changes.

assumptions—Statements taken for granted or considered true, even though they have not been scientifically tested.

attributes—Characteristics of persons or things (e.g., age, eye color).

attrition—The loss of participants during the course of a study. Attrition can introduce bias by changing the composition of the sample initially drawn, particularly if more subjects are lost from one group than another.

average—An ambiguous term generally suggesting typical or normal. The *mean, median,* and *mode* are specific examples of mathematical *averages.*

baseline measure—The measurement of the dependent variable before the introduction of an experimental intervention.

basic research—Discovery research that seeks to add knowledge or support or refute theories.

beneficence—The principle that one should do good and, above all, do no harm.

benefit–risk ratio—The proportion of potential benefits compared to potential risks of an intervention, weighed to determine whether it is ethical.

beta (β) coefficient—Standardized regression coefficient that allows comparison of relative importance of variables in regression analysis.

bias—That quality of a measurement device that tends to result in a misrepresentation of what is being measured in a particular direction. For example, the questionnaire item "Don't you agree that your physician is doing a good job?" would be biased, as it would encourage favorable responses.

bibliography—A list of source materials or references that are used or consulted in the preparation of a work. The references of the bibliography are usually cited in the text.

binary or binomial variable—See *dichotomous variable.*

binomial variable—A variable with only two attributes (e.g., sex, with the attributes *male* and *female*).

bivariate analysis—The analysis of two variables simultaneously to determine the empirical relationship between them. The construction of a simple percentage table or the computation of a simple correlation coefficient would be examples.

bivariate correlation—Analysis technique that measures the extent of the linear relationship between two variables.

box-and-whisker plot—Exploratory data analysis technique to visualize some of the major characteristics of complex data. Sometimes used to display spread, symmetry, and outliers at the same time in a graph.

bracketing—Qualitative research technique of suspending or laying aside what is known about an experience being studied.

canonical correlation—Extension of multiple regression with more than one dependent variable.

case study design—Intensive exploration of a single unit of study, such as a person, family, group, community, or institution.

causal relationship—Relationship between two variables where one variable (independent variable) is thought to cause or determine the presence of the other variable (dependent variable). Three criteria must be satisfied: (1) the cause precedes the effect in time, (2) the two variables are empirically correlated with one another, and (3) the observed correlation between the two variables cannot be explained away as being due to the influence of some third variable that causes both of them.

cell—The box created by the intersection of column and row in a table or matrix. The cell is where the number or information is inserted.

census—An enumeration of the characteristics of some population. A *census* collects data from all members of the population, in contrast to a *survey,* which is limited to a sample.

central limit theorem—A theorem stating that even when statistics, such as means, come from a population with a skewed (asymmetrical) distribution, the sampling distribution developed from multiple means obtained from that skewed population tends to fit the pattern of the normal curve.

central tendency—A statistical index of a typical set of scores that comes from the center of the distribution of scores. The three most common indices of central tendency are the mean, median, and mode.

chi-squared (χ^2)—A test to assess whether observed frequencies of *nominal* data differ from expected frequencies. A nonsignificant value indicates the classes are independent. A significant value indicates an association. Range is zero to infinity.

chronology—A type of unstructured and sequential observation that provides a detailed description of a person's or population's behavior.

citation—The reference to an authority or author of a document.

cluster sample—A multistage sample in which natural groups (*clusters*) are sampled initially, with the members of each selected group subsampled afterward. For example, a sample of clinics is selected, and a sample of patients is drawn from each.

code book—A document used in data processing and analysis that tells the location of different data items in a data file and the meanings of the codes used to represent different attributes of variables. Often a notebook, this document lists all methods used so another researcher could duplicate the work.

coding—The process of transforming qualitative data into numerical symbols. Often done for computer input prior to analysis.

coercion—To compel someone by threat of harm or excessive reward to do something they would not ordinarily undertake (e.g., obtaining participants for dangerous research projects by offering large sums of money).

Cohen's kappa—See kappa coefficient.

cohort study—A study in which some specific group is studied over time, although data may be collected from different members in each set of observations (e.g., a study of the clinical practice of physician assistants who graduated in 1976, to whom questionnaires were sent every five years).

comparative descriptive design—Used to describe differences in variables in two or more groups in a natural setting.

comparison group—Commonly known as the "control group"; a group not receiving a treatment, reward, or intervention.

compatibility—The degree to which the innovation is perceived to be consistent with current values, past experience, and priority of needs.

complete observer—The passive researcher with no direct social interaction in the setting.

complete participation—When the researcher becomes a member of the group and conceals the researcher role.

concept—A term that abstractly describes and names an object or phenomenon, thus providing it with a separate identity or meaning.

conceptual definition—A definition that provides a variable or concept with a theoretical meaning and is established through concept analysis.

conceptual framework—A set of highly abstract, related constructs that broadly explains phenomena of interest, expresses assumptions, and reflects a philosophical stance.

conclusions—Opinion or interpretation of the results or meaning of a study.

confidence interval—The range of values within which a population parameter is estimated to lie.

confidence level—The estimated probability that a population parameter lies within a given *confidence interval.*

confidentiality—Management of data in research so subjects' identities are not linked with their responses. This differs from *anonymity,* in which the subjects' identities are not known.

confounding variable—An uncontrolled variable that may compete with a manipulated variable for interpretive priority. Makes a clear interpretation of the results of a study difficult or impossible.

consent form—A form used to document a subject's agreement to participate in a study.

construct (pronounced with emphasis on first syllable)—An image, idea, or theory that has some general meaning not directly observable

construct validity—The degree to which a measure relates to other variables as expected within a system of theoretical relationships. In other words, *construct validity* is based on the logical relationship among variables (e.g., patients who report they are satisfied with their physician assistant are more likely to comply with treatment).

content analysis—Qualitative analysis technique to classify words in a text into a few categories chosen because of their theoretical importance.

content validity—The extent to which the method of measurement includes all the major elements relevant to the construct being measured.

contingency tables—Cross-tabulation tables that allow visual comparison of summary data output related to two variables within a sample.

control—Rules imposed by the researcher to decrease the possibility of error and increase the probability that the study's findings are an accurate reflection of reality.

control group—A group of subjects to whom *no* experimental stimulus, treatment, or intervention is administered and who should resemble the experimental group in all other respects (also known as *comparison group*).

convenience sampling—Simply entering available subjects into the study until the desired sample size is reached (also known as *accidental* sampling).

copy editor—The person who makes corrections on a manuscript to achieve consistency in style, word usage, and spelling, following the appropriate publication guidelines.

correlation—Consistent relationship between two variables such that one variable can be predicted from knowledge of the other. With a *positive correlation,* both variables increase together, that is, a positive value increase. Positive does not mean good, beneficial, advantageous, or better. With a *negative correlation,* one increases when the other decreases or one variable is high and the other is low. Negative does not mean bad, adverse, worse, or least.

correlation analysis—Statistical procedure conducted to determine the direction (positive or negative) and magnitude (strength) of the relationship between two variables.

correlation coefficient (r)—A statistic that shows the degree of relationship between two or more variables.

correlation matrix—A table that presents variable correlation coefficients. Basically a visual representation of the relationships of two or more variables.

correlational research—Systematic investigation of relationships between two or more variables to explain the nature of relationships in the world and not to examine cause and effect.

cost–benefit analysis—Economic technique that examines costs and benefits of alternative ways of using resources to determine which way produces the greatest net benefit, assessed in monetary terms.

cost-effectiveness analysis—Type of outcomes research that compares costs and benefits of different ways of accomplishing a clinical goal (e.g., diagnosing a condition, treating an illness, or providing a service). The goal is to identify the strategy that achieves the desired result for the least cost.

covariance—the measure of effect by two or more variables.

covariate analysis—See *analysis of covariance.*

covert data collection—Collection of research data without the subjects being aware that data are being collected.

critical analysis of studies—Minute examination of the merits, faults, meaning, and significance of studies.

cross tabulation—A determination of the number of cases occurring when simultaneous consideration is given to the values of two or more variables, such as sex (male/female) cross tabulated with smoking status (smoker/nonsmoker). The results are presented in a table format according to the values of the variables.

crossover design—Experimental design in which more than one type of treatment is administered to each subject; the treatments are provided sequentially, rather than concurrently, and comparisons are made of the effects of the different treatments on the same subject.

cross-sectional study—A study that is based on observations representing a single point in time. Contrasted with a *longitudinal study,* which is based on two or more observations over time.

data—The reports of observations of variables.

data coding sheet—A form for organizing and recording data for rapid entry into a computer.

data collection—Precise, systematic gathering of information relevant to the research purpose or the specific objectives, questions, or hypotheses of a study.

data entry—The process of entering data (usually in coded form) onto an input medium for computer analysis.

data triangulation—Collection of data from multiple sources in the same study.

deception—Misinforming subjects for research purposes.

decision theory—Theory that is inductive in nature and is based on assumptions associated with the theoretical normal curve. The theory is applied when testing for differences between groups with the expectation that all of the groups are members of the same population.

deduction—The logical model in which specific expectations of hypotheses are developed on the basis of general principles.

deductive research—Moving from prior hypotheses to observation or empirical research; other than discovery research.

degrees of freedom (df)—Equal to the sum of the two sample sizes, minus the value 2, ($n_1 + n_2 - 2$). The different rows in the t table, each showing a different value of df, accommodate the changes in the sampling distribution of t as the sizes of samples may vary.

Delphi technique—A method of measuring the judgments of a group of experts for assessing priorities or making forecasts.

demographic variables—Characteristics or attributes of the subjects that are collected to describe the sample.

dependent variable—A phenomenon that is affected by the researcher's manipulation of an *independent variable.*

description—The precise measurement and reporting of the characteristics of a population or phenomenon under study.

descriptive correlational design—Used to describe variables and examine relationships that exist in a situation.

descriptive method—A research plan undertaken to define the characteristics, relationships, or both, of variables, based on systematic observation of these variables.

descriptive statistics—Calculated values that represent certain overall characteristics of a body of data.

design—Blueprint for conducting a study that maximizes control over factors that could interfere with the validity of the findings.

diary—Written record of a subject's observations and feelings, collected by the researcher for analysis.

dichotomous variable—A variable that places subjects into two groups (e.g., male/female).

directional hypothesis—A hypothesis that states the specific nature of the interaction or relationship between two or more variables.

discriminant analysis—A form of regression analysis used to place a variable in a linear combination with other measurements.

dispersion—The distribution of values around some central value, such as an *average*. The *range* is a simple example of a measure of dispersion.

disproportionate stratified sampling—A sampling strategy wherein the researcher samples different proportions of subjects from different strata in the population to endure adequate representation of subjects from strata that are comparatively smaller.

distribution—A collection of measurements usually viewed in terms of the frequency with which observations are assigned to each category or point on a measurement scale.

double-blind experiment—An experiment in which neither the subjects nor those who administer the treatment know who is in the experimental group or control group.

ecological fallacy—Erroneously drawing conclusions about individuals based solely on the observation of groups.

editor—The person in charge of a research publication, who decides which articles are to be published, manages the overall production of the publication, and heads the editorial staff.

effect size—A statistical expression of the magnitude of the difference between two variables, or the magnitude of the difference between two groups, with regard to some attribute of interest.

eigenvalue—The variance explained by each factor, a product of factor analysis. Each factor has a possible total of 1.0, so eigenvalues cannot exceed the number of factors. The eigenvalue shows the relative importance of each factor by the amount of covariance of variables associated with the underlying (unobserved) common factor (which tends to be the most important factor).

empirical generalizations—Statements made on observations or practical experience based on past research.

empiricism—The philosophical doctrine that all knowledge is derived from sense experience.

epistemology—The science of knowing; a branch of philosophy that investigates the origin, nature, methods, and limits of human knowledge.

equivalence—Type of reliability testing that involves comparing two versions of the same instrument or two observers measuring the same event.

ethical inquiry—Intellectual analysis of ethical problems related to obligation, rights, duty, right and wrong, conscience, choice, intention, and responsibility to obtain desirable, rational ends.

ethical principles—Principles of respect for persons, beneficence, and justice relevant to the conduct of research.

ethics—The values or guidelines that should govern decisions in research or medicine. The social obligation the researcher has to his or her subjects.

ethnographic research—A qualitative research methodology for investigating cultures. This method involves collecting, describing, and analyzing the data to develop a theory of cultural behavior.

evaluation research—Has as its objective the description and evaluation of some existing social policy or program (oriented towards program research). Differs from *applied* and *basic* research.

exclusion criteria—Sampling requirements identified by the researcher that eliminate or exclude an element or subject from being in a sample

experimental group—The subjects who are exposed to an experimental treatment or intervention.

experimental method—A research plan undertaken to test relationships among variables based on systematic observation of variables that are manipulated by the researcher.

experimenter effects—A source of bias in experimental research in which subjects react to personal attributes of the experimenter or pick up cues about what the experimenter is seeking and modify their behavior accordingly.

exploratory factor analysis—A method of analysis used to develop scales and subscales.

external validity—The degree to which the results of a study generalize to the population. The process of testing the validity of a measure, such as an index or scale, is conducted by examining its relationship to other, presumed indicators of the same variable.

extraneous variable—A variable, other than the independent variable, that may exert effect on the subject or variable being studied.

F—Designation letter for the value derived from an "F test."

F table—A table of values which represent the percentage points of the "F" distribution.

F ratio—A statistical value used in analysis of variance and other statistical methods.

F test—A test for comparing two or more means: the ratio of variance between groups divided by the variance within groups (error). As the number of observations in each sample (n) increases, the critical value of F increases; smaller differences between the variances of the samples will become significant because variations tend to level out as the proportion of the population sampled increases.

factor—The independent variable in single variable studies. Most commonly used to describe groups of related independent variables within a larger group of variables.

factor analysis—A complex computerized method for determining the general dimensions or *factors* that exist within a set of concrete observations.

fatigue effect—When a subject becomes tired or bored with a study.

feasibility study—A study of whether a research project can or should be performed, as determined by examining the time and money commitment; the researcher's expertise; the availability of subjects, facilities, and equipment; the cooperation of others; and ethical considerations.

field research—A form of research that consists of observations made in nature (the field) and often not easily reduced to numbers.

findings—The translated and interpreted results of a study.

focus group interview—An interview in which the respondents are a group of individuals with some trait in common who are assembled to answer questions on a given topic.

forced choice—Response set using a scale that has an even number of choices, such as four or six, so that respondents cannot choose an uncertain or neutral response.

frequency distribution—A description of the number of times the various attributes of a variable are observed in a sample.

frequency polygon—Graphic display of a frequency distribution, in which dots connected to indicate the number of times a score value occurs in a set of data.

generalizability—The quality of a research finding that justifies the inference that it represents something more than the specific observations on which it was based. Sometimes this involves the *generalization* of findings from a sample to a population.

Gestalt—A psychological theory that the objects of mind are really clusters of linked ideas that cannot be split up into parts. A system of phenomena having properties that cannot be derived solely from the components of that system.

Guttman scale—A type of composite measure used to summarize several discrete observations and to represent some more general variable.

Hawthorne effect—A term coined in reference to a series of productivity studies at the Hawthorne plant of the Western Electric Company (Chicago). The researchers discovered that their presence affected the behavior of the workers being studied. The term now refers to any impact of research on the subject of study.

heterogeneous—Having a wide variety of characteristics; the use of heterogeneous subjects reduces the risk of bias in studies not using random sampling.

history effect—The effect of an event unrelated to the planned study that occurs during the time of the study and could influence the responses of subjects.

homoscedasticity—Descriptive term for the combination of two assumptions: homogeneity of variance and normally distributed dependent variables.

hypothesis—A provisional theory set forth to explain some class of phenomena, either accepted as a guide to future investigation (working hypothesis) or assumed for the sake of argument and testing. A statement to be tested in a study. An expectation about the nature of things derived from a theory.

hypothesis testing—The determination of whether the expectations that a hypothesis represents are, indeed, found to exist in the real world.

inclusion criteria—Sampling requirements identified by the researcher that must be present for the element or subject to be included in the sample.

independent variable—A phenomenon that is manipulated by the researcher and is predicted to have an effect on another phenomenon. A variable whose values are *not* problematical in an analysis but are taken as simply given. An *independent variable* is presumed to cause or determine a *dependent variable.*

index—phenomena used to indicate other phenomena; a values that expresses a relationship between variables or analyses of variables.

indicator—A thing or person that indicates and therefore can serve as a proxy for a concept.

indirect measurement—Measurement of indicators or attributes of an abstract concept rather than of the abstraction itself.

induction—The logical model in which general principles are developed from specific observations.

inductive research—Any form of reasoning in which the conclusion, though supported by the premises, does not follow them necessarily. Research as discovery is used to develop or generate hypotheses. Inductive research is used to move from observation to development of hypotheses.

inferential statistics—Statistical methods that make it possible to draw tentative conclusions about a population based on observations of a sample selected from that population and furthermore make a probability statement about those conclusions to aid in their evaluation; inferential methods include sampling theory, hypothesis testing, and parameter estimation.

informed consent—The process used to inform subjects of the risks, benefits, and goals of research studies.

institutional review—A process of examining study proposals for ethical concerns by a committee representing an institution.

intercept—On a graph, the points where the X and Y axis each equal zero.

internal validity—The extent to which the individual items comprising a composite measure are correlated with the measure itself.

inter-rater reliability—The degree of consistency between two raters who are independently assigning ratings to a variable or attribute being investigated.

interrupted time series design—A study design involving the collection of data at different points in time, as contrasted with a *cross-sectional study.* Also known as *longitudinal study.*

interval scale—Interval measure; the assignment of numbers to identify ordered relations of some characteristic. The interval scale is arbitrarily assigned and at equal intervals but has no zero point.

interview—Structured or unstructured verbal communication between a researcher and a subject, during which information is obtained for a study.

judgmental sample—*Purposive sample;* a type of *nonprobability sample* in which the researcher selects the units to be observed on the basis of his or her own judgment about which ones will be the most useful or representative.

kappa coefficient—A statistical measure of inter-rater agreement. Also referred to as Cohen's kappa. Symbolized by κ.

key terms—See *Associated Key Terms.*

kurtosis—A quality of the distribution of a set of data dealing with whether or how much the data "pile up" around some central point; the quality of "peakedness" or "flatness" of the graphic representation of a statistical distribution.

level of significance—In the context of *tests of statistical significance,* the degree of likelihood that an observed, empirical relationship could be attributable to sampling error. For example, a relationship is *significant* at the .05 level if the likelihood of its being only a function of sampling error is no greater than 5 out of 100.

Likert (pronounced **Lick ert) scale**—A type of composite measurement in survey questionnaires. *Likert* items use response categories such as strongly agree, agree, disagree, and strongly disagree.

limits of confidence—A term used in constructing confidence-interval estimates of parameter values to specify our confidence that the interval includes the parameter value; using procedures for constructing a 95 percent confidence interval, for instance, we would enclose the true parameter value within its limits on 95 percent of such attempts; the higher the level of confidence, the wider the interval.

linear regression—A method of predicting the relationship of the dependent variable to the independent variable.

linear relationship—A relationship between two variables such that a straight line can be fitted satisfactorily to the points of a plot. The result is a linear relationship between the variable.

literature review—A review of prior relevant literature that serves as the basis or beginning point for a research endeavor.

longitudinal study—A study design involving the collection of data at different points in time

Mann-Whitney U test—A nonparametric hypothesis-testing procedure used to decide whether two given independent samples could have arisen by chance from identically distributed populations; a test for comparing two populations based on independent random samples from each.

MANOVA—Multivariate analysis of variance; a general term for analysis using two or more independent variables.

matrix—A two-dimensional organization; each dimension is composed of several positions or alternatives; any particular "score" is a combination of the two dimensions.

mean (M)—The sum of the scores in a distribution of a population or collection of things divided by the number of scores. In common usage, the average.

measurement—A scheme for the assignment of numbers or symbols to specify different characteristics of a variable. Characteristics include validity, accuracy, precision, and reliability.

measurement error—A deviation from accurate or correct measurement. *Random error* is as likely to occur in one direction as the other around the mean. *Bias* is systematic error that tends to occur regularly in one direction, owing to faulty procedure or measurement technique.

measures of central tendency—Statistical procedures (mean, median, mode) for determining the center of a distribution of scores or a typical value.

median—The midpoint or midscore in a distribution. The middle number in a sequence of numbers.

meta-analysis—The statistical integration of the results of a number of independent studies.

methodological triangulation—The use of two or more research methods or procedures in a study.

mode—The most frequent score in a distribution.

mortality—Subjects who are lost to a study or drop out from the study or a group. It does not necessarily mean the death of the subject.

multiple-factor analysis of variance (or multivariate analysis)—A statistical model for testing the consequences of manipulating two or more independent variables in a single research design. Each independent variable (factor) will have two or more levels. The *F* ratio is the statistic used to conduct the appropriate hypothesis tests in multiple-factor designs. Specific techniques include factor analysis, multiple correlations, multiple regression, path analysis, and others.

multiple linear regression—Multiple regressions incorporate more than one independent variable into an equation.

multistage sampling—A process generally used with cluster sampling in which levels (stages) of sampling occur. For example, to study particular traits of patients admitted to local hospitals who are hypertensive, regardless of the admitting diagnosis, all of the local hospitals would be sampled for hypertensive patients, then those patients would be sampled, then study the traits would be sampled.

multivariate analysis—The analysis of the simultaneous relationships among several variables.

Examining simultaneously the effects of age, sex, and social class of patients seen by different providers would be an example of *multivariate analysis*. Specific techniques include factor analysis, multiple correlation, multiple regression, and path analysis, among others.

multivariate analysis of variance (MANOVA)—Extension of the basic analysis of variance design to include more than one dependent variable.

natural setting—Field settings or uncontrolled, real-life situations examined in research.

narrative review—When the reviewer reads and thinks about a collection of relevant studies and then writes some narrative account of whether the hypothesis under consideration seems to be supported by the evidence.

needs assessment—Questions concerned with discovering the nature and extent of a particular social problem to determine the most appropriate type of response.

neopositivism—Empirical scientific method of research that deals with observable facts that must be objectively verifiable via natural scientific method.

nominal scale—Designation of subclasses by assigning numbers or symbols that represent unique characteristics. The weakest level of measurement because it denotes the least information about observations (e.g., eye color: Blue=1; Brown=2).

nondirectional hypothesis—A hypothesis stating that a relationship exists but not predicting the exact nature of the relationship.

nonparametric statistics—Tests that do not directly incorporate estimates pertaining to population characteristics. Examples are chi-squared, log-linear models, and Wilcoxon matched-pairs signed ranks tests.

nonprobability sampling—A sample selected in some fashion other than those suggested by probability theory.

nonsampling error—Imperfections of data quality that result from factors other than sampling error, such as misunderstanding of questions by respondents, erroneous recording by interviewers and coders, or keypunch errors.

nontherapeutic research—Research conducted to generate knowledge for a discipline that does not benefit those in the study; it may benefit future patients.

normal distribution curve—The characteristic values and frequencies of a variable based on empirical observations that are predicted to follow a predicted graphic curve.

null hypothesis—A statement that statistical differences or relationships have occurred for no reason other than the laws of chance operating in an unrestricted manner. The null hypothesis is sometimes stated instead of or in addition to the hypothesis. It is a form of the hypothesis stated in a negative manner.

objectivity—A characteristic of the scientific method; the condition in which to the greatest extent possible the researcher's values and biases do not interfere with the study of the problem.

one-tailed test—A directional hypothesis test that incorporates a rejection region in only one tail of the probability curve used for a given statistic. In setting up a directional hypothesis, the researcher must be very confident beforehand that there is no reason to expect differences in an opposite direction. Used only when there is very good reason to make a directional prediction.

operational definition—The concrete and specific definition of something in terms of the operations by which observations are to be categorized.

ordinal scale—The assignment of numbers or symbols to identify ordered relations of some characteristic, the order having unspecified intervals. Ordinal scales do not represent the magnitude of differences, only order or ranking.

orthogonality—Statistical independence of two or more variables.

orthonormality—A situation in which all variables are normally distributed.

outcomes research—Method developed to examine the end results of patient care; the strategies used are a departure from traditional scientific endeavors and incorporate evaluation research, epidemiology, and economic theory perspectives.

outliers—Extreme scores, which can change the mean and violate homogeneity of variance.

p **value**—The probability value level used to accept or reject a study value as significant or non-significant. For instance, $p < .05$. Thus, if researchers report that a difference was "significant at the $p < .05$ level," they are simply saying that the probability of the outcome was less than 5 percent due to chance.

paradigm—A way of looking at a natural phenomenon that encompasses a set of philosophical assumptions and that guides the approach to inquiry.

paired sample (matched sample)—Two matched samples or groups that are studied before and after the same intervention. Also used to describe a single group that undergoes the same measurement before and after some intervention.

parameter—A characteristic of a population or sample.

parametric test—Statistical test that requires interval data and the assumption of a normally distributed population.

participant-observation research—See *field research*.

path analysis—A form of *multivariate analysis* in which the causal relationships among variables are presented in graphic form.

Pearson's r or Pearson's product-moment correlation coefficient—Parametric test used to determine the relationship between variables.

phenomenon (singular; plural is **phenomena**)—Any object or event, the characteristics of which can be observed.

pilot study—A smaller version of a proposed study conducted to develop or refine the methodology, such as the treatment, instrument, or data collection process.

population—The total number of members (or persons) in a defined group.

population distribution—The frequency with which observations in a population would be assigned or expected.

population mean—The estimate of a population mean (average) based on the mean of the sample and normal distribution.

poster session—Visual presentation of studies at a professional gathering, using pictures, tables, and illustrations on a display board.

power—The probability that a statistical test will detect a significant difference that exists.

power analysis—Analysis used to determine the risk of a type II error, so the study can be modified to decrease the risk if necessary.

practice effect—Improvement of subject performance due to increased familiarity with the experimental protocol.

precision—The exactness of the measure used in an observation or description of an attribute.

prediction—The ability to estimate the probability of a specific outcome in a given situation.

predictive validity—The degree to which an instrument can predict some criterion observed at a future time.

principal investigator—In a research grant, the individual who has primary responsibility for administering the grant and interacting with the funding agency.

probability sample—The general term for a sample selected in accord with *probability* theory, typically involving some random-selection mechanism. Specific types of *probability samples* include *area probability sample, simple random sample,* and *systematic sample.*

proofs—In publishing, the "hard copy" of the typesetter's work. Proofs may resemble the finished pages of the publication or may be "galley proofs": plain, one-column text to be reviewed and corrected (usually by the proofreader and editor) before the pages are laid out.

proposal—Written plan identifying the major elements of a research study, such as the problem, purpose, and framework, and outlining the methods to conduct the study. A formal way to communicate ideas about a proposed study to receive approval to conduct the study and to seek funding.

proposition—An abstract statement that further clarifies the relationship between two concepts.

purposive sample—A type of *nonprobability sample* in which the units to be observed are selected on the basis of one's own *judgment* about which ones will be the most useful or representative. Same as *judgment sample*.

qualitative analysis—The nonnumerical examination and interpretation of observations for the purpose of describing and explaining the phenomena that those observations reflect.

quantitative research—The use of applied mathematics to assist in the research process.

quasi-experimental designs—Research designs that have the characteristics of experimental design but lack randomization.

quota sample—A type of *nonprobability sample* in which units are selected into the sample on the basis of prespecified characteristics, so that the total sample will have the same distribution of characteristics as are assumed to exist in the population being studied.

R^2—Coefficient of determination. Indicates the percent variance of Y accounted for by X_1 and X_2 in combination.

random sample—A collection of phenomena so selected that each phenomenon in the population has an equal chance of being selected.

range—The highest score in a distribution minus the lowest score.

ratio scale—The assignment of numbers to identify ordered relations of some characteristic, the order having been arbitrarily assigned and at equal intervals, but with an absolute zero point. The ratio scale specifies values and differences that are applicable to arithmetic operations and to statements about phenomena. Age is a ratio measure (scale).

references—The specific items or units used as information resources for a study or written report. References can be texts, journal articles, individuals, etc. They are generally noted in the body of a report and listed in the bibliography.

regression analysis—The analysis of the relationship of sets of scores for two variables.

regression coefficient—The amount of increase of one variable with each unit of increase in another.

rejection region (significance level)—A level of probability set by the researcher as grounds for the rejection of the null hypothesis. If a calculated value of probability falls within the rejection region, the researcher will interpret the difference or relationship as *statistically significant*.

relative risk (RR)—A ratio that represents the probability of developing an outcome within a specific period when a risk factor is present, divided by the probability of developing the outcome in the same period if the risk factor is not present.

reliability—The external and internal consistency of a measurement. In the abstract, whether a particular technique, applied repeatedly to the same object, would yield the same result each time.

representativeness—That quality of a sample having the same distribution of characteristics as the population from which it was selected. By implication, descriptions and explanations derived from an analysis of the sample may be assumed to *represent* similar ones in the population. *Representativeness* is enhanced by probability sampling and provides for generalizability and the use of inferential statistics.

research design—The plan, protocol, format, parameters of the research project.

research hypothesis—A statement expressing differences or relationships among phenomena, the acceptance or nonacceptance of which implies the existence of a null hypothesis that is susceptible to a probability estimate.

research methods—The methods used in systematic inquiry into a subject in order to discover or revise facts, theories, etc.

research proposal—Written proposal that provides a preview of why a study will be undertaken and how it will be conducted. It is a useful device for planning and is required in most circumstances when research is being conducted.

response formats—Types of replies allowed by questions (e.g., open-ended versus closed).

response rate—The number of persons participating in a survey divided by the number selected in the sample, in the form of a percentage; the percentage of questionnaires sent out that are returned.

robust—Remaining useful even when its assumptions are violated (said of a statistic).

sample—A collection of phenomena selected to represent some well-defined population.

sample frame—The list of units or criteria composing a population from which a sample is selected. If the sample is to be *representative* of the population, it is essential that the *sampling frame* include all (or nearly all) members of the population.

sample distribution—The frequency with which observations in a sample are assigned to each category or point on a measurement scale.

sampling bias—Inherent bias in a sample. Sources: nonrandom, systematic sampling; incomplete or inaccurate sampling frame; nonresponse. Sampling bias causes systematic error not compensated for by increasing the size of the sample.

sampling distribution—The frequencies with which particular values of a statistic would be expected when sampling randomly from a given population.

sampling error—An estimate of how statistics may be expected to deviate from parameters when sampling randomly from a given population.

sampling frame—The source from which a sample is taken or a list of a population from which a sample can be taken.

sampling ratio—The proportion of elements in the population that are selected to be in a sample.

sampling size—The number of subjects, usually designated as "*n*," in each category, group, etc. used in the research study.

sampling statistics—Calculated values that represent how sample characteristics are likely to vary from population characteristics.

scale—A specific scheme for assigning numbers or symbols to designate characteristics of a variable. *Nominal, ordinal, interval, ratio* are examples of scales. Scales can be single-item or multiple-item measures.

scatterplot—A two-dimensional dot plot that places data in an X and Y grid.

secondary analysis—A form of research in which the data collected and processed by one researcher is analyzed (often for a different purpose) by another. This is especially appropriate in the case of survey data.

semantic differential scale—A specialized type of Likert scale that measures the meaning of an object to an individual. For example:

Outrage	Repugnance	Neutral
1	2	3
Pleasure	Fascination	
4	5	

significance—The level of calculated probability that is sufficiently low to serve as grounds for rejection of the null hypothesis.

single-factor analysis of variance—A statistical model used for testing the significance of difference among two or more means when these means reflect the consequences of different levels of a single independent variable. See *ANOVA*.

skewed—Term used to describe unusual or odd distributions.

snowball sample—A *nonprobability sampling* method often employed in epidemiology research. Each person interviewed may be asked to suggest additional people for interviewing. Used to track down the source of a communicable disease.

specification—Explanatory and clarifying comments about the handling of difficult or confusing situations that may occur with regard to specific questions in a questionnaire.

spurious relationship—A relationship that gives a false impression because it is without a base in theory or common sense.

standard deviation (SD)—The square root of the mean of the squared deviation scores about the mean of a distribution; more simply, the square root of the variance. SD gives a basis for estimating the probability of how frequently certain scores can be expected to occur in a sample.

standard error of the mean—The standard deviation of a distribution of sample means; describes the likely deviations of sample means about the population mean.

standardized score—A value that results from methods of converting values from different distributions into scores that can be compared.

static-group comparison—Studies based on experimental and control groups but using no pretests.

statistic—A characteristic of a sample. Statistics provides the mathematical models for reasoning, providing a framework for reasoning from data so that generalized statements about the data can be made. Types include *descriptive* and *sampling* statistics.

statistical inference—The process of estimating parameters from statistics.

statistical power—The probability of rejecting a null hypothesis that is, in fact, false.

statistical significance level—The level of probability that an association between two (or more) variables could have been produced by chance. Expressed as a "*p* value" and referred to as the level of significance. Arbitrarily set by the investigators, but commonly set at the .05 or .01 level.

statistical test—A test that addresses the question "Could the observed relationship between X and Y have occurred by chance?" Statistical tests state the relationship between variables by some specified degree.

stratification—The sorting of the units composing a population into homogenous groups (strata) before sampling.

survey techniques—Research methods to collect data from populations. These include face-to-face interviews, survey questionnaires (by mail or in person), telephone interviewing, and group interviewing.

systematic sample—A type of *probability sample* in which every *k*th unit in a list is selected for inclusion in the sample: for example, every 25th patient visiting a clinic.

t **table**—A statistical table of percentage points of the "*t*" distribution. Used with statistical analyses that produce a "*t*" value.

t-**test (Student's t-test)**—Test of the difference between two population means, based on the observed difference between two sample means and their distribution.

theory—Statement that integrates a large number of simple laws and their associated variables, contributing to scientific knowledge and generating new testable hypotheses.

two-tailed test—A nondirectional hypothesis test that incorporates rejection regions in both tails of the probability curve used for a given statistic. Also known as non-directionality tests.

type I error—Rejecting a null hypothesis when it should have been retained.

type II error—Retaining a null hypothesis when it should have been the rejected.

units of analysis—The *what* or *whom* being studied, such as individual people.

univariate analysis—The examination of the distribution of cases on only one variable at a time. Usually reported in the form of *frequency distributions, central tendencies* (averages), and *dispersions* (*ranges* and *standard deviations*).

validity—The degree to which a scale is in fact consistently measuring the variable that it was designed to measure.

variable—An observable characteristic of an object or event that can be described according to some well-defined classification or measurement scheme.

variable, dichotomous (also *binary, dummy*)—A variable with only two values.

variance—The mean of the squared deviation scores about the mean of a distribution.

weighted mean—A procedure for combining the means of groups of different sizes.

Wilcoxon test—A nonparametric test for use with related samples.

Wilks lambda—A commonly used test for group mean equality in multivariate tests.

X axis—The horizontal axis on a graph, also called the abscissa.

X variable—Variable plotted on the horizontal axis, usually the independent variable

Y axis—The vertical axis on a graph, called the ordinate.

Y variable—Variable plotted on the vertical axis, usually the dependent variable.

z-**score** (lowercase "*z*")—A commonly used standard score that gives a measure of relative location in the distribution.

Z-**score** (uppercase "*Z*")—A standard score, based on manipulation of the z score, where the mean of the distribution is 50 and the standard deviation is 10.

Research Worksheets

Use these sheets to develop an outline for your research project.

I. Considerations

A. Are there institutional requirements that must be met before you begin your study?

1. Approval by a thesis/dissertation committee?

2. Approval by an Institutional Review Board?

OR

3. Approval by a Human Subjects Review Board?

4. Other?

B. How much time are you planning for your entire study?

C. What are the costs involved?

D. Have you identified the following (as needed)?

1. Consultants

2. Advisors

3. Statisticians

4. Collaborators

5. Reviewers

6. Co-investigators (if allowed)

E. Which style manual are you going to follow?

F. What equipment will you need?

G. What are the purposes and rationales for your study?

II. Identification of the Problem(s) and Development of the Research Questions.

A. Identify the problem you want to investigate. Go from general to specific.

B. Indicate the significance of the problem.

C. Develop research questions, hypotheses, or null hypotheses that will be used to investigate the problem.

D. What is the significance of your questions, hypotheses, or null hypotheses?

E. Can you think of any problems that may hinder your work?

III. Review of the Literature

A. Develop key words for your literature search.

B. What mechanisms do you propose using for your literature search.

C. Identify how you will keep a record of the relevant literature you find.

D. Develop files for your literature and categorize them in some fashion (topic, process, study type, etc.).

E. List key points from the literature that is pertinent to your study.

F. Will you have any problems carrying out your literature search?

IV. Methods

A. Will you do a quantitative or qualitative study?

B. Describe your subjects and sample population.

C. How will samples be drawn or assigned (criteria for inclusion or exclusion)?

D. Describe the design of study you will do.

E. What are your treatment or measurement instruments?

F. Identify your independent and dependent variables.

G. Identify how you will apply controls to your sample.

H. Identify any possible problems with obtaining a sample or carrying out your interventions.

I. How will you keep records of your samples, processes, statistical analyses?

J. Will you need to do a pilot study? Describe it.

K. How will you determine reliability and validity?

L. Can you identify any problems with your methods to include possible limitations, biases, and threats to validity?

V. Data Analysis

A. What statistical analyses will you use?

B. Correlate your choice of analyses with the type of data that will be produced.

C. How will you carry out the analyses? (e.g., a computer program)

D. What will your alpha and p levels be?

E. Who will be your "expert" for statistical analysis?

F. Can you identify any problems with your planned analysis, including limitations of tests?

VI. Results

A. How will you report your results?

B. Will you use tables, graphs, illustrations, figures, etc?

C. How will you put the items in "B" together. (e.g., graphic artist, computer program, etc.)

D. What are the results from similar studies?

VII. Discussion

A. Begin to consider possible

1. Limitations

2. Biases

3. Threats to validity

4. In general, what do your think will be the significance of your results?

5. Will there be applicability to medical practice?

VIII. Publication

A. What journals are you considering for submitting your research?

B. What style does the journal(s) use?

C. Who is the audience of the journal(s)?

D. What will you have to do to turn your research study into an article?

IX. Future

A. Can you develop a research agenda for yourself and future research activities, either related to this study new studies? List possibilities for future reference.

Resources Used and Recommended by the Authors

The latest edition of each of the following resources is recommended.

Alreck PL, Settle RB. *The survey research handbook,* 3rd ed. Boston: McGraw-Hill. 2004.

Campbell DT, Stanley JD. *Experimental and quasi-experimental designs for research.* Dallas: Houghton Mifflin Harcourt. 1963. (A classic on research design.)

Creswell JW. *Research design; Qualitative, quantitative, and mixed methods approaches,* 3rd ed. Thousand Oaks: Sage Publications. 2009.

Day RA, Gastel B. *How to write & publish a scientific paper,* 6th ed. West Port: Greenwood Publishing Group. 2006.

DePoy E, Gitlin LN. *Introduction to research,* 4th ed. Philadelphia: Elsevier Health. 2011.

Harris M, Taylor G. *Medical and health science statistics made easy,* 2nd ed. Sudbury, MA: Jones and Bartlett. 2009.

Lang TA. *How to write, publish, & present in the health sciences.* Philadelphia: American College of Physicians. 2009.

International Committee of Medical Journal Editors. Guide to Uniform Requirements for Manuscripts Submitted to Biomedical Journals. http://www.icmje.org/urm_main.html/. Accessed September 28, 2011.

Kraemer HC, Thiemann S. *How many subjects? Statistical power analysis in research.* Thousand Oaks: Sage Publications. 1987.

Lang TA, Secic M. *How to report Statistics in medicine: Annotated guidelines for authors, editors, and resources,* 2nd ed. Philadelphia: American College of Physicians. 2006.

Locke LF, Silverman SJ, Spirduso WW. *Reading and understanding research,* 3rd ed. Thousand Oaks: Sage Publications. 2010.

Mateo MA, Newton C. Progressing from an idea to a research question. In: Kirchhoff K, Mateo M, eds. *Using and conducting nursing research in the clinical setting,* 2nd ed. Philadelphia, PA: W. B. Saunders; 1999:191–199.

Neutens JJ, Rubinson L. *Research techniques for the health sciences,* 4th ed. Benjamin-Cummings Publishing. 2010.

Richardson L. *Writing strategies: Reaching diverse audiences.* Thousand Oaks: Sage Publications. 1990.

Riegelman RK. *Studying a study and testing a test,* 5th ed. Philadelphia: Lippincott Williams & Wilkins. 2004.

St. James D. *Writing and speaking for excellence: A brief guide for the medical professional.* Sudbury, MA: Jones and Bartlett. 1998.

Strunk W Jr , White EB. *The elements of style.* New York: Bartleyby. 1999. (A classic on writing.)

Vogt WP. *Dictionary of statistics & methodology,* 4th ed. Thousand Oaks: Sage Publications. 2011.

Zeiger M. *Essentials of writing biomedical research papers,* 2nd ed. New York: McGraw-Hill. 1999.

Zinsser W. *On writing well, 30th anniversary edition.* New York: HarperCollins. 2006. (Another classic on writing.)

Electronic and Internet Resources

Many electronic databases are available. The most commonly accessed databases that involve medical research are listed here.

MEDLINE **1966–present**	MEDLINE, produced by the U.S. National Library of Medicine, is a major source of bibliographic biomedical literature. The MEDLINE database encompasses information from three printed indexes (Index Medicus, Index to Dental Literature, and International Nursing Index) as well as additional information not published in the Index Medicus. It contains more than 9 million references to articles published in 3,900 biomedical journals, and this database may be accessed free of charge on the Internet. Two Web-based products, PubMed and Internet Grateful Med, provide this access. PreMEDLINE is a component of MEDLINE that includes the newest citations to articles that have not yet been fully indexed but are in the process of being added to MEDLINE.
HealthSTAR **1975–present**	HealthSTAR, produced cooperatively by the U.S. National Library of Medicine and the American Hospital Association, contains citations (with abstracts where available) to journal articles, monographs, technical reports, meeting abstracts and papers, book chapters, government documents, newspaper articles and clinical practice guidelines. It focuses on both the clinical aspects (emphasizing the evaluation of patient outcomes and effectiveness of procedures, programs, products, services, and processes) and the nonclinical aspects (emphasizing health care administration, economics, planning, and policy) of healthcare delivery.

Nursing & Allied Health (CINAHL®) Now EBSCO	The Cumulative Index to Nursing & Allied Health Literature (CINAHL), produced by CINAHL Information Systems, provides bibliographic access to nursing journals, publications from the American Nurses Association and the National League for Nursing, and from journals in the allied health science fields, including many of the physician assistant journals. Information in the Nursing & Allied Health database is derived from biomedical journals in Index Medicus, nursing dissertations, and psychological and management literature. More than 1,150 journals are covered, including alternative medicine, consumer health, and medical library literature.
HaPI	HaPI, Health and Psychosocial Instruments produced by Ovid, is a database that provides ready access to information on measurements (i.e., questionnaires, interview schedules, checklists, index measures, coding schemes/manuals, rating scales, projective instruments, vignettes/scenario tests) in the healthcare fields, psychosocial sciences, organizational behavior, and library and information science.
AIDSLINE 1980–present	AIDSLINE, produced by the National Library of Medicine, provides comprehensive coverage of research, clinical, and policy issues about AIDS from 1980 to present. Data sources include MEDLINE, Health, CancerLit, CATLINE, AVLINE, the International Conference on AIDS, the American Society for Microbiology, and the Symposium on Non-human Primate Models for AIDS.
Evidence-Based Medicine Reviews	Evidence-Based Medicine Reviews (EBMR), produced by Ovid, provides access to The Cochrane Database of Systematic Reviews and to the Cochrane Database of Methodology Reviews, the Database of Abstracts of Reviews of Effectiveness, the ACP Journal Club, as well as other EB based databases. All contain reviews of current medical research judged clinically relevant and methodologically sound.
PsychINFO®	PsychoINFO, a product of the American Psychological Association (APA) provides references with abstracts for psychology and related disciplines since 1967. PsychoINFO is updated monthly.
ABI/INFORM®	ABI/INFORM, a product of ProQuest, provides abstracts of business and management journals since 1985.
AgeLine	AgeLine, produced by the American Association of Retired Persons (AARP), is a source for references and/or abstracts for many material types related to all aspects of aging and middle age since 1978. AgeLine is updated monthly.
Social Research Methodology Database	Social Research Methodology-Database (SRM) is a bibliographic database containing more than 37,000 literature references on social research methodology, statistical analysis, and computer programs used in the social and behavioral sciences. The database offers an extensive overview of relevant methodological literature published in English, German, French, and Dutch since 1970. Most references are provided with an abstract and are accessible by means of the **SRM-Thesaurus**. The **SRM-Thesaurus**, consisting of sophisticated research terminology, forms a powerful retrieval tool in helping to trace specific methodological subjects of interest for students, methodologists, and social researchers.

Bowker's Books in Print	Records of the U.S. book publishing output available in print as well as out-of-print titles (back to 1979) and forthcoming titles are available in *Bowker's Books in Print*. Online access at http://www.booksinprint.com
CancerLit	CancerLit is a database of abstracts of materials related to cancer published since 1983. References are derived from MEDLINE as well as other references to proceedings, government reports, symposia, theses, and dissertations.
Cochrane Database of Systematic Reviews	Cochrane Reviews offers access to the abstracts and (where available) the full-text reviews of medical research from the Cochrane systematic reviews.
Current Contents Search®	Current Contents Search, a product of Thomson Scientific, provides tables of contents and abstracts of biomedical, agriculture and bioscience journals since 1995.
ERIC	ERIC, the Education Resources Information Center, is a database of more than one million citations and abstracts of educational publications since 1966.

FREE MEDLINE PROVIDERS

Following is a list of websites where versions of MEDLINE are available. Some include the entire MEDLINE database; some are subsets of the entire database. They all have a different search interface. All websites were accessed on April 26, 2011.

Avicenna. http://www.avicenna.com. Includes: AIDSLINE, AIDSDRUGS, AIDSTRIALS, MEDLINE (1990–present), Outline in Clinical Medicine.

Infotrieve. http://www.infotrieve.com/. Includes: AIDSLINE, MEDLINE, TOXLINE.

National Library of Medicine. http://www.nlm.nih.gov/. Includes: AIDSDRUGS, AIDSLINE, AIDSTRIALS, DIRLINE, HealthSTAR, HISTLINE, HSRPROJ, MEDLINE, OLDMEDLINE, PREMEDLINE, PubMed/Medline, and more.

Medscape. http://www.medscape.com/. Includes: AIDSLINE, MEDLINE.

PubMed. http://www.ncbi.nlm.nih.gov/PubMed/. Includes: MEDLIN

Index

Boxes, exhibits, figures, and tables are indicated with *b, exh, f,* and *t* following the page number.